Critical Concepts™ Series . . .

Putting It All Together

Walleyes in the 21st Century

Critical Concepts™ Series . . .

Putting It All Together

Walleyes in the 21st Century

Expert Advice from North America's
Leading Authority on Freshwater Fishing

THE IN-FISHERMAN STAFF

In·Fisherman
An InterMedia Company

Critical Concepts™ Series . . .
Putting It All Together: Walleyes in the 21st Century

Publisher *Stuart Legaard*
Associate Publisher *Mike Carney*
Editor In Chief *Doug Stange*
Senior Editor/Project Editor *Dave Csanda*
Editors *Steve Quinn, Matt Straw, Steve Hoffman*
Staff Writer *Jeff Simpson*
Contributing Staff Members *Mark Dorn, Jim Kalkofen, Joann Phipps*
Founders *Al Lindner, Ron Lindner*
Project Coordinator *Scott Lawrence*
Copy Editor *J.Z. Grover*
Cartoons *Peter Kohlsaat*
Cover *Nelson Graphic Design and Jim Pfaff*
Layout & Design *Scott Lawrence with Jim Pfaff*

Acknowledgments

Bill Diedrich, *electronics usage, Ch. 2*; Bill Koval, *side-scan sonar, Ch. 2*; Bill Diedrich, *GPS, mapping, plotting, Ch. 3*; Bruce Carlson, *underwater cameras, Ch. 3*; Mark Strand, *powerful outboards, Ch. 4*; Grid Michal, *four-strokes, propping, maintenance, Ch. 4*; Bill Diedrich, *boat trailers, boat covers, Ch. 4*; Jim Wentworth, *rigging boats, Ch. 5*; Grid Michal, *maintenance, Ch. 5*; Ron Boggs, *ounce of prevention, Ch. 5*; Bill Diedrich, *boating safety, Ch. 5*; Tom Johnson, *deadsticking, Ch. 7*; Tommy Skarlis, *castaway tactics, Ch. 7*; Bill Koval, *tumbling plastics, Ch. 7*; Scott Fairbairn, *fast-break sauger, counter-current crankin', Ch. 8*; Dave Kidd, *big and fast, Ch. 8*; Dick Sternberg and Dick "Griz" Gryzwinski, *give a rip, Ch. 9*; Bruce Carlson, *shortline trolling, Ch. 9*; Rick Markesbery, *wood 'eye, Ch. 9*; Chip Porter, *thumper jigs, Ch. 9*; Bernie Barringer, *harvest tournaments, Ch. 10*; Scott Richardson with Ted Takasaki, *pro's pointers, visual 'eyes, Ch. 11*; Terry Wickstrom, *off-water research, Ch. 11*; Dave Kidd with Sam Anderson, *hocus focus, Ch. 11*; Jeff Murray and Steve Bissett, *dissecting reservoirs, Ch. 11*; Norb Wallock and Rick Olson, *when the goin' gets rough, Ch. 11*; Tommy Skarlis, *organization, Ch. 11*; Ron Seelhoff with Jeff Murray, *Tiger Woods of walleyes, Ch. 11*; Ted Takasaki, *experience, Ch. 12*; Gary Parsons, *no off season, Ch. 12*; Mark Strand, *pros who guide, Ch. 12*; John Kolbeck, *guide etiquette, Ch. 12*; Jeff Murray, *walleye circuitry, pro to pro, Ch. 12*; Bill Koehne, *amateur turned pro, Ch. 12*; Reggie Thiel, *high cost of crawlers, Ch. 12*; Daryl Christensen, *rivers of gold, epilogue, Ch. 13.*

Putting It All Together: Walleyes in the 21st Century

Printing Edition 10 9 8 7 6 5 4 3 2

Library of Congress Cataloging-in-Publication Data
ISBN: 978-1-892947-10-9

From the Editors— A Word About This Book

This book nearly wasn't. As originally planned, our *Critical Concepts* series on walleyes was to span four volumes. But like so many endeavors, this project seemed to take on a life of its own, easily spilling over into a fifth installment. Truth be told, we had to jump on the lid a bit to squeeze it all home in five.

Chalk that up to the growing complexity of walleye fishing. Once considered a relatively simple application of livebait tactics, it has expanded into a whirlwind of seasonal movements, structural complexity, big-water pursuit, and multiline fishing systems, each of them refined to the *nth* degree. And the sport just keeps on growing, expanding in popularity and precision.

The focus of this final manual deals less with fishing mechanics and more with the psychology of becoming a successful walleye angler.

The focus of this final manual deals less with fishing mechanics and more with the psychology of becoming a successful walleye angler—the aspects of strategy, defining and refining patterns, and making tough decisions under pressure. We delve into the world of competitive walleye anglers, exploring their psyches to see how and why they do what they do. We also examine the rigors of tournament competition and the never-ending search for better equipment that has spurred innovations in boats, motors, tackle, and gear. Every angler benefits from the continuing evolution of fishing tools and accessories, tournament pro or not.

Case in point: boats, motors, and electronics. Thirty years ago, who would have envisioned anglers in 20-foot walleye rigs decked out with 200-plus-hp engines, probing miles offshore despite storms and heavy waves, navigating by satellite navigation, enjoying themselves in relative comfort and safety, knowing that they'd find their way back despite fog, snow, or dark of night? This book examines the rise of the competition-class walleye boat, explains the use of essential electronic equipment, and details the boat rigging process. In the hands of an educated and enthusiastic predator, the end result is a high-tech weapon.

Permit us a minor disclaimer: by the time we print the photo of any depthfinder or boat, another, better, and newer model is likely to be already gracing the tackle shelves or showroom floor. Like computers, walleye equipment is often outdated by the time you read about it. So don't be discouraged if you see a photo of a unit that's not the current rage. Rather than focusing on the latest models, we use photos and artwork to illustrate critical usage *principles* that never go out of style. Apply them, and you can operate any unit or rig any boat to its full potential.

Armed with new knowledge and skills, anglers would seem so powerful that walleyes hardly have a chance anymore. Not so. Just 'cause you can predict their location, detect their presence electronically, and even lower a camera right in their faces, it doesn't follow that you're gonna catch 'em every time. Despite all the technology at your disposal, you still need to make them bite. The best way to do that is to be versatile in your thinking, strategy, and tactics, and to do whatever it takes to catch fish. In essence, be willing to throw the book(s) at 'em, rather than the same old favorite lure or bait. Traditional favorites are nice, but new favorites may lie just beyond the next bite.

Don't Fight the Bite

Ever notice how each branch of the sport of fishing tends to have its own terminology for the gear used to pursue its favorite quarry? Take something like a long, thin, suspending crankbait—a Rapala Husky Jerk, for example—a multispecies lure used in many conditions. Walleye anglers tend to call it a *neutrally buoyant minnow-imitator*. Bass anglers generically call it a *jerkbait*. But to a muskie angler, a jerkbait is a huge chunk of wood sprouting two or three monstrous treble hooks. Communication sometimes breaks down along interspecies lines.

To a walleye angler, a *jig* is a small leadhead sporting a hook, to which some combination of livebait, plastic dressing, or both is attached; an optional stinger hook or rattle; and perhaps some scent or other enhancement. Some traditional jig styles are pretied with hair or feathers, but most are part of a component system featuring many jig sizes, shapes, and colors.

To a bass angler, the component aspect is somewhat similar when small plastic tubes, grubs, and worms are applied to a jighead. They're light-line presentations, akin to walleye jigging techniques. But when bass anglers talk about a *jig-n-pig* combo, that's a whole different ballgame. This system typically features a large, heavy jighead sporting a huge hook and weedguard designed to penetrate cover and yank a bass out of its lair. It's almost always tipped with a chunk of pork rind in various shapes and sizes, though it's also occasionally dressed with plastic—but virtually never with livebait, except by North Country nontournament anglers with no preconceived aversion to using livebait for bass. Figures. In walleye country, anything's fair game.

> *Communication sometimes breaks down along interspecies lines.*

To a bass angler, *flippin'* means using a 7½-foot flippin' stick (long-handled casting rod) and 20-plus-pound line to underhand swing and drop that big jig into shallow cover. *Pitchin'* incorporates the same lure, with perhaps a slightly shorter rod, to underhand sail a lure 30 or 40 feet parallel to the surface, stopping it just above the water, then letting it slip silently into the shallows.

Walleye anglers, meanwhile, tend to use the terms flippin' and pitchin' interchangeably. Mostly, they use an underhand swing to sail a lightweight jig tipped with livebait or a small plastic bait perhaps 10 to 20 feet, either into shallow cover or up to shallow shorelines. And they do it with 6- to 10-pound line and spinning gear—something no self-respecting bass angler would do—unless, of course, he were fishing for smallmouths rather than largemouths. In that case, the tactic would be not only acceptable but effective.

Bass anglers tossing a blade would typically cast a safety pin-style spinnerbait. But walleye anglers fishing a blade would typically vertically jig a heavy metal bladebait in deep water. Walleye anglers fishing a spinner, meanwhile, would generally troll a spinner harness tipped with livebait, weighted with a bottom bouncer, three-way rig, snap weight, or in-line sinker—all Greek to a bass angler.

And then there's that whole sit-down-and-troll-multiple-rods versus stand-up-and-cast-one-rod thing. Especially since walleye anglers tend to motor backward, and everyone knows you're supposed to move in the direction of the pointy end of the boat. Cross the border into Canada, and even walleye fans get confused by the differences (if any) between walleyes, pickerel, and pike. Eh? And don't even bring up that whole business about fishin' through a hole in the ice.

Yet despite our differences, similarities bring us together into one great sport. Bass anglers fishing a jigging spoon would vertically jig a heavy slab spoon in deep water. Walleye anglers jigging a jigging spoon would typically—son of a gun—do the same thing. Guess there's some common ground and potential for communication after all. Perhaps all we need is a good walleye-bass bass-walleye dictionary to help everyone, North and South, get on the same wavelength.

Fortunately for all of us, many anglers are versatile multispecies fishermen, able to cross the lines of communications and speak interspecies dialects. They incorporate many different techniques, some with several names, for many species of fish. They not only catch a lot of different critters in the process but also help foster the notion that all anglers are of the same basic genetic origin, just separated by local conditions. The more you travel, the more you realize this is true.

So, the next time Bubba asks y'all how they're hittin' on jerkbaits, or the next time Sven vants to know vat kind of minners yer usin', remember that we all basically speak the same language, just with a different twang and slang. Put us under the microscope, and basically we're all just the same species, fixin' to get bit.

Dave Csanda
Senior Editor

Contents

A Whole New Ballgame

THE NEXT GENERATION

"...to boldly go where no man has gone before."
—Gene Roddenberry,
Star Trek

Thirty years ago, a futuristic sci-fi cult favorite named *Star Trek* grabbed the attention of the American TV viewing public. Evolving through a succession of television series and a host of big box office theatrical releases, the crew of the starship Enterprise firmly imprinted itself on the American psyche. As we enter the 21st century, that fascination hasn't ebbed.

Over that same thirty-year period, walleye fishing has evolved at a bewildering pace. In the '60s, leading-edge anglers applied the first-generation, green box Fish Lo K Tor (flasher depthfinder) offered by Lowrance, the pioneer of angling electronics. Revolutionary at the time but outdated by modern standards, the locator began to unlock the secrets of the mysterious underwater world. Once anglers had taken their first peek below the surface, there was no stopping the march of technology to assist them.

Today, next-generation anglers revel in a host of electronic wonders that would do the bridge of the Enterprise proud. In addition, larger, faster, safer boats propel them into offshore waters formerly too distant and dangerous to explore. Armed with today's technology, they fish waters their predecessors never tried. What was once considered unthinkable, even unimaginable, has become commonplace.

. . . as a whole, anglers who ignore the monumental offerings of modern electronics will remain largely mired in the limitations of yesteryear.

You can certainly still catch walleyes with the technology of yesteryear; some things will never go out of style or run out of effectiveness. Yet as a whole, anglers who ignore the monumental offerings of modern electronics will remain largely mired in the limitations of yesteryear. Peaceful contemplation and simple tactics are great when they produce fish, but when conditions get rough and tough, it's time to switch into high gear. Enter the 21st-century walleye warrior, armed to the gills with enough high-tech apparatus to swamp the boats of the previous generation.

Modern walleye boats are seaworthy, fast, and have exceptional range. Yet they also troll down slow and maneuver on a dime, allowing anglers to deftly plumb the depths. Their electronic array commonly includes liquid crystal graph plus GPS navigation and mapping, sometimes even side-scanning sonar, videosonar, radio communication, and self-steering electric motors. Coordinating the use of all this electronic gear can become overwhelming.

One consequence is that rigging boats in your garage has become a thing of the past. Nowadays, it takes an electronic genius to run all the wires and connect the gear correctly, prevent battery drain, minimize interference between units, and fuse everything for safety. Plus tack it all down firmly enough to prevent it from falling apart under the punishment of wind and waves. Simply reading, digesting, and semi-understanding all the manuals are about all anyone can hope for anymore.

Faced with such a profusion of technology, we begin this book by offering an experienced look at the current mishmash of high-tech wizardry. Step by step, we examine functions, usage, rigging, and provide an overview of how and why anglers choose—and use—the equipment in question.

THE PSYCHOLOGY OF PATTERNING FISH

Tackle, technique, gear, and gadgets are great, and they can certainly make you more effective if you know how to apply them. But sooner or later, you must use your head—you need to put your thinking cap into the game. This is what separates the angling elite from the rest of the pack when both are equally equipped. The ability to define and refine fishing patterns despite changing weather, the wherewithal to recognize opportunity rather than head back to the boat launch in defeat, the versatility to roll with the punches and come out on top—these are what makes some anglers pros and other wannabes.

Fact is, fish are somewhat predictable, but never a sure bet. Just about the time you think you have 'em all figured out—*wham!*—they throw you a curveball, and you're left with jaws agape, dangling a limp line. Having a solid Plan A is great . . . but don't be distressed if you must switch to plans B, C, D, and beyond to catch fish. Defining and refining patterns is critical to success. We'll show you how it's done.

TOURNAMENT-TESTED TOUGH

Say what you wish about tournaments: some folks love 'em, others hate 'em, while still others dabble or have no feelings whatsoever. All of us, though, competitor and noncompetitor alike, benefit from the eternal push for better equipment spurred by competition. Boat, motor, tackle, and electronics companies would hardly have pushed so hard to develop new and better products if anglers hadn't beaten, broken, outpaced, and outdated equipment as fast as it was designed and manufactured.

Tournament competition has done more than improve equipment, however: it has honed the abilities and spirit of leading-edge walleye anglers to an amazing degree. Ever on the lookout for something new and different to provide a competitive edge, they pioneer new discoveries and refine existing angling systems. Their ability to rapidly decipher patterns far exceeds that of the average recreational angler. They display the stamina to remain mentally tough under tournament conditions, when the clock is ticking and a host of competitors are on their tails. We'll peek inside their thinking and gain an awareness of how competitive anglers function—invaluable insights for everyone who wets a line.

Boat, motor, tackle, and electronics companies would hardly have pushed so hard to develop new and better products if anglers hadn't beaten, broken, outpaced, and outdated equipment as fast as it was designed and manufactured.

Cast for cash? Ever heard of anyone who wouldn't like to go fishing for a living? Neither have we. But few are able to pull it off successfully. Transforming an enthusiastic pastime into a self-supporting career is no easy task. It's filled with loads of hard work, rampant frustration, and unsuspected perils. For those with the hankerin' to give it a try, we offer a realistic assessment of what it takes to make a livin' fishin', which generally means fishin' hard while performing lots of related duties well enough to land sponsors and generate income.

TO EACH HIS OWN

As you look through this book, examining the bewildering array of high-tech equipment now available to walleye anglers, don't simply dismiss it because of estimated cost. If you're a tournament pro committed to proceeding full-speed ahead with the latest gadgets and gizmos, you will certainly take the high-tech route. If you aren't, a more modest, though functional, setup may suffice. The important thing is to digest the principles presented within these pages—equipment installation and usage, fishing patterns, strategy, and more—and to apply them as opportunities arise. They round out the educational spectrum of the modern walleye angler, potentially elevating you to the ranks of the angling elite.

Chapter 2

Understanding and Using Sonar

LIQUID CRYSTAL GRAPHS, FLASHERS, VIDEO AND SIDE-SCAN SONAR

The proper use of electronic sonar is critical to walleye fishing success. Yet many anglers take it for granted, thereby diminishing their fishing potential. To the trained eye, depthfinders (sonar) indicate far more than mere depth; they are your eyes to the underwater world.

Applying the subtle intricacies of sonar usage begins with an understanding of how electronics work and continuous hands-on experience to take full advantage of their technological wizardry. Let's begin by looking at what sonar is and how it works. It will help you select the proper unit(s) for your fishing situations and set you upon the road to success.

POWER

Power determines depth penetration, since a more powerful unit can send a signal deeper into water. For deep fishing, a 3,000-watt unit performs better than a 200-watt unit. But how much power is enough? Bottom hardness, fresh water or salt water, plankton, interference, and receiver sensitivity all affect the operating depth of the unit.

Power determines depth penetration, since a more powerful unit can send a signal deeper into water.

Edge Detection—Power also is important in detecting targets near the edge of the sound (transducer) cone. The most intense (strongest) signal is along the axis of the transducer, an imaginary line perpendicular to the bottom of the transducer and extending to lake bottom. As one moves toward the edge of the sound cone, energy decreases. A more powerful *locator* (a nickname for sonar) detects targets at the edge of the cone better than a less powerful unit.

Target Separation—Target separation—the ability to detect and display objects such as fish, rocks, or weeds—also is a function of power. Most units of midrange frequency have target separation of about 3 inches in shallow water and wider target separations in deeper water. So, if a fish is 4 inches above bottom, the sonar shows the fish and bottom as distinct objects. But if a fish is 2 inches from bottom, the fish and bottom usually blend into one image.

Power affects target separation because a certain amount of energy is needed to drive a sound wave to lake bottom. More powerful locators maintain a smaller target separation into deeper water.

How much power to buy depends on your fishing situation. If you rarely fish deeper than 30 feet and bottom is relatively firm, around 300 watts may be adequate. If you fish soft-bottomed lakes or deeper water, 2,000- to 3,000-watt units work better. The extra power is available when you need it.

PIXELS

An important feature of liquid crystal graphs (LCGs, the most popular units on the market today) are pixels or "picture elements," the little squares that produce an image on the screen. The vertical pixel count (VPC) is the number of pixels in a vertical column from the top to the bottom of the screen.

The VPC determines screen resolution. The better the screen resolution, the more detailed the display. Vertical pixels break the column of water into segments. The more segments and the smaller the segments, the more detail displayed. VPC currently runs about 100 to 300 pixels on most units. In 30 feet of water, one pixel on a 100-VPC screen represents about 3.5 inches. One pixel on a 250-VPC screen at the same depth represents about 1.5 inches.

Pixels cost money . . . Buy as many as you can afford.

Pixels cost money, so you get what you pay for. Buy as many as you can afford. Manufacturers offer models at different price points by offering varying combinations of power and pixels. For most walleye anglers, powerful units with high pixel counts are costly but worth the investment.

OK, so we have an idea of what to buy. How does it work?

TRANSDUCERS

To most anglers familiar with marine electronics, the transducer is the thing mounted on the back of the boat or stuck somewhere in the hull. It's also the thing blamed for poor images, poor high-speed performance, no picture—maybe even for poor weather and no fish! Let's take a look at this small but important object, see how it works, and what we can do to help the transducer perform better.

Transducers come in a variety of shapes, depending on their function. Some look like blocks, others like footballs or hockey pucks. All have one thing in common: they contain a crystal, usually a ceramic crystal, which vibrates in response to an electric current. The crystal converts electrical energy to sound energy and later back to electrical energy. Electrical current traveling from the locator head to the transducer zaps the crystal, which then sends out a sound wave at a particular frequency and direction.

When the sound wave strikes a target such as lake bottom or fish, the sound wave is reflected back to the transducer. The transducer crystal senses the slight vibration of the sound wave and converts this sound energy back to electrical energy. The electrical energy travels to the locator head, where, depending on the type of sonar (LCG, flasher, or paper graph), images are displayed based on depth of the targets.

Transducer discussion usually centers on two closely related items: (1) frequency and (2) cone angle or beam width. Frequency refers to the operating frequency and is usually expressed in kilohertz (kHz). Typical operating frequencies range from 50 kHz to 400 kHz, with the majority of freshwater units in the 50- to 200-kHz range. Each frequency range offers advantages and disadvantages. Manufacturers choose frequencies that best match the performance and function of a particular sonar unit.

Cone angle or beam width refers to the diameter covered in water at a particular depth, generally referred to as the "half-power point," or -3 dB. A simplified but good way to visualize cone angle is to think of it as an inverted ice cream cone (the pointed kind), with the point at the transducer. A narrow cone angle looks like a narrow ice cream cone, while a wide cone angle looks like a wide ice cream cone. Depending on frequency, cone angles typically range from about 8 degrees to 50 degrees. In general, the higher the operating frequency, the narrower the cone angle; the lower the frequency, the wider the cone angle. This is due to the physical limitations of the crystal.

In general, a narrow cone angle—say, one of fewer than 20 degrees—provides more accurate bottom detail but less area coverage, while a wide cone angle

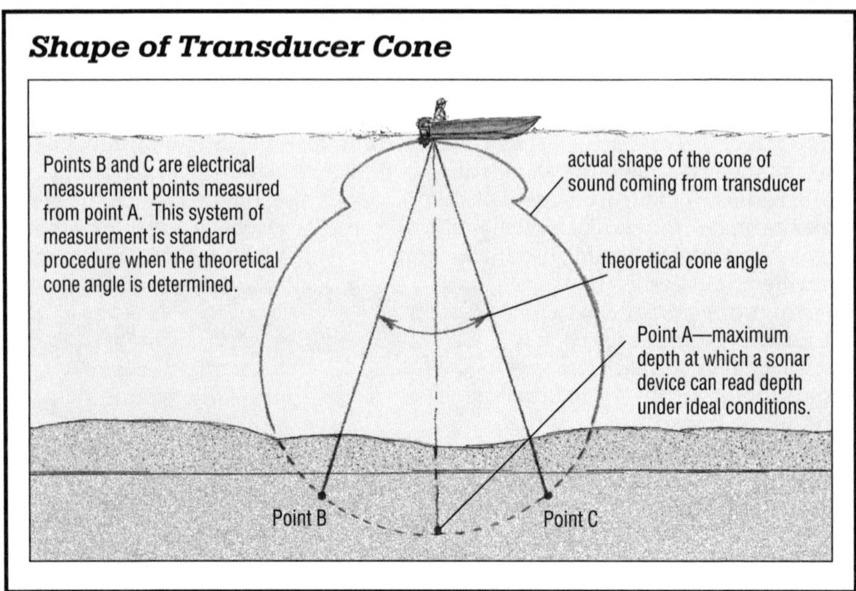

displays a larger area and perhaps more targets. At the risk of oversimplification, if you locate a fish with a narrow-beam transducer, you know the fish is near or under the boat. With a wide beam, you know the fish is somewhere in the lake, and maybe near the boat.

Here are several generalities for the circular area below the boat covered by the transducer (measured at -3 dB): An 8-degree transducer covers an area in which the diameter is about 1/6 of the water depth; a 20-degree transducer covers an area in which the diameter is about 1/3 of the water depth; and a 38-degree transducer covers an area about 2/3 the diameter of the water depth. For example, in 30 feet of water, a 20-degree cone angle covers an area about 10 feet in diameter (30 ÷ 1/3 = 10). If the manufacturer of a sonar unit specifies a cone angle that is, for example, -6 dB or -10 dB, the cone angle is narrower than one measured at -3 dB. For instance, a 20-degree cone angle measured at -10 dB may be about half of that, or about 10 degrees at -3 dB.

In general, low frequencies provide wide cone angles (broader coverage) to cover a broader area. The

Water Depth Versus Diameter of Cone Angle

Water depth in feet	Diameter in feet of circle covered at theoretical cone angles			
	8°	16°	22°	38°
10	1.4	2.8	3.9	6.9
20	2.8	5.6	7.8	13.8
30	4.2	8.4	11.7	20.7
40	5.6	11.2	15.6	27.5
50	6.7	14.0	19.4	34.4
60	8.4	16.9	23.3	41.3
70	9.8	19.7	27.2	48.2
80	11.1	22.5	31.1	55.1
90	12.6	25.3	35.0	62.0
100	14.0	28.1	38.9	68.9
120	—	33.7	46.7	82.6
140	—	39.4	54.4	96.4
160	—	45.0	62.2	110.2
180	—	50.6	70.0	123.9
200	—	56.2	77.8	137.3

downside is that low-frequency systems generally don't work well in water under 10 to 15 feet. Nonetheless, deep water fisherman on the Great Lakes prefer them.

Another tradeoff in frequency called *target separation* refers to the ability to separate or distinguish targets that are close together. High-frequency systems generally offer better target separation than low-frequency systems, a topic we'll discuss later.

Yet another tradeoff is that low-frequency signals penetrate deeper water more weakly than high-frequency ones. But a narrow-beam transducer, such as an 8-degree transducer, can concentrate the sound energy and reach deep water with all the benefits of a high-frequency system. In several hundred feet of water, even a narrow beam covers a significant distance.

Manufacturers often try to make up for shortcomings by producing sonar units that can operate at dual frequencies. For instance, a common dual frequency transducer operates at 50/200 kHz. Another option is a dual beam transducer whose frequency stays the same but whose beam width can be set at either 9 degrees or 18 degrees. Other units offer transducers containing multiple crystals of the same frequency. Each crystal scans to the right, left, or center, thereby creating a wide beam of coverage.

INSTALLATION

Any sonar system is only as good as its transducer installation. Transducer mounting includes transom mount, in-hull mount, trolling motor mount, or portable mount. Transducer shape and function often determine mounting technique.

Transom mounting—High-speed transom-mount transducers typically come in two shapes: a pointed front shape that looks like the end of a football, and a wedge shape that looks like a block with the front edge tapered back toward the top of the transducer. With either style, the boat hull must provide a smooth and continuous water flow off the transom. Air is the big enemy of good transducer reception, because sound travels nearly 1 mile per second in water, but four times slower in air.

Avoid mounting areas where the transducer comes out of the water or where air and water mix, such as areas with strakes or ribs on the boat hull. If you are having trouble finding an area where smooth water flows off the transom, have someone drive the boat while you look over the transom for this smooth water area. The

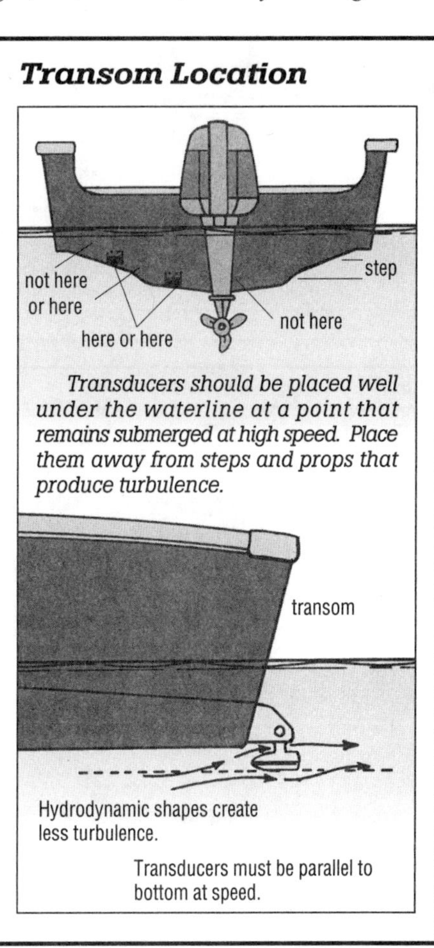

Transducers should be placed well under the waterline at a point that remains submerged at high speed. Place them away from steps and props that produce turbulence.

Hydrodynamic shapes create less turbulence.

Transducers must be parallel to bottom at speed.

best mounting areas should be roughly halfway between the motor and the end of the transom, and no closer than 12 inches to the motor. If possible, route the transducer cable away from boat wiring to avoid sonar interference.

To mount the bracket to a pointed-style transducer, hold the bracket against the transom at the selected location with the transducer face (the bottom of the transducer) parallel to the bottom of the boat. Locate the centerline on the side of the transducer. Find a line halfway between the centerline and the bottom of the transducer. This line should be at the bottom of the transom, which means about

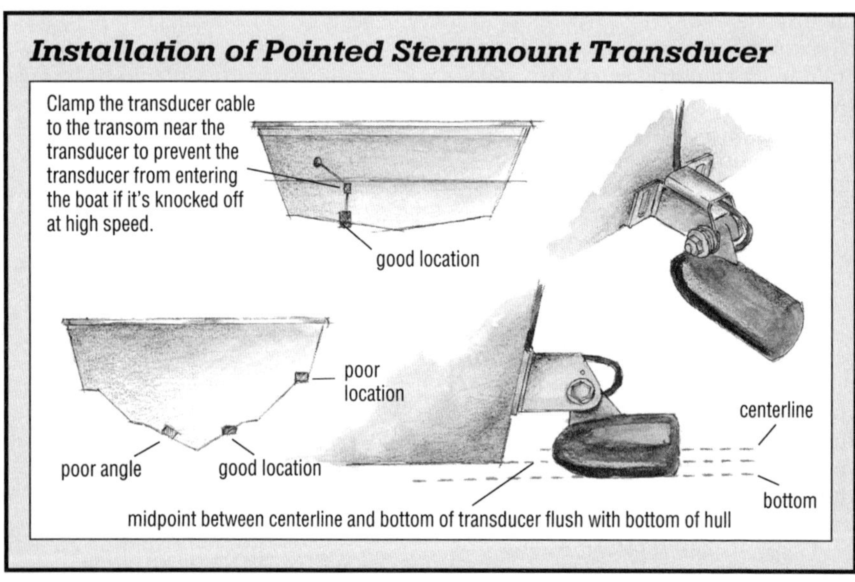

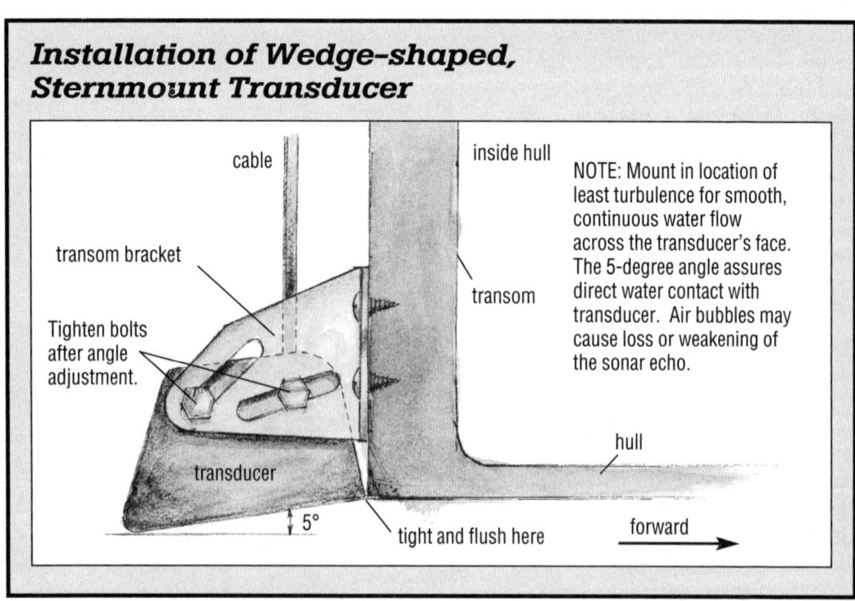

1/8 to 1/2 inch of the transducer will be below the boat hull. Mark the center of the slots on the transducer mounting bracket, and use mounting screws to attach the bracket to the transom or the transom mounting board.

Try it on the water. The goal in any high-speed mount is to get a sonar reading at top speed. Tweaking the mount may be necessary. If you can't get a high-speed reading, try moving the transducer farther down in the water. Also check to make sure the bottom of the transducer is parallel to the boat hull or that the back of the transducer is dropped slightly down (no more than 5 or 6 degrees below horizontal).

> *The goal in any high-speed mount is to get a sonar reading at top speed.*

With a wedge-shaped transducer, hold the transducer with the mounting bracket attached against the transom, the bottom of the transducer flush with the bottom of the boat. Mark the mounting holes so the transducer can be moved up or down for fine-tuning. Attach the mounting screws to the transom, and make sure the back of the transducer is dropped down several degrees. Once you obtain satisfactory high-speed readings, seal any gap between the transducer edge and the boat hull with silicone.

Always follow the manufacturer's instructions. In general, the depth of the transducer and the angle or drop of its back determine the unit's high-speed performance.

In-hull or shoot-through-hull mounting—In this position, the transducer shoots through the hull of the boat. This is a good choice for fiberglass boats, but generally isn't recommend for aluminum or wood hulls because of a loss of sensitivity. In a fiberglass hull, the transducer must be mounted in an area that is solid fiberglass containing no filler material such as foam, plywood, or air bubbles. It also must be mounted far enough back in the hull to remain in constant contact with the water, even on plane. Most manufacturers of fiberglass boats designate an area for transducer mounting.

Make sure the area is clean and smooth, so no air gets trapped under the transducer. The entire face of the transducer must be in contact with the hull. Follow the instructions on the epoxy; if it requires mixing, stir it slowly to avoid introducing air bubbles. Apply a small amount of epoxy to the transducer as well as to the fiberglass. Then gently twist and turn the transducer while pressing it into the epoxy to force out any air bubbles. When the epoxy dries, route the transducer cable to the sonar unit.

Trolling motor mounting—Attach the transducer to the bottom of the bowmount trolling motor housing using the manufacturer's kit, large hose clamps, or plastic cable ties. "Puck-style" transducers frequently are used here. These look like small cylinders about 1½ inches in diameter containing several slots near the top of the transducer for clamps or ties to go through. Make sure the transducer cable is unobstructed when the trolling motor is turning, being pulled up, or let down.

Portable mounting—This usually requires a mounting bracket that hangs over the transom or a suction cup mount attached to the transom. Find an area of clean water flow, and make sure the face or bottom of the transducer is at least even with or below the boat hull. The common mistake made here is in placing the transducer underwater on the transom but failing to realize that when the boat is on plane, the transducer is out of the water. Portable-style transducers read well with a 25-hp motor wide open on a 14- or 16-foot boat.

Select the transducer that best meets your fishing needs. Take the time to carefully mount and fine-tune the system for maximum performance. Follow the manufacturer's instructions or seek the help of a professional installer.

SENSITIVITY

To better understand what's beneath the surface of the water, the first and most important step is to understand the function of sensitivity or "gain" control. Every depthfinder has it.

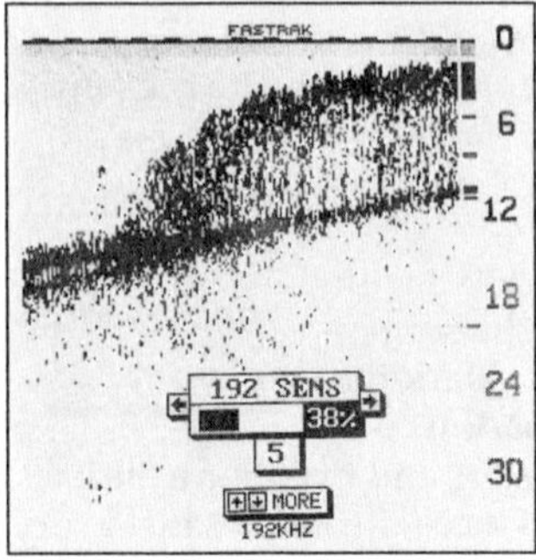

Too little sensitivity

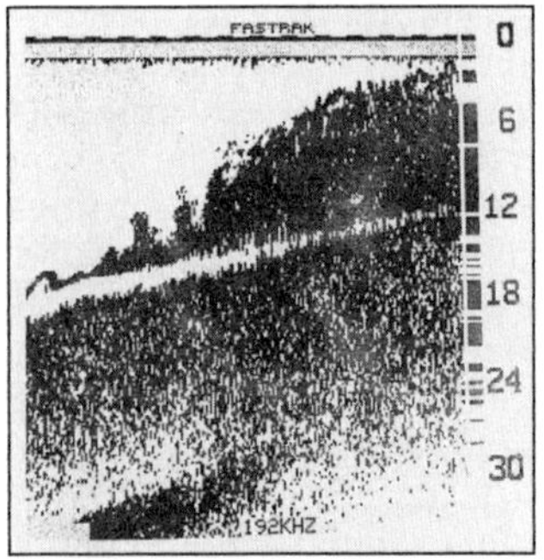

Sensitivity just right

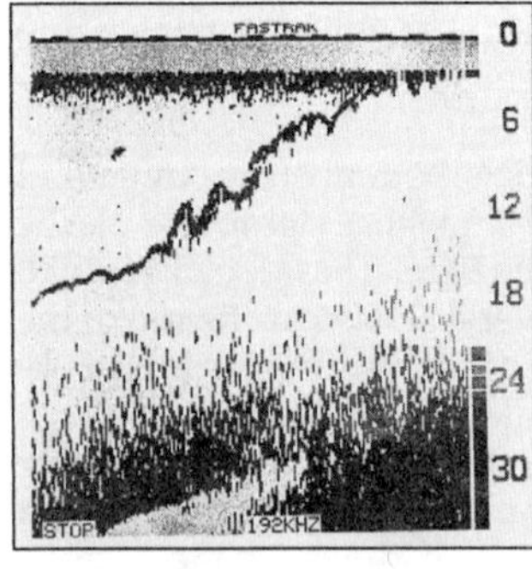

Too much sensitivity

Sensitivity is the most significant control on a locator. Think of it in two different ways. First, think of sensitivity control as you would volume control on a radio. Remember—the volume control does not control the power; that is, turning up the volume does not make the radio more powerful. Instead, turning up the volume enables the radio to pick up weaker signals. The sensitivity control on sonar helps the sonar unit pick up weaker signals. Weaker signals can come from things such as lake bottom in deep water, soft bottom in shallow water, or targets like fish. As in the case of radio, too much sensitivity or too little sensitivity may not provide the performance you expect.

Second, visualize the sound cone emanating from the transducer as a balloon whose inflation is determined by the sensitivity control. The sensitivity setting affects the cone angle (the area covered by the cone) of sound, making it larger or smaller. At a low-sensitivity setting, the cone angle is smaller, similar to a partially inflated balloon. At a high-sensitivity setting, the cone angle is larger, like a more fully inflated balloon. As a result of the increased sensitivity setting, weak sonar signals that lie just beyond the smaller cone angle are now encompassed by the larger cone angle. The area across which the sonar can detect signals increases just as the size of a balloon increases.

In the old days, when virtually every locator was a flasher type, anglers were told to set the sensitivity so the flasher showed a "second echo"—that is, a second depth on the locator scale that is twice the depth of the first. For example, if a locator indicates a water depth of 20 feet, the sensitivity increases until a second mark shows up at 40 feet. This is because the second echo represents a signal that goes twice as far. In other words, the second signal goes to bottom, returns to the surface, gets reflected, then goes down to lake bottom a second time, and returns to the transducer. Because the signal travels twice as far, it is a weaker signal. If the sensitivity gets increased to display this second echo, you can be assured that it displays weaker signals from targets such as fish. In most situations, the strongest signal return is from lake bottom, particularly if bottom is sand or gravel. This signal can be displayed with a low-sensitivity setting, so low that targets such as fish may not show up.

With many LCGs, it's possible to show a second echo on the graph. Place the unit in manual mode and select a depth scale at least twice as deep as the water. Increase the sensitivity to the point where a second print or echo shows on the screen. The problem with this method is that at least half the screen is being used to show the second echo instead of the underwater world you really want to see.

What if the second echo method is not used? Try different sensitivity settings to see what happens. Place your boat over an area that you know has hard bottom, soft bottom, or vegetation. Vary the sensitivity setting and watch the screen. Set the sensitivity high and then low, and compare the screen images. On high settings, you may notice a lot of marks on the screen. These are similar to the static a radio picks up at higher volume. In either case, it's unwanted and useless noise. In the case of low settings, you may barely get a picture on the screen, just as you can barely pick up your radio station at low volume. Make sure your locator is set to the manual mode so you can take control of the unit.

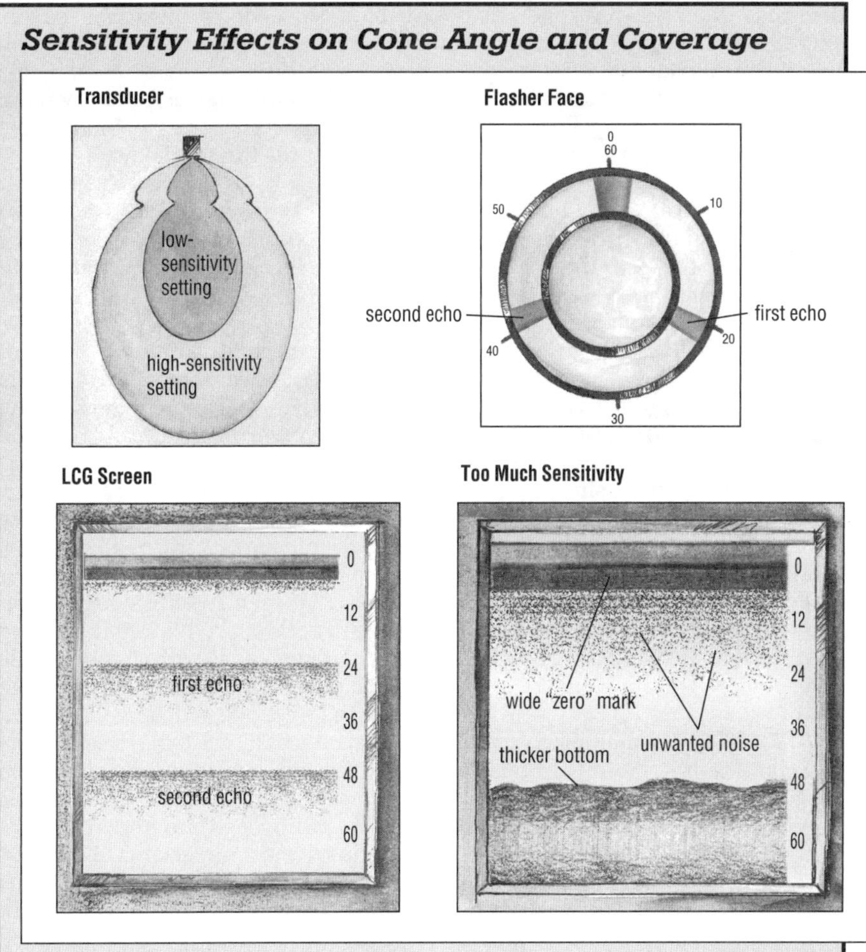

The automatic control, or auto mode, is another option you can use to set the sensitivity on a depthfinder. Manufacturers have made tremendous strides in the improvement of automatic control. In this mode, the locator makes the decision for you. Factors like sensitivity setting and depth scale are selected by the unit. Some manufacturers allow you to make small adjustments to the sensitivity, even in automatic mode. Many experts run their units in auto mode about 90 percent of the time. Problem areas for automatic mode are deep water, soft bottom, shallow water, and dense vegetation.

The problem with both deep water and soft bottom is the weak signal they return. In deep water (operating depth varies, depending on power), the signal travels a long way on its round trip from surface to lake bottom to surface. In its travels, the signal becomes weak and thus hard to detect, translate, and display. In this situation, automatic mode may not increase sensitivity enough. This is when a more powerful sonar can be useful.

With soft bottom, much of the sound energy becomes absorbed by lake bottom—it's like dropping a ball on a mattress: the weak signals from bottom may not be detected by the transducer and sonar head. To improve the sonar reading, the sensitivity may have to be increased manually to a level higher than the one the unit selected in auto mode.

In water shallower than 5 feet, the return signal can be extremely strong because of the short distance traveled. The locator in automatic mode may not reduce the sensitivity setting enough to produce a clear picture. In fact, the whole screen may gray out.

In shallow water over hard bottom, use a low sensitivity, which provides a smaller cone angle. In deeper water or over softer bottom, sensitivity needs to be increased to provide a larger cone angle. Generally speaking, do not increase sensitivity just to create a wider cone—the result may be that you also increase distortion, which can mask important sonar signals.

Weeds provide a slightly different challenge for sensitivity control. In the Midwest, a lot of fishing is along the edges of weedlines or over weedbeds. Locators set in automatic mode have a hard time handling these locations. If the sensitivity is increased to pound the signal through vegetation, the image displayed on the screen is saturated and offers little detail.

Remember—increasing the sensitivity doesn't make the locator more powerful; instead, it increases the sonar's listening ability. The sonar picks up relatively strong signals from the dense foliage because the foliage acts as a good reflector, sending a strong signal back to the transducer.

For whatever reason, in automatic mode, locators seem to select a higher sensitivity setting than necessary to deal with dense vegetation. It's as if the locator has information overload: the result is an overdefined image with a loss of detail. Over heavy vegetation, put the unit in manual mode to reduce the sensitivity.

The sensitivity control is the most important function on your locator.

Place your boat outside the weedbed in deeper water, and then slowly move into the weedbed. Check the screen image in automatic mode, and then repeat the process several times in manual mode, changing the sensitivity settings each time. This should help establish which sensitivity setting works better.

The sensitivity control is the most important function on your locator. Knowing how it affects the locator's display is critical. Head out to your favorite body of water, and place your boat in shallow water, deep water, over hard bottom, over soft bottom, over rockpiles and weedbeds. See how each of these areas gets displayed.

Change the sensitivity setting to see how this affects the information on the display. Decide which settings work best in a given situation. This will help you understand what the sonar unit shows and help you gain more confidence in your unit's capabilities.

BOTTOM COMPOSITION, GRAYLINE, AND ZOOM

Is lake bottom beneath your boat harder or softer than surrounding lake bottom? Changes in lake bottom, whether they're changes in hardness or depth, offer fish-holding possibilities. The change between hard and soft bottom, often called the "transition zone," and minor depth variations on structure, often referred to as the "spot on the spot," are displayed on most locators.

A sonar unit measures the time it takes a sound wave to be sent from and returned to the transducer. The strongest signal is down the center (axis) of the transducer. Signals become weaker as they near the edge of the cone's diameter of sound. Using this and other information, a sonar unit displays bottom as harder or softer than the surrounding area.

To better understand this concept, visualize our previous description of the cone of sound as a pointed ice cream cone with the transducer at the point. Also imagine the sound wave as straight strands of spaghetti extending from the end

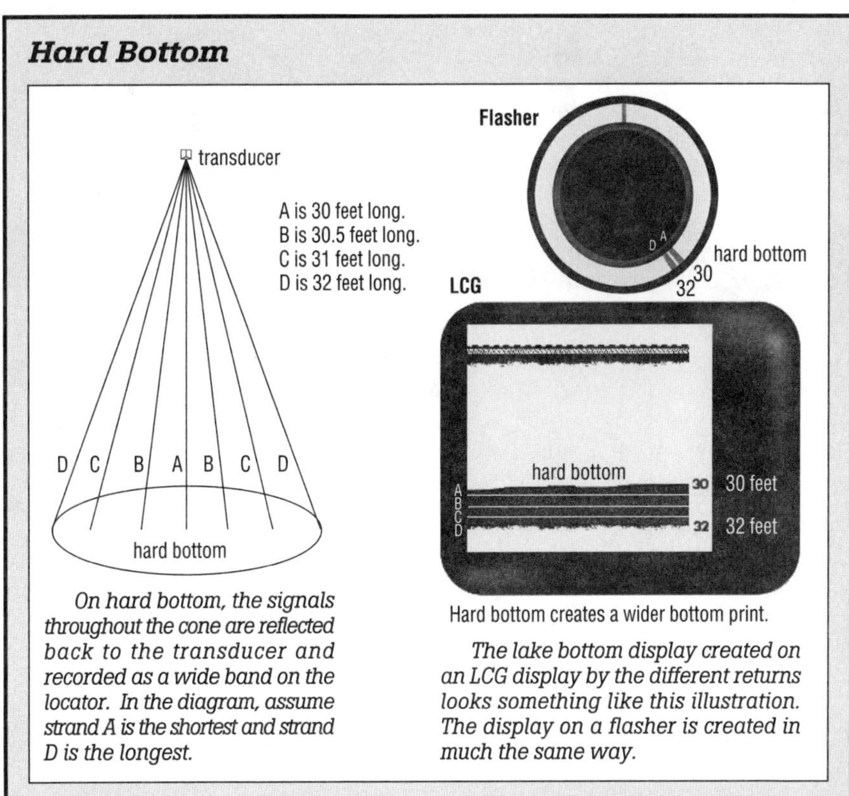

Hard Bottom

On hard bottom, the signals throughout the cone are reflected back to the transducer and recorded as a wide band on the locator. In the diagram, assume strand A is the shortest and strand D is the longest.

Hard bottom creates a wider bottom print.

The lake bottom display created on an LCG display by the different returns looks something like this illustration. The display on a flasher is created in much the same way.

of the transducer, then fanning out and descending to lake bottom. The shortest distance, or shortest strand, becomes recorded first on the display screen when it is reflected from lake bottom. As the sound wave travels out to the edge of the cone, it travels farther. The longer distance is also marked on the locator display.

GRAYLINE

A variation of the hard bottom/soft bottom concept occurs in a bottom detection feature called *grayline* or *clearline*. We'll refer to it as grayline.

The grayline provides a contrasting band on lake bottom and a visual way of detecting relative changes in bottom composition. Grayline is characterized by a lighter band running across the darker bottom print, making objects closer to lake bottom easier to see. The harder the bottom, the wider the grayline band. To adjust the grayline, first adjust sensitivity to the appropriate level. Then adjust the grayline band to 50-50—half the bottom width is displayed as gray, with the remaining (lower) portion as dark.

Even though our discussion has centered around hard objects versus soft objects and their resulting displays on grayline, remember that signal strength reflects the signal returned from a target. Hard objects reflect or return stronger signals than softer objects, but submerged, dense vegetation, while not hard, returns a

Soft Bottom

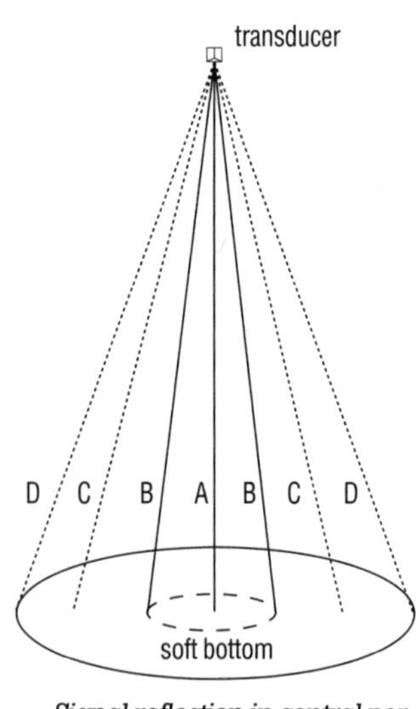

Signal reflection in central portion of cone is sufficient to be detected by sonar.

Signal reflection in outer portion of cone is insufficient to be detected by sonar.

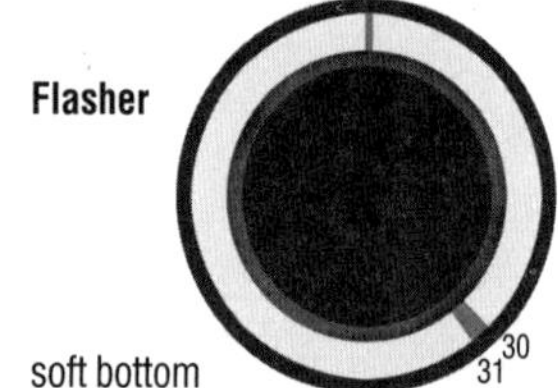

Soft bottom creates a narrower bottom print. The 32-foot signal does not return to the sonar and so is not recorded.

LCG

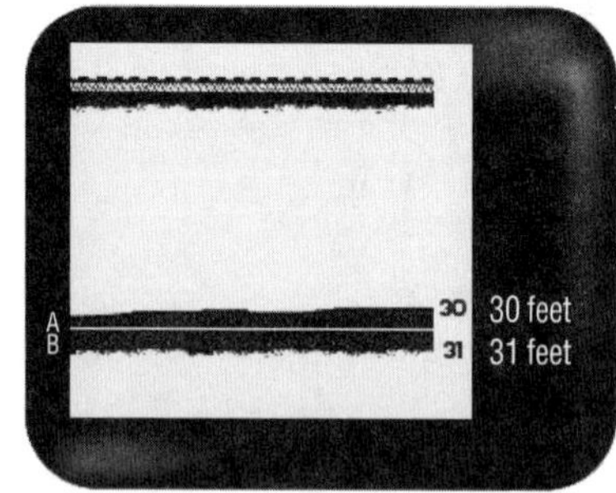

With soft lake bottom, the signal returns coverage of a smaller area because softer bottom absorbs weaker signals near the edge of the cone.

Grayline

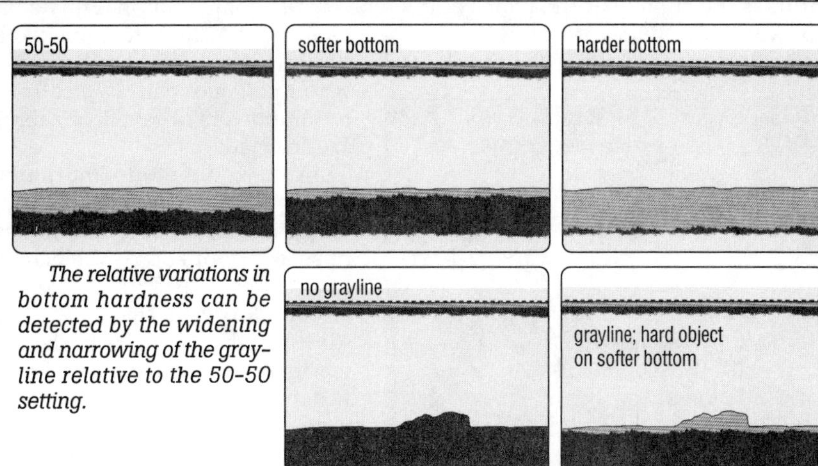

The relative variations in bottom hardness can be detected by the widening and narrowing of the grayline relative to the 50-50 setting.

Grayline also helps to show hard objects on soft bottom and soft objects on hard bottom. Without grayline, changes in bottom were less discernible.

strong signal to the sonar unit, too, often making a weedbed appear gray.

The returning signal can help you determine relative fish size. A larger fish has a larger reflective surface because of its bones, fins, and air bladder. This means that larger fish appear somewhat like harder bottom, returning stronger reflected signals. These stronger signals are displayed by the locator as a wider band.

Larger fish may show some gray on the sonar display as well as the wider print created by a stronger signal. Bigger fish may create a thicker mark than smaller fish. The complicating factor is that the size of the mark depends on where in the cone the fish are detected: fish near the center of the transducer cone appear larger than fish at the edge of the cone because of the difference in signal strength. A larger fish at the edge appears smaller than a smaller fish near the center of the cone.

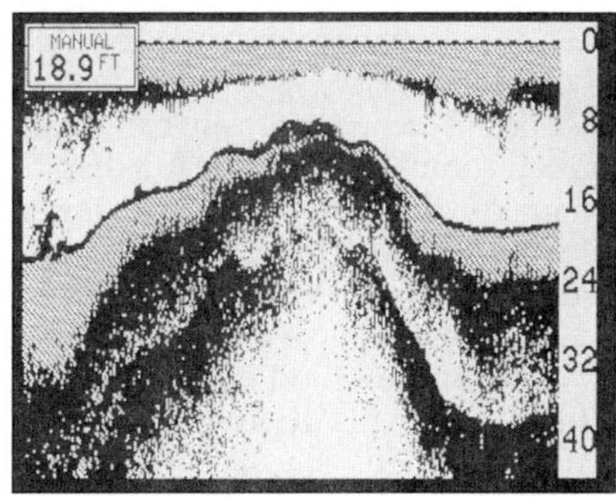

Lake hump shows transition from harder bottom near base to softer bottom near top.

Grayline adjustments on the sonar unit produce changes in the unit's detection or threshold limits. A low grayline setting requires a relatively strong signal from a denser target to trigger the grayline feature. Conversely, a high grayline setting lowers the threshold at which grayline gets displayed. In other words, a high grayline setting causes more of the less-dense targets to gray out.

ZOOM

Another useful tool or feature on LCGs and cathode ray (TV screens) monitors is the zoom feature, which allows the user to zoom in or magnify a band of water. In 40 feet of water, this can be a band from 10 to 20 feet thick. Most often, the zoom feature is used to track or follow lake bottom and a band of water just above it. Typically, different powers or levels of zooming are selected.

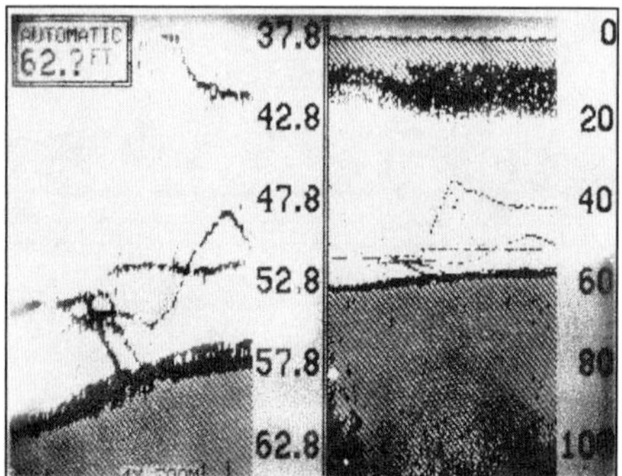

Zoom side (left) shows fish in deep water and emphasizes bottom change.

In the zoom mode, more pixels are applied over a small area to provide greater detail. For instance, suppose a 15-foot zoom is selected. If the LCG has 200 vertical pixels usually spread over 60 feet of water, the same number of pixels in the zoom mode will be spread over a band of water 15 feet wide. This should provide more detail on the screen. Of course, this depends on the unit's ability to electronically detect the objects so they can be displayed.

The zoom feature can help detect the magic fish-holding structure called the "spot on the spot," that unique structural variation on a piece of underwater structure. This spot on the spot can take the form of a small point, hump, depression, or inside turn on the larger structure.

Seeing fish scattered all across a flat or point is unusual; usually, fish relate to unique spots of structure on the flat or point. For instance, at a 40-foot scale setting, a small variation in depth of 1 to 2 feet would hardly be noticeable on the display screen. But when you zoom in on a 10-foot band of water on lake bottom, a small rise or subtle depth change is greatly magnified on the display screen. This minor change now catches your attention. Perhaps you just found the secret spot on the spot.

Zoom screens typically can be set up in two ways. The first method is full-screen zoom, in which the full display screen of the LCG unit is used to show the zoomed-in band of water. With this method, the entire screen may display a band of water from 45 to 60 feet instead of from 0 to 60 feet. A disadvantage of this method is that fish or baitfish above the zoomed column of water aren't shown. In this situation, fish or baitfish above 45 feet won't be shown.

A second method of using the zoom feature is a split screen, in which the display screen is divided vertically into two sections. One section shows the full scale range—say, from 0 to 60 feet—while the other part of the screen shows the zoomed-in feature from 45 to 60 feet. In this way, any suspended targets above 45 feet, such as fish or baitfish, can be seen on the full-scale portion of the screen.

ARCHES, FISH DEPTH, AND THE DEAD ZONE

Do you ever wonder why you don't get the nice-looking "fish arches," those perfect little crescents that you see on simulators? Questions arise: "My locator isn't working right" or "My transducer must be installed wrong because I never get fish arches like that. What do you think is wrong?"

Truth be known, most sonar units don't produce beautiful fish arches. Simulators are designed to illustrate different operating features as opposed to a realistic underwater environment.

Look at how a graph display such as an LCG, video, or paper graph shows information. Keep in mind that a sonar unit measures the distance that a target, such as a fish, is away from the transducer—not necessarily the depth of the target. An object such as a fish could be 35 feet from the transducer but only 32 feet below the surface. It's the 35-foot distance that is recorded on the display.

For the purpose of clarifying fish arches and an example of how the process works, assume that our boat is stationary, the fish is well-behaved and swims right through the center of the transducer cone, and it stays at the same depth as it passes through the cone. We'll pick arbitrary and somewhat unrealistic numbers to illustrate the "arching effect."

Let's assume that our fish is 40 feet below the surface and enters the edge of our cone at 44 feet. The fish is detected at 44 feet, so a mark or indicator appears on the screen. Then the fish moves to a position 43 feet away, then 42, then 41, and finally 40 feet, right below the transducer. Each successively decreasing distance is displayed on the screen in the form of a half arch. Now the fish continues to swim through the cone and exits on the opposite side. This creates the second half of the arch's signature (Figure 1).

Now, let's look at the reality of the situation. First of all, the fish may swim up or down rather than at the same depth, creating more of an angled line or an upside-down J instead of an arch. The fish may just briefly cruise through the edge of the cone, creating only a few target points on the screen with minimal change in distances, so it appears as a short, horizontal line. A fish is displayed, but no perfect fish arch.

One of the most limiting effects of creating the fish arching pattern is the relationship between the actual distance from transducer to target, and, in the case of a LCG, the vertical pixel count (VPC) on the screen. If we assume that a typical 20-degree transducer (measured at -3 dB) is used with a target in, say, 40 feet of

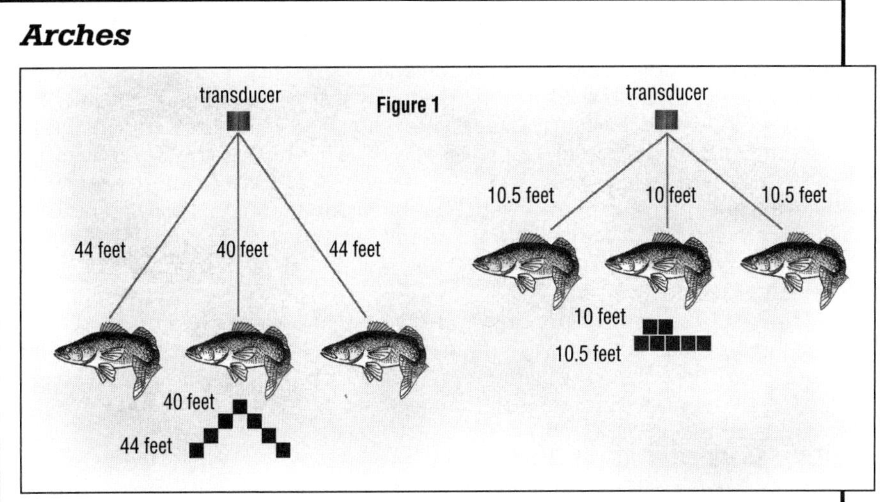

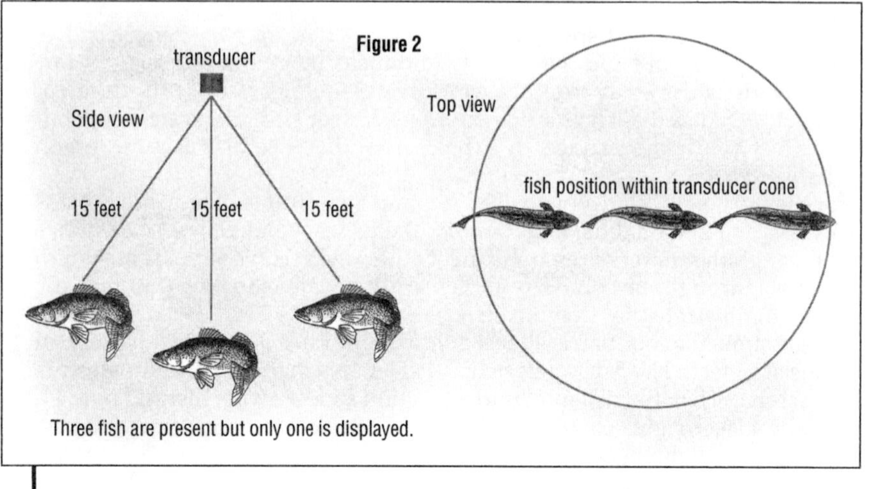

water, here's what happens. First of all, the distance from the transducer along the edge of the cone in 40 feet of water is about 40.6 feet. Let's change these distances to inches to make it easier to see what happens: 40 feet becomes 480 inches and 40.6 feet becomes 487 inches. We have 7 inches of depth difference that we will attempt to display on a screen as the fish moves from the edge to the center of the cone and back out again.

Here's how the vertical pixel count affects the display and the fish arching: let's put our fish in 40 feet of water with a 60-foot depth scale displayed. One pixel on a 100-VPC screen represents 7.2 inches ($60 \times 12 \div 100$). One pixel on a 200-VPC screen represents 3.6 inches, and one pixel on a 300-vertical pixel screen represents 2.4 inches.

Given these numbers, you can see that a screen with a low pixel count will have difficulty displaying any arching. With only 7 inches of difference between the edge and the center of the cone and one pixel representing 7.2 inches, minor differences in depth can't be displayed. The fish will appear as a horizontal line. With the 300-VPC screen, each pixel represents 2.4 inches, so three different pixels representing the depth changes can be displayed. This creates some arching effect.

An increased arch also can be created by going to a zoom screen. In zoom mode, the scale or depth range is reduced, thereby making more pixels available over a smaller area. For instance, on the 300-VPC screen, going to a half-scale zoom (looking at the lower 30 feet on the 60-foot scale), each pixel represents 1.2 inches instead of 2.4 inches.

Unlike LCG displays, paper graphs and video units are less affected by this "pixelitis" and usually provide some arching, because the units generally offer more lines of resolution. Of course, all this depends on having a good receiver capable of detecting minor depth changes.

HOW MANY FISH AND HOW DEEP?

If our boat is sitting still atop three fish, all lying the same distance from the transducer, even though they're at different depths, only one fish will be displayed

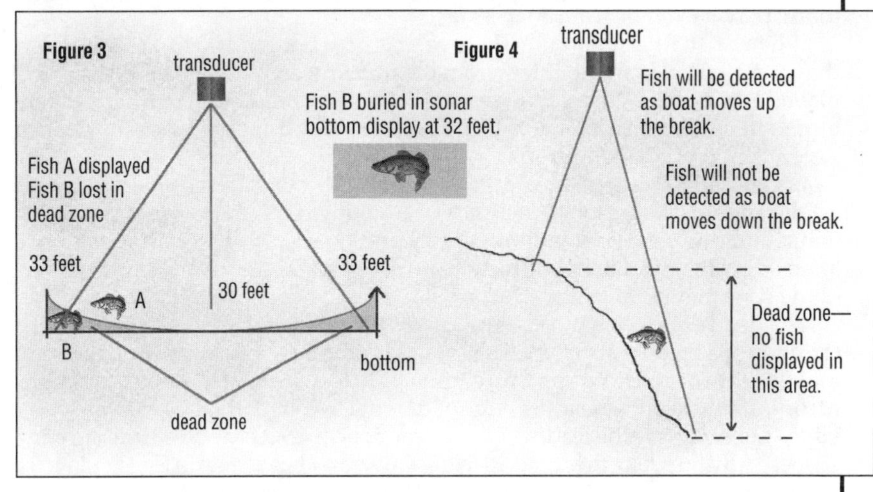

(Figure 2). Remember—sonar only measures distance to the fish, not necessarily their exact depth.

Now assume that we're moving. If we approach three fish, all lying the same distance from the transducer, even though they're at different depths, they simultaneously enter the transducer cone, and initially only one fish is displayed. Then, however, as the boat begins to move toward and over them, each is detected at a different distance from the transducer, so now they appear as separate marks, until they eventually disappear out of the cone. Once again, sonar measures distance to the fish, which continually changes as we pass over them.

A related problem arises because most fish are a bit farther off bottom than they appear, the exception being when a fish is in the center of the cone. This has implications for fishermen, particularly in deep water. Some Great Lakes salmon fishermen see the depth of the fish recorded and adjust the depth of the downrigger to the locator depth, when, in fact, running the lures a bit shallower would be better. Fish see better looking up than down, so it's better to run lures above them than below.

THE DEAD ZONE

The dead zone is typically an area on lake bottom toward the edge of the transducer cone. Consider effective cone angle or area of coverage, which becomes greater or smaller depending on sensitivity adjustment.

Assume we're in 30 feet of water. The shortest distance the sound wave can travel is 30 feet. As we work our way out to the edge of our area of coverage, sound waves travel farther, some 31 feet, some 32 feet, and some 33 feet. This is similar to dealing with hard and soft lake bottom.

As these sound waves return to the locator, the different depths are displayed. If we think of several rows of pixels displaying the 30-foot distance, several more displaying the 31-foot depth, and so on, a wide band is created across the screen, indicating lake bottom. On an old-style flasher display, small light segments were created that in turn created a broader band of light indicating bottom and its hardness.

So now we have this band going across the screen that, according to the locator scale, may be 3 to 5 feet wide. Let's assume it's 3 feet wide. That is, on the locator display it extends from 30 to 33 feet.

When a fish first swims into the area, it is near bottom and toward the edge of the cone. Now it is about 32 feet from the transducer. Where will the fish be displayed? Most likely we won't see it at all because the 32-foot mark is hidden or buried in our bottom display, which covers an area from 30 to 33 feet. The fish is lost in the dead zone (Figure 3).

In general, we can see only targets on the locator that are closer than the shortest distance to lake bottom—in this case, anything fewer than 30 feet away. Don't panic, and don't sell your locator—for the most part, only fish close to bottom are affected by the dead zone. In fact, in 30 feet of water, the dead zone at the edge of the cone may be only 5 or 6 inches.

The dead zone has a more significant effect when you're working a break on the edge of a piece of structure, such as a flat. Suppose you're on the edge of a 20-foot flat with a moderate break extending to 30 feet. As you move down the break (drop-off), the front or leading edge of the cone is longer than the trailing or back edge. Let's assume the leading edge of the cone is 25 feet and the trailing edge is 20 feet. Any target farther than 20 feet away won't be visible on the display. This means that most fish lying on or near the bottom of the breakline won't be detected.

On the other hand, we have a better chance of detecting fish on the break if we work our way up the break from deep to shallow (Figure 4). Now the short or leading edge of the cone is followed by the longer or trailing edge. Fish on the break and fewer than 20 feet away can be detected for a short time. The fish is visible until the leading edge becomes shorter than the distance the fish is from the transducer. Remember—the edges of the cone change continually as you work your way up the break.

PERCEPTION VERSUS REALITY

The engineers designing depth sounders and their features can program a microprocessor to recognize a typical fish signal, sometimes called a *fish signature*. Fish signals assume a variety of forms. Fish detection systems—often called *Fish I.D.* or *cartoon fish*—interrupt the peace and quiet of the outdoors by bleeping out alarms and showing fish-shaped images on your sonar screen. Depth alarms, meanwhile, sound alarms when you enter preselected depths, whether shallow or deep. They can be used as anchor alarms to sound alerts when anchors aren't holding. Just the same, while Fish I.D. alarms have legitimate uses, most veteran anglers prefer to bypass them in favor of interpreting their own signals.

Why? Simple: when the microprocessor can't account for what it detects, it guesses, and it often guesses wrong. Tips of brush or vegetation often are interpreted as fish. It's as if the locator were saying, "Well, this seems like a fishy signal, so let's make the old boy feel good and put a head and tail on it." As a result, you're often fishing for weeds and brush—and they don't bite.

When you buy a locator, make sure the model allows you to turn off the fish identification system in both manual and automatic modes. Running the locator with the fish identification off is best. Use the language of plain pixels. With practice, you will guess much better than the locator about what you're seeing on the screen.

For example, you may know that the old branch hanging over the edge of the point fell off last October. So all those pixels showing up on the screen, you reason, may be the tips of the fallen branch, not fish. The locator doesn't know that the branch fell in the water last fall. Similarly, your fish alarm rings often, but many of its rings are false alarms. If you have kids in the boat, turn on the Fish I.D. system to entertain them. Otherwise, turn it off.

REAL-TIME READOUT VERSUS HISTORY

A technical hang-up or Achilles heel of LCGs is what's called *response time*. This refers to the delay in time between the detection of the return signal and its display on the screen, often referred to as *real-time response*. In comparison to other locator styles, such as flashers, the response time of an LCG is relatively slow. By the time an LCG displays an underwater hump or reef, a boat traveling at 30 to 40 mph may be 50 to 100 yards down the lake. At slow trolling speeds, however, response time needn't be so critical.

To compensate for this slow response time, manufacturers have added "real-time readouts." These are usually in the form of screen options that display traditional flasher faces or vertical bar flashers. It's perhaps not instant real time, but it's much faster than the traditional LCG chart display.

Traditional fast chart speeds have been about 10 to 15 pixels per second. Some newer models operate at 20 to 40 pixels per second. This higher speed moves pixels out of the way more quickly, resulting in faster loading of the next column of pixels. The result is more of a real-time readout at higher speeds, but it's still not up to the speed of a flasher.

At slower chart speeds, fish detected at 15 to 20 miles an hour usually display as single pixels. The problem is, so do other forms of noise and debris. A higher speed screen should at least be able to put two, three, or four pixels on the screen to indicate a possible fish, but probably not arches.

With current technology, there are certain limitations with high chart speed on LCG displays. Fuzziness bothers some anglers. Vertical bar flashers and circular flashers found on an LCG are less affected by technical limitations on the graphic display.

The tradeoff for this lack of fast, high-speed readout is that LCGs retain a history on the screen. Images travel across the screen, displaying what was detected 10, 15, or 20 seconds earlier. Look away from the screen for a few seconds—say, to pour a cup of coffee or select a new bait—look back, and you'll see that a few seconds ago you went over a fish. Flashers retain no such history. Take your eyes off the display for a few seconds, and you may miss a fish—it's only a temporary blip on the screen, and then it disappears.

SURFACE CLUTTER

Surface clutter refers to the black and gray bands appearing across the top of LCG screens. Similar effects are found on flashers, paper graphs, and video units. On LCG screens with a high-sensitivity setting and small depth scale of 15 or 20 feet, surface clutter can account for 20 to 30 percent of the screen. The surface clarity control (SCC) can help reduce the depth of clutter moving across the screen. The control is adjusted so that the return signal is amplified less near the surface than during the remainder of its travel.

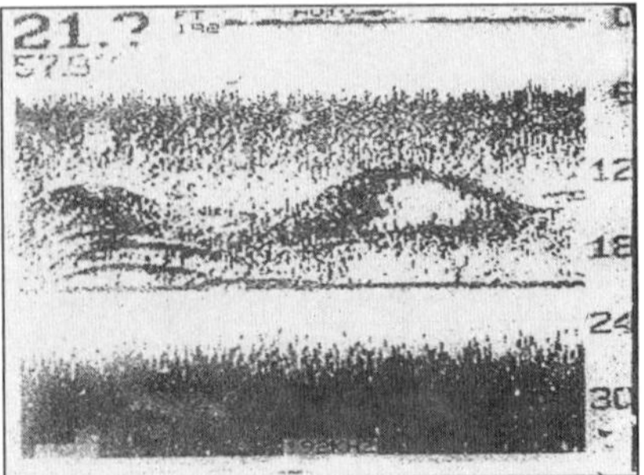

The "hanging icicles" of excessive surface clutter are probably due to a relatively high sensitivity setting.

Normal surface clutter at a reduced sensitivity setting. If the automatic sensitivity mode creates excessive surface clutter, switch to manual mode for a cleaner display.

Another way to think about SCC is to remember that it has a sliding scale or gradient for sensitivity. The sensitivity is lower near the surface and higher when depth increases. This is why the width of the surface-clutter band increases or decreases as sensitivity is increased or decreased. A wide band is often an indicator of a high-sensitivity setting—perhaps higher than necessary.

Keep your SCC on a low setting. Some units don't have adjustments for surface clutter. In shallow water—say, less than 5 feet—the SCC can be placed on a low setting so you can see more of the water column on the screen.

USEFUL TIPS

To reduce electrical interference, wire your sonar directly to your starting battery or to a separate battery for electronics, not to your trolling motor battery. Be sure to install an in-line fuse. Check your manual for amperage. Be sure the nuts are tight on the connecting posts of the battery. More electronic and engine problems are caused by loose connections than by anything else. Replace standard wing nuts with hex nuts, then tighten them down once your wires are on the post.

Swivel-mount brackets are useful. LCG screens are light sensitive and have a narrower viewing angle than other electronic displays. You need to be able to turn and tilt the locator head to improve screen visibility to maximize locator performance. Swivel mounting brackets function as shock absorbers on the water as well as on the road and probably extend the life of the unit.

Removing a locator from a boat to travel safely or to avoid theft is easy with most swivel-mount brackets. Never travel long distances with electronics in the boat; the pounding they receive from the road doesn't do them any good. Place them in a soft-sided cooler.

If your boat sits in the water all season, scum accumulates on the hull and on the transducer. Use a scouring pad (nothing very abrasive) to periodically clean the bottom of the transducer.

CURRENT AND SUGGESTED REFINEMENTS

• Eliminate interference between two sonar units operating at the same time in the boat by using two operating frequencies separated by 50 kHz or more, such as a 150-kHz and a 200-kHz model. Low frequencies, such as 50 kHz or 75 kHz, aren't as useful for most freshwater fishing.

• Increase the maximal chart speed from 10 or 15 pixels per second to 30, 40, or more pixels per second. This helps the real-time display and makes higher-speed searching for fish and structure more efficient.

• Eliminate interference between electric trolling motors and locators without going to integrated systems. Integrated systems refer to sonar and electric trolling motors from the same manufacturer that work as a compatible system.

• Increase screen pixel counts—probably in the area of 500 vertical pixels or more—on top-end units.

READING FLASHERS

Flashers are like the Little Engine That Could. Dismissed as archaic technology by some, they provide quick reads in fast boats. When bottom comes up, flashers point it out immediately. And a flasher fits nicely in the dash.

Some fishermen refuse to give up on them. Some say it's familiarity. Those who learned how to fish with flashers aren't willing to start all over with new technologies—or so the story goes. Whatever the reason, flashers aren't at all bad for bowmount duty, speed reading, ice fishing, small craft, and other specific applications.

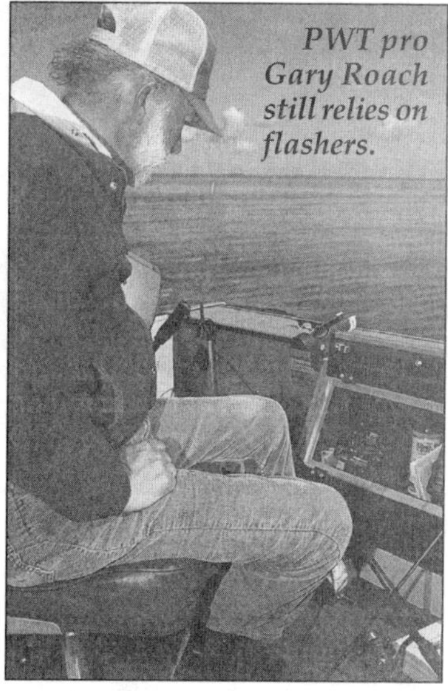
PWT pro Gary Roach still relies on flashers.

Reading a flasher is fundamentally different from reading a Liquid Crystal Display (LCD). It involves making a picture out of an abstraction, as opposed to simply interpreting a two-dimensional picture. Basic guidelines teach you how to read a lot from what seems like a tiny amount of information. As with any depthfinder, familiar water helps acquaint you with the unit. You already know approximate depths, so you'll be able to distinguish bottom quicker.

The bottom line is critical. To avoid mistaking a false echo for bottom, adjust the sensitivity. To clearly identify the bottom line, adjust the sensitivity up and down to create and eliminate echoes. The line that remains on the screen when sensitivity is lowest is true bottom.

A thick line on bottom can mean several things. If the sensitivity is too high, hard bottom reads heavy. If the bottom line is still heavy after lowering sensitivity, the transducer is reading a drop-off. One side of the cone is reading the shallow side of the break, the other the deep side. Steep breaks on rocky Canadian Shield lakes, for instance, can show up on the screen as mostly solid red or

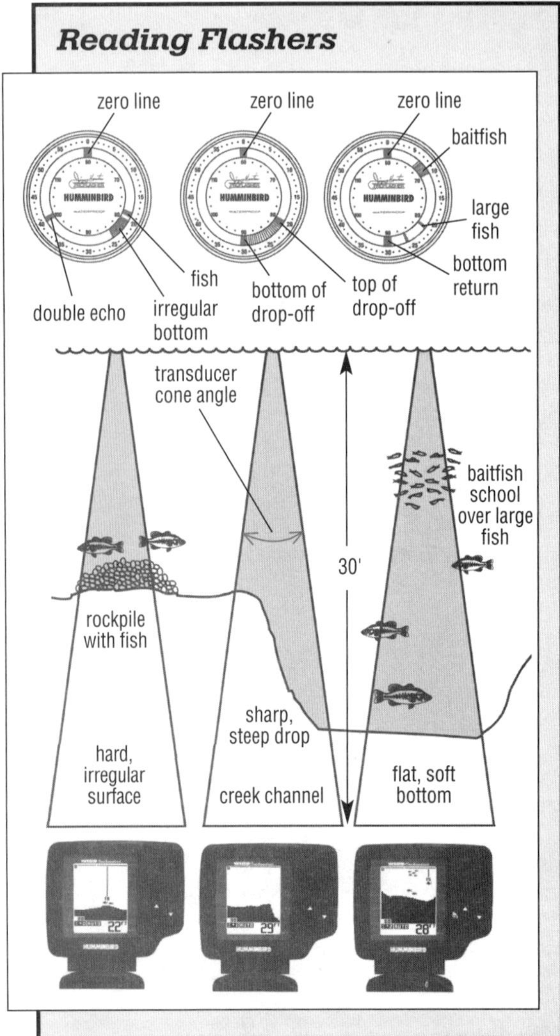

black lines (depending on the make of the unit) extending from the 20-foot mark to the 45- or 55-foot mark, depending on cone angle. Drop a jig down and feel it roll and skid down the break, proving to yourself that it really is that steep. The wider the cone, the wider this band on a break. Anything on or near bottom along this break becomes invisible to the unit. (The same can be true with an LCD in certain circumstances.)

So when you're passing over a submerged 30-foot tree, bottom still shows. Branches appear much the same as weeds—a series of lines that flutter and alter as the boat and transducer move past. These lines are usually less dense than the bottom line, unless bottom is quite soft. Soft bottom returns a weak signal. And the deeper the water, the weaker the signal. The more familiar you become with an area, the easier to detect fish among branches and weeds.

Fish are displayed as lines suspended above the bottom line, anywhere from top to bottom. Small fish appear as thinner, less substantial lines. Big fish may produce thicker lines, especially when they travel directly through the center of the cone. Big fish on the edge of the cone may look smaller. Fish can also be distinguished as a sudden thickness added to the bottom line. Or (especially when you're anchored or ice fishing) the top of the bottom line may begin to flutter, indicating movement tight to bottom within the cone.

As with any depthfinder, you need to adjust the sensitivity to the highest possible setting for the conditions. Back off at the point where bottom clutter begins to distort the bottom line, artificially raising it. When sensitivity is tuned correctly, flashers display the smallest baitfish without cluttering the screen with reflections, false signals, or bits of reflections from tiny particles in the water. As you gain confidence in your ability to adjust the unit properly, you'll feel relatively certain that any flash appearing above bottom is some kind of fish.

High-speed reading is one of the main advantages of a flasher. As the transducer picks up the echo of its sound signal off bottom, the information is displayed almost instantly, thus taking some of the guesswork out of retracing your steps to something interesting that you passed over at high speed.

VIDEOSONAR (CRT)

Why not TV in the boat? You won't get *In-Fisherman* or *Oprah*, but you will get a good lake contour and fish program. Actually, TV has been an option for some time in the form of a cathode ray tube (CRT). Most fishermen think of LCGs as the current locator of choice, but the CRT is another good option. A simple overview illustrates the differences between the LCD and the CRT.

Liquid Crystal Displays (LCDs) come in two basic forms: passive and active. The less expensive systems are passive and are most often used in the sportfishing industry. Several principles of physics apply: (1) light can be polarized; (2) liquid crystals can transmit and change polarized light; (3) the structure of liquid crystals can be changed by electric current.

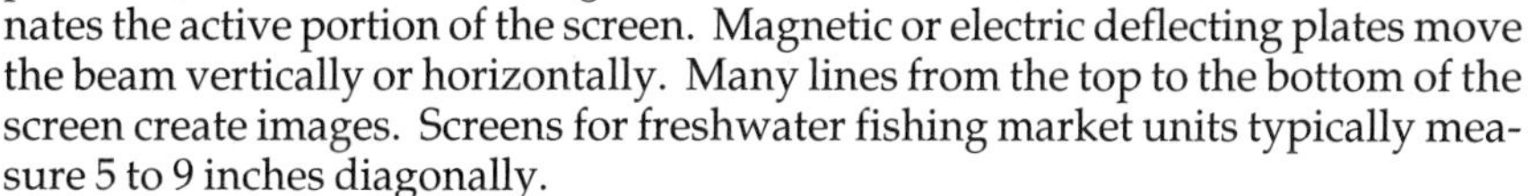

A thin film of liquid crystal is placed between sheets of glass. Filters polarize the light entering and leaving the crystal. When an electrical current is applied to the liquid crystal, the crystal modifies the polarized light. This creates spots where light gets through (light pixels) and spots where light can't get through (dark pixels). These pixels create images on the display.

The CRT or TV screen works on different principles. A CRT works by moving an electron beam created by an electron gun located in the back of the picture tube. Electrons from the gun are accelerated and focused. They strike the screen in a fine beam. Each time the beam makes a pass across the screen, it lights up phosphor dots on the inside of the glass tube. This illuminates the active portion of the screen. Magnetic or electric deflecting plates move the beam vertically or horizontally. Many lines from the top to the bottom of the screen create images. Screens for freshwater fishing market units typically measure 5 to 9 inches diagonally.

CRT screen resolution is measured in terms of "dot pitch" (dp) instead of vertical pixel count (VPC), which is used to measure screen resolution on a LCG screen. CRT screens typically have dot pitches of 24 to 28. The smaller the dp number, the better the screen resolution.

Videosonar systems based on CRT screens are available in monochrome (single color) and color screens. Color screens tend to wash out in bright sunlight, making viewing more difficult. To see the screen in an open boat, you need to use shielding. Viewing in an enclosed area, however, produces an excellent picture. Monochrome screens, particularly green, are easier to see in a variety of lighting conditions.

CRT sonar offers several advantages, one being its wide viewing angle. This makes the videosonar viewable from almost anywhere in a boat under proper lighting conditions. A CRT screen can be seen while standing well off to the side of the screen. In contrast, an LCG screen can only be viewed on-axis.

Another advantage to CRT is fast response time. The time it takes for a returned signal to be displayed to the viewer is measured in nanoseconds. This display speed, combined with rapid sweep speed on the screen, permits high-speed searching for fish. With practice, you can spot and identify fish at boat speeds of 5 to 15 mph or faster. In fact, many people who own CRTs don't use flashers for high-speed running and safety; the CRT's display speed is fast enough.

Expert fisherman feel that with practice, they can detect fish closer to bottom with good CRTs than with good LCGs, although they admit that the differences in ability are minor. Some colors and shadings may help interpret fish signals more easily—for example, with color units, you may be better able to judge the size of fish based on the shadings of the screen images.

Output power for the Si-Tex color CVS-106 Mk II is 2400 watts peak-to-peak, much like similarly priced LCGs. The Genetron GT-9 single-color green screen has 1200 watts peak-to peak power for depths between 50 and 1,000 feet, and 120 watts peak-to-peak power for depths under 50 feet. Genetron feels that their receiving unit is so sensitive that it requires less power at the same depths than comparable sonar units.

CRT systems consume a bit more power than LCGs. CRTs draw about 1600 to 2500 milliamps compared to similarly powered LCGs (500 to 800 milliamps). If the backlighting on an LCG is turned on, add about another 300 milliamps to the current draw. (A milliampere is one thousandth of an amp.)

In conclusion, every locator system has its pluses and minuses. The advantages of a CRT over an LCG system appear to be a faster or more real-time response on the display screen; a wider screen viewing angle; and the ability, with practice, to see fish at higher speeds (5 to 15 mph). In certain situations, a CRT may provide additional information to a trained user.

CRT systems have several disadvantages: the units are weatherproof but not waterproof, and they may require more protected locations than most LCGs. CRT units are larger and deeper—typically 8 to 10 inches deep—whereas LCGs are 3 to 4 inches deep. In some situations, CRTs' larger size can create mounting problems. Color videoscreens, in particular, may need additional shading from direct sunlight. These are generalizations, however, and don't apply to all units. Research and determine your needs before purchasing any sonar system.

READING STRUCTURE AND BOTTOM CONDITIONS

Reading deep structure seems an imposing task for beginning walleye anglers. The abyss below 30 or 40 feet seems a world away, the stuff of Jules Verne, fraught with unknown sea monsters and impenetrable murk.

Hate to spoil the mystery, but you already have all the tools to do the job. The only thing you may be lacking is confidence. Plumbing the depths is no different than fishing shallower, except that generally you need to fish a bit slower and definitely scout out locations first to pinpoint productive spots.

Large structures projecting into deep basins are key fall spots in most walleye waters. They intercept walleyes traveling along the drop-off, holding fish for a while at points, turns, and irregularities in the sloping edge.

When temperature and oxygen are consistent throughout the depths, walleyes encounter few barriers or incentives to lie at a specific depth, unless something's present to concentrate them. In many cases, it's the transition from hard to soft bottom at the base of the drop-off, where the slope's hard bottom fades into the basin's soft muck. Fish sense this edge and lie along it.

Fortunately, you can spot this on electronics and feel it with your slipsinker, jig, jigging spoon, bladebait, or three-way rig. The relative *bang, bang* of harder bottom, transmitted up your line by every lift-drop, suddenly changes to a mushy feeling as your weight oozes down into soft bottom. That's the change. Move slightly shallower, and you feel the bang return. Congratulations. You have just woven your presentation on and off the transition—right where the big ones lurk.

In some cases, this transition occurs right at the base of the sloping drop-off, exactly where it meets the basin. In others, a rim of relatively hard bottom extends out horizontally for 5, 10, 15 feet or more onto the flat. Then suddenly . . . ooze. This transitional edge and the base of the drop offer two options for locating deep walleyes.

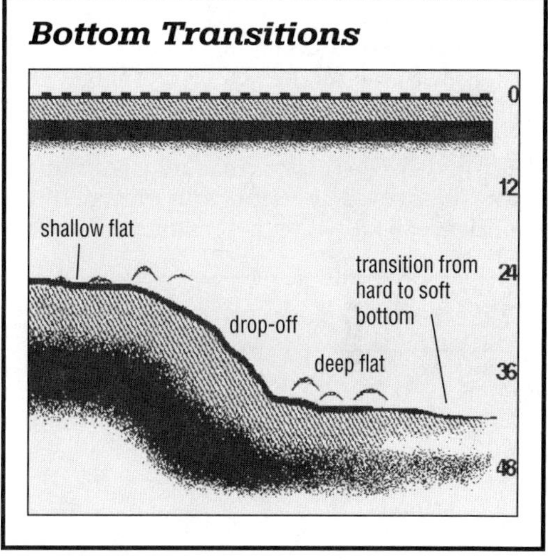

Fortunately, electronics aid in the search. Begin by slowly weaving along the edge of a drop-off, searching for points or turns that may concentrate fish. Hug the deep edge of the slope, moving slightly onto the basin, then slightly back up onto the slope. Repeat. You should not only be able to read depth changes but also changes in bottom consistency.

On a LCG, hard bottom reflects a dark band with probable second echoes at twice the depth of bottom. As you move out over softer bottom, however, the second echo disappears, and the initial bottom reading becomes lighter or dim. That's the transitional point from hard to soft. On a flasher depthfinder, this point changes from bright signals with double or triple reflections to a weak single flash. Same principle.

Walleyes appear as distinctly arched hook marks on a LCG and as solid flash marks on a flasher. Fish lying directly on bottom are tough to see. Those slightly above begin to appear as bumps in bottom. With sufficient separation from bottom, their signals become distinct, clearly marking the presence and depth of fish. Expensive units boast target separation of only a few inches, great for sensing fish near or hugging bottom. Inexpensive units often don't read fish until they're at least 12 inches off bottom.

Now combine sight and feel. Position your boat above the transition edge, lower your jig or rig to bottom, and begin lift-dropping it along, following the edge through the combined use of sight (graph) and feel (finger on the line). Lift-dropping transmits a more distinct *thunk* when your lead touches bottom than dragging, which tends to snag in rock or wood. Adjust line length slightly as needed, using just enough line to maintain bottom contact and interpretation. The shortest, most vertical line typically is most effective. More line decreases feel. It's that simple.

Be sure to use sufficient weight to retain feel and control. For backtrolling in calm conditions, a 3/8-ounce sinker is usually adequate. With any wind, however, 1/2 or 3/4 ounces helps to retain control. Should fish lie at the 50-foot level on a windy day, 1/2-, 5/8-, 3/4-, or even monster 1-ounce jigs may be needed.

Deep water puts a lot of drag on your line, forcing you to move slower than when you're fishing shallow. Thus it's important to focus on key spots. When you locate a potential structure, first spend 5 or 10 minutes running its edges, noting depth at the base of the drop-off, whether the transition to soft bottom coincides with or lies farther off the slope, and which spots indicate the presence and depth of fish. You may save several hours of slow fishing by first locating the fish with your eyes. Now drop your presentation, and have at 'em. You'll have the confidence of knowing they're there, and you can feel the road they travel.

Transition Edges

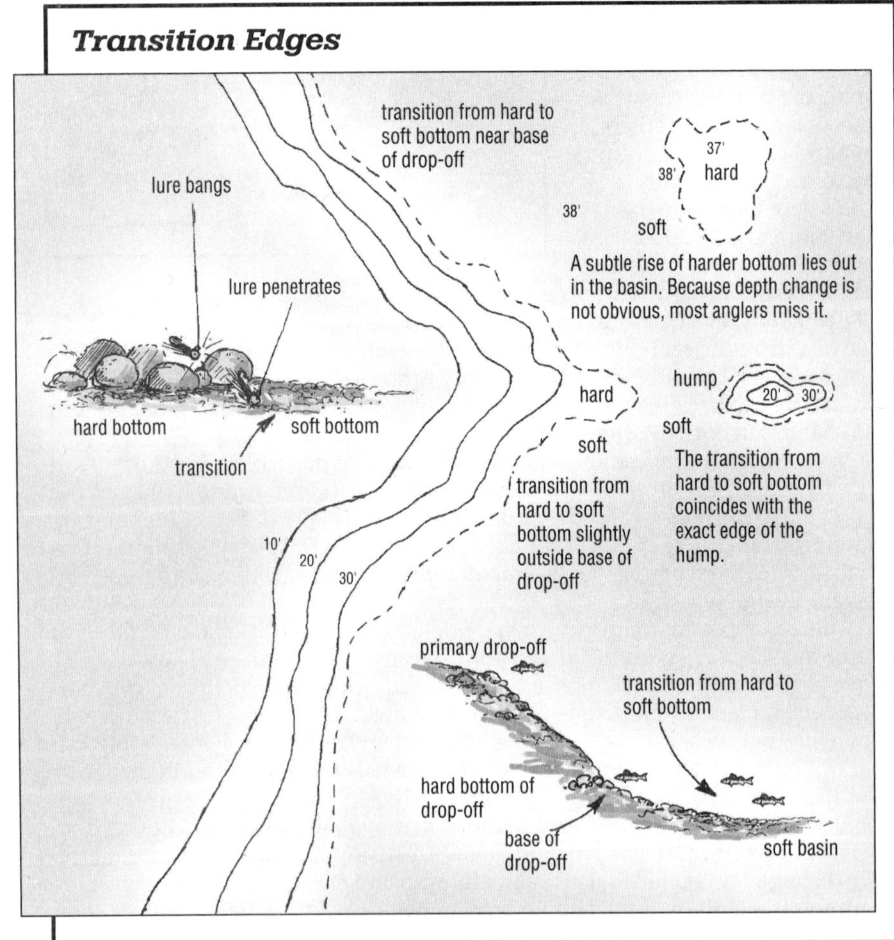

Transitions may lie at slightly different depths on different structures, explaining why the fish are at 38 feet in one spot, 44 in another. It's not just light penetration that concentrates deep fish at certain levels—it's underlying bottom.

SIDE-SCANNING SONAR REVEALS SUSPENDED FISH

Ever troll an area that produced suspended walleyes a few days before but now fails to yield any fish? The usual explanation is, "They must be hugging bottom in a negative mood" or "Maybe the fish just moved." Maybe. Maybe not. They could be right there, and you just don't know.

In lakes where baitfish suspend over open water in summer, feeding on invertebrates and plankton, sometimes they rise quite near the surface. Chances are, walleyes will be right behind, especially when the weather's calm or there's only slight wave action.

These high-riding fish are almost impossible to mark on traditional sonar. Why? Let's look at an example. A 16-degree cone angle transducer reveals an area only 1 foot in diameter at a depth of 5 feet below your boat. Any fish riding this high would likely spook out to the side of your approaching boat.

A side-scanning sonar often reveals the presence of these fish and even suggests how deep to run your lures. Side-scanning technology was first popularized by Bottom Line, which continues to offer several models combining Side Finder functions with depth and bottom interpretation off a single transducer. Humminbird and other companies have introduced models with similar side-scanning functions.

A side-scanning sonar often reveals the presence of these fish and even suggests how deep to run your lures.

Figure 1 details a typical side-scanning setup, with a transducer mounted 6 inches below the water line, scanning parallel to or slightly downward from the boat. Note that the upper half (8 degrees) of the cone angle is out of the water, returning no signal to the unit. The lower 8 degrees scans for fish. Based on this cone angle, fish detected at a set distance are at most only .14 times as deep as their distance from the boat. (There's that dreaded high school geometry rearing its ugly head again!) In this example, fish are detected 15 feet from the boat, and to be seen, must be within 2.1 feet of the surface. Deeper fish, if present, lie outside the cone and are not visible.

Fish detected 30 feet from the boat (Figure 2) must be at 4.2 feet or less—no deeper. (A handy formula: for every additional 10 feet from the boat, fish can be up to 1.4 feet deeper.) So to place lures at or just above the fish's level, start running them 4.2 feet deep or slightly shallower.

After we've experimented at those depths, we have the option to run our lures a bit deeper to try catching fish that may be there but that are undetectable on the side scanner.

Let's say we see two groups of fish, 10 feet and 30 feet out (Figure 3). Start trolling by positioning lures to catch the shallowest, most active fish—those revealed by the closest marks to the boat. In this case, that means setting out lures that run at 1.4 feet or fewer. In general, fish spotted this close to the boat suggest that many fish are riding high near the surface.

Theoretically, any time you see fish 30 feet out from the boat, they can be anywhere from the surface down to about 4.2 feet. In practice, however, waves can break up return signals from distant fish just beneath the surface. Most of the time, the fish you see at 30 feet will be closer to the 4.2-foot level than to the surface. If any number of fish are riding higher near the surface, you should be able to detect them closer to the boat, at shallower depths.

Who says fish depth can't be measured by looking to the side? This system gives the angle and depth on high-feeding, elusive walleyes.

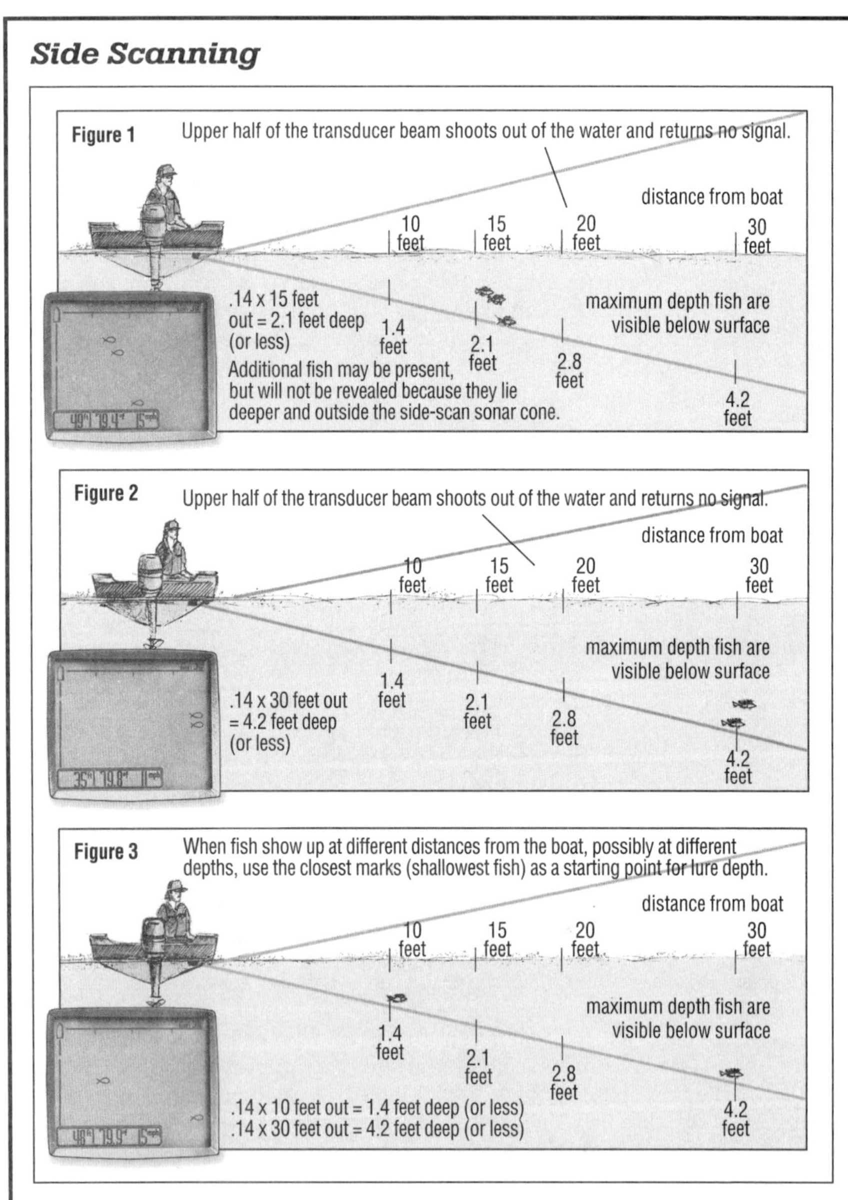

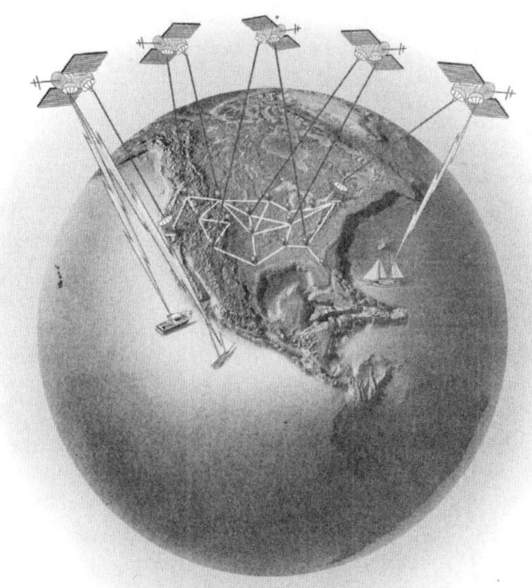

A Quantum Leap Beyond Sonar

GPS, MAPPING, UNDERWATER CAMERAS, AND OTHER ELECTRONICS

The Global Positioning Satellite system (GPS) was created at the request of the Department of Defense. It was first publicly demonstrated during the Gulf War. It depends on a network of satellites located approximately 11,000 miles above the earth that orbit it every 12 hours. With inexpensive GPS receivers, anglers can use this system for accurate positioning (latitude and longitude) to within 20 to 70 feet most of the time.

Selected Availability (SA) was designed to decrease the integrity of the GPS signal and thereby reduce its accuracy for potential enemies of the United States. When SA was in use, you got within 50 to 300 feet of your desired position. When

SA was turned off in early May 2000, the repeatable accuracy of GPS units increased. Now that SA is a thing of the past, you should return to your favorite fishing spots and resave them. This new save will provide much more accurate coordinates for fishing spots. Use the following methods.

HOW GPS WORKS

Global Positioning Satellite systems are the most important electronics connection to fishing since the introduction of the depthfinder. Not surprisingly, the number of sportsmen who own GPS units has skyrocketed.

It's important to understand that handheld GPS units can serve double duty for those of you who are hunters, hikers, and ice fishermen. Among *In-Fisherman's* readers, handheld units will outsell mounted units by three to one this coming year. It's likely, though, that most of you will eventually own both boat-mounted and handheld units.

As has been the case with the introduction and subsequent development of many new technologies, GPS units have advanced quickly in design, while prices have fallen steadily.

Consider, for example, the common price for handheld units. It has fallen from about $500 for the best technology of the day not long ago to about $200—amazing, given how much more refined today's technology is. No more than 10 years ago, countries interested in the weapons delivery application of GPS would have paid millions for simple access to the components we pay $200 for today.

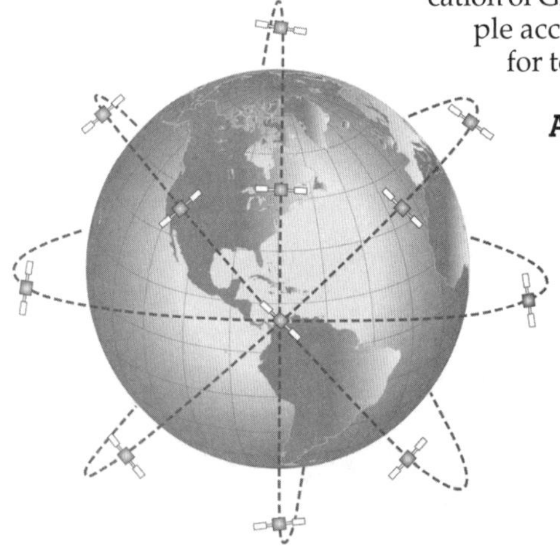

Global Positioning Satellite systems use a constellation of 24 satellites covering the earth in precise orbits about 11,000 miles out in space. As many as 12 satellites are available for signal transmission and receiver reception at any time.

ADVANCES IN RECEIVER DESIGN

The biggest advance in GPS units has been in receiver design. The role of the receiver is to decode satellite signals and display information. Today, some of the most efficient receivers can track as many as twelve satellites, although no more than four satellite signals are ever actually involved in immediate navigation. As we've noted, the good news is that such efficiency isn't much more expensive.

Understanding the differences in receiver design is one of the keys to buying a GPS unit that works efficiently for you. Note again that a receiver must track at least four satellites for the greatest accuracy. Satellites are in a 12-hour orbit, so the receiver needs to continually search for satellites (while some move below and others appear above the horizon), acquire signals, and then select the three or four satellite signals that provide the best geometry for the optimal fix. For some receivers, antenna design also plays an important role in operating capability.

Single-channel receivers—One of the earliest and simplest receiver designs, the single-channel receiver was initially offered as the low-cost choice when the best technology available probably would have cost thousands of dollars. In this design, one channel is available to locate a satellite and to communicate with it. The single channel then locates one satellite after another until it has talked to at least three satellites. This type of receiver is often called a *sequencing* receiver. Older GPS units with a single channel have more difficulty locking onto each successive satellite, as well as processing the information once a lock is complete.

Multiplexing receivers—An improvement on the single-channel design is the multiplexing receiver. Several channels are linked in order to acquire position lock. Instead of just one channel flip-flopping between three or four satellites, at least two channels flip-flop between satellites, attempting to lock with three or four. More satellites are monitored, in turn providing the potential for better coverage. Lock must still be acquired and then dropped when the receiver moves from one satellite to communicate with another.

Multiplexing receivers usually do not work well in vehicles that lack exterior antennas. Even when antennas are used, multiplying receivers often lose lock under canopies of trees or other overhead obstructions. Like single-channel receivers, some multiplexing receivers don't track a course well at running speed.

Continuous or parallel-channel receivers—One of the most common receiver designs in recent years is the parallel-channel receiver, which lies a step beyond single-channel receivers and most multiplexing receivers. At least four channels are available in parallel-channel receivers, each communicating continuously with its own satellite. The receiver dedicates a channel to a satellite so long as that satellite is in good viewing position.

One common design is a five-channel parallel receiver. Four channels lock onto satellites to provide navigation information, while a fifth channel monitors the positions of other satellites in view. If satellite geometry can improve the accuracy of position fix, a new satellite is plugged into the configuration, and the least desirable satellite is dropped.

This receiver design provides efficient satellite lock in many, perhaps most situations. Lock is less likely to be lost under canopy cover and usually isn't lost in adverse weather. Lock usually can't be maintained without an exterior antenna on your vehicle, however.

Twelve-channel parallel receivers—The latest and most advanced receiver design, the twelve-channel receiver offers twelve channels to search through available satellites for the optimal configuration. Four channels then individually lock to four different satellites, while the remaining eight channels continue to monitor other audible satellites. Again, if satellite geometry can improve the accuracy of position fix, a new satellite is plugged into the configuration, and the least desirable satellite is dropped.

All other design characteristics being equal, twelve-channel parallel receivers are most likely to maintain continuous satellite lock, even while on the seat of a vehicle, at maximum boat speed, and under heavy tree canopy or other overhead obstructions.

DIFFERENTIAL GPS

Many fishermen want increased accuracies for positioning. Differential GPS (DGPS) refers to any corrected GPS signal. The most common correction is a service offered by the United States Coast Guard. This system works from a network of towers whose positions are precisely known.

The tower and the GPS receiver both receive a signal from the satellites. The signal determining the tower position is compared to the location of the tower. Corrections are made and sent to the GPS unit, where a radio beacon receiver formats the corrected information and passes it on to the GPS unit, which displays a corrected position.

Used with an inexpensive consumer version of a GPS receiver, differential GPS accuracy is about 30 feet or fewer. High-grade (expensive) GPS equipment can provide accuracies to within 10 or fewer feet. The GPS service provided by the Coast Guard is free, but private pay-for-services systems also are in operation.

The original DGPS towers were located on the East Coast and West Coast, the Great Lakes, and the Mississippi River system. Presently a Nationwide Differential GPS (NDGPS) expansion is underway. When completed, the entire United States should be covered.

WAAS UP?

Wide Area Augmentation System (WAAS), another form of DGPS, was created for the Federal Aviation Administration (FAA). Its purpose is to improve the accuracy, integrity, and availability of the basic GPS system over a wide area. It was designed to help with flight information and traffic management at select airports, making these airports safer and more efficient. Now the WAAS signal is available to the public.

WAAS is based on a system of approximately thirty ground reference stations. Each of these stations determines any error in the GPS signal relative to its position. Data from the stations is forwarded to a wide

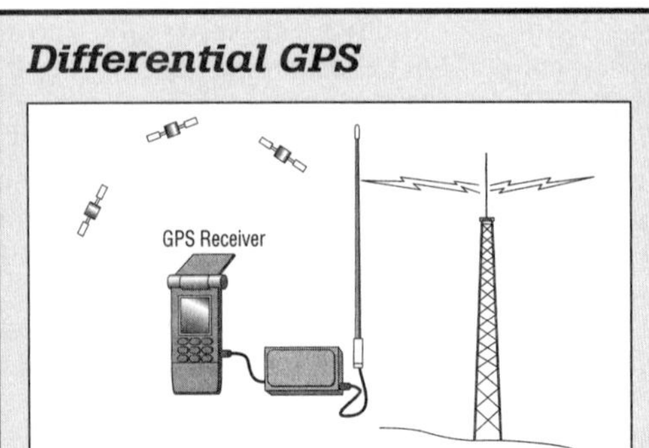

Differential GPS can improve GPS accuracy to within a few yards but requires an additional differential GPS receiver to acquire signals from the differential beacons, which correct signal error.

Satellite Differential GPS Comparison

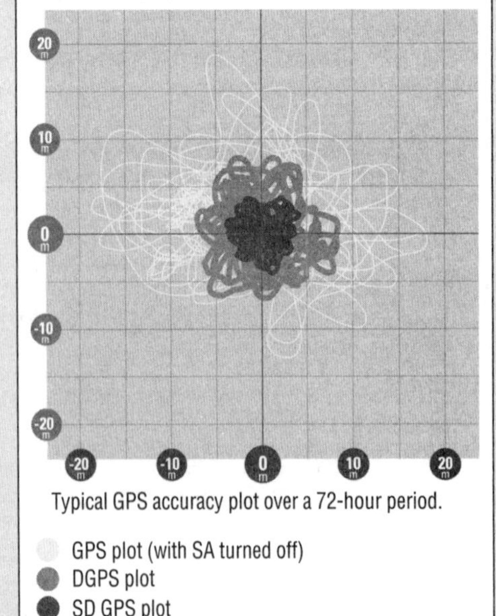

Satellite Differential (WAAS) technology provides accuracy of less than ten feet.

area master station, where corrections are calculated. This data is then put into a format for uplink to a GEO (Geostationary Earth Orbit) communications satellite, which remains in a fixed position in orbit rather than rotating around the earth, as a GPS satellite does. From a GEO, these signals are forwarded to the user in an aircraft or on a boat.

Raytheon is a primary WAAS contractor, but the technology is in the public domain, so other manufacturers can now take advantage of the system. Raytheon has introduced several WAAS GPS receivers to the consumer market. Suggested retail prices for these receivers run between $1,000 and $2,000.

The accuracy of the WAAS system is similar to that of the tower system, perhaps a little better. With top-end systems, accuracies to within 10 feet or fewer should be available for both horizontal and vertical measurements.

Fishermen who use GPS are looking for better positioning accuracy. Boat control is the ultimate determining factor. But you've got to be realistic: running out into the middle of a large lake, such as Mille Lacs, Winnebago, or Erie and being able to stop over a table-sized rockpile because you have 1-foot accuracy just isn't going to happen.

Boat speed, wind and wave action, and current make such pinpoint accuracy improbable. Most fishermen have a difficult time holding a boat within 10 to 20 feet of an underwater structure. We need better boat control more than we need more accurate GPS.

GPS MAPPING

Tired of pulling out lake maps and navigational charts? Maybe it's time for a chart plotter or electronic mapping system—an electronic display of a lake or river and its shoreline. You can see where you've been, where you are, and where you're going.

Some mapping systems also provide navigational information, such as buoy markers, reefs, channels, and water depths. Others provide shoreline details for lakes, bays, and islands.

Two ways to manage and display electronic maps are the chart-by-chart and seamless methods. The chart-by-chart method, which basically represents a digital version of many individual maps spread out together, introduces the problem of varying scales once map borders are crossed. The seamless method provides the feeling of one continuously scrolling map with no changes in scale.

Chart plotting—In 1983, Navionics developed the first marine electronic chart plotter, the GEONAV. Chart plotters are available in permanent-mount units and portable, handheld units. Some mapping systems are self-contained—that is, they're ready to use without additional purchases. These may be in the form of a Global Positioning Satellite (GPS) system and mapping combination or a sonar-GPS-mapping system. Other systems are no more than map readers, much like VCRs. They display a built-in map or map files read from a cartridge inserted into the unit.

When a GPS system is linked to a mapping system, the user's position is marked on the screen (and map) by a symbol or icon. Movement is traced across the screen by the icon. When the icon gets near the edge of the screen, it recenters itself, much as you trace a route along a highway map with a pencil.

Other plotter screens are moving map screens on which the icon marking position stays at or near the center of the screen while the map itself moves across the screen. This is like placing a pencil on the roadway of a map and then pulling the map forward beneath your pencil. In both systems, a plot trail (path of dots) shows where you've been.

Background maps—Some mapping systems offer a built-in map of the forty-eight continental states. Some show only the outline of the states. Other units include maps that illustrate large bodies of water and major highways. Detailed maps make a system easier to use and allow for zooming into an area for more detail. Many units have plotter scale ranges from 2,000 to 3,000 miles down to 0.5 mile or less.

Mapping cartridges—Cartridges for mapping units are usually created from government charts. Raster charts are scans from paper charts, which are displayed on a screen, reproducing the original documents. The raster format is inflexible and memory intensive.

Vector charts are also made by scanning originals to create raster files. Then the files are vectorized—that is, put into a vector format. In vector form, data can more easily be compressed for loading and display. Information is stored in different layers: coastlines on one layer, contour lines representing depths on another, buoy markers on yet another.

Mapping Cartridges

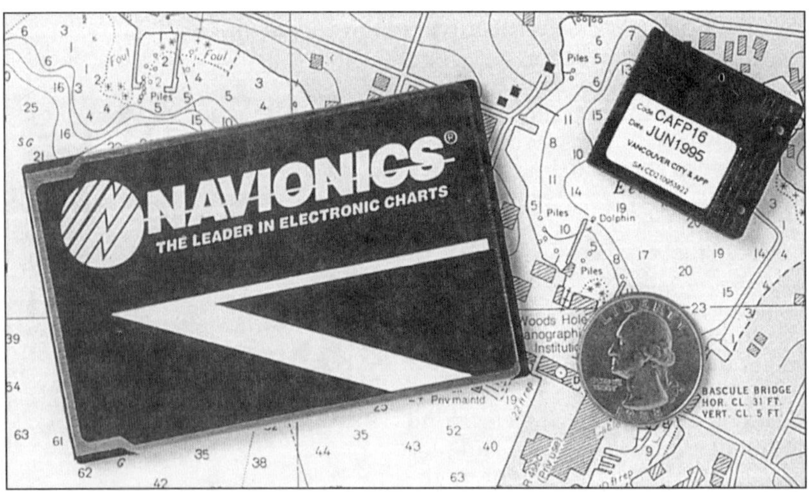

Most plotters use small, credit cardlike mapping cartridges that contain hundreds of square miles of charts. Individual cartridges covering just about any area of the world's waterways can be purchased from either the plotter's manufacturer or the two leading electronic chart producers, C–MAP and Navionics. Maps like the C–MAP chart shown here are displayed on your plotter as vectorized charts.

A cartridge may contain 100 layers of files. Layering allows elements to be displayed or hidden upon command. For instance, names and contour lines may be displayed,while buoy markers remain hidden. The vector chart data can be supplemented, enhanced, and updated with more factual information. Vector charting represents the future of electronic chart-making, according to leading manufacturers.

The word *seamless* often appears in the terminology of electronic mapping. When a cartridge is made, ten to over 100 maps may have been used to create its map. The transition from one map to another is seamless if the borders between maps do not show; the cartridge appears to have been created from one large map rather than many small ones. Cartridges created from different paper maps often present unique challenges to cartridge makers because of their different scales.

Mapping detail—The quality of map detail is related to at least two factors: the map file in the cartridge and the display screen. In the case of a common Liquid Crystal Display (LCD), screen quality is determined by the absolute number of pixels, the pixels per square inch, and the screen's ability to react to light. Coarse display screens—that is, screens with fewer pixels—may not adequately display all the information on a cartridge, particularly the small details. In addition, some cartridges display only bodies of water of 1,000 acres or more, while others display 20-acre duck ponds.

Before purchasing an electronic mapping system, insert a cartridge that covers an area you're familiar with, and check it for detail. Look at the display screen in sunlight as well as in low-light conditions. Check the zoom ranges of the display screen to see that they're small enough. The unit should at least zoom down to 0.5 mile. Some units go down to 0.1 or 0.2 mile.

Finally, keep in mind that zooming down to a small scale may not really enhance detail. "Zooming in" may mean that what you saw at 2 miles is only bigger at 0.2 mile, with no additional detail. Different levels of detail should appear at different zoom or scale levels. For instance, contour lines, small reefs, and islands that may not appear at a 50-mile scale should become visible at a 10-mile scale.

CD-ROM mapping—How'd you like to see maps on your GPS screen that show roads, back roads, roads to your lake, the locations of small trout streams, buoy markers indicating the approach to Great Lakes harbors or other designated navigational waters—or better yet, lake contour lines? Even though GPS mapping for the sportsman is less than 10 years old, this is all possible.

GPS mapping appeared on the sporting goods scene in the mid '90s. At that time, maps available in GPS units were quite basic and often called background or base maps. They displayed freeway systems, state roads, large and midsized lakes, rivers, and large to medium towns. Background maps typically covered the entire United States and parts of Canada and Mexico. Then most manufacturers introduced cartridges designed to provide more detail for designated areas of the background map. Small streams, ponds, and towns were included, and even some drainage ditches and dirt roads. Shoreline detail was enhanced.

Like other technologies, data storage and transfer in GPS units changed rapidly. Manufacturers went to CD-ROMs. Now, instead of buying a handful of cartridges to cover all the areas of your outdoor activities, one or two CDs covers the entire country in high detail. The only catch is that you need a computer.

When you load the CD into your computer, the mapping program appears on the screen, and the area you select or outline on the screen gets transferred to a GPS unit. This transfer is done with the help of a data cable. (Note: hand-held and permanent-mount units, for the most part, use the same system). Some programs allow users to create their own maps. You can choose the type of detail to be displayed. Selections can display or not display items like small streams, rural roads, streets, street names, and navigational aides. Lowrance's Map Create is one such program. Other manufacturers offer specialized CDs. Garmin, for instance, offers *Road and Recreation* and *MetroGuide U.S.* Most CDs cost $100 to $200.

Once the data for an area is selected, the information is transferred to a "flash memory" system or to a blank cartridge in the GPS unit. Typically, units have 2–8 MB of memory, which depending on the detail displayed, can partially or entirely include a state the size of Minnesota. For most people, this is adequate coverage—most of your favorite lakes can be included in a map of that size. In other words, it isn't necessary to have sufficient memory capability to cover most of the United States on one map. These created maps can be stored and resurrected whenever needed.

Some tournament fisherman find it easy to get their individual tournament lakes on a map as small as 1.5 MB. To do so, outline, for example, Saginaw Bay, Winnebago, Leech, Mille Lacs, Oahe, and Fort Peck individually, but save them as one map. These map-creating and memory-storage systems are in use at the present time.

As you might expect, another new system has appeared on the block. In 2001, with the new X series of sonar-GPS units, Lowrance uses multimedia cards (MMC), which offer a wide range of available memory. Memory sizes of 8, 16, 32, and 64 MB are available on cards like those used in digital cameras.

The GPS mapping system for the X series operates much the same as it did in previous units. The difference is that the mapping information is transferred from the computer to the multimedia card through a card reader. The multimedia card is then inserted into the slot in the sonar-GPS case; there's no need to bring the sonar-GPS unit into the house. Multimedia cards also are used to record sonar and GPS data, just like old paper graphs. The stored information can then be played back through the system for review.

Besides storing the day's fishing structures and routes, the unit can play back information through the locator as if it were a VCR. In the playback mode, adjustments can be made to the sensitivity, gray-line, zoom, and depth ranges, just as if you were back on the water. It's a great way to learn more about both your electronic gear and the body of water you just fished.

Suppose on a cold winter night you want to play at fishing. Get out your loca-tor-GPS unit, connect it to the computer, turn it on, and insert any MMC that recorded your fishing exploits (or turn on the simulator). Your electronic unit is now interactive with the computer, giving you control of all the operating functions on the sonar and GPS. It's a great way to keep your sonar-GPS skills sharp during the off season.

GEEPERS KEEPERS!—ADDITIONAL FEATURES

Originally, mapping data in general and data showing the outline of a particular lake or reservoir gave fishermen a sense of where they were on a lake. This was useful on a new lake and invaluable in fog or rain. Lake displays provided familiarity as well as safety. By marking important points like boat ramp, rocks, and reefs, anglers found it easy to go to a fishing spot and return again, even in bad weather or at night. They could always see where they and their boat or snowmobile were on the displayed lake.

An interesting feature of the CD-ROMs offered by Fishing Hot Spots and Waypoint Technologies is their ability to display GPS coordinates. When the desired lake is brought up on the computer screen, you can move the mouse to a particular location, and the GPS coordinates of the chosen spot appear on the screen. Marking underwater points, inside turns, and sunken islands is easy. This information is readily transferable to a GPS unit, either by hand or by using a data cable attached to your computer and GPS.

These CDs contain only lake map images, 30 to 50 lakes to a CD, with little or no regional information. The CDs from GPS manufacturers such as Garmin, Lowrance, and Magellan contain information about an entire region or country. By zooming in on a lake, you can find information about the lake but not necessarily in the detail that appears on lake CDs.

The newest level of information offered is contour lines for selected inland lakes. Companies such as C-Map and Navionics have constructed offshore, Great Lakes, and selected large inland lake and reservoir maps with contour lines. Attention is also being paid to smaller inland lakes. Navionics purchased map data from Fishing Hot Spots and has formatted the information to work in newer GPS units. Garmin is also formatting data to work in its units. This information is available on cartridge, CD, and website.

C-Map and Navionics format their mapping data to work in the GPS units of several manufacturers, as well as in Raymarine's new WAAS unit. Lake Master (Waypoint Technologies), another inland mapping manufacturer, is formatting its own data to meet specific GPS units. LakeMaster's ReelBottom technology offers precise contour maps of larger inland lakes right on your GPS screen.

Most mapping systems allow the user to choose a variety of display features. Buoy

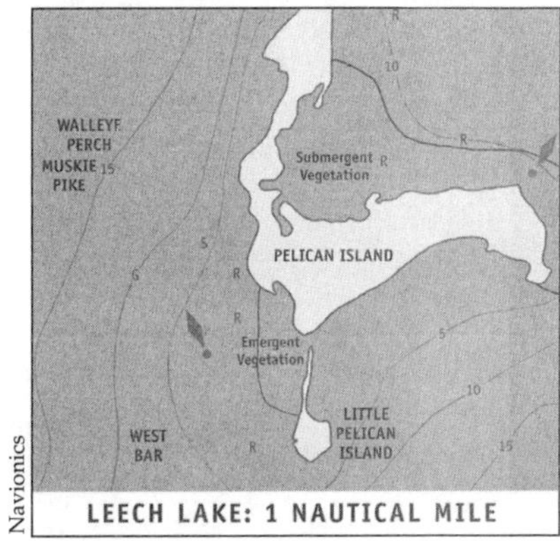

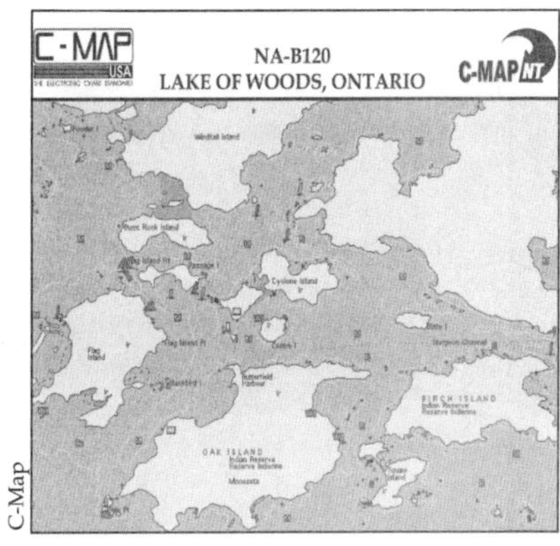

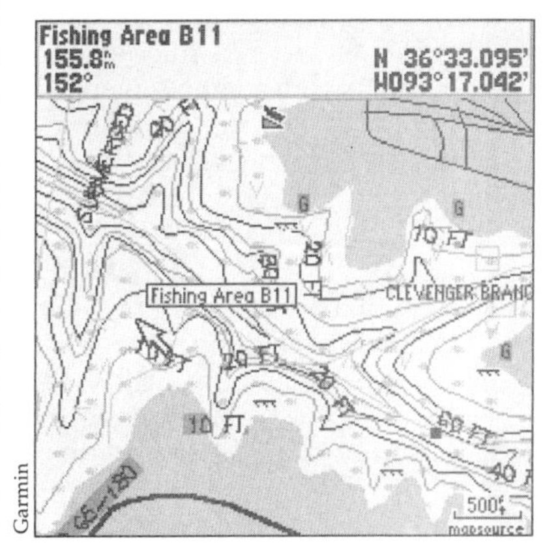

markers, depth soundings, and contour lines can be selected or deselected so that only the information you want is displayed. When a mapping system is interfaced with a Global Positioning System unit, waypoints and other icons can be overlaid on the map display. The icons stay in position until the user chooses to remove them. For the boater, these electronic charts are a navigational aid, not a replacement for official paper charts.

The cursor, usually a small crosshair, is another useful feature found on some GPS receivers. The cursor, for instance, can be placed on a far island or bay, and the position coordinates as well as the distance to that island or bay can be shown on the screen. When the cursor is activated, the display system centers around the cursor rather than the position icon.

Advantages of a mapping system—For bodies of water such as the Great Lakes and offshore waters, electronic charting eliminates the need for large, bulky navigational charts. These charts should be available, however, just as a compass should back up a GPS unit.

On inland waters, a mapping system makes navigating from point A to point B easier. It also makes learning to use a GPS easier because your movement and position can be seen relative to land masses and other familiar reference points.

With some GPS mapping units, it's possible to place icons on the screen to mark fish or interesting structure being displayed on sonar. Then you can return to fish these locations and get a sense of position relative to land.

Don't overlook the safety feature. An angler, particularly on a strange body of water, can become disoriented in fog or other severe weather. Unless a route has been entered in the GPS unit to return to the boat landing or harbor, only a straight line will appear on the screen from point A to point B. This route could travel over a point of land or across several islands. With a chart plotter, it's possible to see the obstacles you need to avoid in the fog to get from point A to point B.

Map datums and accuracy—Accuracy, particularly in mapping systems, is affected by datums. A datum is a geographic frame of reference used by cartographers (map makers) to define a chart's coordinates. Because the earth is projected on a two-dimensional map as flat, while its actual shape is somewhat ellipsoidal, different reference points around the world require different datums.

In the United States, most new GPS units and maps are configured to World Geodetic System 1984 (WGS 84). An older configuration still in use is the North American Datum 1927 (NAD 27). Most newer GPS systems list as many as 100 or more different datums from around the world in their menu. It's important that the GPS datum and the map datum be matched. Otherwise, errors of several hundred feet to 0.25 mile can occur.

Even though technology marches onward, the oft-repeated warning, "The fish won't have a chance," still doesn't apply. Despite all the gadgets and gizmos, we still have to encourage the fish to bite.

THE PLOT THICKENS

The Global Positioning System (GPS) story has heretofore read something like "there and back again." Anglers fishing big waters have used GPS technology to navigate to distant fishing spots and, perhaps more important, to return. The confidence gained from knowing your unit will direct you home in wind, rain, and fog spurs a continuing pursuit of open water trolling bites for suspended fish. Without GPS, most Great Lakes walleye anglers would more likely still be bank runners instead of offshore explorers.

The ability to run from A to B and home again isn't the only thing GPS units provide, though. Like Alice in *Through the Looking Glass*, you enter a new world through GPS—the world of big water walleye movements. What follows are a few tips for getting the most from your unit while locating, tracking, and trolling big water systems across North America.

Locating walleyes—When you're heading out onto a big lake in search of suspended fish, use grid patterns to locate gamefish and baitfish. Begin by running parallel courses, 0.25 mile apart, at speeds that allow you to spot fish. Combination liquid crystal depthfinder and GPS plotter units allow for simultaneously marking fish and keeping track of the navigation course on the split screen of a single unit. The plotter feature draws and indicates successive paths, much like the old Etch-a-Sketch you probably played with as a child.

Double back along a parallel line, 0.25 mile away, examining a systematic grid. Note large gamefish or concentrations of small baitfish—both indicate possible fish locations. Don't start fishing until you see something promising.

It's possible to do this from scratch, but most anglers aren't averse to getting a few latitude-longitude combos where fish have been taken recently from their buddies, then punching them into their units and hitting ENTER and GO TO WAYPOINT to use as a starting point in their search.

Getting numbers usually makes it easier to locate fish quickly, but you can expect them to have moved somewhat from the last sighting. But at least you're in the neighborhood. The rap among purists is that it's no longer necessary to earn fish location as in the old days, when considerable searching was almost always necessary, even though general fish location was known. Today, few secrets remain. But almost everybody gets numbers, if they're available.

GPS LINGO:	
SOG	*Speed Over Ground*
COG	*Course Over Ground*
DTG	*Distance To Go*
BRG	*Bearing*
TTG	*Time To Go*
WPT	*Waypoint*

Marking and staying on pods of fish—Begin upwind of a group of fish, and set out lines for a downwind trolling pass. Avoid long passes. Generally troll 1 mile or less, usually less. Try to determine a specific location or pod of large fish based on those you've caught during previous passes. Most good units offer an event marker that allows you to punch in a caught fish, which then appears as a symbol. Every time you catch a fish, punch in the event. After you troll well past the event point, pick up your lines, return upwind, and make another pass.

Repeat productive trolling paths as exactly as possible to find the most fish. Often big walleyes are located within a few feet of where fish were caught on the previous pass. This is a key to heavy limits instead of smaller-sized fish.

In practice, tournament pros generally make parallel passes on each side of their first productive pass to determine the extent of the school and the size of the fish. You may not catch as many fish on successive passes, but then again, you may score big and learn something. In any case, you're gathering information for later use. When you have it prior to competition, you can minimize scouting and maximize fishing time.

Gridwork

Plotters indicate a history of recent movement, such as successive scouting passes. Maintain intervals between passes, establishing a 1/4-mile grid. Note that the split-screen feature enables you to observe the path and look for fish simultaneously.

Once you locate and catch suspended walleyes, repeat trolling passes as accurately as possible to continue catching them. Note that overlapping passes produce fish where event markers pinpoint their location.

Repeat Trolling Passes

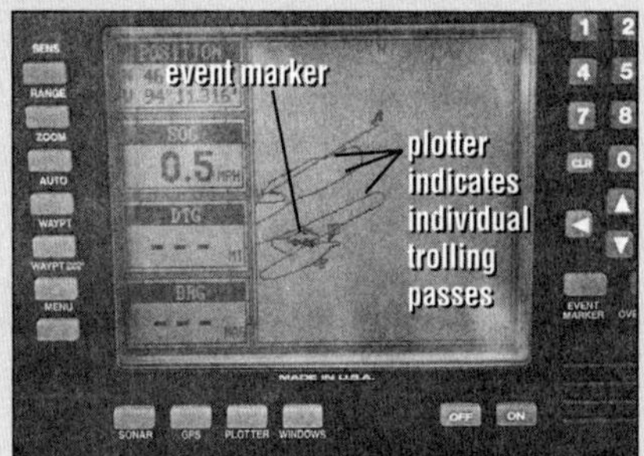

The Plot Thickens

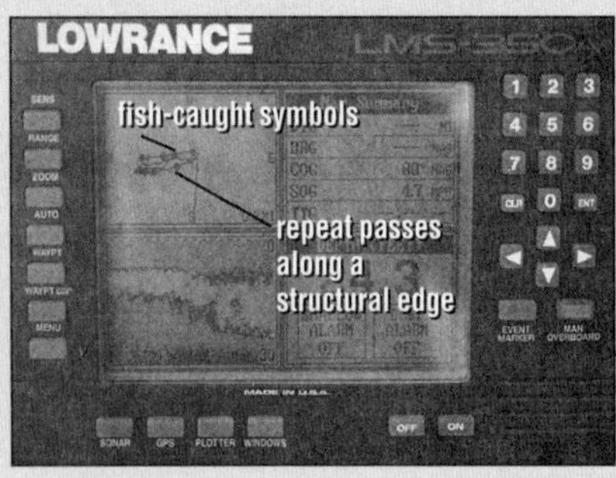

For every fish caught on this structural element, an event marker indicates its location. Multiple passes along the drop-off edge produce fish in the same limited area. Note how the event markers overlap, almost blacking out the screen. Obviously a good spot. Store this waypoint in the unit and store the latitude and longitude in a notebook.

Plotters and numbers—Successive trolling passes amass a huge amount of information. For example, you may notice that if you return to a certain latitude and longitude, then troll downwind 0.75 mile, you catch good fish until you leave the area. After a few days, you may note that the caught-fish symbols (event markers) are overlapping and beginning to blacken your screen, especially when you're fishing the edge of a structural element like a deep hump that tends to hold fish within a certain limited area. Wherever the plot thickens—wherever pass after pass along the same line produces walleyes—that's where you want to be. Follow the path. Wandering off reduces trolling success.

When walleyes hold along a distinctive edge of a large structural element, use

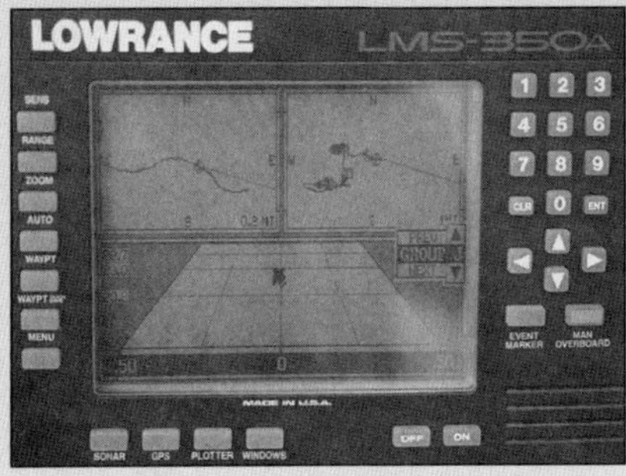

Show Me the Way to Go Home

A collection of waypoints provides a history of suspended fish movement and a valuable reference for returning to productive structures. The most important waypoint, however, is the harbor mouth you departed from, which indicates your direct path home.

your plotter feature to return to within 50 or 100 feet of the edge. Or simply punch in the latitude and longitude (coordinates) of the spot, and save the spot as a distinct entity. Most units can store a number of spots—waypoints—as numbers. Some units allow you to give them names, too. Thus waypoint #34 on your GPS can also be referred to as WALLEYE HOLE, or some such name. Practically speaking, most anglers don't take the time to punch in names for locations of suspended fish, because they expect them to keep changing. But a key reef or hump may be worth a permanent entry. Most anglers also keep a written logbook of prime latitude-longitude locations, just in case their electronics zap the coordinates into the stratosphere.

By the numbers—GPS units determine location by latitude and longitude, in degrees, minutes, and seconds—even tenths of seconds. That's accurate! When your longitude begins to roll over from 94 46 322 to 94 46 323 while you troll the productive section of your favorite drop-off, you might expect to get another bite about the time 323 (32.3 minutes) appears on your screen. This is as true for repeated paths over suspended fish as for following the edge of huge midlake structures, such as the famed mudflats of Lake Mille Lacs, Minnesota. Keep your line at the productive depth, follow the edge, and be ready when your number comes up.

Tracking walleyes—Plotters allow you to retrace a boat path over hours and miles. Play back your plot to see where you've been, where you've caught fish, and where you haven't. Study fish-location coordinates, not just during one day on the water but over several days, weeks, and months—a tactic that provides a history of fish movement and clues to long-term seasonal migration.

In the short term, for example, you may find a suspended walleye school generally drifting southwest at 1 to 2 miles per day, but then be unable to relocate them in the expected area the next day. Conditions changed—wind, current, baitfish movement, something—but you still have a starting point for relocating them. Even if your GPS lacks a plotter, you can proceed to the last known location (latitude and longitude), then begin a grid search. The fish should be within a few miles. A few hours may be needed to relocate them, but most of the time, your paths will cross. Do this day after day, year after year, and you become good at predicting walleye behavior.

Numbers game—Offshore walleye fishing has always been about increasing your odds for catching fish. Now it's also a numbers game with GPS coordinates becoming an integral part of the hunt. Coordinates give you a starting point and provide a reference to what's happening. As you follow, mark, and catch fish, repeating successful trolling passes, the plot thickens. Yet it's easy to see where this story's headed: the thicker the plot, the better the spot—at least 'til the fish move. Then the game's afloat once again.

SCOUTING AND MAPPING STRUCTURE

A plotter screen starts out like a blank sheet of paper, with a blinking + sign or similar icon to indicate your current location. When a waypoint—the coordinates of a distant location—is called up for navigation, a dotted line connects your present location to the waypoint destination. You then navigate along the path, with the plotter icon following the line.

While this feature of plotter screens is most commonly used, other features are also useful. One traces the outline of a piece of structure to determine its shape. As your boat moves, the GPS receiver lays down a series of dots—a plot trail—on the plotter screen, like Hansel and Gretel's trail of bread crumbs through the forest. Fortunately, aquatic creatures won't eat your electronic bread crumbs.

Trying to fish or to map an unfamiliar structure in high winds can be difficult, whether you're casting, trolling, or drifting. But if you use a sonar unit to follow a particular depth—say, the 15-foot level along the drop-off edge—your GPS plotter will simultaneously sketch the shape of your path and the shape of the structure. To make an effective plotter image, however, you need to maneuver the boat at least 8 to 10 mph.

Select a plotter scale close to the size of the structure being mapped. In other words, don't use a 5-mile-wide screen to trace and map a structure that's 200 feet long. A 0.1- or 0.2-mile screen will show vastly more detail. You can always change the scale of the plotter screen later, when you move down the lake. Once your plot trace of the structure is complete, zoom down to a small scale to show the structure in more detail.

As you trace the edge of a structure, place an icon (symbol) on the screen to mark areas where the edge of the structure turns. These points are potential fish locations. Once you establish a completed trace of a structure, you can observe both its corner points and the plot trail connecting them. That gives you the outline of the structure.

If you continue trolling around or along the structure, the plot begins to look like a spiderweb. That's due to the combined effect of multiple plot trails. Eventually you may need to clean up or erase the plot trail. Once you've erased it, however, you lose the basic shape of the structure. Any icons you placed on the screen remain there after the plotter trail is erased, indicating formerly located corner points. Icons can also be used to indicate spots where you located or caught fish.

Some plotter screens have a feature called a cursor or crosshair that looks like the one on a rifle scope. When returning to a previously mapped structure, move the cursor to the position indicated by the previously stored icon. Once you've moved it, a comment like GO TO CURSOR appears. Once you've selected it, you can follow directions to the cursor location, fine-tuning your navigation.

Plotter units typically make a finite number of plotter points available on the screen—generally 500 to 2,000. When a plotter runs out of points, it begins to erase points laid down at the beginning of the trail in order to have room to add new

Fishing Structure Using GPS

FIGURE 1

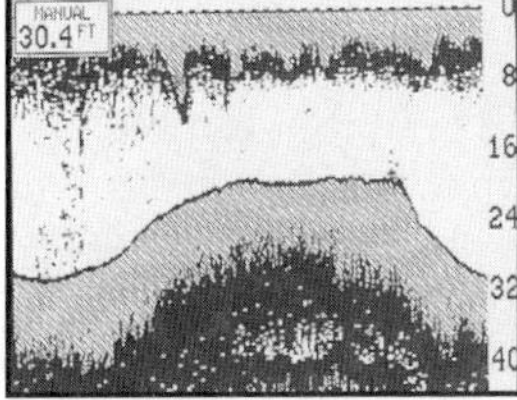

FIGURE 2

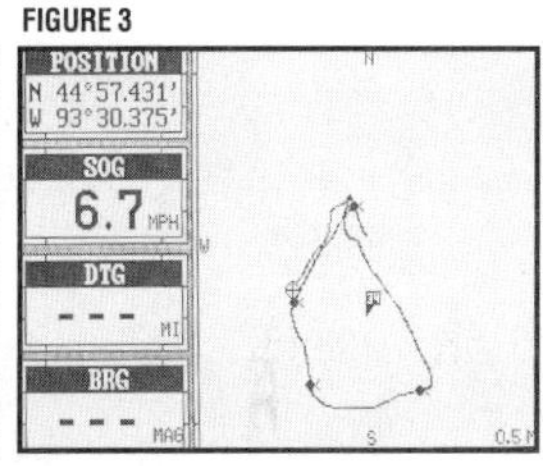

FIGURE 3

FIGURE 4

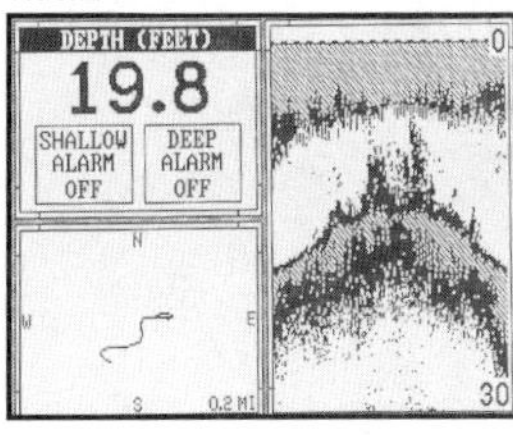

FIGURE 1 A midlake hump topping off at about 18 feet shown on a sonar screen.

FIGURE 2 A plotter trace of the midlake hump. The plotter scale setting is 0.5 miles. The trace was created by following the 20-foot contour line with the aid of sonar. Combination sonar and GPS units can be programmed to show depth on the plotter screen. Corner or anchor points are indicated by fish icons. These are placed at points on the screen where the structure changes direction. Plot trails can now be erased, leaving the corner points intact for future tracing.

FIGURE 3 The start of a second trace around the structure. This could happen during a second trolling pass around the structure. Repeated working or tracing of the structure creates a spiderweb of many plot lines. These lines can be erased.

FIGURE 4 An integrated sonar and GPS screen is sometimes called a "windows" or "group" format. The angler just crossed over a midlake hump with weeds growing on top. A plotter trace is being started with the aid of the sonar section at the 20-foot contour level.

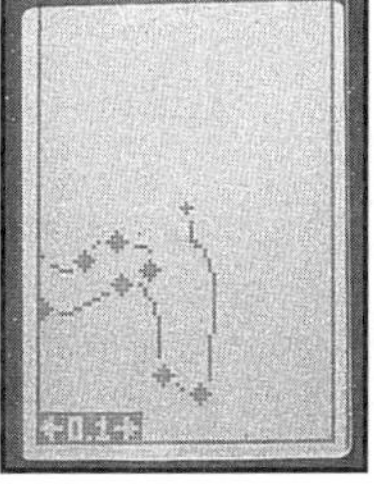

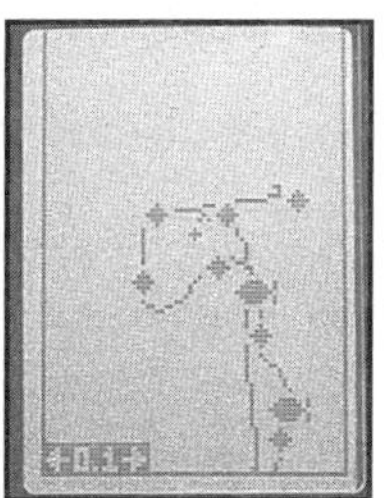

FIGURE 5

A plot or trace on a handheld unit. The screen indicates a 0.10-mile-wide screen. No corner point icons have been placed on the screen. The complete plotter image will be lost if the screen is cleared.

FIGURE 6

Same piece of structure. This time, corner icons (small diamonds) have been placed on the screen at critical turns in the structure.

FIGURE 7

The same plotter screen with the plot trail cleared or erased. You can retrace the structure using the icons as guide points. The screen appears more compressed because the plotter scale was changed from 0.10 miles to 0.15 miles.

FIGURE 8

A piece of structure with a long arm running off its south end. Diamond icons have been placed at the corners. Fish icons have been placed where fish contact occurred.

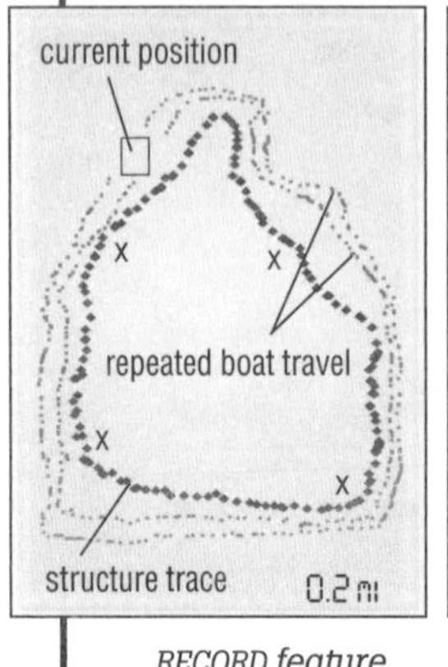

points. If you don't store corner points as icons, you risk losing the early portions of your plotter trail and any key spots previously located.

Units have update rates for processing and placing new information on the screen. These may be every 1, 2, 5, 10, or 30 seconds. Slower rates make the limited number of plotter dots last longer, while faster rates provide more detail. Generally use the fastest update rate possible.

By establishing icons on corner points, you can return to a structure weeks later with a picture of its shape and the location of its key features.

The simultaneous use of sonar and GPS plotter works well. Units with both features offer two forms of data: depth and shape. Even in the worst weather, they give you a complete picture of the area being fished and how best to fish it.

Once you find a good spot, why risk losing it? Punch it in for future fishing—it's the shape of things to come.

GPS TIPS & TRICKS

The growing popularity of GPS systems leads to questions and problems for new users. The following suggestions describe even more and better uses for your GPS unit.

Shopping for new receivers—Many new twelve-channel receivers are available for between $150 and $250. When you're comparison shopping among brands, also consider the cost of accessories. Three common ones are external power cords, carrying cases, and mounting brackets. Others might include external antennas (rarely needed with twelve-channel designs), PC upload-download kits, and rechargeable batteries.

Making scale changes for improved accuracy—Anglers often complain that they can't get as close as desired to their destination when they use their plotter or map page. Using the 5-mile scale worked fine for navigating the lake, but as they approached their

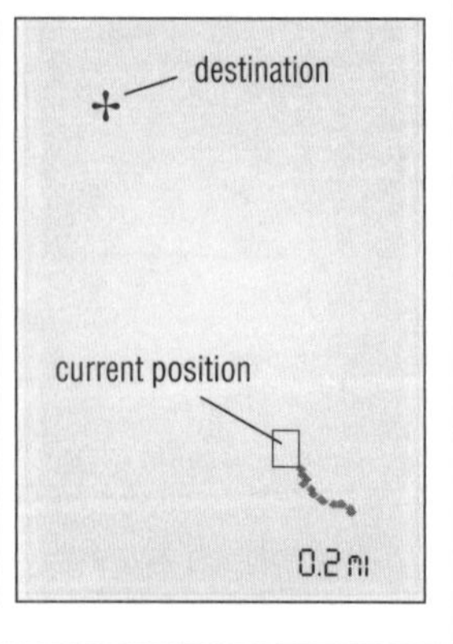

destination, they were unable to pinpoint the location precisely.

Simple remedy: when you're within 1 mile of a destination, zoom down to a smaller scale, such as from 5 miles down to 0.5, 0.2, even 0.1 mile. Now the entire screen represents a smaller space, and it's easy to navigate to the spot.

Outlining structure on the plotter screen—When attempting to determine the shape of an underwater structure, you can use the plotter or map screen to help you visualize it. Turn the RECORD feature off, if necessary, and choose the depth you're interested in. Let's say it's 15 feet. Drive your boat around the structure, using your depthfinder to maintain the 15-foot contour. This causes an outline of the structure to be drawn on your screen.

Move at a speed of at least 5 mph to create a better trace or track line on the screen.

If your unit has freestanding icons—symbols independent of waypoints—place an icon on the screen anywhere that there's a distinct change in the edge of the structure. This helps define key corners and turns that may attract walleyes. Troll or cast around the structure, periodically erasing the plot trail but following the icons on repeat passes.

Another option is to complete the initial plot and then turn off the RECORD feature on the plotter screen. This eliminates the clutter drawn by repeated passes around the structure. The current position symbol still indicates your location.

If you receiver doesn't have a TURN OFF RECORD feature, you can usually get plotter updates by time or distance on most receivers. The update rate indicates how often a dot is placed on the screen, such as every 3 seconds, or every 0.1 mile. When tracing the initial track around the structure, set your update rate as fast as possible. When following or repeating the trail, set the update rate as slow as possible, such as every 30 minutes, to avoid cluttering the screen.

Use the same strategy for open water trolling. To repeat a successful trolling run, retrace it on the plotter screen just as you retraced the edge of the structure. Just remember to turn your RECORD feature back on, and change your PLOTTER UPDATE feature back to a faster rate when you leave for a new location.

Using the plotter to navigate around a lake—Use a similar tracing technique to move about a new lake without getting lost—a particularly helpful feature on big Canadian lakes that have many islands. Adjust your update rate as necessary. With a lake that's 20 or 30 miles long, you can reduce your update rate from about every 3 seconds to every 10 seconds to ensure a complete record. A plotter screen has only a limited number of

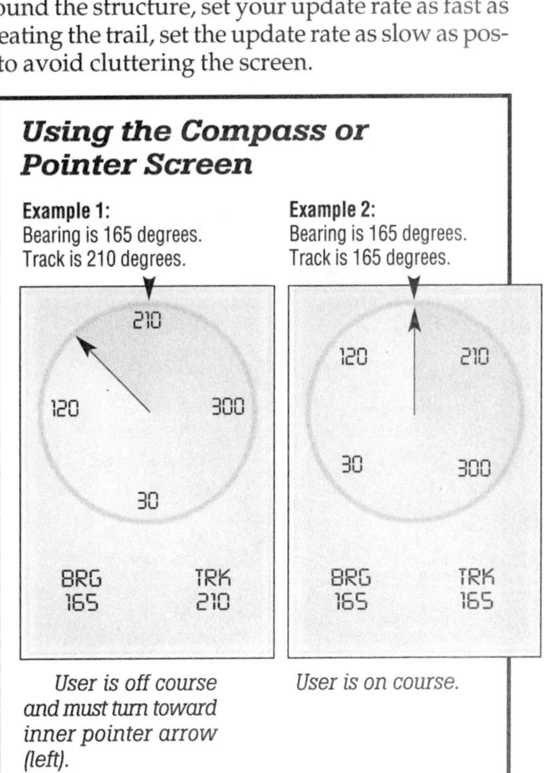

Using the Compass or Pointer Screen

Example 1:
Bearing is 165 degrees.
Track is 210 degrees.

Example 2:
Bearing is 165 degrees.
Track is 165 degrees.

User is off course and must turn toward inner pointer arrow (left).

User is on course.

dots available for a trace. Don't lose the first half of the day's trip if the unit runs out of dots—slow down the update rate to extend the unit's memory.

You can also put freestanding icons on the screen to indicate key locations like narrows, islands, or inlets. When you return, just connect the dots, steering from one icon to the next, all the way back to camp.

Some manufacturers have a track-back feature that's like a combination of plotter screen and icons. After a trail has been established, the track-back feature breaks down the trail into segments and connects them to form a route. On most units, you can create a route using the ROUTE feature.

Using the compass or pointer screen—Once a GO TO command has been punched in, the arrow on the compass or the pointer screen indicates the direction you need to follow; this is often called *the bearing*. Your current direction of travel, often called *the track*, is indicated at the top of the compass screen.

For example, if your destination lies at a compass heading of 315 degrees (bearing), and you temporarily must steer around a big rock sticking out of the water, your current track may temporarily change to 280 degrees. Once you clear the rock, you gradually turn back to a compass heading of 315 degrees. Always turn toward the compass or pointer arrow. Once both are lined up at the top of the screen, you're back on course.

If you travel past your destination, the pointer arrow will rotate 180 degrees and point straight down. Turn around and head back to your destination.

Locking in on satellites—Once a receiver has been initialized, locking on a satellite is rather fast with the new twelve-channel parallel receivers—typically 30 to 60 seconds. Occasionally, however, a receiver seems to lock up, unable to find a position. Turn it off, then on again—this works most of the time. Make sure you're in a position that allows a clear view of the sky and satellites; even new receivers can't pick up signals through concrete jungles or rain forests.

Still having problems? Check the datum setting. The wrong setting can make it hard to lock onto a satellite.

Coordinate Systems

Typical datum selections in menu	Position formats
WGS 84	DEGREES MINUTES N 44°54.968' W 93°30.276'
N American 1927	
	DEGREES MIN. SEC. N 44°54'58.1 W 93°30'16.6"
N American 1983	
Adindan Mean	UTM 15 0460172E 4973757N
Arc 1950 Mean	
	STD MGRS 15TVK 60172 73757
Ascnsn Isld '58	

Typical datum selections in menu

Position formats

Positions several hundreds yards farther off than normal—If positions are consistently off, check the datum setting. Most receivers default to WGS 84. If by some mysterious finger punching, you've selected some other datum, it can lead to errors of hundreds of yards. (Different datums are used to compensate for curvatures of the earth in different parts of the world.)

Map coordinates different from receiver coordinates—Most likely it's datum-setting problems again. Reset to the datum specified on the map.

DISTANCE TO GO (DTG) off by thousands of miles—You bring up the waypoint to your favorite fishing spot, and the DTG says 13,200 miles rather than the expected 5 miles. In most cases, the waypoint was entered in error. In North America, the latitude is north, the longitude west. Inadvertently, the latitude west may have been entered as latitude east, and you're navigating to Russia or China.

Position coordinates in a strange format—Most receivers offer a variety of formats to express waypoints in latitude and longitude. Most are in DM (Degrees, Minutes) or DMS (Degrees, Minutes, Seconds). North 44 degrees 54.94 minutes, W 93 degrees 30.3 minutes in DM is the same position as N 44 degrees 54 minutes 56 seconds, W 93 degrees 30 minutes 18 seconds in DMS. There also are British, Irish, Swedish, and other coordinate systems. (These are not the same as datums.) Make sure that your unit is set on the desired system and matches your map coordinates.

Sightseeing—Your GPS can help you navigate back roads and find scenic spots. *GPS Companion* is a series of handbooks that provides coordinates for thousands of towns, waterfalls, mountain summits—even golf courses. These are available from The Aviation Company, 800/423-2708.

These tips and suggestions should make your GPS receiver even more effective. To keep in practice, though, see if you can still manually line up some of your old fishing spots, using landmarks, just as you did in the good old days. In cases of power failure or equipment breakdown, it's helpful to know where you are and to be able to navigate back safely without electronics. When fishing large or unfamiliar waters, carry a compass, just in case.

HANDHELD GPS

An increasing number of GPS users are switching to handheld units. Some are first-time buyers, while others are upgrading their units to improved technology.

Handheld GPS units presently take two forms: (1) a basic unit (non-mapping) that stores waypoints (saved locations), allows some routing, and indicates direction of travel or bearing to a destination with a navigation or "plotter" screen; 2) a mapping unit that includes all the above features and displays them on a screen with a map that you've chosen. A few color models also are available.

Prices for the basic systems range from $100 to $250. Price points are often an indicator of available features. Generally, less expensive units include less memory, so fewer waypoints can be stored, fewer plot trails can be saved (if a plotter screen is available), and fewer operating features are included. Uploading and downloading information, such as waypoints from or to a computer, may not be possible on low-priced units. Shop around for a handheld GPS that offers the features most important to you at a price you can afford.

Most basic units have memories capable of storing 100 to 1,000 waypoints along with icons or event markers. Many receivers allow you to name and number your waypoints. Most of the newer units are twelve-channel parallel receivers. These perform on both water and land.

Many GPS screen menus contain a feature called *waypoint averaging*. Waypoint averaging collects data on the incoming latitude and longitude every few seconds. Incoming data is averaged, and over time, a significant amount of error is averaged out. This provided more accurate readings for waypoints, an important feature before May 2000, when SA was still in effect. In order to use waypoint averaging, however, the unit must remain stationary for a period of time, the longer the better. Five to 10 minutes provide satisfactory results.

Mapping units are capable of doing everything that basic units do, but they also display locations and plotter trails on their screens. These maps show lakes, streams, towns, and roads in varying degrees of detail. Like console versions, handheld mapping units come in two versions: those with built-in maps whose details can't be further enhanced, and those with background maps whose details can be improved by inserting map cartridges into the unit. Some units can also download data from a computer. Typically, you can outline a region of interest from the map displayed on the PC monitor. Information that you don't plan to use should be eliminated. If you're just going fishing, eliminate city streets, parks, and restaurants. Too much information causes clutter and makes the screen difficult to read.

Mapping units have become popular. Besides offering all the advantages of basic GPS units, they let you see your location relative to points, islands, bays, or roads. This is particularly useful in fog, rain, or snow. It also provides a certain degree of confidence and security when you're fishing a large body of water for the first time—you always know where you are.

Be sure to compare the accessories that come with different units. Some come packaged with a DC adapter cord (cigarette lighter plug-in), which allows you to run it off a boat, car, or truck battery. Determine if computer cables and CD-ROMs are included or must be purchased separately.

OTHER ELECTRONICS

"I can't believe you've been seeing other electronics besides me," the weeping, beeping GPS scrolled in big block letters to the walleye angler behind the console. "You don't love me anymore!"

"Baby, you gotta play the field if you wanna win at this game."

Other than sonar and GPS, the most popular electronic devices on walleye boats are electric trolling motors. MinnKota and MotorGuide dominate the mass market, with appearances by Mercury-Mariner, OMC, Pinpoint, and a few other players. Most walleye anglers with console boats run 24- or 36-volt, long-shaft, foot-control models off the bow, allowing them to jig two rods simultaneously. If the wind gets too strong, they switch to a kicker outboard for boat control. Walleye anglers with tiller outboards prefer to remain in the back of the boat and run transom-mount, hand-control electric motors in tandem with splashguards to deflect the waves. When the water gets rough, they shift back to the outboard for precision trolling and drifting. A surprising number of anglers mount electric motors on both front and back, using whichever best suits conditions.

To keep these electronics running, onboard battery chargers, often called smart chargers, plug in at the dock or while the boat is on the trailer, thereby eliminating the hassle of carrying a separate charger.

Walleye anglers tend to use tiller control motors when backtrolling from the transom but switch to foot-control motors when fishing from the bow. Why? Because foot control permits the simultaneous use of two handheld rods, typically in a forward trolling mode. Hands-free steering like MinnKota's AutoPilot (maintains a set direction and speed) and Pinpoint's depth tracking (combines the motor with sonar to maintain a specific depth) increase trolling efficiency.

To keep these electronics running, onboard battery chargers, often called *smart chargers*, plug in at the dock or while the boat is on the trailer, thereby eliminating the hassle of carrying a separate charger. They sense the level of charge in each battery and shut off when they reach maximum charge. No timers or guessing. Some electrical systems are capable of charging off the engine alternator, keeping you powered up even on remote multiday trips. Neptune, Lester, Dual Pro, Guest, Dual Phase, and Professional Mariner are among the leaders in this category. Exide, Navigator, and other companies offer deep-cycle trolling motor batteries and marine starter batteries in varying capacities.

A word of warning: with all those multiple gadgets drawing current from your standard starter battery, it may have too small a reserve to keep up with the drain. If you fish small lakes, don't run long enough distances to recharge the starter battery with the alternator, and experience frequent starting problems due to lack of juice, you may need a new or larger starter battery. Anglers with abundant electronics may wish to upgrade from a group 24 or 27 to a group 31 battery (larger and longer) with more storage capacity. The battery requires a longer mounting bracket than a standard one to mount it to the floor. Ask your marine dealer for further details.

Add a battery gauge that warns you when batteries need a charge if your electrical system lacks battery-charge indicators. For emergencies, most In-Fisherman staff boats are rigged with jumper cables so that the outboards can be jump-started from the trolling motor batteries in case the outboard's starter battery runs down—which happens when we mistakenly leave one of our gizmos on for a few days. Jumper cables have bailed us out on more than one occasion, particularly when batteries fail unexpectedly.

Larger Great Lakes boats often have autopilots for hands-free steering of the main engine. We haven't seen many of these on small boats yet, and we don't really expect to. In a small boat, you need to respond to each wave, so letting go of the steering even for brief periods isn't a good idea. Autopilots are useful for slow trolling, however. Units like the Autohelm SportPilot, designed for boats from 18 to 27 feet, have applications but are probably more than you need.

Some charter boats have RDF (radio direction finder) units that lock into radio signals and point a course toward the source. These offer legitimate safety features—for example, locating a boat in distress or zeroing in on a safe harbor, even when you lack latitude and longitude readings. Mostly, though, they're used by charter captains, who lock in on radio chatter from people who say the fish are bitin'. Next thing you know, several big boats are bearing down on the location. Big Brother is listening.

Scotty offers "black box technology" for downrigging. This introduces subtle electric fields into the water through the downrigger cable. Commercial fishermen use it to attract salmon in the waters of the Pacific Northwest, though as far as we know, no research has been done on it with inland species like walleyes, and it may be illegal in some states.

In most waters, anglers don't use electric downriggers much for walleyes, but they occasionally use them for other species like trout and salmon, or for walleyes on big lakes like Lake of the Woods. Cannon downriggers have a bottom-tracking feature that hugs contours, provides easy depth control, and offers auto retrieval—all the good stuff that takes the work out of fishing cannonballs. No more hand-cranking the heavy balls up and down.

BAND FOR LIFE

Anglers are discovering the wisdom of going to sea on inland waters with marine band radios. Like so many safety items, these may not seem important until a crisis develops.

On big water, marine band radios should be mandatory safety equipment. It's too easy to get lost or stranded without landmarks to navigate by. Besides locating someone who can help you, marine band radios can provide you with weather reports, let people know where you are, allow you to talk to your buddies, and alert you to fellow anglers in distress. Plus you can listen in to fishing reports, of course. Because unwanted company can tap into your chats about productive locations and techniques, some captains have now switched over to cellular phones.

In-Fisherman Professional Walleye Trail (PWT) anglers are required to carry fully functioning marine band radios and adequately fixed antennas on board. A prescribed channel is set prior to each tournament, and radios must remain locked to that channel. Many times, pro anglers have come to the rescue of other boaters and each other. In case of a breakdown, one pro may hail another to bring his fish to the scales.

How fishermen install and use VHF radios varies tremendously, and the garbled messages that sometimes come across the airwaves leave much to be desired.

The first problem is usually the antenna. Most folks purchase a good radio but either don't know about antennas or settle for the least-expensive model they can find. Buy a ñ6Db antenna with a price of $60 to $100. Although your local marine dealer may stock cheaper antennas, don't skimp. Height is a major component of how far an antenna's signal can carry. The higher the transmitting and receiving antennas, the farther apart they can communicate. VHF is a line-of-sight form of communication. So while a 3-foot stainless steel antenna is fine, it won't carry as far as an 8-foot model. If you fish big water, you need an 8-footer.

The second most common problem is the proximity of the VHF antenna to the radio. If they're closer to each other than 3 feet, a range of problems may occur, from garbled signals to no transmissions at all. Keep these components at least 3 feet apart.

Another major source of failure is installation of the PL259 connector to the end of the antenna wire. The connector must be installed and soldered properly for maximum performance. Carefully follow the instructions that come with the antenna or radio. The connection between the antenna wire and the fitting that plugs into the radio is crucial to clear transmission.

The fourth most common problem may not stop transmission totally, but it can be very frustrating. Your VHF's proximity to other electronics has a major impact on what can be transmitted and received, and its quality. Problems such as a rhythmic ticking can occur when the antenna wire on the VHF runs alongside transducer wires or behind your sonar-locator. To avoid this, make sure the antenna wire is separated from the transducer and GPS wires. For maximal performance, run them down the opposite side of the boat.

A VHF radio should be wired directly to the boat battery rather than to the power buss under the console. With this rigging system, you still have a VHF radio for safety if any fuses blow or the system malfunctions. A VHF radio may be the only way to get help in an emergency.

Two additional malfunctions occur occasionally, and both are operator errors. When the radio microphone is left out in an all-day rain, transmission problems occur. Keep the microphone under the console or protected by a plastic bag.

Another operator error is more common than most of us want to admit. When two fishin' buddies are talking, one may toss the microphone between the windshield and console. If it lands with the transmit button depressed even slightly, all communications within range cease on that channel.

In summary, keep the radio and the microphone dry. Keep the antenna up when fishing. Make sure the connections are soldered. Mount the antenna away from the radio. Run the wires away from transducer cables and other wires. Connect the VHF radio directly to the battery.

A VHF radio may save your life. Once you reach another boat or someone ashore and you aren't facing an emergency, you can switch to another channel and save the day by talking with a buddy.

UNDERWATER CAMERAS

Few technological developments have stirred as much recent controversy in some portions of the the fishing world as underwater cameras. On one side, proponents say that the cameras open new worlds of enjoyment and insight for those curious about what's going on below the surface of a lake. On the other, detractors claim that the cameras make fishing so easy that fish populations are becoming threatened.

In-Fisherman contributor Dr. Bruce M. Carlson has experimented with cameras and offers some of his observations about their basic technology. Dr. Carlson is the chair of the Department of Anatomy and Cell Biology at the University of Michigan in Ann Arbor. He's an avid angler and a former fishery biologist and ichthyologist.

Most of the time, Carlson uses his cameras on a North Country lake with extremely clear water— typical Secchi disk readings there are between 20 and 25 feet. His systems use a waterproof camera lowered into the water and connected by cable to a battery-powered black-and-white or color TV monitor. Depending on the camera, the picture is displayed on a small TV screen or a monitor within a virtual-reality headset.

Carlson: "My impression is that despite the technological inconvenience still associated with underwater cameras, they open an unparalleled window into the underwater world. In a lake I know intimately, having spent thousands of hours studying it with a paper graph recorder while fishing, I was continually surprised at the difference between my impression of bottom type and distribution of vegetation and what I saw through the camera.

"There is, for example, a living room-sized area in about 35 feet of water where whitefish congregate year after year. From both graph tracings and feeling bottom with bottom bouncers, I assumed bottom was covered with rubble. But it really resembles a moonscape, with smooth sandy stretches punctuated by boulders several feet in diameter. The area also was full of whitefish. Eventually I was no longer surprised by seeing fish where I already knew they should be, based on vast fishing experience. On the other hand, lake topography and bottom composition continually surprised me."

Carlson surmises that the most effective underwater range of a camera is between one-third and one-half the Secchi disk reading—some 6 or 7 to slightly more than 10 feet in this extra-clear Minnesota lake. In a modestly clear Michigan lake, however, his view was so restricted that other than close-ups of underwater vegetation and a few sunfish, he couldn't see much of interest.

To use his cameras, Carlson stays in the same spot, slowly drifts, or uses a motor. "It works best to pick a drift in a light wind that will take the boat along the length of a bar," Carlson says. "Anything more than passive drifting requires a second person to operate the motor, because the person using the camera is so occupied that accurate boat control and simultaneous viewing is difficult, especially when depth varies.

"The most effective viewing is with the camera is within 1 foot or less of bottom. The reflection of light off bottom creates a narrow vertical zone of excellent viewing along bottom. But again, you must constantly adjust the length of cable leading to the camera to keep it from banging into rocks or stirring up bottom sediment. While you're moving, the field of vision is relatively narrow, and fish typically put in no more than cameo appearances. You see them, and the camera passes by or the fish move."

For Carlson, the most informative aspect of using the camera lies in his discovery of how vegetation is positioned. Moving along a weededge, he can quickly see how pockets and points in vegetation stop and gather or funnel fish. An intuitive angler can literally see the trees in the forest, observing, as a hunter might, that certain stands of vegetation offer distinctively different habitat—and that this habitat changes, becoming more or less appealing as the season progresses.

"I was impressed, too, by how much life is found in the deeper zone beyond the weedline," Carlson says. "All those little puffs of sediment made by darters shooting away. But what are all those small pits in bottom sediment in deeper water? Hours of observation are needed before many aspects of the biology of deep waters can be understood."

One of the biggest technical difficulties with underwaters cameras is seeing the picture they transmit on a screen in sunlight. "Encasing the screen end of a TV monitor in a dark bag helps but is far from ideal," Carlson observes. "An advance in this regard is the newer version of viewing screens housed in a tubular plastic viewing case that serves the same purpose as a black bag. Still, the best time for viewing, given prevailing light conditions during the day, is during the half hour before sunrise and after sunset. The light is strong enough then to provide a good view of bottom in depths as great as 35 feet. During this period, images on the screen are particularly crisp.

"Night viewing wasn't effective without lights. Even full moonlight wasn't strong enough to allow viewing. With lights,

Fisheye

vegetation stood out in sharp relief, but reflections from plankton and small suspended particles were distracting." Many cameras today are available with infrared or colored light to assist in viewing.

Cameras can help anglers better understand readings on sonar. "Verify the presence of fish with the camera, and then immediately check the reading on your sonar unit," Carlson says. "Even fish stationary on bottom read differently from rocks or other debris. Bottom substrate changes also become easier to read when you can verify what you're seeing with the camera. Start, for example, by viewing atop a sand and gravel hump. Check the bottom reading. Monitoring the camera again, move down the drop-off. See how the substrate changes—the transition from gravel and sand to silt? Check the change on your sonar. Watch how the grayline widens as you move over softer bottom?"

One of the most controversial aspects of the underwater camera is its potential as a fish finder. Carlson: "Whenever I lower the camera onto a spot that I know is a good area for walleyes, I see at least one walleye. On the other hand, whenever I let the wind blow me randomly away from spots I have previously identified as fishy areas, I rarely see fish. For an angler unskilled in finding fish, using a camera to locate fish is going to be futile.

"For anglers skilled at knowing where fish should be, however, I don't see an overwhelming need for a camera, except to verify what can already be inferred from lake maps and sonar. But the cameras are a wonderful learning tool. I don't think it's inappropriate to learn all you can about the lake you're fishing. Cameras, like sonar and lake maps, are a tool that, if used properly, can increase that knowledge.

"I'm uneasy about locating major schools of fish and then fishing for them. Still, it's not much different from finding fish with sonar, except that now you can identify whether the fish are whitefish, walleyes, or suckers.

"Two mitigating factors exist in this regard, though," Carlson continues. "First, it's almost impossible for a boat angler to fish for the fish he sees on the camera. Doing both things at the same time is almost impossible. Second, while you're using the camera, you can't be catching fish. The technology is time-consuming enough to give the fish an even chance over the course of a day of fishing."

An angler on ice has more control than an angler bobbing in a boat. Once a camera's set up under the ice, you can monitor how a fish responds to a presentation. The technique is a potential extension of the sight-fishing we practice in shallow areas of clear water lakes.

The problem with ice is the limits it imposes on camera mobility. Once you've set yourself up in an ice shack and planned a few major moves for the day, fine. The proficient ice angler is often more mobile than that, however—no time to pack and unpack a camera at each new hole, not when the object is to cut as many holes as possible in pursuit of fish. It takes time to set the camera in a hole near your main fishing hole and then to point the camera at your lure while you fish.

As prices continue to fall, cameras are becoming a presence on the ice scene, used mostly to identify fish marked on sonar and to learn about bottom makeup. For these purposes, cameras are inspiring to use—a means for finding answers to questions about what's happening below. What you learn may eventually lead to increased fish catches. It's also possible that you may be able to identify winter congregations of fish that will become vulnerable when they weren't before.

Efforts to ban cameras are clearly futile. For what purpose—without data that proves harm—would we surrender a technology that allows us to explore brave new worlds and go where only scuba divers have gone before?

Chapter 4

Investing in the Proper Equipment

SELECTING THE RIGHT BOAT, MOTORS, AND TRAILER

Walleye boats are often marketed as multispecies boats to appeal to more anglers. Rigged and ready for big water walleye fishing, these boats offer amenities like bowmount trolling motors. Following the bass boat trend, they have become bigger and faster. High-performance pads, positioned aft of the normal deep-V, result in better handling and faster speeds. These pads also make boats more stable at rest.

With huge livewells, baitwells, and wide gunwales for mounting rod holders and accessories, these boats are great for muskie and pike, striper, crappies, catfish, bass, and, of course walleyes. Regardless of whether you're a serious walleye tournament angler, a weekend warrior, or a sometimes-angler with a family, choices are plentiful in today's walleye-multispecies boats.

THE 75-PERCENT SOLUTION

Prospective boat buyers often ask our opinions of this or that boat or the differences between similar models from competing boat companies. "Which is better?" The answer is more obvious once you ask, "Which boat is better for me?"

Overall quality—Many good or adequate boats are available to walleye anglers. The main difference between a good boat and an also-float can be summed up in two words: design and construction. At In-Fisherman, we use our boats often and in a wide variety of conditions, so we tend to lean toward industrial strength instead of saving a few bucks with lesser components.

If you're a serious and frequent angler, a little overkill is fine—even desirable. The first time you get caught on the lake far from port in substantial wind, you'll be glad you invested in a seaworthy craft rather than one that may not handle the conditions.

If you fish only occasionally and don't travel long distances across big water in changeable weather, you may not need a heavier grade aluminum hull, abundant waterproof storage, or premium components like seat mounting bolts and electrical systems. Adequate may be good enough, and additional expense can't be justified.

All boats of equal size aren't necessarily equal. Make sure you're comparing apples with apples, not apples and plums. You get what you pay for.

Frequent fishing style—This important question is often missed by many fishermen. In essence: how and what do you fish for, most often? Walleyes? Multispecies? Even if you fish a little of everything from rivers to the Great Lakes, what you tend to do most often is the key.

The market for walleye boats that can alternately take on Lake of the Woods, Gull Lake, and a 100-acre lake continues to expand. One boat may never be able do it all, but a tournament-ready walleye boat comes close.

If you fish big water, such as giant reservoirs or large natural lakes much of the time, steer your selection toward at least a 17- to 18-footer, preferably a 19-footer or longer, so you can handle the long runs and the frequently rough conditions. Such boats call for high horsepower, generally 150 to 225, with console steering.

If you can come up with something that suits your fishing style 75 percent of the time, is adequate for another 15 percent of conditions, and probably not a good fit for the remaining 10 percent, consider it a good compromise.

Once you select the basic hull and motor, add accessories like kicker outboards, electric motors, electronics, and gadgets galore.

The dollars add up fast, frequently topping $30,000 for a fully rigged fishin' machine. You'll also need a tow vehicle with considerable power. And consider where you can stow the boat when it's out of the water. Will it fit in the garage? Oops!

That's not the boat for you if you fish small lakes and rivers with poor boat launches, shallow stretches of water with obstructions, lakes with horsepower restrictions, or have a limited boat budget. In these cases, you're better off with a small, aluminum 14- to 16-footer. In fact, you're probably best off with a johnboat or a 12-foot cartopper, along with a small matching outboard. Maybe a pontoon if you fish only one small lake with your family.

Again, after you determine the basic hull and motor, add accessories to the level of your desire and budget.

If you fish many in-between conditions, ranging from large to small waters, the choice becomes more challenging. Ask yourself what size and style of boat would handle most conditions, most of the time. If you can come up with something that suits your fishing style 75 percent of the time, is adequate for another 15 percent of conditions, and probably not a good fit for the remaining 10 percent, consider it a good compromise.

Many 16- to 17-footers fit this description. They're a bit small for frequent big water use but sufficient if you accept the fact that weather will sometimes keep you off the water. They also run small rivers pretty well if the water level doesn't get too shallow, and they can be launched even from poor accesses, if you invest in a good trailer.

Console steering versus tiller outboard—Hands-on tiller steering is more responsive to precise trolling maneuvers like traditional backtrolling. Consoles are less responsive, often requiring a kicker outboard to slow down and troll at speeds too slow for an idling engine. Consoles have sufficient power to move big, heavy boats, however. But they also guzzle gas and oil.

If you can't visualize fishing with a steering wheel, stick to familiar tillers. You can switch to a transom electric in calm conditions without having to move from your seat. Console boats usually run best off the bow with a powerful electric for precision trolling. For in-between conditions—winds of 20 to 30 mph—consoles require sea anchors and controlled drifts, whereas midsized tiller outboards (35 to 90 hp) handle backtrolling quite well. It's those in-between conditions that challenge console boat-control maneuvers the most.

Fiberglass versus aluminum—Personal choice comes into play here. Fiberglass is generally a little heavier and more expensive. Curvatures can be molded into fiberglass more readily to alleviate spray and pounding. Durable aluminum might be a little wetter due to limited spray-deflecting hull curvatures (Tracker Marine's new Tundra aluminum manufacturing technology is an exception), but aluminum takes abuse better from rocks and shorelines. Fiberglass has in recent years made considerable inroads into the competitive tournament market, while aluminum still dominates among the weekend angling crowd.

The times are a-changin', at least for many of the pros. Glass boats have been accepted, primarily because they offer roominess, comfortable ride, more variety in color schemes, and attractive prices.

Admittedly, pros demand more of their boats than recreational anglers fishing small lakes. And guides run the same rigs as pros. The boats used in many amateur walleye tournaments are similar to those seen at a typical PWT event—larger, fully equipped, and identical to the pros'. This is no coincidence. One boat may never be able do it all, but a tournament-ready walleye boat almost does.

Interior layout—Number and position of livewells, rod racks and storage, seating arrangements, raised decks versus lower seating, battery storage—all are matters of personal preference. Nearly any combination of equipment can be installed in any boat, but first select the proper floor plan and general layout to suit how and where you fish most often.

Open aluminum boats with multiple pedestal seats are popular with guides

and anglers who fish with 3, 4, even 5 anglers in the boat most of the time. They offer room to move, plus room for equipment. Adding even one side console eats up space; an opposite-side console claims more.

But for long runs in rough water, sitting farther back in the boat and hanging onto a console can cushion thousands of waves, block spray, and help keep you warm. (Walk-through windshields are a blessing in cold, damp, windy weather.) Competitive anglers who mostly fish with two anglers in the boat, sometimes three, often favor consoles. Families, however, quickly overrun boats equipped with casting decks and few seating positions.

Raised decks elevate you to great casting positions in calmer water. Is that where you want to be, though, when you're bouncing in big waves? Or would you rather be down inside? Walleye boats with raised decks—actually, they're multispecies boats—have higher gunwales than bass boats. Where do you want your kids to be when they're fishing or roaming around the boat? Tough questions that need to be answered.

In the end, all aspects of boat design should be considered: hull, layout, engine requirements, standard features, ease of rigging. Narrow your choices to a prime few. Research. Then shop at local marine dealers, comparing not just properties of the boats but service reputation and rigging expertise. Then factor in overall price.

Remember, however, that your total cost is more than dollars. If the boat doesn't perform to your expectations and demands, do you care how much money you saved? Perhaps even worse, how much money did you squander on a rig too big or impractical for your needs?

You're gonna be married to this partner for some time, and beauty is more than skin deep. (Though ugly goes straight to the bone!) Don't be lured by metal flake and gadgets when what you really need is the right personality plus a good dose of home cookin' to be compatible over the long haul and to be able to weather the storms. At least 75 percent of the time.

TO EACH HIS OWN

Each boat has its own personality. It should meet individual needs, which means it's got all the bells and whistles you need to make each trip a pleasure. Some boats are sold "as is," while others can be modified. If you're a serious angler, make sure that your new boat includes timers for the aerator pumps, ability to trim your outboard from several positions in the boat, possibly hydraulic steering, a kicker outboard that has a bracket to hold it in position in rough seas, and a T-H Marine system for freshwater livewell pickup when you're underway.

The list continues, but remember—you're only talking a few dollars more, and over the life of the payments, those extra dollars per month will boost resale value, an important consideration.

Make sure the trailer adequately handles the weight of the boat, outboard, fuel, batteries, gear, and anchors. Trailers are rated for the load they carry. A typical 1,500-pound boat becomes 400 pounds heavier with a V-6 outboard. Three or four batteries add 200 more pounds; a 40-gallon tank adds 240 pounds; a kicker, 100 pounds; a bowmount, 40 pounds; boxes of jigs, spoons, and tackle, 200 pounds; anchors add more, as do raingear, life jackets, extra props, and oil. Add it up, and then make sure the trailer supports the weight with adequate carpeted bunks, a spare tire, and probably a dual axle setup with built-in shock absorbers.

Buying a walleye boat was never this easy, based on recommendations of walleye pros and manufacturers. At the same time, boat buyers never have had so many options. Shop early and ask questions.

MULTIPLE PERSONALITIES

Chameleons adapt to their environment by adopting strikingly different colors when exposed against different backgrounds. Modern walleye anglers equip their boats and gear to do much the same.

Watch versatile walleye anglers zip around big lakes and fish different kinds of areas, displaying various profiles in dissimilar spots. Why? To be most effective, they match presentation tactics to local conditions. Livebait rigging, vertical jigging, casting, forward trolling, backtrolling, controlled drifting, downrigging, planer board trolling, anchoring—all theoretically possible on the same body of water during a fishing day. Certainly all are fair game over the course of a fishing season.

Livebait rigging, vertical jigging, casting, forward trolling, backtrolling, controlled drifting, downrigging, planer board trolling, anchoring—all theoretically possible on the same body of water during a fishing day.

Modern shape shifters have all the necessary equipment to let them shed their skins and take on new personalities in an instant. Boat hulls are designed not just as multiple-presentation walleye boats, but as multi-species craft. Stand up and cast for walleyes, but it works just as well for pike, muskie, or bass. Troll open water for walleyes—remarkably similar for salmon, steelhead, or brown trout. Vertical jigging for walleyes isn't much different from working deep for crappies. And anchoring for walleyes certainly smells like a catfish tactic.

Walleye hulls designed for big water performance are deeper at the bow than bass boats. You don't just cross waves, you fish in them. Hulls are usually 17 to 20 feet long, and comfort and performance improve with every inch, increasing your ability to cross wave tops without crashing into their crests. Anything larger is more difficult to trailer. Anything shorter is better suited to smaller waters and calmer conditions. They have the gas capacity and power to traverse long distances in rough water, plus the boat control needed to fish in all conditions—the best of all characteristics without sacrificing fishability.

Powerful 24- or 36-volt bowmount electrics allow you to vertical jig or livebait rig in substantial wind and waves or at near-standstill speeds in calm conditions, plus provide suitable speed for forward trolling spinner rigs and crankbaits without resorting to noisy outboards. Once upon a time, you needed to backtroll with an outboard to accomplish this, but no longer, unless you prefer the control of a midrange

Casting

Raised casting platforms aren't quite as high as they are on bass boats, yet they allow easy casting. If decks were level with the gunwales, you could fall off in big waves.

Controlled Drifting

Controlled drifting spreads lines and baits across the length of the boat. Use minor corrections with an outboard or electric to correct the angle of drift. Great for fishing flats.

Backtrolling

Traditional backtrolling uses an outboard or transom electric to slowly move and direct the boat through waves, presenting lines and baits almost vertically beneath the boat. The flat transom slows progress to a crawl, allowing pinpoint control.

Forward (Power) Trolling

Power trolling spinner rigs is easiest with powerful 24–volt bowmount electric motors. Plenty of power and speed to get blades turning.

35- to 90-hp outboard to the get-up-and-go of a more powerful console engine.

Rather than attempting to slow troll with a monster engine, you can operate a 9.9- to 15-hp kicker outboard either with a tiller control at the rear for hands-on response or with a tie to the console via a tie bar for steering wheel control; it's strictly a personal choice. Those who prefer a large tiller outboard to a console setup use splashguards to deflect spray in rough conditions, and they use a transom electric for pinpoint control when waves barely lap at the hull. Every situation is anticipated, every angle covered.

Rod holders strategically located along the gunwales position multiple rods for simultaneous presentation. Electronics are viewable from all around the boat, including GPS navigation for plotting trolling passes and running from point A to distant point B and back without fear of getting lost in fog or darkness. Nowadays, it's almost always possible to get there from here, though you should always exercise good judgment in the face of wind and weather. Call for assistance on the marine band radio if you encounter a problem. No need to take chances.

Examine the accompanying photos. Note the similarities in rigging and hull design, despite the variety of manufacturers. Any of these boats performs all of the described tasks, and more models are introduced each year.

There's more than one way to catch a walleye—or pike, bass, trout, panfish—but you don't need more than one boat if you rig it right. A leopard can't change spots, but chameleon walleye anglers do it all the time, and very successfully.

Planer Board Trolling

After lures are out and running, attach angled planer boards to your lines, let out sufficient line to cover a wide swath, place rods in holders, and troll forward. When fish strike, reel in, detach the board, and land the walleye.

Downrigging

Downriggers present crankbaits, spoons, or spinner rigs in deeper water than you usually can fish with other forward trolling techniques.

Livebait Rigging or Vertical Jigging

Precision vertical presentations off the bow are possible with foot-control electrics. Anglers sometimes fish two rods simultaneously.

Anchoring

Anglers commonly anchor off the bow in large waves to fish shallow, windswept rocks. High bows cut waves and deflect water to the sides instead of over the bow.

PRECISION MANEUVERS FOR BIG WATER BRUISERS

Slip, slide, and away. You can't fight wind, but you can make it your ally.

Big boat maneuvers provide a lesson in compromise—working with wind and waves rather than trying to overpower them. The bigger the boat, the harder to control unless you're equipped to do it right. The following pages offer tips for controlling big boats on big water.

KICKERS, TILLERS, AND TIE BARS

Some anglers like PWT participants prefer hands-on control for big water trolling, using tiller kicker outboards from 10 to 15 hp. To facilitate this standing approach, they add handle extensions, either factory-available kits or modified extensions.

Other pros prefer to steer the kicker from the console while trolling for suspended fish, using factory-made, detachable tie-bar kits to link their big outboards with kickers, simultaneously steering both. The tie bar either mounts in front of the motors inside the boat, where it's easily reached, or on the back of

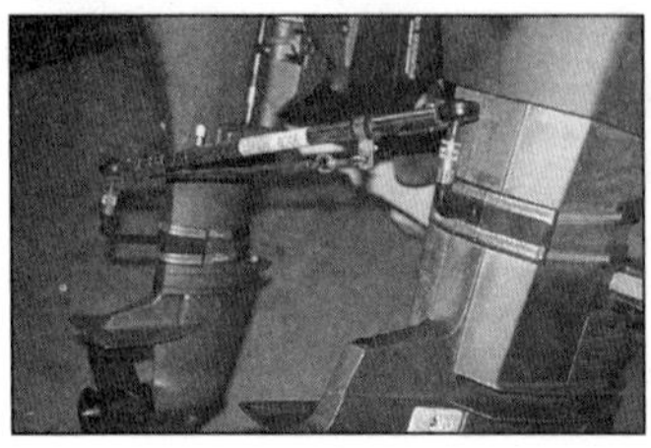

Tie rods connect the main motor to kicker motors, making console steering of the kicker possible. Connect a detachable tie rod (Goldeneye Products) between your main motor and kicker, and both motors will move simultaneously. The tie rod also pivots, allowing each motor to be trimmed up or down.

the motors, where you must lean precariously over the back to attach and detach it. With an inside mount, however, the tie bar can remain attached even while moving at high speed in calm weather. In wind, detaching the tie bar and securing the kicker with a safety strap prevents the motor-mount bracket from breaking when the kicker bounces up and down during long runs across rough-and-tumble water.

A kicker tiller handle extension makes steering from a standing or sitting position more comfortable.

Some anglers with console steering boats and big outboards like the option of fishing from the transom, using a transom-mount electric or kicker outboard to backtroll, hover, or controlled drift. To properly achieve this, however, a boat should be equipped with splashguards—typically installed on most walleye boats that have tiller steering. The flat transom slows backward movement against waves, while adjusting reverse thrust and turning the outboard or electric trolling motor makes precise maneuvers possible. In strong waves, splashguards prevent water from splashing over the transom.

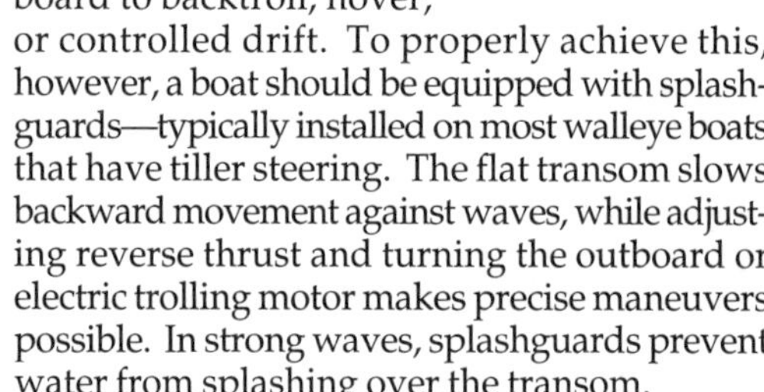

Most console-steering boats lack splashguards, which reduces their backtrolling ability, but this can be remedied with controlled drifts by trolling downwind with sea anchors or using the bowmount electric whenever possible. Larger console boats offer more power, range, and handling ability in rough water than small boats with tiller outboards under 100 hp, but they sacrifice precision control in winds of 20 to 40 mph, when electrics may be inadequate.

Console and tiller rigs each offer advantages, though both are adequate most of the time. It comes down to this: if you fish large bodies of water or angle for suspended fish most of the time, you probably should consider console steering, high horsepower, and a boat over 18 feet long. But if you primarily fish small waters, place a premium on precision boat control, and only occasionally venture onto bigger waters, then a 16- to 18-foot tiller-steering boat with less horsepower should suffice.

CENTER-TRANSOM SEA ANCHOR

PWT angler Greg Horoky, winner of the 1994 Lake Erie Eastern Pro-Am, controls his trolling speed with a large sea anchor attached by a sliding metal ring to a short rope spanning the transom eyes. The sea anchor slides along the rope, centering itself, and keeps the transom parallel to the waves instead of angled, as a sea anchor is when tied off one corner. Some pros use two small sea anchors, one at each corner. These slow downwind drifting and trolling passes. Horoky opens or closes his walk-through windshield to decrease or increase wind resistance, depending on whether he wants to move a little slower or faster.

HOW SLOW?

Lake Erie charter skipper Jim Fofrich, Jr., uses two sea anchors, one lowered along each side, to control forward trolling speed when he uses the big inboard engine on his 27-foot Sportcraft. One or more sea anchors work on 16- to 20-foot boats, too. For downwind trolling, attach a sea anchor off a bow cleat, perhaps another on the other side of the bow. For controlled drifting, attach one off a bow cleat and perhaps a second off a transom cleat. For backtrolling, hang a sea anchor off the bow eye.

What about trolling upwind or crosswind? Why fight it? Go with the wind to minimize line tangles and maximize control.

FOR BIG, BIG BOATS

Walleye anglers trolling from boats over 20 feet long attach kicker outboards to their transoms or main engines, using retractable lift brackets (available from motor manufacturers) to raise their engines out of the water at high speed. Electric motors designed to be mounted to main outboards and steered via consoles are available, too.

MinnKota's Navigator trolling motor mounts to outboard motors. A control box allows you to set the amount of thrust and to change prop direction.

MORE POWER!

Ever think about putting that 200-hp outboard motor on your 16-foot square-stern canoe? You might go real fast—to the bottom of the lake. Boat manufacturers are required to post horsepower ratings on boats under 20 feet that use outboard engines. Ratings were developed by professional boating organizations. Central to this group is the American Boat and Yacht Council, an organization that solicits information from

the United States Coast Guard, and boat manufacturers, insurance companies, and others. They suggest, encourage, and evaluate boating standards for the industry.

The actual determination of the outboard horsepower a boat can use depends on several mathematical formulas and a table developed over the years. Boat design, however, has a major influence on how the formula is applied.

Outboard Boat Horsepower Capacity

The following table is used to determine the appropriate horsepower rating.

					Remote steering and 20" transom	No remote wheel steering or transom less than 20"	
						Flat-bottomed, hard-chined boats	Other boats
If the factor is	thru 35	36-39	40-42	43-45	46-52	over 52	over 52	over 52
H.P. capacity is	3	5	7.5	10	15	(2 x factor) -90	(0.5 x factor) -15	(0.8 x factor) -25

Flat-bottomed, hard-chined boats—reduce horsepower capacity one increment for factors through 52.

Raise horsepower capacity to nearest 5-horsepower increment if factor is over 52.

Hard Chine

transom height

Soft Chine

chine

Example: a boat hull whose factor (length x transom width in feet) equals 120. Assume the boat has a transom height of 20 inches, remote wheel steering, and soft chines. Since the factor exceeds 52, take 2 times the factor and subtract 90 (2 x 120 - 90 = 150). The maximum horsepower rating for the boat is 150.

Take the same boat hull and transom but change the steering to tiller. The chart now says to take 0.8 times the factor and subtract 25 (0.8 x 120 - 25 = 71). The maximum power for this boat is 75 hp. We are permitted to raise the horsepower to the nearest 5-hp increment, according to the table.

Consider a hard-chined, flat-bottomed boat with a transom height of 15 inches, a length of 11' 9", and a transom width of 4' 8". The factor is 11.75 x 4.67 = 54.87 or 55. Take 0.5 of the factor and subtract 15 (0.5 x 55 - 15 = 12.5). The horsepower is 12.5. Then raise the rating to the nearest 5-hp increment because the factor was over 52. So this boat can be rated for 15 hp.

Motor requirements for inflatable boats, canoes, kayaks, and sailboats are covered under different regulations, and ratings for boats over 20 feet are determined by the boat manufacturer.

Exceeding your boat's horsepower capacity is unsafe and against the law.

One determining factor is the chine of the boat. *Chine* is the place where the side of the boat meets the bottom. Chines are described as hard or soft, depending on the sharpness of the angle formed by the side and bottom. For instance, the flat-bottomed riverboat or johnboat is considered a hard chine because the sides meet the bottom at nearly right angles. Many modified V-hulls are considered soft chines because the meeting of the sides and bottom have been rounded, even though the side still appears to meet the bottom at almost a right angle.

Other factors enter into appropriate outboard horsepower: length of the boat and transom width and height. Boat length, measured in feet, is the distance from the bow to the stern, excluding handles and other fittings. Transom width, measured in feet, is the distance across the transom. If the boat doesn't have a full transom, such as a setback motorwell, the width is measured where the beam is broadest in the back quarter of the boat. Transom height is the vertical distance from the top of the transom, or bottom of the transom cutout, to the bottom or keel. A final consideration is steering type, either remote (wheel steering) or tiller (hand) steering.

Each of these factors plays a role in horsepower ratings. In the case of chines, a flat-bottomed, hard-chined boat is somewhat less stable when turning, so adjustments must be made in horsepower rating. Length, transom width, and transom height affect the size of the boat's hull. Steering type affects weight placement as well as control. Tiller boats have added weight near the transom because the operator sits there, whereas in remote steering, the operator and his weight are forward of the transom. More important, the operator has better visibility and control of the boat, particularly under adverse conditions. As a result, rating factors are more generous.

Some simple arithmetic: a number called the *factor* must be calculated. The factor is the product of the length of the boat in feet times the transom width in feet. For instance, a boat 17' 10" long with a transom width of 6' 9" has a factor of 17.83 x 6.75 = 120.35. Rounded off to the nearest whole number, the factor becomes 120. Consult the accompanying chart to determine horsepower capacity.

PRECISION TROLLING WITH POWERFUL OUTBOARDS

Today's bigger outboards are quieter, smoother, and use less fuel than those of earlier generations. For speed and safety, many pros run 200- and 225-hp engines on their big, water-worthy boats. The trials they put their equipment through can benefit you.

Manufacturers have different names for technologies that inject fuel directly into their big two-stroke engines: Mercury has OptiMax; Yamaha has HPDI; and OMC (Johnson, Evinrude) has FICHT.

Keith Kavajecz, who runs Mercury motors, takes advantage of an optional accessory that allows his 225-hp Opti-Max to "troll down" better.

"It's called the Smart Craft Gauge package," Kavajecz says, "and it makes a big engine a fishable engine. With Smart Craft Gauges, we can control idling revolutions per minute

(rpm). A typical big outboard—anything over 135 hp—will idle at just under 1,000 rpm. With the props we run on those engines, that moves us along at 3 to 3.5 mph—too fast for walleye trolling most of the time.

"With Smart Craft Gauges, I can adjust the idle all the way down to 450 rpm. That gets me down into the 1.5 mph range, a good speed for summertime crankbait fishing. It's still too fast for some presentations, like coldwater conditions in spring and fall, or pulling spinners. But summer trolling often is best in the range from 1.5 to 2.5."

There are inherent advantages to controlling the boat with the main gas outboard. One, the control's in the middle of the transom, rather than off to one side, as it is for a kicker. "Let's say I'm contour trolling in a big wind," Kavajecz says. "If the wind blows me in too shallow, I can punch the throttle for all that horsepower, and the big prop can push me quickly back out to the right depth.

"Two, the OptiMax is much quieter and smoother than older big engines. The new engines emit more of a low hum, a steady, droning sound, which I think spooks fish less than the staccato *blap-blap-blap* of older engines."

SmartTach and SmartSpeed are specifically designed to display information sent from the electronic control module (ECM) built into each Mercury OptiMax. These gauges feature both text and graphic displays to provide the standard readouts anglers are accustomed to, along with fuel management data and engine alarm conditions.

A key feature is the system's new method of controlling idle speed. This should have several applications for walleye anglers—for example, being able to troll at a constant low speed, even with 150- to 225-hp motors, without having to continually adjust engine rpm or shift in and out of gear.

Mode select buttons on SmartSpeed will engage the Troll Control, an exclusive Mercury feature that allows for setting a target rpm or boat speed with the touch of a hand. When Troll Control is selected, engine rpm automatically drops to a preset level as low as 400 rpm. This allows walleye anglers to integrate big motors into many presentation scenarios not previously possible. These high-tech engines can run all day at low rpm without a cough or sputter.

All three common speed-measuring devices—a paddle wheel, a pressure tube gauge, or the speed feature on GPS—can be integrated into the SmartSpeed gauge, so the most accurate readout can be selected for the speed range being used. As a bonus, this high-tech gauge can display current GPS course.

In addition, SmartSpeed provides multitank fuel- and oil-level readings, current fuel-range capacity, along with air and water temperatures. It automatically defaults to display boat speed, time of day, and fuel level.

With the SmartTach gauge, anglers can see engine rpm, trim level, fuel flow, and water pressure at a single glance. Also available through this gauge are engine temperature, battery voltage, engine hours, and engine default data—whew!

In other words, these new high-tech instruments provide more information than you can possibly use (or probably want). The Troll Control offers a number of other low-speed boat-control options. We may, in fact, be seeing a new trend away from four-stroke kicker outboards as add-ons to main outboard engines. Everything you need to do can be accomplished with one engine at the push of a button.

As good as the new engines are, Kavajecz isn't ready to get rid of his kicker. "The kicker still has an important place," he says, "especially in clear, shallow water."

AND HERE'S THE KICKER

Big news in kickers is a model from Yamaha. The four-stroke T8 is an 8 hp with distinct advantages, according to PWT pro Jim Bell.

"This is the first kicker ever designed for the walleye or kicker market," Bell says. "A couple things make it better. Dropping a kicker always has been difficult. You had to lean out over the back of your boat to grab the manual bracket. Tilt systems were available, but they placed the motor even farther back, maybe 5 to 6 inches. So an already too short tiller became even shorter. Long extension handles became necessary.

"The new T8 has a power tilt system. An extra-long tiller handle doesn't require an extension. A major weak spot on other kickers is the bracket that holds the motor up out of the water. That bracket is designed for a 12- or 14-foot boat, not the pounding we put our equipment through. On the new T8, the bracket was redesigned to be much stronger."

The motor itself has been designed to maximize power, or "thrust," over top-end speed. "We're not driving our boats with the kicker," Bell says. "What we want is thrust. We want to move the boat, not make it go fast. This engine has a high-thrust lower unit that's exactly what we need."

The exhaust is redirected when the T8 is put in reverse. "We reverse troll with our motors," Bell says, "and with a standard configuration prop, in reverse the exhaust still comes out of the hub of the propeller. That creates air bubbles, and the prop tries to bite into that water. By redirecting the exhaust away from the direction of travel, reverse thrust has been increased by about 60 percent."

FOREWARNED IS FOUR-ARMED

Back in the '60s, Homelite had a 55-hp, four-stroke outboard. It was durable, clean, economical, reliable, and because of these traits, it appeared on many rental boat fleets. But unfortunately, it didn't have a wide dealer network. There simply wasn't a demand for it as there is now in the "greening of America." The engine's demise was before its time.

Fast-forward nearly four decades. Public outcry has rightfully demanded the reversal of worldwide pollution, and recreational boating must be part of the solution by reducing contaminants dumped into the water, especially by two-stroke outboards.

A two-stroke engine, whether it's in a weed eater, personal watercraft, chain saw, or outboard, accomplishes one cycle of its operation in one revolution of the crank. From the bottom of the stroke to the top, and back to the bottom again, fuel is drawn in through intake ports, pushed ahead in the piston to create an explosion, then travels through exhaust ports on the other side of the cylinder.

To create more power, a "looper" system was devised that uses in-rushing fuel from the intake port to push burned gases out the exhaust port. Unfortunately, some of the unburned fuel exhausts with the burned fuel . . . right into the water.

By comparison, four-stroke technology accomplishes its operation in two rotations of the crank. Fuel is drawn in through an open intake valve, the valve closes, compression and detonation follow, an exhaust valve opens, and all the burned gases exhausts into the atmosphere, not the water. No unburned fuel remains.

The EPA determined that marine engines contribute 2.6 percent of the ozone (smog) created when discharged hydrocarbons and nitrous oxide mix with sunlight. The agency has decreed that by 2006, 75 percent of current emissions must be eliminated. At one point, the industry thought about plopping an automobile engine atop a lower unit to meet the requirement. But . . . this was a "weighted" requirement. If the biggest sellers were midrange engines, four-stroke technology could be applied there, while big gas guzzlers that didn't meet EPA specs could continue to be manufactured, so long as the line as a

Four-Stroke Cycle Operation

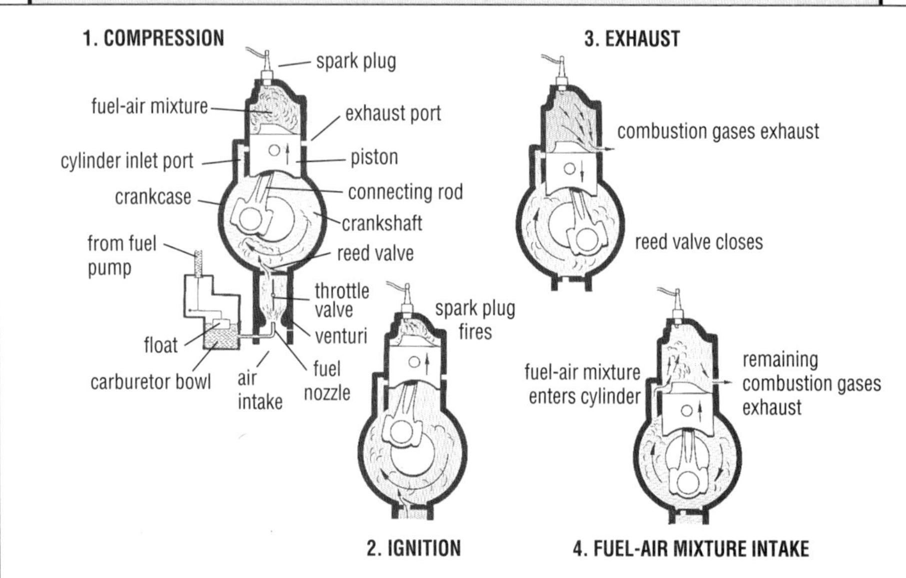

Two-Stroke Cycle Operation

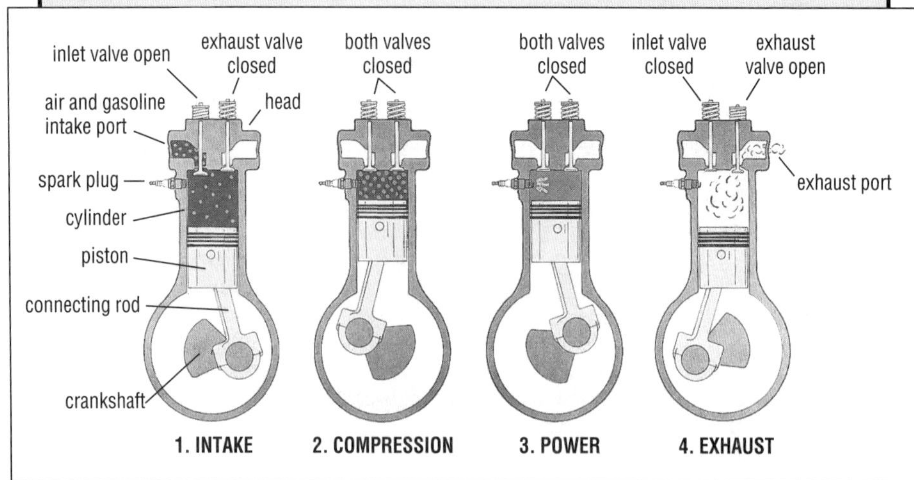

whole met allowable average emissions. This compromise gave the industry time to create alternatives to four-stroke weightiness and slow spool-up times.

Unusual alliances were formed: OMC and Suzuki, Yamaha and Mercury. Suzuki began producing the four-stroke 60/70 horsepower models for OMC. Yamaha used their powerhead on Merc's lower unit. Honda hung right in there with an entire lineup of EPA-compliant engines.

The benefits of four-stroke technology, according to Honda, are many:

• Oil is recirculated, not discharged into the water. As in cars, oil isn't mixed with fuel.

• Better fuel economy. Commercial fishermen in Nova Scotia average half the fuel. And at the low speeds common to trolling, fuel savings are even better.

• Longevity. Only while starting does metal-on-metal contact occur. Oil creates a fluid film on internal components.

• Honda builds millions of car engines and applies its technological advancements to outboards.

• Four-strokes have about the same number of parts as two-strokes.

Meanwhile, OMC, relieved of the pressure of developing new midrange engines, concentrated on reducing the emissions of their larger engines by using the FICHT fuel injection system. Mercury gained the same relief and went with the Orbital DFI. As an aside, several fuel-injected engines are on the market, but they all still use the "looper" approach; only the FICHT and DFI explode unburned fuel completely, like four-strokes, but without their complexity.

According to OMC, fuel injection accomplishes the following:

• Improves two-stroke fuel economy by 35 percent.
• Has a great power-to-weight ratio.
• Provides superior acceleration.
• Reduces two-stroke oil consumption by 50 percent.
• Eliminates oil filters.
• Provides silky-smooth operation.
• Is quieter at wide-open throttle.
• Is available with higher horsepower.
• Meets EPA standards.

Four-strokes continued to improve, however. Technology led to tuned exhaust stacks and multiple exhaust valves. Engines with quick spool-up times like those of two-strokes are now available with twice the fuel economy of two-strokes: cost differences between two-strokes and four-strokes are becoming almost negligible, and the four-strokes' quiet running is astounding. The biggest problem seems to be with starter bendixes: folks forget that their engines are already running when they reengage the starter. Four-strokes seem to run better at higher rpm, making a 70-hp four-stroke comparable in power to an 85-hp two-stroke.

But the larger the engine, the less the power-to-weight ratio. For an example, an 80- to 100-hp four-stroke Yamaha HDFI weighs 358 pounds, while a 90-hp two-stroke weighs 252 pounds. The 90 hp, therefore, offers 1 horsepower per 2.8 pounds, while the 100-hp, four-stroke offers 1 horsepower per 3.6 pounds.

Eighty extra pounds on a light boat make a huge difference. If, however, the boat is heavy or carries a heavier complement of passengers and equipment, the 80-hp Yamaha may be even a better bargain than the 90-hp two-stroke. The Suzuki/OMC 70 hp shows 254 pounds for the two-stroke, and 319 pounds for the four-stroke. That's 3.6 pounds per horsepower for the two-stroke versus 4.6 pounds for the four-stroke.

If you want an engine with midrange horsepower, you are probably better off serving yourself and the atmosphere with a four-stroke outboard. The price isn't scary, the responsiveness is great, and the gift to nature is marvelous. Ditto for the little fellers, all the way down to 5 hp. It's when you get into the big engines that power-to-weight isn't in your favor.

Options of fuel injection with "looper" technology—FICHT and DFI—used to be the best ways to approach your power purchases. In 2001, however, Yamaha introduced 200- and 225-hp four-strokes that were lighter in weight, more fuel efficient, and able to troll down slower than most people anticipated. So the age of big four-strokes is definitely upon us. The coming years should see a growing shift toward this technology.

Nice things about four-strokes: you don't have to mix oil with your gas, either by hand in a remote tank or through a mixing system. They're also quiet, troll down slow, and you don't breathe any fumes. Just change your engine oil as often as recommended by the manufacturer, as you do with your car. Both four-stroke and two-stroke engines need "by the book" maintenance, but especially the four-strokes. Simply put: more parts equal more specialized maintenance, but less often.

PROPER PROPPING

We get countless letters from folk about prop and "power prop" or "speed prop" information. Three, four, or five blades? Aluminum, stainless steel, or composite? The days of big engines with two-blade props are behind us; almost nothing over 6 hp has fewer than three-blade props.

In theory, a prop with a given pitch propels your boat forward by the number of inches the pitch designates. Example: a 13-inch (diameter) by 21-inch (pitch) will move your boat ahead 21 inches each time the prop completes one revolution. With a 2:1 gear ratio and an engine turning at 5,000 rpm, you advance 21 inches x 2,500 rpm in one minute. That's 52,500 inches, or 4,375 feet in one minute. That's 262,500 feet in one hour, which (whew!) translates to 49.72 mph. Again, all this is theory.

Propeller blades can't achieve 100 percent adhesion, however, so slippage has to be factored in. Boat-dependent slippage can be figured at 10 to 20 percent, but most runabouts experience a 12- to 14-percent loss, making a 49-mph boat a 42 (actual) -mph boat.

Part of the price of your boat engine went to computer prop design and testing aimed at achieving the best all-round performance at a reasonable cost. Each manufacturer has different requirements, and because of gear case design, prop diameter is somewhat limited. Diameter is a function of thrust, and the greater the pitch, generally the smaller the diameter.

A simple example is the V-4 engine, which pushes a runabout easily at 5,500 rpm using a prop with a 13¼-inch diameter and 17-inch pitch. Put the same engine on a deckboat, and it needs a prop with a 14-inch diameter by 13-inch pitch to

achieve the same horsepower. Nothing mythological about props—just choose the pitch and diameter that allow you to achieve the manufacturer's top rpm with normal load (the amount of weight usually in the boat). Easy? But there's one qualifier.

With just you in the boat, let's say that your 115-hp engine is turning at 5,500 rpm with a 13¾-inch x 17-inch pitch, three-bladed aluminum wheel. That's easy. But say you're rarely in the boat by yourself. With passengers, the engine may only turn at 4,400 rpm.

A quick way to compute the correct pitch for your normal load is to use the following formula: 1 inch of pitch = 100 rpm per blade. If you go to a 13½-inch x 15-inch prop, you pick up 600 rpm and max out at 5,000 rpm. Drop to a 14 x 13, and you're back up to about 5,600 rpm at wide-open throttle with a normal load. That's not a dangerous rpm rating for the engine. Keep in mind, however, that when you're running the boat with only yourself aboard and the engine's rev limiter reads in the upper rpm reaches, you need to ease back on the throttle to be properly propped for a normal load.

It's not reasonable to spend the afternoon swapping props back and forth to suit your normal load. Props are available, however, that shift pitch as they pick up rpm. If your needs fluctuate wildly enough to warrant $600 for such a prop, go for it.

ALUMINUM VS. STAINLESS

Stainless is heavier than aluminum and uses centrifugal force to help turn a prop with a larger pitch, hence generating more speed. Stainless props generally cost over $400, versus around $100 for aluminum. Stainless isn't what you'd use in shallow, rocky rivers, because stainless is unforgiving and gear sets are fragile. Solid contact with a Paleozoic Era stone generates many tiny pieces of gears. If you're boating in this type of environment, stick with aluminum props, which bend easily when they hit rocks. Then have them repaired as needed. Composite (plastic) props also are available, along with composite props featuring replaceable blades.

With the current emphasis on walleye boating and offshore outboards, manufacturers have expanded their propeller lines to include 4- and 5-blade models. These props allow offshore rigs better prop grip as they bounce off waves. They also permit mounting engines higher for more speed while retaining good handling characteristics.

The tradeoff of performance props is their cost. If you have budget constraints, stick with what the boat and engine manufacturers have developed. The faster you want to go beyond the manufacturer's specs, the higher the cost. Once you decide to go with a high-performance prop, though, and you take your new stainless prop to the prop shop for blue-printing or blade-thinning, have the prop ventilated with a 3/8-inch hole

---

Spun Hubs?

Sometimes prop hubs are spun by hitting less moveable objects, like rocks. Sometimes age takes its toll on compounds and adhesives. And sometimes thermostats stuck open will not allow heated water to flush over prop hubs.

Spun prop hubs don't require prop replacement. The center hub has been "de-vulcanized," causing the prop shaft to spin within the propeller. Take the prop to a prop shop or to a dealer for repair. The cost is usually $35 to $40, half to a third the cost of a new aluminum prop, or one-tenth the cost of a new stainless prop.

Use the following terms in discussing propellers with dealers, mechanics, and rigging experts.

• *Diameter*—The width of a circle outlined by the tips of the blades. Diameter used with pitch measurements determines the correct prop for different boating applications.

• *Pitch*—Theoretical distance that a prop moves forward in one revolution. In the water, a prop moves forward about 80 to 90 percent of the theoretical pitch. The difference between theoretical and actual pitch is called *slippage*, and it's necessary to produce thrust.

• *Through-hub exhaust*—Allows engine exhausts to exit through a hub of the same diameter as the gear case.

• *Over- and through-hub exhaust*—Engine exhaust exits through and around the prop hub, providing enhanced acceleration for high-performance fishing hulls.

• *Ventilation*—The result of air bubbles in the prop "working area" from surface air or exhaust gases drawn into the blades. These air pockets cause a prop to lose bite or thrust. The engine rpm may climb wildly and the boat may lose speed. Ventilation is most common in high-transom mountings, extreme trim-out, or sharp turns.

• *Cavitation*—Boiling of water caused by low pressure conditions near the gear case or propeller. Excessive cavitation may require propeller replacement.

drilled strategically into the hub at the base of each blade. Now your prop can bring you onto plane faster than a rocket.

PROP SHOPPING

Most fishermen probably realize a boat that plows and doesn't plane quickly or get out of the hole efficiently isn't necessarily underpowered. But knowing what to do next is another matter. With that in mind, OMC developed a troubleshooting checklist for fitting the right prop to any outboard:

1. Find the recommended rpm range for your outboard. Check the specification page of your owner's manual or ask your dealer for the operating range.

2. Using either your old or new propeller, make several test runs to determine maximum rpm and boat speed. Vary the trim angle to find the optimal performance.

3. If the wide-open throttle rpm is above the recommended rpm range, install the next higher pitch propeller and retest.

4. If the wide-open throttle rpm is below the recommended rpm range, install the next lower pitch propeller and retest.

5. Engine height can significantly affect boat performance. Consult the manual, and contact your dealer for specific recommendations.

Finding a good prop doesn't mean you should stop testing. Test as many props as possible, especially considering the wide array of materials and designs available today. Arriving at the perfect prop for your unique combination of engine and hull—the one that moves you farthest and fastest in the recommended rpm range—can add years to engine life, save a few C-notes in gas, and get you to the walleyes sooner every trip.

Any time boat performance is unsatisfactory, consider testing props. Of all possible remedies, changing props may be the quickest and least expensive. Marinas may allow you to test various propellers on site, especially if you bought your boat there or make it clear that you intend to purchase any new prop through them.

LOOK, MA—NO HANDS!

MinnKota, first to introduce self-steering electric trolling motors (the Auto Pilot series), offers a Cordless Remote Control option for PowerDrive models and Riptide saltwater bowmounts. Another feature, Quick-Response steering, quickly rotates the motor for faster remote-control turns. (Weak or slow turns can be a problem with some servo-operated remote models.) "Touch the steering pad for a smooth turn, or hold the button down for more than a second for power turns," explains Tom Rogers, product manager for MinnKota. The cordless MicroTouch foot pedal works on a radio frequency within a 24-foot radius and doesn't require a clear line of sight to the trolling motor to operate.

Pinpoint Corporation took self-steering trolling motors to the next level. Special microprocessors work together with the motor to keep the boat at a specified speed, automatically compensating for wind and waves, to stay on track and hover, crawl, or zip as desired.

Original Pinpoint models had a high-resolution liquid-crystal graph (LCG) on the head that displays fish and depths. A built-in digital flasher was located along the side of the display, and the graph featured instant review of the area traveled for up to 300 yards. Newer versions tie in to LCG for an integrated system. All models come with shafts up to 60 inches long, an important feature for walleye fishermen, who fish more open water than bass fishermen and who endure bigger waves from higher decks.

Pinpoint's TDP series can track bottom, creek channels, or a shoreline through an array of transducers built into the motor casing. Press DEPTH TRACK when it's critical to stay over a certain depth. The motor senses the nearest shoreline in SHORE TRACK and maintains an established distance.

The Nautamatic TR-1 is a 12-volt motor with hydraulic arms that, with the aid of a computer, a compass, and a handheld remote, provides remote-control kicker-motor operation from anywhere in the boat. The TR-1 keeps the kicker on a set heading and can interface with GPS to follow an established route or head for a particular waypoint. Newer models also sense the rpm of the motor and with the aid of the computer can maintain an established speed, compensating for wind.

With a trolling motors on the bow and the Nautamatic Marine Systems TR-1 Autopilot remote control on the kicker motor, a boat can accomplish almost anything with the smallest amount of participation from those on board. According to PWT pro Marty Glorvigen, the TR-1 makes any technique that doesn't require an anchor easier to perform. "I found it helped in ways I never would have imagined.

"In so many walleye fishing situations, the thrust on the bowmount is maxed out, so boat maneuverability goes out the window. The TR-1 allows me to set forward momentum with the kicker, so it just hovers in the wind. Now the bowmount is maneuverable again. If I want to go sideways to the wind to work a breakline, the thrust of the front trolling motor goes directly into the wave, while the kicker moves you perpendicular to the wave. Thrust and direction are controlled with a remote.

"The system works for backtrolling, quartering into wind, forward trolling, pitching jigs to shore—for anything," Glorvigen says. "It's sophisticated, yet simple to operate. Remote control gives me the latitude to work from any station in the boat. Bringing a fish to the back corner to net, I can concentrate on the fish and at the same time kill the motor with the remote control. In current, I can stay in one spot in an eddy. A gyroscope adjusts for rocking motion or wind, keeping the bow pointed in the direction I set it."

Nautamatic TR-1 Autopilot steering enables fingertip control of the kicker motor's speed and direction.

Dale Stroschein, a PWT championship qualifier and professional known for his expertise in trolling tactics, carries both systems on board. "Advanced trolling techniques become a one-man operation," Stroschein says. "That's the primary advantage to running the TR-1 and Pinpoint together. It's like having an invisible first mate. Previously, I had to constantly monitor my course. Now, I can sit in the bow and tie crawler harnesses or whatever, keeping my lines in the water and fishing effectively at the right speed and depth. When I first put these systems on my boat, I was lost. I had too much time on my hands, because these systems freed me up in so many ways.

"On the navigational side, the TR-1 is GPS compatible," Stroschein says. "Bring up the coordinates for any route, and it follows them. The interface isn't complicated.

"In the past, when I had to leave the bow to adjust a rod in a holder or net a fish in the back of the boat, wind and waves blew me off course. Now, I can leave the bow without losing fishing time, and my extra rods are fishing effectively while I'm landing a walleye. I'm no longer dead in the water after hooking a fish. The Pinpoint continues to track the hot depth range to a T. When it deviates, the motor speeds up to regain that contour.

"The Pinpoint has more than enough power," Stroschein continues. "I've had no trouble with it. It's built to take a hit and to stand up to big waves. I like to work out of the bow, so my big concern has always been getting blown off a contour when the trolling motor prop rises out of the water. But by using both systems together, I can let the Pinpoint steer and follow a depth contour and set the TR-1 to run straight at low speed. I find it easier to compensate in rough water now, because I can steer the kicker from the bow.

"This takes walleye fishing into a whole new realm, adding hours of fishing time, even over the course of a single day. It's expensive to put both systems on a boat, but I don't think the combination can be fully appreciated until it's used. It's like GPS—I never felt I needed it, but now I don't feel I could live without it."

Tony Puccio, another PWT pro, recently demonstrated the effectiveness of the TR-1. "Being able to do other things while trolling is the biggest advantage," he says. "But it's really helpful when I have a big fish on. I can get the net, stand and wait, and nobody has to man the motor."

THE ELECTRIC HORSEMAN

Select an electric motor with the proper thrust for the job. Lightweight 14-foot aluminum boats may need only 36 pounds of thrust, but a fully equipped 18- to 20-foot walleye rig needs more power. Think 75 pounds of thrust or more on the bow.

You might get away with a powerful 12-volt unit on the transom, but the bowmount usually calls for a 24-, 12/24-, or 36-volt system. Electric motor catalogs often list maximum boat length and weight for electric motor models. Treat those as conservative estimates, and move up at least one size.

Make sure your bowmount has a long enough shaft to accommodate the high bow of most deep-V aluminum or high-performance fiberglass walleye hulls. In general, 48 inches is minimum. Some units come with optional 50- to 60-inch shafts, which are a bit more cumbersome for retracting and securing, because motor companies don't provide longer mounting brackets with their extra-long shafts.

Usually it's necessary to retract the motor and then slide the shaft upward to securely position the lower unit on the bracket, then clamp it down securely, using a Rod Saver strap or bungee cord for running across rough water. MinnKota's Genesis series, however, eliminates this hassle. Simply touch the proper button on the foot pedal, and the bowmount automatically retracts to a solid position for transport. Ditto for a button on their Vantage

Bowmount Electrics Point the Way

Powerful 24– and 36–volt bowmount electric motors opened a new dimension to big water boat control. Anglers like Bruce Samson, shown here, can sit in the bow and deflect moderate waves rather than try to backtroll and hover into them. The system works because of the increased power of modern motors and higher bows to take bigger waves on walleye boats compared to bass boats. The system's ideal for livebait rigging, vertical jigging, or power trolling in calm to moderate conditions.

transom-mount tiller series. Effortless—almost too good to be true.

Make sure your selection is long enough for transom mounts, too. A 30- or 36-incher may not function as well as the optional 42-, for example.

Bow versus transom? Personal choice. Most times, smaller boats operate fine with a transom-mount motor. Anglers with large tiller outboards often use both. Big console steering jobs generally have a mega bowmount on the nose and a kicker outboard on the transom for slow trolling.

BOAT CONTROL WITH ELECTRICS

Electric motors don't just move boats. They position them for fishing. Whether casting or trolling, electric motors used in conjunction with depthfinders and visual orientation help keep lures and baits on target, in the fish zone.

Most walleye applications involve trolling techniques. Apply an electric motor with periodic changes in thrust and direction, interspersed with shutting off the motor and allowing the boat to drift. An electric provides precision control in calm or light wind. When wind and waves become too strong for an electric, switch to an outboard.

Electrics excel when finesse and stealth are needed: shallow water, clear water, fussy fish, precise structure, hovering in place. Tap your toe on a bowmount foot control to change speed and direction, leaving both hands free for two-fisted jigging or rigging. Or reach back to fine-tune thrust and steering on a transom mount, while dangling a live nightcrawler, minnow, or leech on a livebait rig and jigging with the other hand. Use an electric for subtle changes in direction as you drift across flats or along edges of contours. In calm to modest wind, it's tough to match the control an electric offers, even for the most seasoned veteran.

Strong winds provide the biggest challenge to boat control with an electric motor. Some anglers point the kicker straight forward and set the kicker outboard in forward gear at low speed to nearly neutralize the force of the wind. Then they use a powerful bowmount electric up front to steer, hover, and provide the last little bit of oomph to overcome the force of the wind. That takes practice, but it provides a way to overcome those in-between conditions that console boaters hate: wind too strong for electrics, but with precision tactics like backtrolling required to catch fish. Dual thrust control—outboard and electric—solves the problem.

Open water trolling typically is handled with a kicker outboard, main outboard up to 90 hp, or larger engine slowed to trolling speed by a trolling plate or sea anchors. Forward trolling in big wind with an outboard typically doesn't provide much challenge to boat control. It's possible, however, to incorporate an electric motor into the boat-control equation under calm conditions, particularly for trolling low-speed lures like spinners or minnowbaits.

CHOOSING, USING, AND
MAINTAINING BOAT TRAILERS

You see them on the highway throughout the season: trailers with tinkertoy wheels, groaning under the weight of the 18-foot boats they're carrying. Trailers made from the back ends of logging trucks, bouncing along, carrying 10-foot johnboats. Trailers so well-matched that it's hard to tell where the boats end and the trailers begin. And, of course, trailers jacked up alongside the road, delaying vacation trips. In other words: consider the requirements that make for a good trailer, along with some do's and don'ts for trailer use.

The boat package—The boat trailer serves two important functions: to transport

Sam Anderson

the boat and to protect its hull and other equipment during transport. The boat trailer usually is the last item considered in the boat package, so it's where budget cuts usually get made. Marine dealers may also suggest putting a little less of a trailer into a boat package as a way to be more price competitive. This thrifty approach to trailer buying shows up in the disabled trailers along the highway, the four-letter words at the ramp site, and the damage sustained by boat hulls and equipment.

Determining trailer capacity—First, consider trailer size. Make sure you have enough trailer for the boat; that is, make sure the carrying capacity of the trailer is adequate. The carrying capacity is the total weight of the boat, engine, full fuel tank, batteries, and gear stored in the boat, such as tackle boxes and anchors.

Assume a deluxe aluminum 18-foot boat weighs 1,400 pounds, a 115-horsepower engine about 350 pounds, and thirty gallons of gas, 350 pounds. Tackle boxes, boat gear, batteries, trolling motor(s) can easily add another 400 pounds. This setup needs a trailer with a carrying capacity of at least 2,500 pounds—double the original boat weight. The trailer's carrying capacity determines the frame and tongue strength as well as axle and tire size. These structural items provide a boat trailer that can protect the boat's hull and equipment and that provides easier and safer towing.

Trailer dimensions—Trailer length is determined by measuring the straight-line distance from the center of the transom to the bow eye in the front of the boat. The trailer length can then be determined by checking the boat length against the manufacturer's trailer specifications. Length is not the only consideration. Eighteen-foot boats can have from 75- to 95-inch beams. Boat length and width determine the trailer dimensions best suited for the boat.

Manufacturers recommend that 5 to 10 percent of the gross carrying weight should be supported by the trailer coupling ball. In the carrying capacity example, the trailer tongue weight at the ball should be in the range of 125 to 250 pounds (5 to 10 percent of 2,500 pounds). Redistributing gear in the boat or moving the winch stand a bit can alter this tongue weight. Proper tongue weight helps to eliminate fishtailing and strain on the towing gear.

National Marine Manufacturers Association (NMMA) certification indicates that the trailer, including winch stand, safety chains, and lights, meets national safety standards set by the NMMA.

One axle or two?—Larger boats may require a tandem-axle (two-axle) trailer for greater carrying capacity. The four wheels also provide greater safety and control if a tire blows. Many fishing pros who trailer up to 50,000 miles a year prefer this system. A tandem trailer, though, is difficult to move around in the garage or driveway after it's unhooked.

"The breaking point for a second axle is about 20 feet in length or 3,500 pounds in weight," says Chip Schwein of Eagle Trailers. "Any boat heavier or longer than that should be pulled on a tandem-axle trailer. But that doesn't necessarily mean that shorter and lighter boats won't benefit from a tandem, too. These trailers ride and handle much better than single-axle models, and despite what many boat owners believe, they're just as maneuverable as singles."

Tire size—"The smallest tire most boaters should consider is 13 inches," Schwein says. "Smaller tires turn much faster than those on the tow vehicle, so they wear out quicker and are much more vulnerable to failure. Those interested in ordering a custom trailer might even consider one with tires and wheels that are interchangeable with their tow vehicle to ensure better handling and availability."

Tires are rated according to their load capacity. This includes not only the weight of the boat and motor but also the batteries, fuel, and other equipment that will be carried in the boat. Note, too, that trailer springs and frame are usually compatible with the original tires and wheels, but they may not be with upgraded ones. Be sure to check the trailer capacity when you're upgrading tires to prevent overload.

Trailer brakes—"Laws about trailer brakes vary by state," Schwein says, "but even boat owners living in states with high weight allowances should have a brake on every axle, particularly if they're pulling heavy loads. Brakes are becoming even more critical because tow vehicles are becoming smaller and lighter, while boats are growing larger and heavier. Brakes are the best way to protect your boat and vehicle, as well as other vehicles on the road."

Most trailer manufacturers would prefer a strong recommendation on the use of trailer brakes.

The need for brakes is determined by individual states, so standards vary from state to state. The most common weight requirement for brakes is a Gross Vehicle Weight Rating (GVWR) of 3,000 pounds (total weight of the boat, motor, gear, and trailer). In Minnesota, the GVWR for brakes is 3,000 pounds or more. In Ohio, it's 2,000 pounds. Dealers and consumers need to know the trailer brake requirements of their states.

Most trailer manufacturers would prefer a strong recommendation on the use of trailer brakes. A set of brakes for a single-axle trailer costs $400 to $500—somewhat less when ordered as part of the trailer package, a bit more if added later. Disc brakes probably will be available in a few years. Remember, 2,000 to 3,000 pounds of towed weight can dramatically increase the stopping distance of even the biggest sports utility vehicles.

Rollers or bunks?—"Roller trailers are convenient for launching and loading small boats," Schwein says, "but they don't offer the same hull protection as bunk models. The biggest problem with rollers is the small amount of support area that makes contact with the hull. Usually, only the top 1/2 inch or so of each roller provides any boat support. Bunks, on the other hand, cradle the bottom of the boat for maximum support.

"Our custom-welded frame bunk trailers offer more than just superior support," Schwein adds. "Each trailer is designed for a particular boat model with a Computer Aided Design program to ensure a perfect fit. Loading a boat on a custom bunk trailer is easier than backing a truck down a ramp. The bunks assist in centering the boat on the trailer so that it ends up in the right position every time—a real time-saver for anglers who frequently load boats in swift current or heavy wind." Side guide arms or bunks, available as after-market kits, are a big help in loading boats onto the trailer, too.

Accessories—Good trailers include bearing protectors, plug-in wiring, and waterproof lights. A bolted-on trailer coupler (hitch) is preferable to a welded hitch because it makes maintenance and replacement easier. A complete trailer package contains a tongue jack (at least for larger boats and trailers), transom tie-downs, spare tire and carrier, and, where necessary, a transom saver.

Trailer finishes are either painted or galvanized. A good paint job lasts a long time. Galvanized trailers are popular around salt water, but obviously they'll last a long time around fresh water, too. Galvanized trailers, though, are usually more expensive than painted trailers.

USING THE TRAILER

Tie it down—"Safety always should be the primary consideration," Schwein says, "but most boat owners don't give it much thought. The tie-downs on most rigs, for example, are inadequate for extreme situations, like rear impacts. A pair of transom straps rated for 800 pounds probably aren't enough to hold a heavy boat in a collision. Always look for the heaviest straps available, and use them every time the boat is trailered.

"Another security feature few boat owners employ is a bow strap," Schwein adds. "Some may believe that the winch strap or even the safety chain is enough to secure the bow to the trailer, but they exert only forward pressure on the bow eye. In a collision, they may actually propel the boat forward through the winch stand and into the back of the tow vehicle. A bow strap that exerts pressure toward the stern is needed to secure the boat.

"The whole idea here is to unitize the boat to the trailer as much as possible," Schwein concludes. "This is achieved by maximizing the amount of boat surface area in contact with the trailer, and using the appropriate number of tie-downs to minimize boat movement. The end result is a more comfortable and safer tow, and better protection for the boat."

Secure everything—Upgrade the license plate holder, then secure the plate to the holder with a coat of epoxy. For trailers that don't include a plate holder, rivet the plate to the trailer frame. Check for enough clearance between the bottom of the plate and the ground when you're backing down a steep ramp.

Secure, seal, and tighten everything else on the trailer while you're at it. Bolts work loose and rivets pop out at the most inopportune times unless you head off trouble before it happens. And when you've finished tightening, make sure to

Most boats spend more time on a trailer than on the water. Is your trailer up to the job?

drop the appropriate-sized wrenches or sockets, or both, into a toolbox in the boat or tow vehicle for repairs on the road.

TRAILER MAINTENANCE

Trailer maintenance is at worst a euphemism for emergency repairs and at best something done the night before a long road trip. Doesn't have to be that way. Take time to jack up the trailer and place the frame on blocks. Clean, inspect, and repack bearings with a good marine-grade grease. Grease the hitch, tongue jack, rollers, and other moving parts, too.

Check that the trailer's secure, then crawl underneath to inspect the springs and shackle bolts for wear or cracks. Make sure the bolts are tight, and apply a little grease to the springs. Adjust the bunks or rollers so that they fit the hull when the boat is properly aligned on the trailer. Check the wiring, particularly exposed wiring, then clean and grease the bulb sockets with dielectric paste.

Schwein recommends greasing trailer bearings before the boat goes into winter storage and again when it comes out. Carry an extra set of bearings in your tool box, just in case. With proper maintenance, you'll probably never need them. They're only expensive when you break down on the side of the road without them.

HELPFUL HINTS

• Cross the trailer's coupler safety chains when attaching them to the towing vehicle. In this position, if the coupler comes off the ball, the trailer tongue and coupler should land on the crossed safety chains rather than on the highway, where it can skid out of control. Be sure the bow safety chain on the trailer is attached to the boat.

• The jack stand and spare tire carrier should be mounted on the right (starboard) side of the trailer. In this position, the boater (driver) is out of the flow of traffic when pulling over to the shoulder to unhook the trailer or remove the spare tire.

• Check tire pressure on the trailer wheels and spare tire regularly.

• Make sure the trailer towing package, including the trailer ball on the tow vehicle, meets the load and towing classification.

• Use transom tie-downs to prevent the boat from bouncing on the trailer, which causes both boat and equipment damage. If it's necessary to swerve, or if you are forced to the shoulder or ditch, the boat can slide or tip off the trailer without tie-downs, increasing the chance for serious accidents.

• Launching and loading techniques vary with the style of boat as well as the type and angle of the boat launch. Whether you choose to winch the boat on or drive it on, experiment to find the right combination of trailer alignment and water depth. A few practice launch and loads are necessary. Just don't do it on the Fourth of July weekend.

Many boaters back the trailer too far into the water for loading. If the roller or bunks are 5 or 6 inches under water, the boat may float around on the trailer, making it difficult to center it. Start with the tops of the rear bunks or rollers just under the water. Other reference points might be the depth of the wheels or fenders in the water.

If the boat ramp is not horizontally level, try angling the trailer on the ramp if there's room. The trailer wheel on the high side of the ramp should be angled so that it is in slightly deeper water, helping to level the trailer. In severe cases, tie an additional line near the back of the boat and have someone pull the boat sideways to the high side as the boat is loaded in order to center it on the trailer.

The boat trailer is an integral part of your boating package. Shop for the trailer as carefully as you shop for the boat and motor. If you do, the trailer isn't likely to leave you high and dry at the ramp or along the road. And the big investment you made in the boat and motor will be protected. Live by the adage, "If you don't fish well, at least look like you do."

DEEP-CYCLE AND MARINE STARTING BATTERIES

The deep-cycle batteries used to power electric trolling motors are designed for repeated draining and recharging, unlike start batteries, which are designed for short jump starts. Purchase 12-volt, high-amperage, deep-cycle batteries and a marine starting battery that will handle the abuse of pounding in waves. Charge but don't overcharge batteries for peak performance.

Proper care of marine batteries means extended cycle life—the number of charge-discharge cycles the active material in the battery can complete. Take care of your marine batteries, and they'll take care of you.

What constitutes proper care and maintenance of a 12-volt marine battery? Bob Griffin, a technical engineer with Exide, recommends that you remove the caps and check the electrolyte levels in every cell before each recharge. The liquid should be approximately 1/4 inch below the filler tube on the inside of the cap. "If levels are too low, the capacity of the battery to accept recharge is reduced," Griffin says. "If the level is too high, the electrolyte can spill through the vent caps.

"If you need to add water, use distilled," Griffin continues. "Impurities like iron and chlorine in tap water may reduce battery life substantially. Then check the electrolyte with a hydrometer—a big glass eyedropper containing graduated float beads. The number of beads floating indicates the specific gravity range, which should fall between 1.265 and 1.280 in a healthy, fully charged marine battery."

No-maintenance gel cell batteries are sealed, so you can't test them except with a voltage gauge. They're convenient, but some folks feel they don't last as long as traditional batteries in colder northern climates, particularly when stored for long periods in the cold.

Recharge all batteries immediately after use or at least as soon as possible, even if the battery is only drawn down 20 to 30 percent. "The most detrimental time for internal components of the battery occurs when the discharged electrolyte is exposed to the battery plates," Griffin explains. "The corrosive effect of the electrolyte is much greater on battery components at this state of charge.

"Recharging should be done only in well-ventilated areas, since lead-acid batteries produce excess explosive hydrogen-oxygen gases during recharge," Griffin warns. And no smoking!

Batteries should be stored in a cool, dark spot, not in the deep freeze of a backyard, unless connected to a smart charger designed for long-term storage. Before storing or using a marine

Anglers who use their electric trolling motors for long periods or in wind and waves know that they never have enough juice. Some use four or more 12-volt batteries to run trolling motors and other electronic boat accessories. Batteries must be stored so the boat remains well balanced.

battery, check electrolyte levels, then monitor the charge with a voltmeter. Fully charged lead-acid batteries should read 12.6 volts across the terminals. Immediately after charging, readings may be higher, even if the battery is properly charged. And during discharge, readings will be substantially lower than 12.6. Give a battery ten minutes after use to show a proper reading.

How long should a marine battery last? Depends on how it's treated and on the quality of internal components. Deep-cycle batteries are designed to withstand hundreds of deep charges, unlike automotive batteries. Some batteries are rated by cycle life, which is usually measured in the hundreds. One cycle is one complete discharge and recharge, so if you use up the charge capacity of a battery in a day and the battery is rated for 300 cycles, you should get 300 days of work from that battery.

New on the scene are 12-volt nickel-zinc batteries from Evertroll. Considerably more expensive than traditional lead-acid batteries, Evertrolls are touted to last longer and recharge quicker. The new technology requires a specialized charging system; each battery comes complete with its own internal smart charger. Just plug it in. Caution: nickel-zincs are great for moderate climates, but the jury's still out about their effectiveness in cold northern climes.

ONBOARD CHARGERS

The days of taking your battery out of the boat each night and carrying it into the motel to charge it are over. At the very least, use a 100-foot extension cord to get you close enough to an outlet to avoid the battery shuffle. If not, changing motels is easier than toting batteries. No one appreciates battery acid on the carpet, at home or away.

So you have 110-volt power to the boat. What about all those batteries—one for the electrical system and a couple more for 24-volt motors? Can you justify saving a few bucks by carrying portable alligator-clip chargers—more than one charger, remember—and connecting and reconnecting them at every charge cycle? Can you depend on getting a good electrical connection after repeatedly clipping onto often-corroded terminals? Can you trust the gauges that indicate charge level?

The solution to the battery shuffle and charger runaround is mounting an onboard charger in a storage compartment and connecting it to each battery. Popular models come equipped with a wiring harness to connect the charger to one, two, or three batteries, depending on what's needed. Many serious anglers either use the double hookup to their trolling motor batteries or the triple hookup to charge the start (cranking) battery for their outboard and electrical system as well. (Anglers with 36-volt systems may elect instead to charge the three trolling motor batteries.)

Premium units are designed to charge deeply discharged trolling motor batteries at a higher (faster) rate (typically 10 amps), and the crank battery perhaps

at a lower rate (around 3 amps). Theoretically, all you need do is run your extension cord to the boat, be it at the dock or on the trailer, plug in the charger, and sleep soundly, knowing your system will be fully charged the next morning. Colored lights indicate the level of charge at a glance.

The best onboard chargers include some sort of "smart" feature that independently reads the degree of charge in each battery and tapers the level of charge as it nears maximum. This not only prevents your battery from boiling, greatly extending its life, it also ensures a full charge every time. You can leave the unit plugged in for days or weeks—even all winter in storage.

Once a battery's fully charged, a smart charger reduces the level of charge to an ultralow maintenance level, barely supplying enough potential to the battery to keep it fully charged without damage. Left off the charger, a battery typically loses about 1 percent of its charge per day. Leave your boat sitting idle for a couple weeks, and your batteries may not handle a full day of heavy trolling-motor use in windy conditions. Low-level maintenance charging eliminates the problem.

So now you want to invest in an onboard charger. Smart move. They're not cheap—often $200 to $300—but for a serious fisherman, they're an investment in ease and confidence. Which one to buy?

Different manufacturers design their chargers with slightly different charging philosophies. Dual Pro, a longtime marine industry leader, claims peak performance by rapidly raising charge levels with a traditional transformer charger, then tapering them down toward the end of the cycle to a final level somewhere around 15 volts. This results in a fairly quick charge.

Transformer units incorporating linear charge are susceptible to variations in voltage input, however, possibly affecting amperage output and level of charge. Tie a bunch of tournament boats to a dock for the night, have everyone plug chargers into the same circuit, and the next day everyone's level of charge will be adversely affected by even a small drop in voltage.

Guest chargers, by comparison, incorporate *switching technology* and are designed to charge batteries in three stages, from bulk (rapid charging to 75 percent capacity) to absorption (tapered charging to about 98 percent capacity) to maintenance (float stage). Ultimately, the charge reaches a level of about 14.2 volts.

Guest chargers are designed to avoid even a slight overcharge and to promote longer battery life by avoiding any potential damage. (Lead-acid batteries accept a charge up to about 14.7 volts, gel batteries, less.) Their units are not susceptible to incoming voltage regulations, ensuring a consistent charge each time.

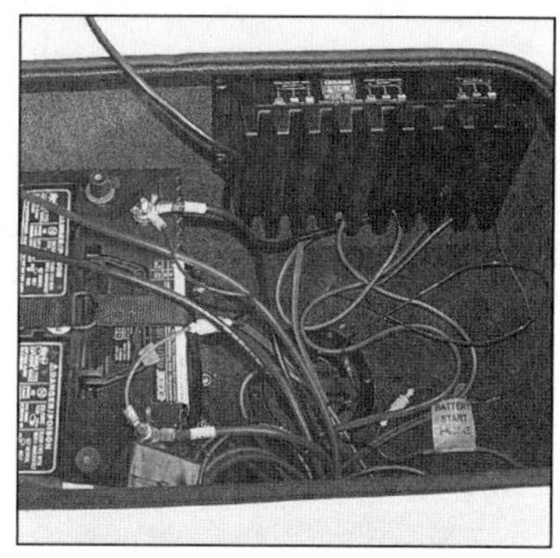

Onboard chargers demand only that you plug them in. All battery connections are prerigged and ready for charging.

Chargers typically are quite heavy, requiring several mounting bolts. All waterproof chargers should be capable of withstanding exposure to water in the bottom of the boat.

Chargers should incorporate reverse polarity protection, in case a set of wires is hooked up incorrectly. This feature protects equipment from short circuits and sparks—the last things you want near gas tanks.

GOTCHA COVERED!

Boat covers. Some boats don't have them. Some covers look like giant balloons, and try to lift boats off their trailers, while others fit like latex gloves.

Is a cover necessary? What fabric or materials? Effective tie-downs and cover support systems? Maintenance?

Consider four reasons why a boat cover is necessary:

(1) Reduced theft of boat contents when the boat's parked. An electronic boat system called Undercover C.O.P. (800/588-5578) for boats up to 21 feet long can be installed in the boat cover drawstring or hem rope.

(2) Improved gas mileage when towing the boat. Estimates vary, but a 5 to 15 percent improvement is reasonable.

(3) Reduced wind, rain, dirt, mildew, and ultraviolet ray damage to the boat's interior.

(4) Improved safety. Minnow buckets, landing nets, buckets, and clothing don't blow out, causing driving hazards.

FABRIC

All boat covers must provide air circulation. Without this feature, mildew coats everything in the boat. Either the material itself must breathe or the cover must be vented.

Cotton is a classic boat cover material. It's breathable and as it becomes wet, the fibers swell, making the material more waterproof. Because cotton absorbs moisture, it also eliminates sweating in the boat. Cotton covers, however, shrink when wet and stretch when dry, they're not durable, and they require maintenance. A cotton cover for a boat with a windshield can run approximately $18 per boat foot. For a 17-foot boat, that's $306.

Another common material is a 30%-70% cotton-polyester blend. Cotton stretches with heat; polyester shrinks with heat. Cotton provides breathability, polyester, durability. Waterproofing such as Scotchgard or Aqua Tite often is necessary because water pooled up on a cover causes the cover to stretch. The material then loses its water-blocking ability, and water seeps through. This treated material costs about $21 a boat foot. Our 17-foot boat cover would cost $357.

Another alternative, a 100-percent acrylic material frequently referred to as Sunbrella, is slightly more durable and more waterproof than a cotton-polyester blend. Cost is $25 per boat foot, for $425.

Urethane-coated polyester is becoming a popular material for boat covers. It's breathable, more durable than polyester, yet costs a bit less. Often referred to as Top Gun, this material currently appears to be the fabric of choice.

Occasionally, boat covers feature a cotton-polyester blend with a vinyl laminate. This durable, waterproof cover doesn't breathe, so vents must be added to provide air circulation. The material is a bit more expensive than Top Gun.

Some anglers opt for a discount store one-size-fits-all cover, and the price is right. Cheaper material is used, however, and covers are mass produced, so the fit is usually poor, providing less boat protection.

If a custom cover is your choice, put all accessories on the boat that will be in place when the boat is towed, because reinforcement material is added where the cover rests on accessories, such as locators and trolling motors. Or remove these accessories before trailering. The best cover fits as smoothly as possible.

A good boat cover sometimes has small tabs or pieces of fabric sewn to the fabric where tie-downs attach to cover loops to prevent them from rubbing against the boat. Tabs may not be necessary, so consider the type of webbing loops on

---

the cover and the type of tie-downs used.

If rub marks occur in spite of precautions, the problem may be caused by a trailer that's too narrow. As a result, the tie-downs are pulled down and inward, marring the boat's finish.

One way to avoid this is to use a mooring or travel cover that attaches to the boat with snaps on the splash rail. This type of cover can be used on the boat when it's tied to a dock.

TIE-DOWN SYSTEMS

Tie-downs usually consist of pieces of rope or bungee cords that attach to grommets or loops on the boat cover and then to the trailer. Good rope tie-downs hold the cover securely but are harder to put on and take off, particularly when your fingers get stiff in cold weather. Bungee cords are easier to put on and take off but allow the cover to move, creating wear spots. Adjustable bungee cords provide a better fit but still allow some slippage.

Another part of a good tie-down system is the draw or hem rope that runs around the boat and through the edge of the cover. When pulled tight, this cord snugs the boat cover to the hull and prevents the ballooning seen on some trailered boats. Ballooning stresses the material, causing the cover to shred and tear.

Just as important as the cover is the system that supports it in the center of the boat. A good support system prevents puddling and allows the water to run off. A large puddle causes stress on the cover, causing it to stretch, leak, and tear.

Support systems may incorporate a prop pole—a pole that fits into a pocket or hole in the cover and sits on the floor of the boat. Some covers use bows made of wood or fiberglass to form a series of bowed supports under the cover. Arranging the pedestal boat seats also provides support. Puddling is hard to prevent, but puddles can be kept small with good support systems.

The two main enemies to boat covers besides improper tie-downs are rain and leaves. Leaves and pine needles deposit a slightly acid solution on the boat cover; unchecked, these eats holes in the cover. Prevent this by washing occasionally with a hose and water. Be sure to wash the cover prior to off-season storage. Then apply a waterproofing solution.

If your boat cover has vinyl windows, be sure they don't touch the supporting frame. Frames are usually made of aluminum, which can scratch the windows. Aluminum also conducts heat that can damage vinyl windows. Repair all rips immediately—"a stitch in time . . ." If your boat gets wet, remove the cover so the boat can dry out; a small oscillating fan helps.

A boat cover that works for you will be designed by an experienced person who can tell you which material is best for your situation, where to reinforce the cover, where to build pockets, and where to place tie-downs. That person will be proud of his work and will continue to work with you after the cover is sold. If you just spent $10,000 to $25,000 for a boat, saving a hundred dollars on a cover may not be the smartest choice.

Chapter 5

Planned Right, Rigged Right

BOAT RIGGING, MAINTENANCE, AND SAFETY

You finally have the boat of your dreams. Between your purchase and fantastic fishing trips lie some important decisions. How will your "dream machine" be rigged? What accessories will you need, and where? Who will do the work?

Professional rigging is not cheap, but fighting problems inherent in a quick-and-dirty rigging job is about as much fun as a backlash on every cast. Knowing your equipment will work under all conditions provides the security only a properly rigged boat can give. Whether you do the rigging yourself or hire a private rigging shop or marine dealer, decisions about how the boat is rigged can be as important as the boat, motor, and trailer.

A well-rigged boat is a collaboration between you and the rigger. Tell 'em how much you want to spend so the job can be tailored to meet your budget. Rigging fees, including accessories, can go from several hundred to several thousand dollars. Perhaps a basic rigging will get you on the water this season; next year, you can add or modify.

To save time and eliminate errors, provide a sketch that shows where the equipment should be placed. Discuss your fishing style and species fished for with the boat rigger. If a lot of equipment will be added, the rigger may need to revamp or upgrade the wiring.

Begin in the front of the boat and work your way back. Decide how you will fish in the bow. Will you stand up or sit down most of the time? Do you prefer to lower your bowmount electric motor with your right or left arm? The style of trolling motor (foot-control versus hand-control) introduces factors that affect use, space, and the way the trolling motor is mounted. Do you have a 12- or 24-volt motor? Trolling motor location determines where the sonar unit is mounted—is there enough room to mount the sonar? Can the locator be seen and adjusted from your primary fishing position?

Now move back to the console or tiller and again visualize fishing operations you will perform from that position. Can the sonar or GPS unit be operated and adjusted while you're fishing as well as while you're running wide open? Should the pedestal base be moved slightly to make running the tiller easier?

If a marine radio is used, can it be operated conveniently as well as heard? Is the radio waterproof? If not, it must be mounted in a protected location, which may mean adding an auxiliary speaker. Do you need a long or a short antenna? Placement is important. Do you want to be able to raise and lower the antenna from the driving position? The antenna should not affect your ability to set the hook or to net fish.

If you plan to run a small gasoline kicker motor or a transom-mount electric, which side of the transom should it be mounted on? When either motor is in the up position, does it interfere with other boat operations? Will you be using splash-guards? Think through the placement of rod holders. Consider whether you want to be able to reach the rods from the console or tiller. This is particularly important if you're fishing alone. Place your holders where the rod handles won't interfere with storage compartment doors or other equipment. Will you be using downriggers? Decide where you want to work them from and whether they'll be manual or electric.

Weight distribution plays a major role in performance and boat handling. Consider it from front to back as well as from port to starboard. Battery placement must complement fuel tank placement so the boat isn't too stern heavy or bow heavy. Fishing alone with ten tackle boxes creates a different weight and balance than fishing with two or three people in the boat.

Onboard chargers are becoming popular. They offer fast, convenient charging systems built into the boat—just plug them in. Onboard charging systems can be supplemented by the alternator on the engine. The alternator or charging system of the big engine can be wired to charge trolling motor batteries while you're running from spot to spot.

Use determines the primary placement of equipment. But equipment should be removable for service or warranty work—you shouldn't have to tear up half

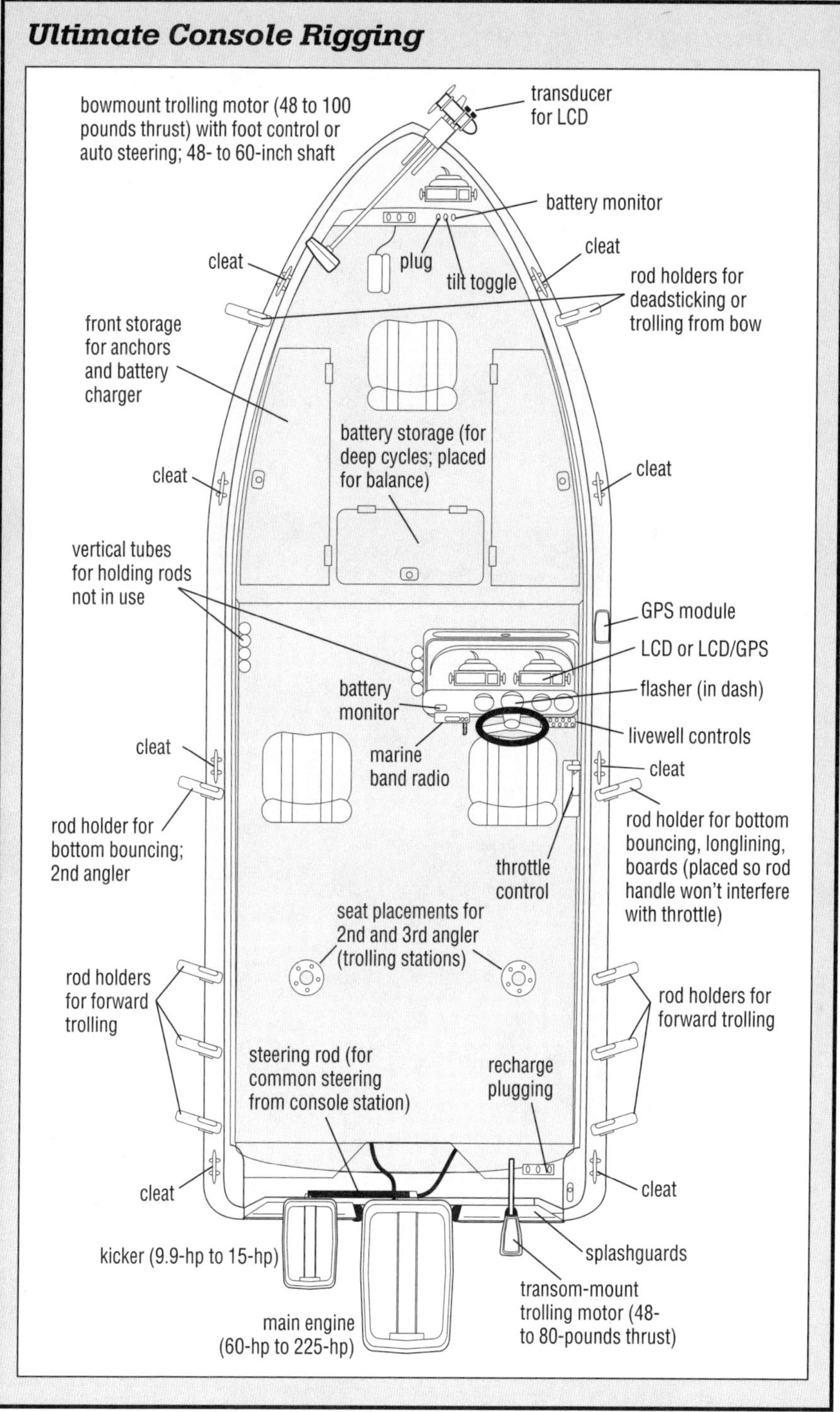

transducer for LCD
bowmount trolling motor (48 to 100 pounds thrust) with foot control or auto steering; 48- to 60-inch shaft
battery monitor
cleat
plug
tilt toggle
rod holders for deadsticking or trolling from bow
front storage for anchors and battery charger
cleat
battery storage (for deep cycles; placed for balance)
cleat
vertical tubes for holding rods not in use
GPS module
LCD or LCD/GPS
flasher (in dash)
battery monitor
livewell controls
marine band radio
cleat
cleat
rod holder for bottom bouncing; 2nd angler
rod holder for bottom bouncing, longlining, boards (placed so rod handle won't interfere with throttle)
throttle control
seat placements for 2nd and 3rd angler (trolling stations)
rod holders for forward trolling
rod holders for forward trolling
steering rod (for common steering from console station)
recharge plugging
cleat
cleat
kicker (9.9-hp to 15-hp)
splashguards
main engine (60-hp to 225-hp)
transom-mount trolling motor (48- to 80-pounds thrust)

Ultimate Tiller Rigging

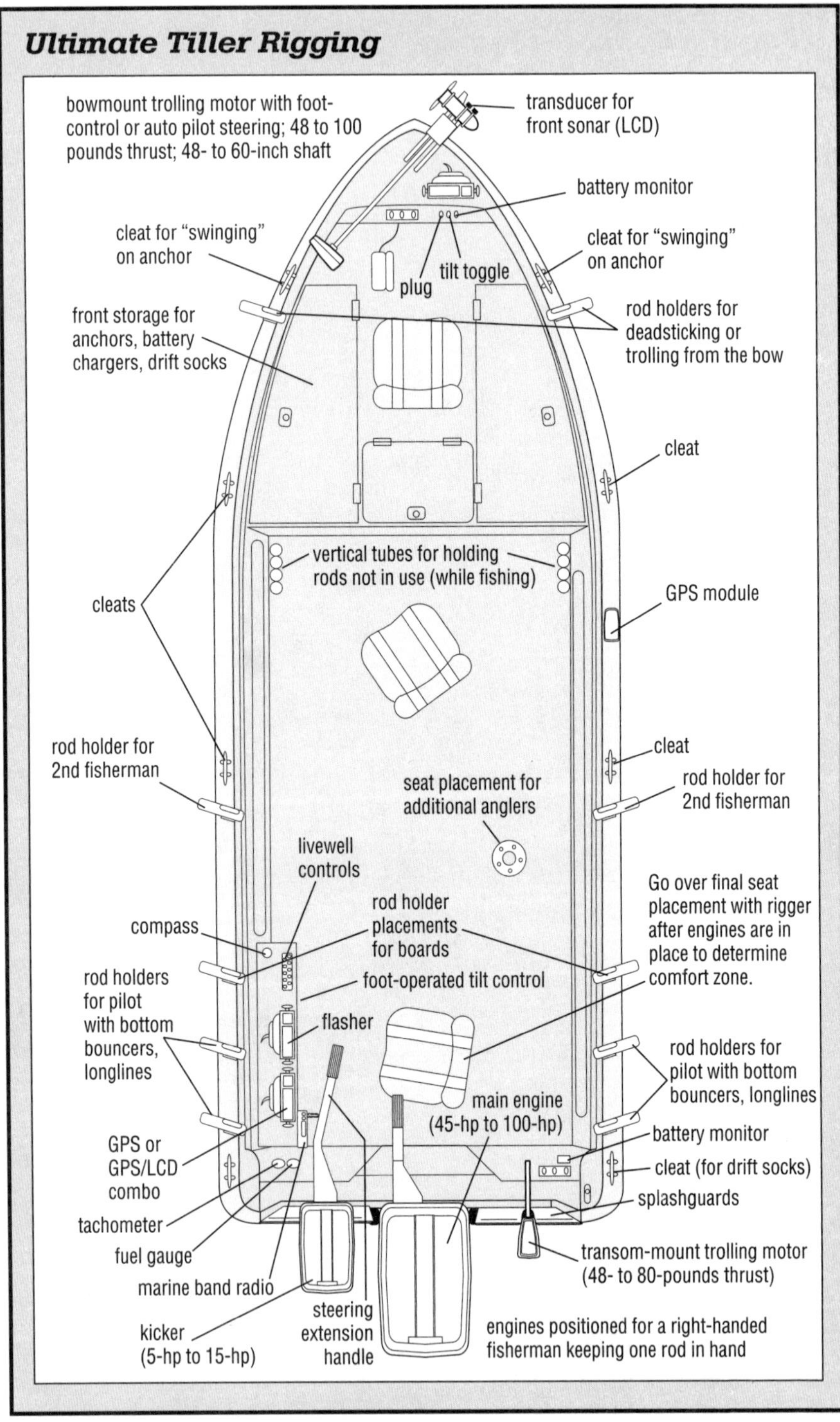

the boat to get at something. Place GPS modules, transducers, and marine radios in positions where they can be easily removed. Talking things through with your boat rigger helps avoid frustrations.

Boat manufacturers use only the fuse sizes their engineers recommend. Your rigger may alter these if longer wire runs demand larger-diameter (gauge) wire. Make sure all fuses are labeled, or match the fuse patterns on the fuse block diagram.

Correct propping and engine mounting are part of the rigging process. Both alter the performance of your boat. If top-end speed is more important than trolling speed, the rigger may place a higher-pitched prop on the engine. Transducer placement is also critical. The single largest cause for poorly performing depthfinders is improper transducer placement. A good rigger places a transducer where turbulence will be eliminated or minimized across its face. Call the electronics manufacturer with any questions.

A well-rigged boat, whether simple or complex, is a joy to fish from.

A well-rigged boat, whether simple or complex, is a joy to fish from. You only need to fish from one that has been thrown together quickly and cheaply, in which half the equipment shuts down after hitting the first big wave, to appreciate the difference. Remember—you're on the water to enjoy fishing, not to run through a high school physics experiment. Choose a good boat rigger who knows the idiosyncrasies of different boats and equipment, and then work closely with him.

FUNCTIONAL ACCESSORIES

Sonar and GPS units should be installed on swivel mounts that are visible from all locations. Front-and-center placement for trolling motor batteries is essential to a balanced boat. Cleats, too, should be placed on the balancing points (port and starboard on the bow) for using the wind to cover water from an anchored position—change the rope from one cleat to the other to alter swing position. Cleats for drift socks should be placed at three other locations along the sides for dual socks or balancing the drift according to wind direction.

Adding a hydrofoil on the cavitation plate of the main engine can make steering easier and help some boats get on plane quicker and stay on plane at lower rpm. Adding a flasher is a safety feature. It's critical for seeing bottom in heavy weather, even on familiar waters. Flashers announce bottom changes at high speeds faster than LCDs, so using one as a back-up to the LCD is a good idea.

Extension handles on the kicker make it possible to troll from a standing or sitting position. Other modern refinements, such as the Nautamatic TR-1 Auto Pilot, make it possible to steer the kicker from any position in the boat. Make certain the kicker is matched properly with hull size, so speeds of at least 5 mph into the wind are possible. Kicker placement (right or left on the transom) is finally determined by your dominant hand (right or left handed) and steering function. If you intend to steer the kicker from the console (with special linkage rods that join the two engines), place the kicker on the opposite side in most cases to balance the boat.

Minor rigging details can minimize the possibility of broken equipment, even physical injury. When fishing, it's critical at times to have rods out of the way but within reach. In heavy winds, while trying to control the boat, you shouldn't have to get into the rod locker. Use PVC pipe to create vertical rod holders in out-of-the-way locations. Having or creating enough storage space is critical for keeping items dry and out of the way.

BOAT RIGGING PROBLEMS AND SOLUTIONS

"I've seen lots of changes in the rigging business over the last 25 years," reminisces master boat rigger Jim Wentworth, who's rigged, repaired, and redesigned all manner of boating equipment since the early days of marine electronics. "Back

when Al Lindner and I set out to rig his old Lund 315 tri-hull—adding a locator, electric trolling motor, livewell, and bilge pump—it took about eight hours and a few gadgets to transform it into the ultimate fishing rig of its day.

"By comparison, the boat I rigged for Al last year didn't even exist in our imaginations a decade, much less a quarter century ago. Today's larger, faster, more seaworthy boats incorporate a wealth of electronics, and with them, a whole new set of challenges.

"Many boats now come prerigged from the factory. But when anglers start adding or substituting larger, more powerful, more complex electronics, there's no guarantee the combination will perform as it was originally intended."

According to Wentworth, the most important considerations you make after purchasing a boat are selecting the right equipment and matching it with the proper rigging. That goes far beyond simple placement of electronics and gear. It's using topnotch components to form an integrated system, mounting everything to withstand abuse and corrosion, and ensuring that the electrical system comes under total system management.

The main power system is primary and vital. "Say a guy comes into the shop complaining he can't get the expected amount of power from his front trolling motor," Wentworth says. "I look at the rig and find he has a 24-volt motor on the bow and a 12-volt on the back. That's unbalanced. Any draw on the back motor reduces the amount of charge on one battery, affecting the 24-volt performance of the bowmount. He'd be better off with a 24-volt motor on the transom, too.

"Lack of power can also originate from inadequate wiring to the bowmount. It should be multistrand 6-gauge wire to transmit current without heating up. Anything less—8- or 10-gauge—sacrifices efficiency to heat buildup.

"Keeping trolling motor batteries totally separate from the rest of the 12-volt electrical system is important so that electrical interference from the trolling motors affects depthfinders and radios less. Also, the two trolling motor batteries used in a 24-volt system discharge at equal rates and always provide equal power, creating a balanced system.

"Add locators, marine bands, livewells, bilge pumps, stereos, electric downriggers, and all the assorted equipment found on high-tech walleye boats, and a tremendous demand is placed on a 12-volt system. The wiring must be sufficient to withstand not just the demand of each component but the combination of many items in simultaneous use."

According to Wentworth, at least 10-gauge wire is necessary from the primary system, branching out to lighter wire, depending on the needs of each component. And everything must be properly fused to prevent electrical shorts. If something overheats and melts a wire, an electrical arc presents the possibilities of fire and cascading problems throughout the electrical system.

For bowmount trolling motors, Wentworth uses 50-amp circuit breakers, which admittedly can overheat and pop under heavy use, particularly when plowing through heavy weeds. But they cool down and can be reset, saving the system from disaster.

"Then there's the question of sufficient power," Wentworth says. "Simultaneous use of multiple units—livewells, radios, depthfinders—drains the capacity of the starting battery. Keeping the charge as high as possible is critical. The alternator on the outboard should do this if it's run occasionally. The alternator is voltage regulated and current limited; it runs until it charges the starting battery, and then shuts it off. If the big motor isn't run much during normal fishing conditions, a heavy-duty starting battery is needed to provide more reserve.

"I specialize in installing a loop charging system, which uses the outboard's alternator to charge the trolling motor batteries in conjunction with the starting battery. With additional wiring and plugs, you can connect trolling motor batteries, or banks of batteries, into a configuration with the starting battery that charges them without causing short circuits. Then the alternator can read charge levels and react accordingly, charging as necessary. The system operates at peak power constantly. And should you leave your outboard key on or otherwise drain your starting battery, you can jump-start the outboard off the trolling motor batteries—a great safety feature.

Splashguards

Most anglers think of splashguards in terms of comfort. Keeping spray off purple knuckles and icy feet while backtrolling is great, but safety should be your primary reason for attaching splashguards to a boat. When you're trolling or navigating with the waves in rough weather, a sudden stall can spell disaster. Without power, a big wave breaking over the transom of the average walleye boat is no laughing matter. Even with power, having wet feet over many fathoms is simply not funny.

Splashguards also protect a boat's interior, storage areas, and the on-deck equipment while loading and unloading on a steep ramp. But ask walleye fishermen, and they'll say splashguards make backtrolling possible in rough seas, and that's all they need to know.

Wave Wackers and Walleye Masters splashguards are constructed with 1/4-inch Lexan, a polycarbonate material that's tougher than Plexiglas and designed to withstand heavy forces. Models are 16 to 20 inches high and offer rubber-lined, custom-fit cutouts for transom-mounted trolling motors and kickers.

Splashguards on big console-steering boats enable backtrolling into big waves without getting too wet. Splashguards like Wave Wackers are custom-made to fit numerous boats.

Rigging Tools for the Unholiest of Boats

Placing transducers is tricky. Perfect placement on one boat may be off by inches on another, even if both hulls are almost the same. One hull may be carrying a different outboard; maybe, too, it's placed differently to accommodate a kicker. Perhaps one boat is loaded differently or has more or heavier passengers. Many things can make similar hulls act differently in the water. For that matter, no two hulls are exactly the same to begin with.

"Reading at speed" requires perfect transducer placement. Perfect transducer placement on the transom means out of bubble trails created by projections, edges, strakes, or steps. And the 'ducer must always remain submerged. That narrows the window to the deepest part of the transom, yet it must avoid any disturbance caused by props or steps.

The easiest way to avoid problems with placement of transducers, especially on the transom, is to avoid affixing them permanently.

Wille's Transducer Mounter holds two transducers and reduces the number of holes in the transom by six. The portable model can be fastened over the drain plug on some boats with an adapter that accompanies the unit. This eliminates drilling altogether. It's a solid, lock-tight method for securing portable transducers, and it can be removed quickly at day's end.

The Rig-Rite Transducer Plate, made of a special polymer called *star board*, can be drilled and redrilled many times and holds epoxy well. It comes in four sizes and is durable enough to outlive three boats. Model 920 is the smallest (12 inches long) and holds three transducers on a horizontal plane using only two screws in the transom. Model 910 is the largest (18.5 inches long by 8.5 inches wide) and can be secured (with four screws) vertically above the waterline.

The primary advantage of portable plates is being able to tweak transducer position without having to remove screws or repair screw holes in the hull. Sometimes just turning a transducer slightly improves its read a lot.

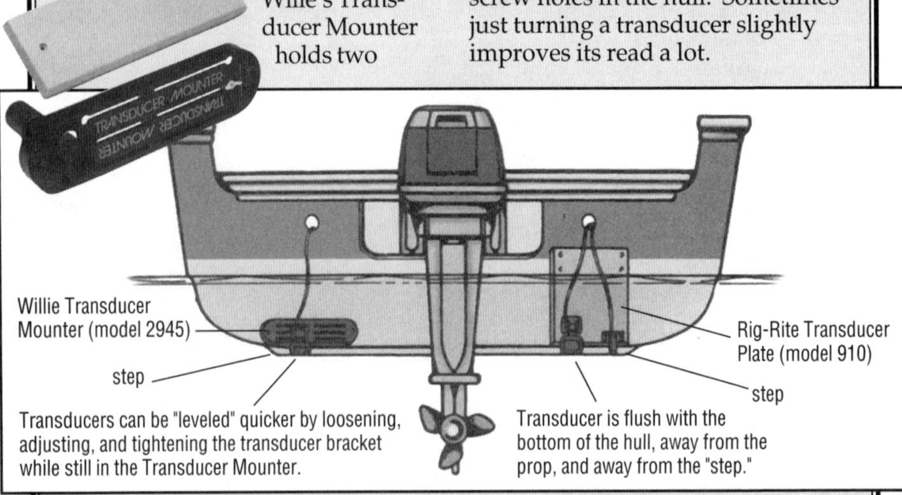

Willie Transducer Mounter (model 2945)

step

Transducers can be "leveled" quicker by loosening, adjusting, and tightening the transducer bracket while still in the Transducer Mounter.

Rig-Rite Transducer Plate (model 910)

step

Transducer is flush with the bottom of the hull, away from the prop, and away from the "step."

"Even so, a battery charger is needed for the times the boat sits idle on a trailer or at the dock, and no serious angler uses anything less than an onboard charger. Just plug it in, and it automatically reads the charge level on each battery and tops it off properly. You can even leave your livewell running all night at the dock, with no problem the next day."

TOTAL SYSTEM MANAGEMENT

"I believe in having the ability to monitor and control the electrical system," Wentworth observes. "I install gauges for reading the charge of each battery at any time, giving you the ability to react and charge as necessary. I also like regular lead-acid batteries, because they provide some degree of control, although it's necessary to open them occasionally and top off the water to preserve the electrolytes lost by repeated charging.

"I prefer total system management, in which I monitor and inspect everything myself. Because one little thing—a bad connector, a faulty fuse, a crimped wire, a wire rubbing against the hull and wearing away the insulation, a bad battery cell—can cause system failure. Even no-maintenance systems require periodic checkups—like frequent inspections for wear, corrosion, pinched wires, and loose connections. A corrosion protectant should be sprayed on battery terminals to prevent contact problems.

"And then there are the things the average person fails to consider, like electrical interference between electronic components. For example, just running a transducer cable along the shaft of a bowmount motor may create interference on the depthfinder, due to overlap of electric fields. That's hard to eliminate, though interference between components can be minimized through proper placement and correct wiring. Depthfinders, for instance, should never be attached to trolling motor batteries, even though they draw little current.

"Mount marine radio antennas as far away as possible from other components. Even then, other electronics may have to be turned off for the best reception. And don't coil up the antenna cable neatly for easy storage, because that affects the signal-to-noise ratio. Check the installation with a standing wave-ratio meter to ensure the best performance. Placement of GPS receivers, on the other hand, typically isn't critical."

Wentworth insists that improperly mounted transducers are the most frequent cause of sonar problems, even though they come from the factory prerigged. Moving the transducer makes all the difference between high-speed reading and getting nothing at all.

"Then there's weird stuff that drives folks crazy, like electromagnetic fields from one type of unit causing havoc with another," Wentworth says. "Radio-frequency interference between the marine band and the power trim seems like the last thing to worry about, but every piece of electronic equipment—for that matter, the air around us—is permeated by electric fields of all sorts. Sensitive electronic equipment is subject to interference from outside sources. And in a boat, all sorts of electronic equipment is sometimes crammed into a small space. Running ground wires directly to the battery is a possible but not necessarily guaranteed solution to electronic gremlins.

"You know who really has problems?— the guy who decides to update an old boat with powerful new equipment."

"You know who really has problems?—the guy who decides to update an old boat with powerful new equipment. The original wiring might be inadequate for today's power demands. Undersized wire, poor grade or improperly crimped connectors (some connections should be soldered and water-proofed), wrong fuses or circuit breakers—the wrong balance of components, rigged not in harmony but discord, causes trouble.

"The more variables you introduce, the less control you have, and the more opportunities for frustration. Rig right, plan for all contingencies, monitor every gadget and battery, and even then, carry a good fire extinguisher."

ROD HOLDER PICKS AND PLACES

Rod holders are supposed to make fishing easier and more fun by becoming an extra pair of hands when yours are occupied with a tiller or steering wheel, or when you need to set a rod down. But rod holders become a hindrance if improperly placed, or if models chosen are designed for techniques or equipment you don't use.

One rod holder is not as good as another. Most designs appear as an answer to regional applications or to specific types of equipment. Even rod holders made in walleye country may be manufactured with some other species in mind.

According to Mark Dorn, In-Fisherman PWT tournament director, over 50 percent of all PWT pros use Tempress Fish-On or R-A-M rod holders. "They hold both spinning and baitcasting rods equally well," Dorn says. "They're versatile in terms of the number of angles they can be locked into, up and down and side to side. That's an advantage for walleye fishermen, who may be deadsticking, bottom bouncing, and trolling cranks all in the same day."

Other models popular with walleye pros include the Berkley Rod Holder, the Roberts Deluxe, and the Wille Hercules, for similar reasons. They're versatile, work with both spinning and casting gear, and swivel through a wide range of adjustments. With all these models, the holder itself can be pulled and stored when not in use, and the mounts are primarily flush with the surface of the gunwale.

Most pros like to place six holders, three on each side, near the back of the boat for trolling, and one on each side in the bow for deadsticking and vertical jigging. In a console boat, all six trolling holder placements would be from the steering wheel (where the pilot can reach one rod from his station) back to the transom. The bow holders should be positioned within a comfortable reach from the bow pedestal seat or chair position.

When drifting or forward trolling with bottom bouncers, rods should be spread evenly from amidships to transom. When trolling, the rods farthest forward (with the heaviest bouncers) must be at a 60- to 90-degree angle to the gunwale, the next set at a 45- to 60-degree angle, and the rods nearest the transom should point straight back. This creates a "V" formation that covers slightly more water. In-line planer boards cover even more water, and all rods can be set at a 60- to 90-degree angle to the gunwale.

Planer-board trolling with bouncers or crankbaits demands spacing, too, though grouping holders as close to the back of the boat as possible can be an advantage. Anglers need just enough room between rods to get them up and out of the holders without whacking each other or tangling.

The bow holders should be positioned within a comfortable reach of the bow standup seat or chair. Correct placement is determined by what's comfortable and how the angler prefers to stand or sit. For vertical jigging with two rods, you should place a holder within easy reach on either side for quickly stashing one rod when a fish is hooked with the other. When dead-sticking, you often turn away from the rod to jig on the other side of the boat. Holder placement should make a visual check easy with a quick glance over the shoulder. The tip of the rod should point out at an oblique angle to your line of vision so you can check easily.

If your boat lacks rails, you have two options: side mounts or flush mounts on the gunwale. Either is fine, providing the mount itself is flush with the surface of the gunwale so that nothing that could break a rod protrudes when holders are not in use.

Jim Kalkofen, executive director of the PWT, prefers the rail mounts that come with his Fish-On holders. "Mounts set into or bolted to the side of the gunwale can't be moved," Kalkofen says. "With rail mounts, all I need to adjust the position of several rod holders is a screwdriver, a pliers, and about two minutes.

"Permanent placements are, by necessity, a compromise. Rail mounts make it possible to temporarily group holders near the back, where three rods can be reached from a single seat when trolling with boards. Later, the holders can be spread out, allowing wider coverage for drifting and holding the boat perpendicular to the wind with drift socks."

Consider the type of equipment most often used, and choose a holder that accommodates it best. Then place holders for function and comfort.

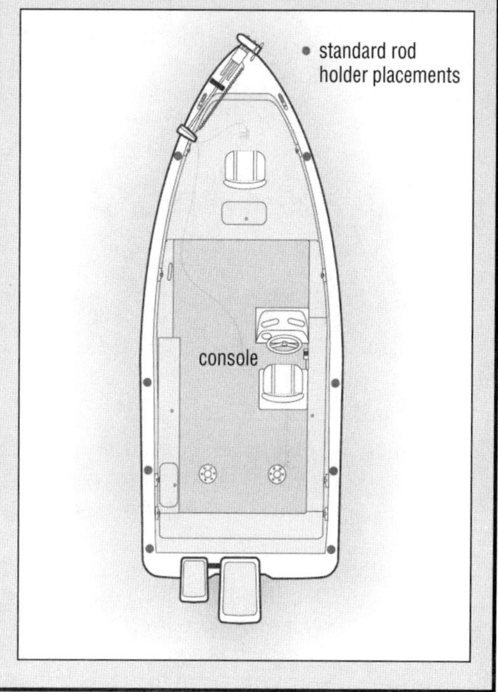

TWO BILGE OR NOT TWO BILGE?

Two bilge pumps are better than one. A single pump can burn up or get clogged just as a series of waves starts washing over the transom. A backup is more than a good idea—it's a potential lifesaver.

The now time-honored best method of bilge-water control centers on float switches. A float switch rises as water collects in the hold, turning on the bilge pump automatically. When the water level descends below the intake valve, the float switch turns the pump off. Handy, indeed. Having one pump on a float switch and a second on manual is an adequate system for most walleye boats.

"We offer bilge pumps with a float switch and three wire leads running to a

three-position switch on the dash," says Mitch Pixley of Mayfair Marine, a division of Johnson Pumps of America, Inc. "Pumps can be set on automatic, manual, or off."

Float switches have been around for years. Newer on the marine scene, however, are sensor systems. Rule Industries has a series of automatic pumps that electronically sense the presence of water in the hold. "Once engaged, the pump keeps running until the water is removed," says Steve Tilders of Rule Industries.

Automatics provide a margin of safety for boats parked in the water overnight or boats trailered during a downpour. Didn't pull the plug at day's end? Or forgot to put it back in? Either way, you're covered. You don't even have to remember to turn the pump on or off. A true no-brainer.

Rule also offers a Deluxe 3-Way Panel with a remote sensor that transforms any bilge pump into an automatic and offers the convenience of manual operation, as well as the battery-saving option of an off position.

Dual bilge pumps remove water from your boat quickly. Ask your boat rigger about adding a second pump for safety.

When the pump is in operation, a small LED lights up on the panel.

"Automatic pumps that don't sense for water work in a cycle," Tilders explains. "When you set it on automatic, the pump turns on every 2.5 minutes. A manual or on-demand switch is a good back-up." When you're backtrolling and take a huge wave, you don't want to wait 2 minutes for the cycle to come around again.

Rule also offers a new anti-airlock feature on some of their pumps. Most pumps start up with air bubbles in the valve. These new models shut off automatically when an airlock prevents intake, then turn on again when the bubble is cleared.

Mayfair has another interesting backup feature: a cartridge pump. "It has a removable motor cartridge," Pixley says. "If a motor burns up, you just pull it out of the pump and snap in a new one in seconds. Pump failure is usually due to clogging, not motor problems. But this feature makes it easier for customers to service their own units and to carry back-ups in case of emergencies."

In case of complete power failure, a hand pump is useful. In fact, it's a must. Friends and family depend on us to be prepared, to be good sailors in the event of sudden squalls and unforeseen disasters—a rock ridge rising suddenly out of 80-foot depths. Beckson Marine, Inc. offers a hand bilge, the Thirsty Mate 136 PF, which pumps over 13 gallons per minute, 1 gallon for every four strokes. The PVC body is durable, and a removable foot allows for easy cleaning. (Beckson also offers a full line of motorized pumps.)

Check the bilge system when buying a new boat. Some boats are underpowered for removing water. Most walleye boats (16- to 19-foot modified V-hulls) should probably have at least one pump rated for 750 to 1,000 gallons per hour (gph), though manufacturers' specs often say otherwise. You may find that the boat you want has only one 360- or 500-gph pump. Check the buyer's guide to see if two pumps can be installed as an option. (Ranger boats, for example, offer optional dual 1,000-gph bilge pumps.) If not, see about having one installed, or install an extra pump yourself.

REINFORCEMENTS SAVE THE DAY

As walleye boats grew larger, outboard engines more powerful, and GPS lured anglers into the magic of offshore angling, a new challenge arose: getting there and back again safely. Anglers who were willing to test the endurance of their equipment soon found weak links in the system. The incredible pounding that running over miles and miles of turbulent water produced took its toll on everything not designed for the long haul. Repairs ran from the aggravating—loose screws and wire connectors—to the frustrating— seat pedestals ripped out of the floor and phantom electrical problems caused by corrosion—to the downright dangerous—cracked hulls, shorted-out electrical systems, fractured trolling motor kicker-outboard brackets.

In many instances, professional walleye angler the test pilots of the waves—discovered flaws in mar equipment design, and relayed the information manufacturers, who followed up with design chang to alleviate the problems. Top-line pros today demar strong, durable, and dependable equipment. The take extra measures to reinforce components that migh otherwise fail at the most inopportune moments. It': not just time and money on the line—15 miles offsho in 7-foot waves, your life's on the line, too. You can't afford to cut corners.

Forget flimsy accessories designed for the mass-market consumer who uses his equipment a couple of times a year. You need the best: heavy-gauge stainless steel screws and bolts to fasten everything down; T-nuts and bolts instead of screws for mounting pedestals; rod holders that withstand the punishment of trolling in big waves without fracturing; heavy-gauge electrical wiring to trolling motors, backed up by circuit breakers or replaceable fuses (carry spares); and everything in your electrical system on fuses in the event of a short—fire and water don't mix.

Walleye pros with large console boats typically run kicker outboards for slow trolling. In the up position, kickers bounce on their mounting brackets with every wave. Strapping them down on cross-lake runs with Rod Saver Kicker Motor Tie-Down ratcheted safety straps prevents them from bouncing. Most pros also add additional safety cables or chains—just in case. Trolling motors require bungee cords or Velcro straps to prevent them from bouncing. Ditto for rods laid along the tops of storage compartments.

Electronics must be securely mounted with dependable brackets and stainless steel hardware. Ultra-Mounts, Johnny Ray swivel mounts, or R-A-M Mounts make it possible to position units for optimal viewing. Your electrical system should feature an Altus or similar battery gauge to indicate the percentage of charge. Don't get caught on the water without power to start the outboard, work your trolling motors, and power your electronics, GPS, or marine band radio.

Your tool kit should be filled with spare nuts, bolts, screws, fasteners, electrical connectors, wire, fuses, switches, vinyl electrical tape, screwdrivers, wrenches,

The first year pro Keith Kavajecz clamped a 9.9 hp to his walleye boat, he went through seven clamp brackets. This is an extreme example, but many more pros have had broken brackets—or worse yet, their kickers vibrate loose from the fiberglass transom and backflip into the depths.

Essentially, 9.9-hp outboards were designed to push smaller fishing boats, and they did so just fine for decades. Then, trollers who wanted precise slow-speed control switched their small outboards onto their bigger, newer boats, with the results just described: unforeseen punishment of the mounting brackets.

Position the kicker where it best suits your fishing style. Most tiller handles are on the starboard side of the kicker, making them easily accessible when motors are installed on the port (left) side of the boat. Many pros, however, use an electric-start model and steer from the wheel, so the tiller handle isn't a factor. If this is your choice, a second remote control can be rigged near the driver's console.

Once the kicker is clamped on, drill through the transom and bolt on the motor with stainless steel hardware. Better yet, first bolt a steel bracket onto the transom, then clamp the screws onto the bracket. The recessed bracket accepts the clamp screws so they can't vibrate loose. Then drill and bolt the kicker onto the transom. If your kicker is a multipurpose outboard that you want to easily remove for use elsewhere, simply tighten the screws and go to plan B. Plan B is to support the kicker's midsection from below while cinching down the motor with a strap.

Pounding and bouncing at high speed across miles of open water was too stressful for early brackets, so they were beefed up and re-engineered for strength. The force that killed them, however, came not from rough water but from

running through swells. The kicker's lower unit pointed almost straight out from the transom; as the boat came down hard, the lower unit snapped up. Then, when the boat bottomed out, the lower unit smashed down, placing an extraordinary amount of force on the bracket.

What to do? Install a support that holds the engine in the up position, then strap it down so the motor can't move. The accompanying photos show a metal rod bracket that PWT pro Steve Poll made for several other PWT pros. (Similar versions are available at marine dealers.) A coated metal wire attached to the motor makes it easy to lift the support bar. An adjustable strap that fits into the holes is snugged up for running and can be removed and dropped into the boat while trolling.

pliers, nut drivers, wire crimps and clippers, bulbs, and spare depthfinder cords. Rusty Duck or similar lubricant can keep things working smoothly and electrical connections rust-free. Add whatever else you can anticipate that will provide safety, security, and peace of mind.

Reinforcement also means being prepared with enough life jackets, a throwable cushion, flares, horn or whistle, heavy rope for towing or anchoring, a big enough anchor to hold in heavy seas, and a sea anchor to position the bow into the wind should you become adrift. If you haven't assisted in a big water rescue or tow, you don't realize how essential proper equipment is to doing the job safely and successfully.

An angler who only fishes small inland waters may consider all of this overkill, and in some cases, he's probably right. What's more worrisome, however, are marine dealers with the same attitude. If they don't occasionally rig boats for traveling anglers, they don't understand, because they're probably rigging boats only for the casual local angler. When a comment from a boat rigger goes something like, "Harry must be really tough on his equipment. Look at all this extra heavy-duty stuff he wants on his boat," expect that something on this guy's rigging job will fail during the course of the season. "Good enough" isn't good enough.

Because today's boats are so complex, the average person can no longer properly rig the electronics and gear in a few evenings in the garage. A professional is needed, and for most folks, that means their local marine dealer. We're not suggesting you should mistrust their ability; just don't assume they'll give you top-of-the-line service, because they often try to cut costs with inferior components and less rigging time just to make a sale. Talk to the salesman and boat rigger, and assure both of them that you want to beef up everything and are willing to spend more money to get it done right. Reach an understanding before you put the boat in the water and find you're disappointed.

Even if that happens, there's still hope. But retrofitting is usually more expensive than doing it right the first time. Talk to another marine dealer. See if they're on the same wavelength as you are. Or go to a custom boat rigger, a person who specializes in doing work for demanding customers—someone whose only job is rigging boats properly. You get what you pay for. The added cost is more than worth it in peace of mind, dependability, performance, and safety. Over the course of owning your boat, freedom from problems will more than pay for the initial investment.

LIVELIER LIVEWELLS FOR HEALTHIER WALLEYES

Most modern walleye boats contain one or more livewells to keep fish lively. Anglers use their livewells to maintain fish in a fresh and healthy condition for later cleaning and eating. Where culling is legal, anglers sometimes sort fish during the day, replacing caught walleyes with either larger or smaller specimens. Some hold fish a short while to make sure stressed fish are releasable, or they wait for better light to take photos before releasing fish. Livewells also keep minnows aerated, eliminating the need for extra buckets and coolers.

Tournament anglers, meanwhile, require dependable livewells to keep fish alive and in releasable condition, earning live-release weight bonuses and eliminating dead-fish penalties, which can make the different between losing or winning, between cashing a check or not—and over the course of a season, qualifying for the PWT Championship (or merely watching it on TV). Many problems can be avoided with a little precaution and investment.

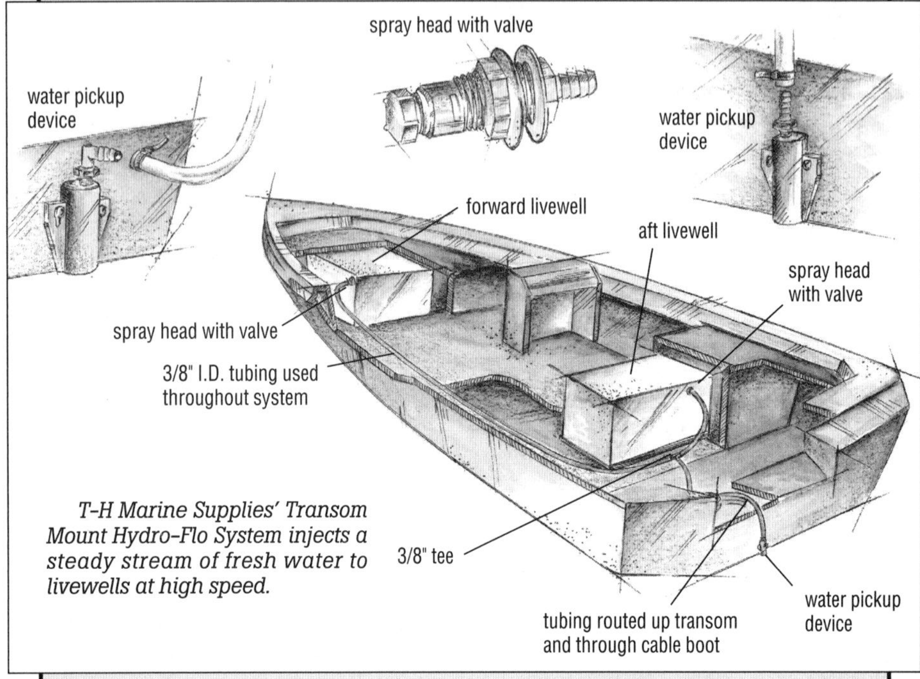

T-H Marine Supplies' Transom Mount Hydro-Flo System injects a steady stream of fresh water to livewells at high speed.

KNOW YOUR FLOW

Livewell pumps inject a flow of surface water into a livewell. Standard models simply have on-off switches, while more deluxe versions have auto timers that allow you to set frequency and duration of aeration cycles. More fish or warmer water temperatures require a steadier supply of fresh water. Dual through-transom pumps provide a back-up in case one pump jams, malfunctions, or burns out.

Airlocks are the biggest hassles with pumps. Typically, a pump works fine until you take off down the lake, leaving it on. When you reach your next location, an air bubble has crept into the system, causing the pump to lose prime. As a temporary fix, you can turn the pump off, then quickly back up the boat, forcing water into the intake to clear the bubble. Then restart. In the long run, however, replacing the pump with an anti-airlock model is a better option. Your marine dealer can offer guidance.

When you're heading down the lake at full speed, livewell pumps temporarily lose prime. But a separate aerator pump can recycle water and aerate livewell water while you're underway. T-H Marine Supplies' Pro-Air System is one example.

Deluxe boats are often equipped with dual aerators that have timers similar to those used with livewell pumps. Be aware that many livewells drain at least partially while you're on plane. Prior to a long run down the lake, temporarily plug one or all livewell overflow drains with a rubber twist or snap plug to maintain full water level during transport and aeration. Remove the plug once you arrive at your destination, allowing fresh water to cycle again.

To obtain a steady stream of fresh water to livewells during high-speed runs, consider adding a freshwater pickup system. T-H Marine Supplies offers its Hydro-Flo System in either through-hull or easy-to-add transom-mount versions. Basically, a tiny scoop grabs water off the bottom of the hull under speed and sends a stream through a long plastic tube into the livewell.

Oxygenation Systems of Texas offers add-on kits using portable oxygen tanks to insert pure oxygen into the water via a diffuser hose similar to a garden soaker hose. New water isn't pumped in. Instead, existing water is slowly injected with oxygen.

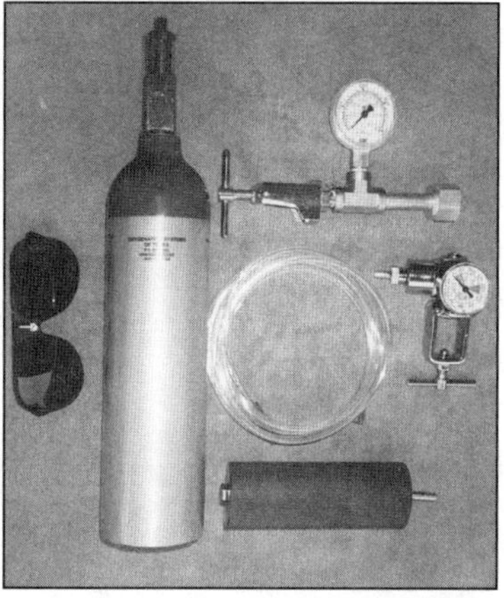

Oxygenation Systems of Texas offers Oxygen Edge livewell kits that trickle oxygen directly into livewell water. Use your livewell pump to fill the livewell, then shut it off and turn on the oxygen flow.

The theory is that air is only 21 percent oxygen, and no matter how much air is pumped into warm water, maintaining 7 or 8 parts per million (ppm) of oxygen, the level necessary to support a livewell containing several fish at stress-free levels, is difficult. By bubbling in pure oxygen, establishing 12 ppm (saturation) is feasible. Stress caused by oxygen starvation rather than by square-cornered livewells appears to be one reason fish get beaten up in livewells.

Oxygenation Systems of Texas sells Oxygen Edge livewell oxygenation kits for about $300, depending on your boat model. Oxygenation tanks are easily refilled at welding supply houses, and provide about 80 hours of oxygenation between refills for about 1¢ per hour. Tanks must be strapped down, but they require minimal installation. Get past the initial investment, and the cost is negligible. In general, livewells positioned toward the back of the boat tend to cushion shock better on rough rides.

Minimizing handling of fish in livewells has its own technologies, too. Loki's livewell dip net allows easy removal of walleyes from wells with minimal handling. Anglers have also experimented with placing fish in large mesh bags much like laundry bags, then simply lifting them out at weigh-in time; this technique cushions fish and makes removing them quick and easy. But we've seen few proponents of the bag-and-grab system.

Adding Walleye Formula Catch and Release or a similar chemical to livewells tends to calm fish and helps replace the natural slime coat lost during handling, thereby minimizing infection. Adding salt in low quantities does the same. But these strategies work only when water is being recirculated—a flow of new fresh water quickly dilutes and eliminates any benefits of the system.

If your boat lacks a livewell, add-on cooler kits from pump manufacturers like Attwood, Mayfair, and Rule provide livewell capability with minimal remodeling. Larger Toho-Rig Livewells are designed to straddle the interior of johnboats. Whichever kind of livewell system you use, install intake filters or steel mesh strainers on the intake and drain to keep minnows in and miscellaneous debris out of your pumps. A livewell pump—or a bilge pump, for that matter—jammed with a snail or a piece of monofilament spells disaster.

Investing in a good livewell system will keep fish healthy. If you're a tournament competitor, it'll pay for itself, maybe even the first time out.

REVOLUTIONIZE YOUR WALLEYE BOAT

Over the years, In-Fisherman staff members and PWT anglers have revolutionized the way walleye boats are rigged. The following photos depict notable rigging options.

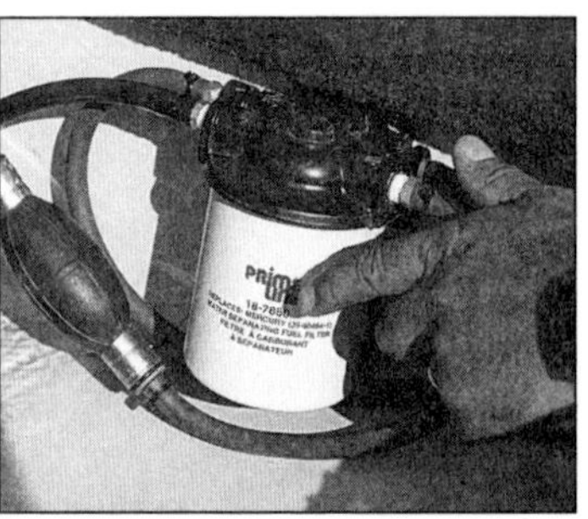

In-line water-separating fuel filters remove water from the fuel before it enters the engine.

Durable and secure electronic mounts like R-A-M mounts absorb shock and vibration. They're also easy to adjust to nearly any angle from which you wish to view your flasher, LCD, or GPS.

Autopilots maintain the exact course you set—perfect for open water trolling while you're rigging rods, baiting hooks, setting planer boards, or catching fish. Simply point your boat in the direction you want to go, turn on the autopilot control switch, and let go of the wheel. An autopilot also can be used in conjunction with GPS, steering you to waypoints.

With kicker lifts like Goldeneye's Panther lift, your kicker motor can be raised and lowered with the touch of a button. The mount also provides added support, although strapping down the motor when boating in big waves is suggested.

Add a no-skid material to spots on your trailer and boat that you frequently step on, to prevent slipping and falling.

Some boats come with more dashboard instruments than cars display. Gas gauge, tachometer, motor trim gauge, water temperature gauge, and a compass are helpful boat instruments.

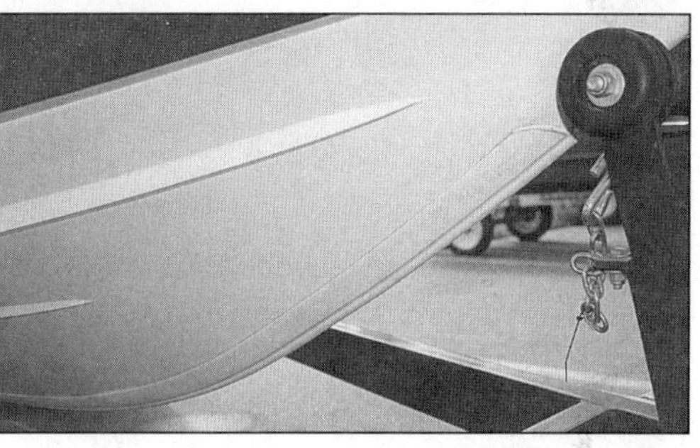

All modern motors are rigged with a safety kill-switch that could save your life.

Protect your boat keel from rocks and other damaging debris by adding a TECH 5 Keel Guard.

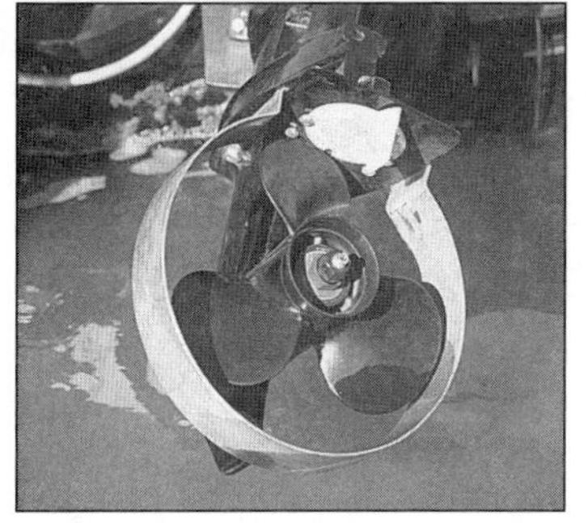

Anglers fishing rivers and wing dams should consider a rock guard for the kicker motor to reduce damaging encounters with rocks.

Anglers rigging and jigging from the bow, particularly with two rods, should consider installing rod holders to provide a secure place to set rods while lines are still in the water, to prevent snags, and to keep fish from pulling the rods overboard.

Tubular rod racks like this one from Osprey Products fit under the deck of the boat and hold rods snugly, preventing them from bouncing, tangling, and breaking.

Hydraulic and electric jack plates make raising and lowering your engine easy while fine-tuning your boat ride. A transom saver positioned between the motor and trailer prevents your motor from bouncing and damaging the boat transom while being towed on the trailer.

Motor trim switches located on the motor, floor, console, and bow make trimming your main motor easy and convenient.

Anglers fishing from the bow should consider built-in forward baitwells for easy access to lively bait.

Warrior Boats' hydraulic Pro-Tiller steering system makes handling big horsepower tiller engines effortless. With the touch of a button, steer the motor left or right, using the foot- and thumb-control pads.

Rigging your boat with remote oil-reservoir access makes adding engine oil easy. Position a small object like a pocket knife between the two cap tabs to loosen tight-fitting oil reservoir caps.

Mounting an LCD and flasher side by side enables simultaneous viewing of bottom and fish.

Some anglers, like In-Fisherman Professional Walleye Trail pro Bruce Samson, elevate and shade their bowmount sonar for easy and more comfortable viewing.

The aluminum rod rack from Messenger Bait Accessories holds up to 8 rods and fits into Springfield Taper Lock bases—good for storing and protecting multiple trolling rods. It features Berkley rod holders with lock rings to keep rods in place.

Add an adhesive strip of Velcro to keep rods secure.

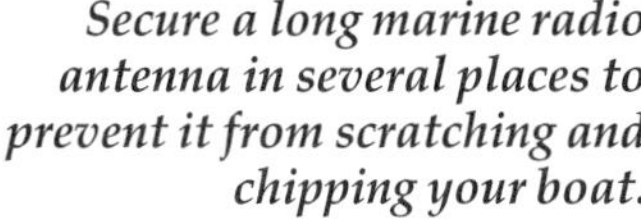

Secure a long marine radio antenna in several places to prevent it from scratching and chipping your boat.

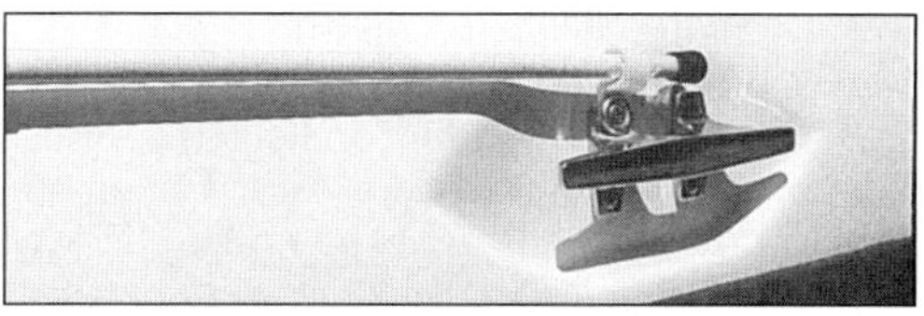

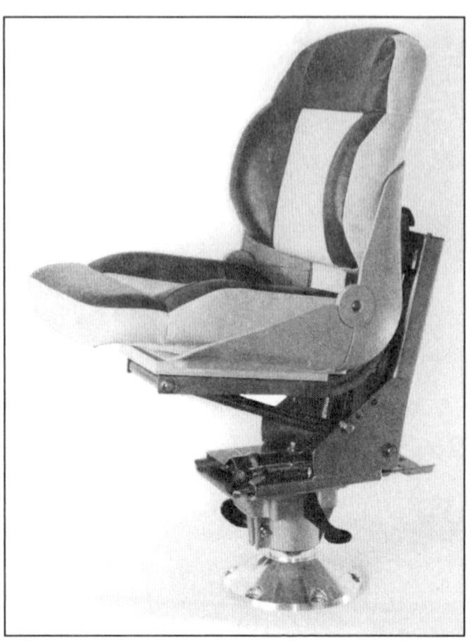

Install a seat near your kicker-tiller motor to make trolling more comfortable.

Suspension seats like Estes' Glyde Ryde prevent jarring blows to your back when you're traveling in rough water.

IS THE BOAT READY?

You've survived another winter. Signs of spring are about. Now most of us can no longer walk on water. Like the bear, the boat comes out of hibernation. How well things work and what needs to be done depend on how much effort you put into your fishing machine last fall. Here's a checklist for the boat, engine, and trailer.

The boat—A good scrubbing followed by a waxing is in order. If the boat was stored under a boat cover, wash the cover in water and a small amount of mild detergent. After it has dried, check to see if any repairs are needed.

Check the fluid level in the batteries. Batteries tend to discharge over several months, so they need recharging. Clean the battery terminals and connectors, then connect the wires to the batteries. (Note: Marine dealers tell us that one of the most frequently diagnosed problems is loose wing nuts on battery terminals.) Consider replacing the wing nuts with regular hex nuts and lock washers. Tighten them down with a wrench. With power in the electrical system, check accessories like navigation lights and livewell and bilge pumps. If equipment is dead, recheck connections and fuses.

A few swipes across the transducer face with a nonabrasive scouring pad removes any dried-on algae from last summer. Take the prop off the electric trolling motor and check for fishing line wrapped around the shaft behind the prop. Finally, check the condition of fire extinguishers, throw in life jackets, and top off the gas tank.

The engine—Depending on what was done to the engine last fall, some of these jobs may or may not be necessary. Change the lower unit oil if this wasn't done at the end of the season. In any case, check the oil level by dropping the engine to the down or run position, then remove the top breather plug on the lower unit.

Insert something like a wire tie or twist tie into the plug hole. The oil level should come up to about a half inch from the hole.

Check the engine oil reservoir, and top it off if necessary. Grease any fittings. (These usually are near the steering pivot areas.) Remove the prop to make sure no line is wrapped around the shaft, and put a little spline grease on the shaft. Then replace the thrust washer, prop, and prop nut.

Back your boat into the water or put engine muffs on so that the engine can be run. Cross your fingers, and fire up the engine. Run the engine for 5 to 10 minutes to burn out any storage solution that may have been put into the engine last fall. While the engine is running, watch to see that an adequate stream of water is coming from the small discharge hole behind the engine. (Note: If the water pump impeller breaks, it often occurs during this first start-up after a period of storage.) Check for gas line leaks, too.

The last, best, inexpensive maintenance is changing spark plugs. This usually isn't done in fall because plugs may become fouled by the engine storage mixture.

The trailer—Make sure the wheels go around smoothly; that is, check the wheel bearings. Jack up one wheel at a time and give it a spin. Check for noise and wobble. Either probably indicates bad bearings. If the bearings haven't been packed and the seals replaced in a few years, maybe you should do so, to save yourself from the "jacked up, pulled over to the shoulder" scene popular along highways in summer. If the wheels have Bearing Buddies, give them a squirt or two of grease. Examine the insides of the tires for grease streaking on the tire and rim, which indicates a blown rear seal. Check tire pressure, and don't forget the spare.

With larger rigs on the road, more trailers have brakes. Check your brake fluid level. If it's low, add fluid, but also look for brake line leaks, usually at points where the line comes out of the reservoir. Checking brakes' condition and diagnosing their problems are somewhat difficult, and usually require two people. Better to consult your marine dealer.

Clean the connectors on the wiring harness, using sandpaper or a wire brush. Then hook them up and check the trailer lights. If the lights aren't working, chances are you've got a burned-out bulb. Direct your last check to the winch stand. Make sure it's solidly attached and the webbing or rope is in good condition.

TROUBLESHOOTING WITH
THE MOTOR DOCTOR

Grid Michal (alias the Motor Doctor), an *In-Fisherman* columnist specializing in addressing motor problems, offers the following advice on motor problems:

1. When your engine doesn't start, remember that only three things make it work: spark, fuel, and compression. Most "no-start" problems are due to the kill lanyard not being attached to the control box. The fuel line wasn't hooked up, or on a system with separate six-gallon tanks, was hooked up in reverse. Somebody grabbed a can of last year's fuel and hooked the engine to it. Totally corroded battery cables were attached to corroded battery posts by loose wing nuts. Clean those battery connections within an "inch of their life," as your mother used to say. Use a stainless lock washer under the wing nut. Spray corrosion sealer on the terminals *after* making your attachments. These are things you need to discover *yourself*, with no tattletales watching. Put that kill lanyard back on firmly. Make sure the primer bulb arrow on the fuel line points toward the engine and that you're using fresh fuel and an outboard manufacturer's TC-W3 oil.

2. When you get it started, and no tell-tale water comes out the side, investigate to see if a mud-dauber wasp may have built a spy station in the discharge hole. Before you take your engine to the dealer for what you assume will be major water pump work, run a piece of weed-eater line up the discharge hole while the engine's running to clear out the mud. And while we're on the cooling system, thermostats of late have been made of different metals in different countries and reset differently in different types of water, so don't be alarmed if you see water discharging from the discharge hole while the overheat alarm goes off. Slow down, put the engine in neutral, let it idle for 10 seconds, shut it off, let it cool down, restart, and go slowly until you can have those funky thermostats checked.

3. If you think you've grown weaker over the summer because the steering's harder to turn, the problem more than likely is in the stainless ram, which may be rusting solid in the engine's tilt tube. Don't attempt to break it free by twisting the steering wheel, or you'll break the helm and cable. The steering ram needs to be driven back through the tilt tube, the tube reamed clean and lubed, and the inner parts of the ram cleaned and lubed. Considering the liability involved, this isn't a job for the inexperienced.

4. There's nothing more infuriating than having the engine shut down on the water. Look at your primer bulb. Is it flat? If so, there's a fuel restriction ahead of the bulb, most often in the fuel pickup check-ball in the fitting that comes off the fuel tank pickup or in the pickup screen itself (most often from aluminum shavings present when the tank was built). If this is the case, let everything sit until the bulb resumes its proper shape, then head slowly to where you can get the pickup tube cleaned or repaired. If the primer bulb is still the proper shape, does squeezing it repetitively keep the engine going? If so, the VRO or the fuel

pump is shot. If your engine bogs down on acceleration, try engaging the choke-primer for just an instant. If it picks up speed, your carbs are fouled and need to be removed and cleaned. If you continue running the engine hard with a fouled carb, you'll end up with a melted piston from lack of fuel lubrication, and that's far more expensive than cleaning the carb. Many boaters use STP Fuel Injector and Carburetor Cleaner in their fuel year-round to prevent this problem.

5. If your engine's RPM accelerates fine but moves the boat ahead only slowly (assuming you've untied yourself from the pier), you probably haven't broken anything major. Remove the prop and check for a spun hub. You'll see rubber shards where the rubber bushing meets the center of the prop. Any prop shop can re-hub it, saving you close to 75 percent of the cost of a new prop. While the prop is in the shop, have them check your thermostats. Often a thermostat that's stuck open causes the hub to devulcanize.

Finally, every manufacturer has a different sequence of alarms that warn of problems. Check your owner's manual to determine what the buzzers are saying—overheat, low oil, fuel restriction, oil restriction, over-rev, water flow? Familiarize yourself with the combinations of warning buzzers and gauge indicators so you know what the engine's telling you.

10½ MISTAKES THAT CAN QUICKLY KILL YOUR BOAT'S ENGINE

Simple maintenance and operational procedures can eliminate 95 percent of repetitive major repairs. Here are 10½ mistakes to avoid.

1. *Use the least expensive TC-W3 Oil you can find.* The cheaper, the better. Quicker piston-cylinder wear means more big-dollar repairs for your cheerful mechanic.

2. *Buy the cheapest lowest-octane fuel from discount service stations or seldom-used marinas.* See if those high-tech knock sensors really do their job and retard the timing before you melt a piston.

3. *Stop lubricating your tilt-tube steering ram.* It's always better to let it seize with rust so you twist on the steering wheel until the helm breaks, too. Then you can get a whole new steering system.

4. *Keep the same gear oil in the gear case and the same crankcase oil in the engine.* Cars can go 7,000 miles between changes, and you'll probably sell the boat before you've gone 7,000 miles on the water.

5. *Don't repair a bent prop.* It's a marvelous lesson in geometry when you see how a prop shaft going in an ellipse can wallow out seals and bearings and dump all the gear oil into the lake.

6. *Keep your water-separator filter forever.* You didn't leave the gas-fill cap open, so where would water have come from? Your fuel supplier wouldn't have had a problem in his tanks . . . would he?

7. *Don't treat your fuel with additives or cleaners.* Gas is gas, and there's absolutely no reason to consider preventive care for it if your engine's running fine now.

8. *Ignore those warning lights and alarms on your dash.* They're probably just gimmicks the manufacturer added to make more money on his boat.

9. *Recognize that warming up your boat engine before leaving the pier only wastes gas.* There's absolutely no difference between your car's engine and your boat's engine.

10. *Always start the engine in neutral with the throttle wide open.* Don't worry about those strange metallic noises coming from the engine compartment.

10½. *"Zing" your engine repetitively in neutral.* It's a joy to see the look of astonishment on bystanders' faces when a connecting rod piece flies airmail back to the manufacturer for repair.

WINTERIZING THE WATER CHARIOT

Another boating and fishing season comes to an end. Come spring, when the rig rolls out of storage, you want the engine to fire up with everything in working order. What you do now can lead to a trouble-free start next spring.

The outboard deserves the most consideration because it's the most important component and most expensive to repair when not treated right. Winterizing the engine is important during any period of extended storage, but it's even more critical in cold weather.

First, a gas stabilizer should be added to the gas remaining in the tank. Then the engine should be run for 10 or 15 minutes to ensure that the stabilizer reaches all of the fuel system. Run the engine in the water or out of the water with engine muffs.

Next, introduce a fogging solution to the carburetor throats, a procedure that's easy to somewhat difficult, depending on your engine's design. Some engines have a convenient valve to which a fogging spray can be attached, while others make you remove the air intake box to reach the carburetors. Add fogging oil until the engine is really smoking, which tells you that the upper cylinder areas are well lubricated.

Sometimes mechanics run a special fogging mixture through the engine to accomplish about the same thing. You probably will want to scale back on their formula so you can make it in a standard six-gallon gas can: a 50:1 gas-oil mix—1 quart of fogging oil, 5 ounces of Stabil gas stabilizer. (For a two-gallon can: 2 gallons of gas, 5 ounces of outboard oil, 11 ounces of fogging oil, and 2 ounces of Stabil.)

Connect the special fuel mixture to your fuel line, and run the engine for 5 to 10 minutes. Finally, tilt the engine down as far as possible and turn it over several times. Don't run it—just touch the key switch, allowing any water left in the system to run out.

If this seems like too much work on a cold fall day, perform at least minimal maintenance. Pull the plugs, disconnecting and labeling the plug wires for each cylinder. Squirt fogging oil into each cylinder through the plug holes, replace the plugs, leave the wires off, and turn the engine over several times. Then reconnect the plug wires.

The other engine part needing special attention is the lower unit. Lower-unit oil should be replaced at least once a season. Doing so eliminates any water in the lower unit. Water usually separates from oil and runs out the drain hole first. If you find more than a tablespoon of water in the oil, check its lower-unit seals. If water is present and freezes, seals can be ruined—or worse, the lower unit could crack. If the lower unit is left empty all winter, condensation occurs and bearings rust.

While you're on this end of the engine, remove the prop. Check for fishing line wrapped around the propeller shaft. Place spline grease on the shaft before putting the prop back on. Grease any fittings. Then place a small amount of grease on the steering arm and turn the steering mechanism a few times to work it in.

Occasionally, the livewell and bilge pumps can create storage problems in cold weather. Flip on the livewell and bilge-pump switch for a second or two to expel any water, and add 1 or 2 cups of nontoxic antifreeze to the livewell system.

You have two options for storing batteries in winter. You can either pull them from the boat or disconnect them, leaving them in the boat. In either case, label the wires, because they all look alike in spring. If the batteries are easy to get at, taking them out is a good idea. Remember, however, that batteries emit explosive fumes that can be ignited by a flame or spark, producing a serious explosion. Storing a vented battery in the vicinity of a heating system is dangerous. Remember to recharge batteries several times over the winter, too.

If you prefer to leave batteries in the boat and don't have a smart charger to maintain voltage level over the winter, make sure they're fully charged, then disconnect the wires and label them. Disconnecting the wires eliminates the possibility of any small current draw on the battery, which is important, because even a small current draw discharges the battery, allowing it to freeze and become damaged. In spring, when you return the batteries to the boat, clean the terminals and wire connectors for good contact. Then charge the batteries.

TRAILERS

Too often, periodic trailer maintenance gets overlooked. During the boating season, a familiar sight along the highway is a boat trailer jacked up because of a shot wheel bearing. Before storage, jack up each wheel and give it a spin. Check for any wobble or unusual noise that may signal a bearing problem. After two or three years of normal mileage, pull the wheels, check the bearings, and replace the seals.

Bearing Buddies, grease fittings attached to cups that cover the ends of an axle, work well if they're maintained properly. A couple of squirts of grease in the Bearing Buddies during and at the end of the season usually are adequate. Remove and clean the Bearing Buddies every few years. For slightly more money than the buddy system, Liqua-Lube's liquid hub lubricating system provides years of worry-free trailering with minimal maintenance.

When you store the boat, pull the drain plug and tie it to the tiller handle or steering wheel, where you'll see and reinsert it before launching. Raise the bow of the boat or trailer so any water drains.

If all this sounds like too much work, contact your local marine dealer. Take your boat to your dealer in early fall—during late fall, dealers are busy winterizing and repairing. Spring is even worse, with repairs and new boat rigging.

FUELED AGAIN?

Chemistry goes to work on walleye rigs during winter storage, fueling owners' discontent with their outboards. Classic fuel dete· ·· starvation problems arise. Gas mixed with oil loses its octar 50 percent in 30 days. Fuel becomes gummy, then evapora completely, leaving an oil residue that becomes harder and hard· and harder as each day passes. Oil residue blocks the passag· of fuel through the carburetor and into the engine, creating a variety of problems, depending on where the buildup occurs— the mechanical equivalent of clogged arteries.

Rule of thumb: the less often you use your boat, the more you need to use fuel additives.

If you use the engine manufacturer's TC-W3 oil, you won't need Carbon-Guard or the like. Winterizing preservatives like LubriMatic Gas Stabilizer or Stabil slow your fuel's deterioration, reducing the risk of engine detonation

The less often you use your boat, the more you need to use fuel additives.

and powerhead destruction. Products like STP Fuel Injector and Carburetor Cleaner help keep carburetor passages clean of gum and fuel residue.

Not all engines need the same type or amount of chemical cocktail added to their fuel tanks. Think it through. Analyze your motor use. The more you use your boat, the less you need to depend on additives. But if your boat sits idle over the winter, its gas deteriorates, and when you try to start it on a cold day in February or March, you may experience problems that could have been prevented.

COLD WEATHER CRUISIN'

Some folks put their boats away for the winter after winterizing them. Others have learned that fine fishing continues until ice floes choke rivers and ice sheets cover lakes.

Not much difference between humans and engines when the weather gets cold: the colder we get, the stiffer and less efficient we become. Gasoline loses its volatility, too.

On outboards and inboard-outboards, everything that tilts or swivels has grease, which hardens with the cold. Movable parts move more slowly in cold weather. Remember this when you need to tilt the motor or steer to avoid an obstacle. Shifting becomes more difficult, too.

Seals stiffen and shrink. You may notice oil seeping around the prop shaft or tilt and trim rams. Some engines dump fuel out the bottom crank seal, and others blow compression out the top crank seal. Obviously, the colder the weather, the more tantrums your seals may throw. Racing the engine won't cure these problems. Seals that were marginal during summer are likely to need major repairs.

Engines with carburetors, instead of fuel injectors, have more difficult times starting and running in cold weather because fuel resists movement through the carburetor. Puddling of fuel becomes the norm instead of the exception. Extremely cold pistons and cylinders have greater tolerances, making it more difficult for them to draw the fuel to the area of combustion.

Be patient with the starting process, and try not to use your high-speed warm-up lever more than necessary. When a piston speeds back and forth rapidly while the engine's cold, it expands more quickly than the cylinder and transfers its aluminum to the cylinder walls. When the engine locks up due to improper warm-up, it's commonly known as *cold seizure*. The piston damage makes it difficult (due to screwed-up tolerances) to draw in fuel, regardless of ambient or internal temperatures.

In northern climes, you should change thermostats for ones that open when the operating temperature becomes warmer. Thermostats that are too cool can cause cold seizure even during normal use. Too cold an operating temperature, and combustibility suffers, decreasing fuel economy. Cold oil causes excessive drag on internal parts in a cold-running inboard. Don't ignore cold-weather engine needs.

What about the cooling capacity of oxygenated fuels? In theory, these fuels burn hotter, like high-test gasoline with reduced octane. Most engines are resilient enough to take the modest increase in heat generated by higher oxygen levels.

OPEN WATER FISHING IN COLD WEATHER

When your boat sits in -20°F temperatures for extended periods, warm it in a heated garage before heading out to an icy river on the first warm (20°F) day. Make sure the engine starts and the electrical system functions. With larger console engines, steering cables may have stiffened in extreme cold, locking the steering. Turn the wheel to ensure it works, instead of resorting to a torch later.

When your boat sits in -20°F temperatures for extended periods, warm it in a heated garage before heading out to an icy river on the first warm (20°F) day.

Let the engine warm. Look for the telltale small stream of water shooting from the rear of the engine housing. Check for a frozen water-pump impeller. Run the livewell pump continuously—or not at all.

When you're ready to pull the boat out of the water, be sure the engine is warm. If you've been trolling all day, run at medium to three-quarter throttle for a few minutes to warm the engine. This ensures that water will run out instead of freeze when you pull the boat from the water. After trailering, tilt the engine down to allow water to run out. Turn the engine over briefly to expel any remaining water in the cooling system. Pull the boat plug to allow any water to run out, and make sure the livewell is drained. You may wish to add a cup of nontoxic antifreeze to the livewell when you head home.

AN OUNCE OF PREVENTION IS WORTH
A POUND OF WALLEYES

Little glitches take you off the water to search the back country for fixes. If you fish tournaments, little glitches can knock you out of the prize pool. Prepare for glitches before they happen. Carry spare parts or quick-fix gear.

Duct tape—What quick-fix artist would leave home without it?

Needlenose pliers—Arguably the easiest hook removers available. They also serve as a makeshift crimper, wrench, cutter. If your old pliers have been rusting in the bilge for a few months, pick up a new pair. And pack a couple screwdrivers while you're at it.

Spare fuses—Many late-model boats no longer use in-line fuses; breaker switches are the norm. You still need to carry fuses. Outboard motors typically have a main fuse under the cowl. Your fishfinder-GPS units generally have low-amp, in-line fuses, too. Check your owner's manual for appropriate fuses.

Extra oil—Automatic oil-mixing systems are a feature on many outboards. It's easy to forget to check oil level, however. Carry an extra quart of two-cycle oil in the boat, and you'll never have to listen to the low-oil beeper again.

Spare propellers—Jamming your bowmount motor into the pier while pulling up to dock is a quick way to break a plastic electric-motor

PWT pro Dan Plautz tightens up after a long day on rough water.

prop. This $20 part should be purchased the same day you buy the motor. A spare prop for the main engine costs considerably more, but it's likely you'll eventually need to repair or replace it. Even a $20,000 walleye boat can be crippled by a single tap of the propeller on rocks. Purchase spare prop nuts, thrust washers, and cotter pins, too. Carry a prop wrench like the Quicksilver floating plastic wrench.

Replacement pumps—When you anchor in big waves, your bilge pump gets heavy use. If the pump quits running, you quit fishing. Live-release tournaments also take a heavy toll on livewell pumps and recirculators. Lose a pump, and you lose your fish.

More than 90 percent of pumps in fishing boats are manufactured by three companies: Mayfair, Rule, and Attwood. Check the make of the pumps in your boat and buy back-ups. Bilge and livewell pumps usually differ in the angle of their inlet and outlet ports. Livewell outflow plumbing may be sized for a particular water volume from the pump. Be sure you match pump style and gallons-per-hour of flow to your particular boat. Remember, pumps are open to the water. Plug the through-hull intake, or pull your boat out of the water to install a new unit.

Light bulbs—The lights on the boat trailer are sure to do something weird in the next year or so. It seems bulbs burn out while the rig is sitting in the driveway. Carry a few trailer bulbs (usually #1157) or a replacement light assembly in the glove box.

Grease gun—Ever tried to replace a boat trailer wheel bearing after dark alongside a mosquito-infested swamp? Ever tried to find a replacement wheel bearing in Resume Speed, North Dakota? LubriMatic sells an inexpensive, downsized grease-gun kit that includes marine grease. Use it regularly on trailer bearings. It can rescue sticky steering and swivel brackets on your outboard, too.

Electrical repair kit—Power cords get pinched and tangled. Old connectors wiggle loose. A small kit containing electrician's tape, a stripping-crimping pliers, a couple of short lengths of wire, a few assorted connectors, and a tube of silicone sealant is a must.

Fasteners—A generous handful of stainless steel screws, nuts, bolts, and washers comes in handy. A rod holder wiggles free—no problem. Uncle Milo sits on the fishfinder bracket—a simple fix. Add a cordless drill-driver, and you can mount or dismantle most accessories on your boat.

Additions for Tournament Anglers

Livewell plugs—Water sloshes out the livewell overflow as you run from spot to spot. A tight plug keeps the livewell full and reduces empty space for sloshing for better fish survival. Find a plug to fit the overflow opening inside the livewell. If you can't, plug the outside opening through the hull.

Backup fishfinder and accessories—Tournaments are brutal on sensitive instruments. Modern fishfinders are rugged, but anglers are even more rugged. Thieves also pose a threat to electronics. Just in case, carry a moderately priced backup unit. Carry appropriate fuses for all your electronics. Extra swivel bases and gimbal mounts are wise add-ons. Floating debris, even ice chunks, can rob you of a speed-impeller wheel or transducer.

Prepare for glitches, and you beat them before they beat you.

SAFE BOATING IN ROUGH WATER

The fish were biting. *In-Fisherman* contributor Dick Sternberg and his companions were fishing on the midlake flats of Lake Winnibigoshish, a large lake in northern Minnesota. Suddenly a huge black cloud appeared over the horizon, moving fast. Lines were quickly pulled in and the fishermen headed for shore—6 miles away.

But the storm was moving fast. Suddenly they were surrounded by a huge white mass of rain driven by 60-mph winds. The initial blast caught the bow and turned the big Lund Pro-V away from the storm.

Initially they had to run with the storm. Huge following waves were close to breaking over the back of the boat. Sternberg knew he had to try to turn around and head into the storm. He steered the boat around in a trough between waves, and with the help of his Global Positioning System (GPS), he slowly worked his way back to shore.

Shore wasn't pretty. Trees had blown across the harbor mouth, while others lay across boats and trailers. But ahead stood land, solid land.

ANTICIPATE AND PREPARE

How should fishermen in small inland fishing boats prepare for and ride out a storm?

First, anticipate and prepare for extreme weather conditions. Anticipation means learning to recognize and understand basic weather patterns. Preparation means taking time to make sure your boat has basic safety equipment on board and that you understand how to use and adapt this equipment to your advantage.

Weather is complex. Weather experts can only make percentage calls, and they're sometimes wrong. We can't all be weather experts, but we can learn to recognize conditions that warn us of threatening weather while we're on the water.

We can't all be weather experts, but we can learn to recognize conditions that warn us of threatening weather while we're on the water.

For inland boaters, the inherent violence of a thunderstorm is a primary concern. Thunderstorms occur most frequently in summer, usually in late afternoon or early evening. Typical conditions include a falling barometer and hot, humid days. The fishing is hot, and so are you. Experience warns that a storm is near.

These storms are the result of a strong cold front colliding with an existing warm front. The air that rises rapidly from this collision forms tall clouds with anvil-shaped tops, often above 30,000 feet. The cloud base may look like rolling balls of dark cotton, their darkness usually because of rain. The leading clouds are usually cumulus, which transform into ominous-looking cumulonimbus. When you see this type of cloud structure, the safe and prudent thing to do is to head for shore.

If thunder and lightning are present, it's possible to predict the approximate distance of the storm. Lightning travels at the speed of light, so we see it as it happens. Sound travels much slower, about 1,000 feet per second. This means that it travels 1 mile in about 5 seconds. To determine how far away the storm is, count the seconds from the time you see the lightning until you hear the thunder, then divide by five. That gives you the distance in miles that the storm is from you. Example: It takes fifteen seconds from the time you see the lightning until you hear the thunder. Fifteen divided by 5 is 3, so the storm is about 3 miles away.

SAFETY ITEMS

Anglers should include a number of safety items in their boats. First and most important is a personal flotation device (life jacket). Wear it. A radio is useful to pick up local weather. The AM band of a radio starts to break up with static when a storm approaches your area, providing a warning. Marine band radios offer weather channels. Use them. If you have access to the TV Weather Channel, check it before you leave home.

Useful equipment includes a compass, GPS, flare gun, and sea anchor—a device dragged through the water to slow the boat and keep the bow pointing upwind. A minnow bucket makes a good emergency sea anchor.

You're caught in a storm, out in the middle of a huge lake, surrounded by high winds and big waves. You wish you were back in your vehicle, drinking coffee, keeping dry, and watching the storm as a spectator instead of a participant. What choices do you have?

Let's say that you've had a few minutes of warning. To prepare for deteriorating conditions, make sure everyone in the boat is wearing a life jacket.

• Put on raingear.
• Stow away as much gear as possible.
• Empty livewells to decrease the weight of the boat by as much as 300 pounds. A lighter boat rides higher in the water and is more buoyant.
• Put anything that can help you stay afloat where it will be easily accessible if you're thrown into the water—a clothes bag, minnow bucket, cooler, or boat cushion.
• Arrange passengers so they balance the boat—nobody in the bow seat, because the bow should be as light and buoyant as possible.
• Position everyone on the floor of the boat to keep the center of gravity low.

WORKING WAVES

Now let's consider three situations: (1) heading into the waves and storm, (2) going with the waves and storm, (3) traveling parallel to the waves, or at right angles to the storm.

Into the waves—Assume that you're heading in the direction of the storm, the recommended direction to travel. Try to take the oncoming waves so that the bow intersects the face and direction of the waves, somewhere between 30 and 45 degrees.

If the boat is bow heavy, move passengers and gear farther back. Check your speed. Moving too fast can drive the bow of the boat into the base of the oncoming wave, bringing water over the bow and into the boat. Remember too, that a tremendous amount of pressure is put on the hull, causing potential damage to the boat. A slight "up trim" on the engine helps keep the bow up.

Find a safe speed at which you can still make progress. It may be necessary to increase speed as you move up the face of the wave, to decrease speed as you move down the backside. Adequate forward speed is necessary to maintain steering and boat control.

If you find you can't head in one direction to get to shore, you'll have to travel in several directions. Your course might first be 45 degrees NE, and then at some point, you change direction to 45 degrees NW. By continuing this zigzag pattern, you can work your way north in an indirect but safe way. This pattern is called *tacking*, a common sailboating technique.

Going with the waves—In the next case, let's assume that you must run with the waves and storm to get back to the harbor. You might find that running with the waves when they're coming from directly behind you works quite well. It might be better, however, to run at an angle of 30 to 45 degrees to the waves—the tacking previously mentioned.

You have two primary concerns when running with the waves: (1) a following wave that moves up on the stern of the boat may catch up with you, break over the stern, and swamp your boat. A following wave can look mighty big when you glance over your shoulder while running up the back of the next one. At proper boat speed, however, the following wave can't catch you.

(2) The boat travels too fast from the crest of the wave to the bottom. Your bow may dig into the base of the next wave, drastically slowing the boat. The following wave may then drive onto the stern of the boat, shoving the bow deeper into the wave, and causing the boat to turn sideways in the trough (the low point between two waves), often resulting in your losing control of the boat. Correct speed and total concentration on your part are essential.

The most dangerous situation occurs when the bow is driven into the base of the next wave, so that the following wave catches the stern of the boat. The stern may then flip over the bow—a cartwheel, in plain English, and *pitchpoling*, in boating terms. By any name, it's serious.

As you approach shore, conditions change in shallower water. The shallowing lake bottom begins to slow the bases of the waves, forming breakers. Tops of waves move forward faster than the bases, breaking free from them. These nasty piles of water breaking over the stern of a boat can swamp it. Again, boat speed is critical. Be alert. Don't relax until you're at the dock—better yet, on the trailer.

Running parallel to the waves—The last direction of travel is running either between the waves or parallel to them. Avoid traveling parallel to the waves. Riding a boat parallel to the wave places the boat at the top of the wave, on the side of the wave, or in the trough. This type of sideways rolling action can cause the boat to overturn. So what are your choices to avoid this?

The most dangerous situation occurs when the bow is driven into the base of the next wave, so that the following wave catches the stern of the boat.

Assume the storm is blowing north-south, and you want to go east. We're back to tacking, sometimes referred to as *quartering points on the compass*. By way of illustration, assume that you're heading due south with the waves, but you need to get to a point east of your position.

A good way to accomplish this is to run southeast, then northeast, then southeast. Repeat this pattern of crossing waves until you reach your destination on the eastern shore. In other words, use a tacking motion, covering a quarter of the compass face, northeast to southeast. When it's necessary to change boat direction for the next tack, turn the boat quickly into the trough of the wave. Then begin your course up the next face or backside of the wave.

Can GPS help? Absolutely. If you have remembered to save the location you

Angle of Approach

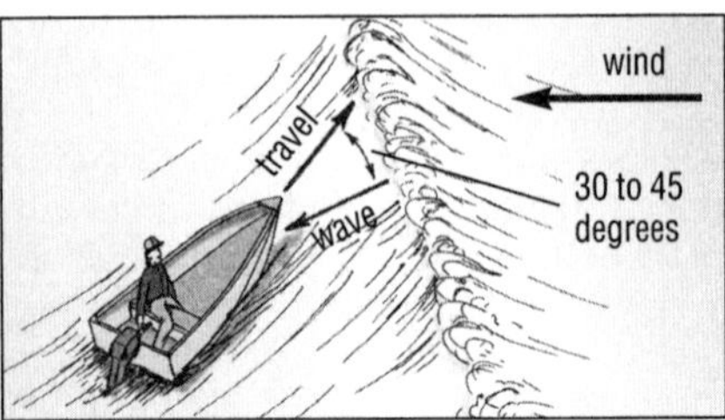

Approach large waves at a 30- to 45-degree angle to prevent the wave's crest from breaking over the bow.

Direction of Travel—Coming or Going with the Waves

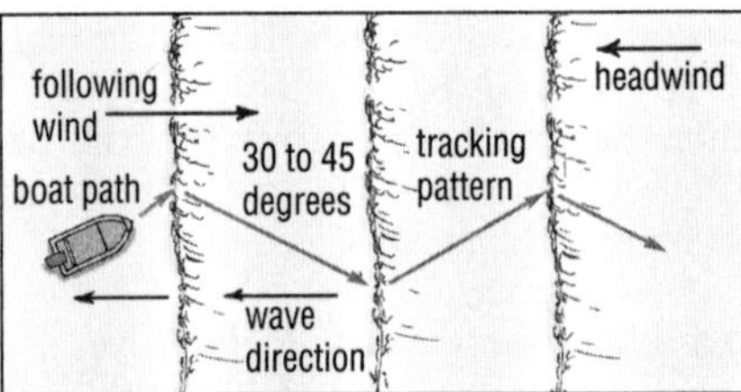

Use a zigzag tacking pattern—first left, then right—to move upwind without heading directly into big waves.

Tacking Pattern

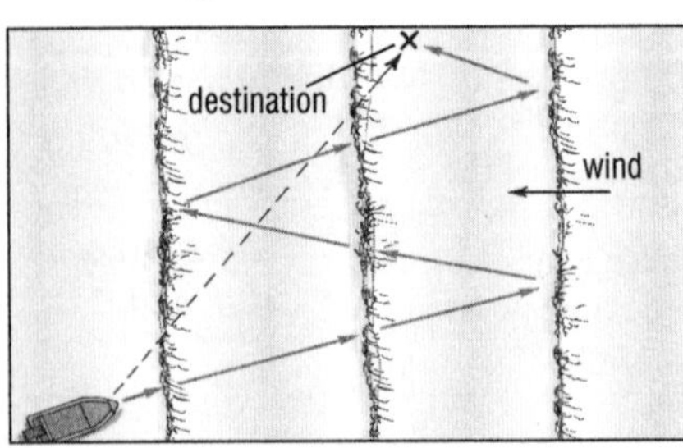

Use an angled approach when trying to move parallel to waves.

Beware of Following Waves

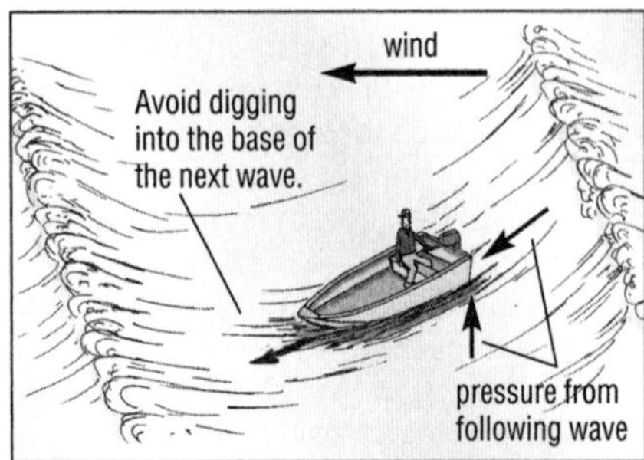

If you proceed too quickly down a wave when you're moving with the wind, the bow may dig into the base of the next wave. Water and wave pressure against the transom or bottom of the boat can then cause the following wave to wash over the transom, which can turn your boat sideways, flip it, or push the nose down into the water. Use a zigzag tacking pattern—first left, then right—to move downwind without heading directly into big waves. Adjust speed as necessary.

Almost Home

As the boat approaches shallow water near shore, the base of the wave is slowed by lake bottom, while the top of the wave moves forward at a faster rate, forming a breaker that can rush over the transom, swamping the boat. Proper boat speed is critical to avoid being overcome by a following wave top.

launched from, bring up its waypoint—its electronic address—and execute a GO TO command. Now you have a direction in which to head. A good plotter screen makes this easy, even when visibility approaches zero. As a safety check, make sure your GPS maintains satellite lock in bad weather. Some units have difficulty doing this under adverse conditions. Test your unit's effectiveness during the next hard rain or snow.

Remember that GPS operates in a straight line, so it will point over reefs and other obstacles. Mark these hazards ahead of time on your GPS. Icons work great for this. Another safety procedure is to store waypoints for several harbors, so you have different choices to head to. Why go 10 miles if you can find safety 2 miles away? The advantage of GPS over a compass is that you are always given a direction to move in to get to a specific spot, even in a storm. But don't forget your compass; the GPS unit can fail.

MOTOR FAILURE

What if the motor fails? Now you've lost boat control and you're at the mercy of the storm. In most cases, your best choice is a sea anchor tied to the bow and thrown into the water. The sea anchor offers enough resistance to keep the bow pointing into the waves.

At least two items in a boat can serve as improvised sea anchors: a minnow bucket and a drift sock. Be sure to always carry a piece of rope, preferably about 50 feet long. Tie one end of the rope to the bow, the other to the bucket or drift sock. Warning: most drift socks are set to operate close to the boat on a 10- to 15-foot line, which is too short. A short hookup keeps the bow of the boat down in the water instead of allowing it to ride quickly up the face of the next wave.

A third alternative is a regular boat anchor. Tie the anchor to the eye on the front of the boat, letting out less rope than the depth of the water, so you don't catch the bottom with the anchor. Suspended in the water, the anchor slows the boat and keeps the bow moving into the wind. Lightweight anchors with large surface areas, like the Water Spike, work well.

What if everything goes wrong and the boat swamps? Stay with it and grab anything that floats—cooler, minnow bucket, clothes bag, boat cushion. Do not leave the boat. Thanks to to flotation specifications that boat manufacturers must follow, boats today are designed to stay afloat.

Check your boat for the necessary pieces of safety equipment, pay attention to the weather, and don't take chances. One more fish isn't worth the risk of losing a lifetime of fishing. Give yourself a margin of error. When things get tough, you can make it back if you can stay calm and focused.

Do yourself, your fishing companions, and your family a favor. Enroll in a boating course. You can be a boater without being an angler, but unless you're a shore angler, you can't be an angler without being a boater. Call 800/336-BOAT for the boating course nearest you.

Defining and Refining Patterns

CATCHING FISH VS. CATCHING LOTS OF BIG FISH

In-Fisherman founder Al Lindner says that the difference between a good fisherman and a great fisherman is attention to detail. A good fishermen, for example, may fish productive structures with a likely lure or bait, often catching good fish, and occasionally big ones. A great fisherman, however, moves beyond that plateau to evaluate fish location and behavior and correctly match lures or baits to the fish's mood and surroundings. A great fisherman carefully observes what the fish are doing, how they're responding, and continually experiments to improve success by tiny degrees—a whisker here, a percentage point there. By the time he or she is done improving the odds, the sum total of all those little things adds up to one big thing: increased efficiency. Getting fish to respond effectively results in consistent catches of bigger fish.

Fish location is not the mystery it once was. Nowadays, educated anglers more often than not fish in the right places. Many of those anglers would be distressed, however, to learn how many fish they're fishing through with few results. Simply being in the right place isn't a guarantee of success; if the fish don't bite, a near miss is as bad as being miles off. Fishing in the right place at the right time with the right lure or bait, however, is about as good as it gets.

This chapter focuses on two principles: 1) learning to read and adapt to the signals fish provide us by evaluating their response (or lack of response) to our angling efforts, and 2) fine-tuning presentation approaches to match the prevailing conditions. It's much more than simply fishing in the right kind of place with something that should work—it's bridging the elusive gap between hope and success so that fish respond to your best efforts.

MULTIPLE PATTERNS, VERSATILE TACTICS

Spring walleye location and behavior are driven by spawning instinct, so patterns are similar or at least predictable in most bodies of water. Walleyes are drawn to the best combinations of shallow broken rock and current, fancasting their eggs among the crevices. Locate prime spawning habitat, and you'll find fish.

Once spawning is complete, however, walleyes' priorities shift from spawning to feeding, and they adjust their location and behavior accordingly. Postspawn walleyes may linger near spawning areas as long as sufficient forage and cover are available. When those ebb in one spot and begin to develop elsewhere in the warming lake, river, or reservoir, walleyes disperse to distant sites with better combinations of seasonal habitat. Food and comfort are the driving forces in a walleye's life during the summer season or seasons. In-Fisherman divides these up in the following way:

Presummer—The transition period between fish spawning and setting up in summer patterns is typified by fish movement, temporary patterns, and scattered or small groups. Water temperatures commonly range from the mid 50°F to the mid 60°F range. Weeds are developing, baitfish are spawning, and insects are beginning to hatch. Walleyes begin to display their first summer schooling behaviors as they gradually gather in areas with good combinations of food, depth, and cover. Fish activity becomes concentrated along the edges of major main lake structures in natural lakes and reservoirs. In rivers, as water levels recede, walleyes disperse downstream, away from dams, moving from formerly flooded shoreline cover to midriver current breaks.

Summer peak—At some point, summer habitat, weedgrowth, forage production, walleye schooling behavior—the entire aquatic environment—suddenly explode into peak activity, marking the arrival of true summer patterns. In-Fisherman refers to this as the Summer Peak, when every aspect of fishing hits high gear. A lake suddenly appears alive with fish schooling in classic areas and responding to traditional presentations. Water temperatures of about

Multiple Patterns

Multiple locational patterns are common during the Summer Period, due to an abundance and variety of habitat and food. Walleyes simultaneously inhabit weeds and woodcover atop flats; patrol the edges of the first drop-off from main lake structures; suspend or roam the open basin; lie at the base of deep structure, just above the thermocline; move into shallow current inlets, atop rock reefs, or along shorelines at night or on windy days. Recognizing available locations is the first step to contacting fish.

Determine which areas will produce at different times of day or under varying weather conditions. For example, the deeper the fish, the more likely they'll be daytime feeders. The shallower, the more likely they'll be active during low-light conditions—at dusk, dawn, night, or during reduced sunlight penetration caused by wind or rain. Fish in between, such as those located along the primary drop-off, may be in a neutral feeding attitude and therefore catchable with appropriate presentations. Shallow feeders may offer only a narrow window of opportunity when they're active and aggressive.

Determine which areas to fish at which times of day. Select an appropriate presentation. Deep fish may require vertical jigging or live-bait rigging. Cast crankbaits or jigs, or longline troll minnow-imitators over shallow flats. Walleyes along a drop-off may fall to livebait rigs, jigs, crankbaits, spoons—a variety of systems. Fish in woodcover may hit weedless jigs. The better you adapt to depth, cover, and aggressiveness of local groups of walleyes, the more consistent your catch.

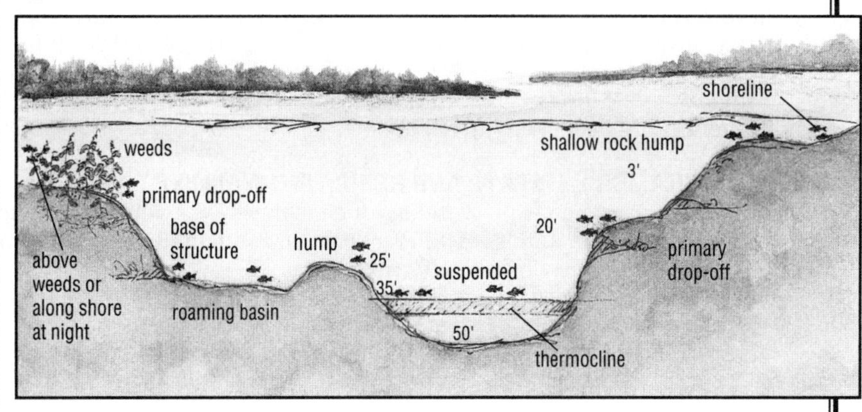

68°F to 72°F are good indicators of this condition. It's a great time to be fishing.

Summer—After the first explosion of Summer Peak activity, summer patterns settle in for several months. Water temperature, food production, and weed-growth (when present) reach maximal levels in all bodies of water. Walleyes often have many choices for suspending or roaming: shallow cover, edges of points and humps, moderately deep drop-offs, and shallow basins. The formation of summer thermoclines separates the warm, oxygen-rich top layers from the cold,

oxygen-poor depths, so walleyes tend to stay shallower than 30 to 35 feet during most of the summer, in most (but not all) bodies of water.

In summer, several simultaneous patterns become common, with schools of fish feeding at different times of day, depending on depth, cover, forage type, water clarity, and weather conditions. Several days of stable weather seem to promote active feeding throughout the day. Severe cold fronts tend to curtail fish activity, except sometimes for brief flurries at twilight or at night. In general, deeper fish tend to respond better during the day, shallower fish in low-light periods, at night, or during windy conditions that reduce sunlight penetration and provide walleyes with a multisensory edge over their more visually oriented prey.

But that doesn't mean fish in all habitats behave similarly. Quite the contrary, in fact. Walleyes have been stocked or have expanded into so many different habitats that no such thing as universal behavior exists anymore—particularly in summer. Summer habitat varies greatly in different types of water, resulting in diverse patterns of walleye behavior. Fortunately, if you understand the choices offered by different aquatic habitats, you can predict walleyes' location within them. And once you locate the fish, you can select appropriate presentations.

Postsummer—As summer wanes and waters begin cooling slightly, fish seem to sense the wane of forage abundance and begin feeding with a sense of urgency. This may last for a week or two before Fall Turnover begins sending summer patterns into disarray. Prior to Turnover, however, postsummer fishing can be excellent. Classic structures, drop-offs, and weedlines focus fish activity. Weeds have begun to thin slightly, making it easier to fish deep weedlines. Current breaks in rivers provide the last fling of great summer fishing before fish begin moving to and concentrating in deep holes in fall.

DIFFERENT SUMMER HABITATS AND RESULTING WALLEYE PATTERNS

Summer is a time when walleye behavior challenges even veteran anglers. Note how the following examples of different habitats result in variations in summer walleye location, behavior, and effective tactics.

Deep, clear natural lakes (*Mesotrophic natural lakes, plus late oligotrophic rocky waters of the Canadian Shield*)—These are nature's classic walleye gems, with plenty of suitable rock spawning sites to support self-sustaining fisheries. Weeds often are present in sufficient numbers to support summer weed patterns, but weeds do not choke the shallows. Abundant forage is available throughout the system, often including suspended ciscoes over deep basins. Bass, pike, muskies, and panfish share the environment with walleyes.

Several coexisting patterns are the rule on these waters. Classic points, humps, and drop-offs along the edges of prominent main lake structures hold fish anywhere from the first drop-off or weededge down to the top of the thermocline. Livebait rigging and vertical jigging are classic tactics, but anglers also should probe weedlines with jigs and crankbaits, troll crankbaits in open water for suspended fish, and cast or troll atop weedbeds and along shallow rock structures during twilight periods, at night, and in windy conditions for fish that become active in the shallows. This is a time when your versatility is invaluable. You need to select the correct pattern and type of presentation for segments of the walleye population that become active at different depths, on different types of structure or cover, at different times of day.

Shallow, fertile natural lakes *(Late mesotrophic and early to mid-eutrophic stocked walleye lakes, often referred to as prairie lakes or farm country lakes)*—These are primarily soft-bottomed lakes with very little deep structure. The basin is often like a featureless, soft soup bowl. The shallows may feature considerable thick weedgrowth down to about 8 to 12 feet in stained waters; in darker fertile waters, weeds may be limited to clumpy growth in less than 4 to 5 feet of water. Sloping shoreline flats are the norm, often extending into the basin. Gradual but not prominent depth changes may extend around the lake.

Many walleyes suspend in such waters during summer, especially when shad forage is present. If it is, troll open water with crankbaits and planer boards. If the water's dark, walleyes often remain within 10 feet of the surface. When they move shallow, they push baitfish against the outer edges of weeds or against shorelines that have prominent rocky lips dropping immediately into several feet of water. Flip weedless jigs tipped with leeches to prominent shallow structures.

If weeds extend down from 5 to 10 feet, they may host walleyes all summer. This is common on lakes artificially maintained with walleye stocking, where the fish inhabit the environmental niche more commonly occupied by largemouth bass. Focus along deep weededges to find the bulk of the population.

Clear, hard-bottomed reservoirs *(Highland, canyon, hill-land, and portions of plateau reservoirs)*—These impoundments are the manmade equivalents of clear natural lakes, and many of their patterns are similar. Thermoclines may develop between about 30 and 40 feet in mountain lakes or be deeper or even absent on the large, windswept waters of open prairies. Weeds are mostly absent because of water level fluctuations; flooded terrestrial vegetation or woodcover may range from a lot to almost none.

In summer, walleyes roam up and down these reservoirs, bumping into points, humps, or timberlines, typically relating to areas for a short time before moving on in search of roaming forage like shad, ciscoes, or smelt. Shiners and other minnows may relate more closely to shallow cover or structure, providing walleyes with additional food. In calm conditions, fish the deep tips of points or the edges of humps, using livebait rigs or jigs. Or troll open water with crankbaits for suspended walleyes. On deep canyon reservoirs, fish the points or the humps where tributaries intersect the main lake or vertically jig sand slopes or rubble piles where broken cliffs have deposited rock at the base of canyon walls.

When the wind blows, mudlines forming along shorelines draw walleyes quite shallow to feed on disoriented baitfish. Cast jigs or crankbaits into the shallows, flippin' around rocks or woodcover. Forward trolling or drifting with bottom bouncers, spinners, and nightcrawler harnesses is probably the most common reservoir tactic, used anywhere from the extreme shallows down to about 25 feet.

Fertile, soft-bottomed reservoirs *(Lowland-wetland and flatland impoundments, sometimes called* flowages, *often in swampy or forest terrain)*—These manmade equivalents to fertile natural lakes often have minimal structure and feature predominantly shallow water habitat because stained or dark water results in reduced light penetration. Troll crankbaits and planer boards in the open basin for suspended fish, especially where shallow cover is absent.

In contrast, timbered flowages with abundant woodcover often host walleyes on flats less than 10 or 12 feet deep. Find the areas of best cover and proceed from tree to tree, dipping a weedless jig tipped with a leech or minnow along the trunk. Where cover is scarce or scattered, troll diving crankbaits across prominent main lake flats, occasionally contacting and deflecting over woodcover. In less stained waters, walleyes may drop into old river or creek channels; trolling channel edges and intersections with bouncers-spinners-crawlers or crankbaits is an excellent tactic. In dark waters, shallow woodcover and even the outer edges of shallow weedgrowth often hold walleyes in fewer than 8 feet deep during summer.

Large, deep rivers *(Middle-aged river stretches)*—Big rivers experience falling water levels in summer, but long stretches often retain enough depth (4 to 8 feet) and flow to host walleyes. Here fish don't necessarily need to move to deep holes at bends, because plenty of suitable depth and habitat are available even on straight stretches. Focus on visible current breaks formed by shoreline points, islands, and manmade structures, like bridge pilings, roadbeds, concrete walls, and especially wing dams with 4 or 5 feet of water flowing across their tops.

Try standard vertical jigging and three-way rigging along the front faces and tips of points, islands, and wing dams. Nightcrawlers are great summer baits. You can also cast diving crankbaits right up on the tops of wing dams and rock points, using quartering downstream retrieves to bang and bounce them across boulders and woodcover. Troll diving crankbaits along stretches of riprap, too. At night, cast crankbaits from shore toward tributary intersections, where walleyes are drawn upstream into the feeder creek to feast on minnows.

Small, shallow rivers *(Adult and mature river stretches)*—Smaller rivers offer more limited options in summer. As water levels drop, shoreline cover dries up, and shallow stretches become too shallow for fish to use consistently. Walleyes migrate up- or downriver and stack into the deep pools often associated with river bends. Drift holes with three-way rigs tipped with livebait, or longline troll diving crankbaits up- and downcurrent, scratching bottom to trigger strikes. Johnboats and canoes may be best suited to fishing small rivers fraught with rocky rapids and shallow stretches, where you need to wade to pull your boat across the shallows.

Great Lakes *(Aqua giganticus—great big water)*—Great Lakes basin areas less than 100 feet deep, preferably 30 to 70 feet deep, often host dynamic offshore fisheries for suspended and basin walleyes. Abundant suspended forage like shad, ciscoes, smelt, and alewives, coupled with cool water, help grow monster fish. Huge schools of walleyes are continually on the move. They can be located and relocated by electronics, by pinpointing groups of successful boats, or by talking to anglers on marine band radio.

Angling versatility, an open mind, and the ability to react to different habitats and conditions are essential keys to consistent summer walleye fishing success.

Trolling crankbaits, spinner-crawler harnesses, or flutterspoons covers water aggressively to locate schools of suspended walleyes. In summer, trolling speeds of 2 to 4 mph generally are best. Spinners are most effective at the lower end of the speed range. With spoons or some cranks, you can proceed up to and occasionally a bit faster than 4 mph. Planer boards or diving planers spread multiple lines to the sides of the boat, reaching out to any fish that are spooked by the boat's approach. Constant experimentation with style, shape, color, trolling speed, depth, and other lure factors helps determine productive combinations. These, of course, can change by the day or by the hour.

In summer, secondary fisheries occur in bays and rivers attached to the Great Lakes, mostly for smaller or juvenile fish. Larger adults prefer cooler water and suspended baitfish in summer, but they return in late fall and winter to bays and rivers, where they usually spawn in spring.

FACING OFF WITH SUMMER WALLEYES

Successful summer walleye fishing involves more than merely fishing structure, drop-offs, and rocks. Differences in summer habitats result in vastly different combinations of location and behavior. Forage opportunities and potential fishing patterns make summer the most diverse and challenging fishing period of the year. Your ability to recognize and adjust to several concurrent patterns and to fish them during optimal times of day and weather conditions goes a long way toward insuring fishing success. Likewise, versatility—your ability to switch from casting to trolling, from livebait to artificials to combos, from fishing structure precisely to covering open water efficiently—is critical to success.

From shallow to deep, day to night, fair weather to foul, summer walleye fishing is challenging, yet rewarding.

TIMING DAILY DEPTH PATTERNS

Walleye fishing has evolved into a three-dimensional chess game. We now pursue fish horizontally, laterally, vertically—anywhere from the shallows to the depths. Today's anglers must think spatially. Shades of Isaac Asimov, Gene Roddenberry, and Buzz Lightyear!

When you think about it, though, walleyes don't simply operate in three dimensions. Like everyone else on earth (and elsewhere), the walleye is affected by a fourth dimension—time. Walleyes' behavior definitely depends on time of day (or perhaps more correctly, on amount of light penetration). Seasonal movements throughout lake, river, and reservoir systems also correspond to an annual timetable. In short, time is definitely a critical dimension. Shades of H. G. Wells!

But all walleyes in any lake do not do the same thing at the same time. On any given day during summer, walleyes in a typical natural lake usually display a variety of location patterns and feed in different kinds of areas. Moreover, they do these things at different times of the day. This versatile species adapts to every available physical and temporal niche in their environment.

The result is that we may find some walleyes using shallow weeds, others along

the first (primary) drop-off, others at the base of a secondary drop-off above the thermocline, still others suspended or lying across the basin—and who knows where else? Now we add the time factor—measured not by a wristwatch, but by how sunlight penetration changes during the course of the day. Changing light levels activate walleyes, once they sense them.

For example, walleyes using shallow water generally become most active during low-light levels—sunrise, sunset, or night. The rest of the day, extreme light penetration in the shallows tends to suppress activity, except when wave action, clouds, rain, or other factors diminish light. We simplify all these factors by saying that shallow walleyes bite best in low light.

Say we experienced a good burst of shallow walleye activity at first light, where we've found that longline trolling minnow-imitators, pitching jigs, or casting slipbobbers in 5 feet of water is productive. But the clock's ticking. After an hour or two, the action subsides along shallow rocky shorelines and riprap and atop shallow reefs. Walleyes have either left the areas completely and shifted deeper, or they're hunkered down under some other cover. You could argue that they're trying to avoid the discomfort associated with the increased light level, but it's more likely that their feeding efficiency is dwindling rapidly where light is penetrating deeply.

Now the sun has risen a bit higher in the sky. Sunlight is penetrating shallow flats, perhaps to the first drop-off. The light levels at those depths fall within a range in which walleyes can prey effectively on available forage species. You suspect that fish activity is better at those levels—perhaps 10 to 20 feet—and shift your focus there. Livebait rigging, jigging, casting cranks—whatever—produces some nice fish from about 7:30 to 9:30 a.m. Then it's deadsville.

What happened? Similar deal. With the sun now well overhead, light is blasting down into the water, illuminating it so that minnows can see the approach of the nasty walleyes. Schools of minnows now flit and flee, no longer vulnerable in the semidarkness, where only an hour ago, walleyes pounced like silent ninjas out of the gloom. Theoretically, walleyes using these depths now settle into a resting, waiting, or unresponsive posture.

About this same time, though, walleyes lying in deeper water—say, 25 feet-plus—are finding the increased light level to their liking. They prowl the deep perimeters of midlake humps, or slash into suspended schools of ciscoes just above the thermocline. These deeper fish become active when shallow fish are likely to be unresponsive to your best efforts.

Lunchtime. Break out the sandwiches. Noon to about 4 p.m. can be notoriously difficult on many waters during summer, with the exception of a possible suspended bite. Better put on more sunscreen; those UV rays are really bearing down on both you and the fish. Seems like the fish went into hibernation. Perhaps the wind will come up to turn 'em on? Unfortunately, it doesn't.

Late afternoon: the sun dips toward the west. You bump into a flurry of fish on a deep hump or the tip of a deep point. Things are happening in reverse; the deeper fish are beginning to turn on again. You bide your time until prime time.

Suppertime. Are you going to leave the lake for a bite or stick it out till nightfall? Already, you've shifted your focus a bit shallower and have picked up a few more 'eyes along a deep weedline; coincidence or not, it was along the western shoreline, where a bit of shade is developing along the deep weedline. Can't leave now. Things are just starting to get good. Anyone have a candy bar?

About 8:30 p.m., fish are prowling the deep weededge in earnest. You're putting together a good catch—fish are obviously turning on.

An hour later, the setting sun is touching the tops of the trees, and the bite continues. But as it really gets dark, the weedline bite slows. What to do? Head for the shallows or the boat launch? Hey, one's right on the way to the other.

So you end the day as you began, longline trolling or casting the 5-foot depths. Walleyes have reactivated at those levels, finding light penetration—or lack thereof—to their liking. Minnows and perch are vulnerable in the darkness to walleyes with night vision and vibration-sensing capabilities of scary proportions.

About 11 p.m. It's time to head for the boat launch to get some sleep before prime time again at sunrise. Prime, at least, for shallow 'eyes. Deeper fish come later. To infinity, and beyond.

COVERING WATER—THE ODDS GAME

Talk to top anglers, and a common theme arises: to be successful, you must be efficient, presenting appropriate baits or lures in front of as many sizeable fish as possible during the course of the day. Maximizing potential bites generally triggers real ones. Time spent with lures or baits in the boat, in the air, or descending into the fish zone is time wasted. Time spent in the fish zone, however, converts efforts into results.

That shouldn't suggest, however, that you should never run around and look with your depthfinder; never cast; only troll, keeping your lure or bait in the water every possible instant. Exploring and casting are integral parts of fishing. Do as much looking as it takes to locate potential structure or fish, even if that means spending significant time without a lure in the water until you locate a suspended school of walleyes or fish lying off the tip of a point.

Cast where casting is the most logical and effective method or where trolling is difficult, impossible, or wasted effort. Just don't spend more time than necessary with lures out of the fish zone.

Fishing is a judgment call, and no two anglers do things exactly the same. Seldom is there only one way to catch fish. But the common theme is that whatever you do, do it as effectively and efficiently as possible to maximize your chances of success.

The concept of coverage is most obvious when trolling. This suggests effectively presenting as many lines and lures (or baits) as practical (or legal) in the fish zone for as many hours of the day as possible. When open water trolling, you need to truly saturate productive depths and areas with multiline setups of crankbaits, spinner harnesses, and/or spoons. You need to keep your baits in front of the eyes and noses of walleyes for every possible instant, not trolling out of the school and continuing onward for several miles of fishless water. Lures presented in fishless water aren't successful.

Pull baits or lures past enough fish, and some have to bite.

Precision Tactics

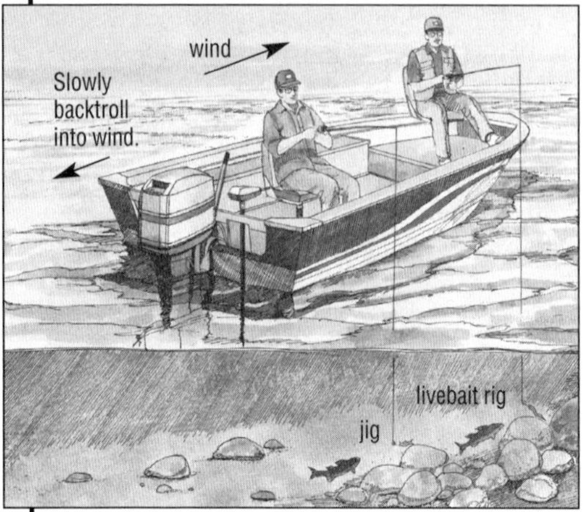

Vertical precision tactics probe the edges of distinctive structure to tempt fish to bite. Characteristics: slowness, finesse, frequent incorporation of livebait.

Coverage Techniques

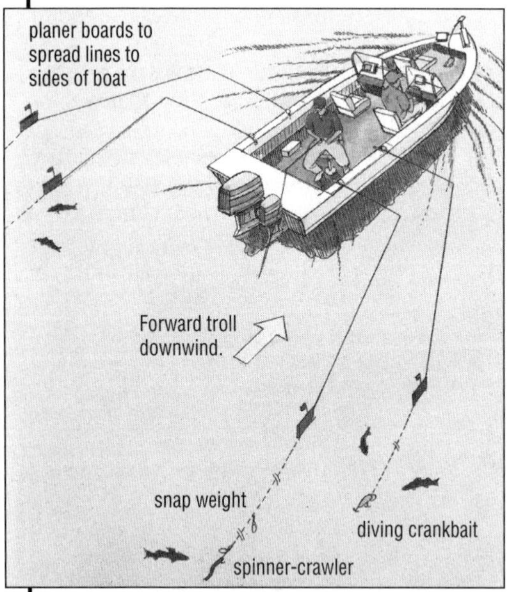

Horizontal coverage tactics strain large areas to contact fish that are suspended or spread across flats and basins. Characteristics: faster speeds to trigger strikes; less precision for small spots, though depth control has inherent precision.

When working a weededge, you need to keep jigs, crankbaits, or livebait rigs tickling the fringe. Minimize snagging while you rustle walleyes out of the leafy canopy. When livebait rigging the tip of a point, follow the lip of the drop-off around and through the school of walleyes lying there rather than meandering up and down at random depths, only occasionally passing through the level or location of the fish.

When fishing a river, you need to vertically jig along the edge of the eddy where calm meets swift water, where walleyes lie waiting for a passing meal. When casting a crankbait across the tops of weeds, wood, or rocks, you need to make occasional contact, caressing bottom or cover without frequent snagging.

Coverage is more than simply keeping lines or lures in the water. It's keeping appropriate baits in the fish zone as much as possible. It's easiest to understand when you're effectively trolling lures in relatively open water, because the lures or baits are down there working for you all or most of the time. When casting, some of the time your casts cover the water correctly and effectively. Then, unfortunately, you must reel up, recast, and reposition the lure or bait once again.

Casting is inherently not as efficient as trolling because of all the additional time required to get the lure or bait into and back from the fish zone. But if the sum total of those short intervals of proper coverage is well adapted to conditions, the results may be better than additional hours of trolling lures under less appropriate conditions.

To cast or to troll? Read the circumstances, predict fish location and activity based on the body of water, season, weather, time of day, cover (or absence of cover), depth, type (or lack) of structure, available forage, and a seemingly endless array of other factors. Then select an appropriate presentation, and either fine-tune it (if it's working), or switch to plan B, C, or D. The fish will tell you what works—and what doesn't. In summer, you can typically fish a little faster than in spring or fall, expanding your coverage by triggering strikes rather than tempting bites.

Tournament anglers have a set number of hours in which to determine and fine-tune patterns. By their own choice, they subject themselves to nervous tension and anxiety while the clock winds down. The recreational angler doesn't experience the same type or level of stress—unless, of course, he has only limited time or opportunity to fish, feels pressure to get his boat partners on fish, has a ton of yard work and projects to do back home, has dinner reservations with the family in a few short hours, or feels some other time constraint that puts a premium on time management and effective coverage.

Fishing is supposed to be fun, relaxing, an escape from reality, and treasured time spent in the majesty of the outdoors. The reality, however, is that usually some outside influence is conspiring to put a stop to your fishing. We're not suggesting that you run around like a madman and stress yourself trying to gain an extra three minutes of effective coverage in your fishing day. But don't squander your opportunities, either. A little extra coverage could mean one more bite. And that bite could be a big one.

MAKING CRITICAL CHOICES FOR WALLEYES

How many times have you fished the same rig or jig all day? How often have you used your favorite presentation instead of experimenting with one less practiced or less preferred? Have you ever felt lost on the water, unable to choose a proper approach?

Guilty on all counts? Through preference, sheer laziness, or lack of understanding or direction, you avoid making choices or make the wrong ones. Versatility can be a double-edged sword—you've got the luxury of choices, but with choices, but you still have to make them.

Among the armada of versatile anglers float those who have difficulty selecting the tactics to apply. They have all the recommended gear, but they can't put their myriad choices into practice. You can buy tools, but you can't buy the experience needed to use them.

BASIC GAME PLAN

Establishing successful fishing patterns is a process. Each time you fish, you run through a system of decisions: choosing a general area of a lake-river-reservoir, selecting appropriate seasonal habitat, determining how fish relate to it, choosing likely presentations and boat control based on fish position and mood, and then fine-tuning

or switching a presentation to maximize your catch. It's not leaving the dock with something tied on the end of your line and predetermining that you'll use it all day. Even if it was successful in the past, being flexible meanings being willing to change it when it isn't working. And that means catching more fish.

Veteran anglers make a series of choices without even realizing they're making them. Say you run the boat out to a midlake hump and tell your partner that you recommend a leech along the drop-off. Sounds like a basic plan, but many

Ten Generations of Fishing Decisions

Forget about the legendary six degrees of separation between every human on the planet. Here, with a quick sketch, we can easily depict ten generations of choices a fisherman goes through to match tactics to fish position and mood. For the sake of simplicity, we traced only 2 sets of either/or options through 10 generations of decisions. Had we filled out the entire chart, the tenth level would have shown 2^{10} choices—or 1,024 options, all told. Some of those options would have been good, others poor; some very good, others a total bust. Some tournament winners, others also-rans.

The scary thing is, our graphic depicts some relatively fundamental choices. Each level of choice was an either/or—only two choices. In reality, each step could have many more choices, each leading to further decisions and consequences. And we could have extended our number of generations well past 10.

For the jigging option, for example, we could have chosen between types and sizes of minnows, jigging motions, probing the weededge versus penetrating it, penetrating the edge slightly versus extensively, and so on.

Now consider how intimidating this decision process is for an inexperienced angler who tends to reach a point somewhere in the general ballpark and then leaves it at that. It's also easy to see why you can become totally lost when moving from a familiar body of water to one offering different habitats. If the fish are exhibiting totally different behavior, it becomes necessary to work down unfamiliar paths, using unfamiliar tackle.

While not meant to intimidate, this example sheds light on the thinking process successful anglers use. The further you proceed down the decision path, the more fish you'll catch.

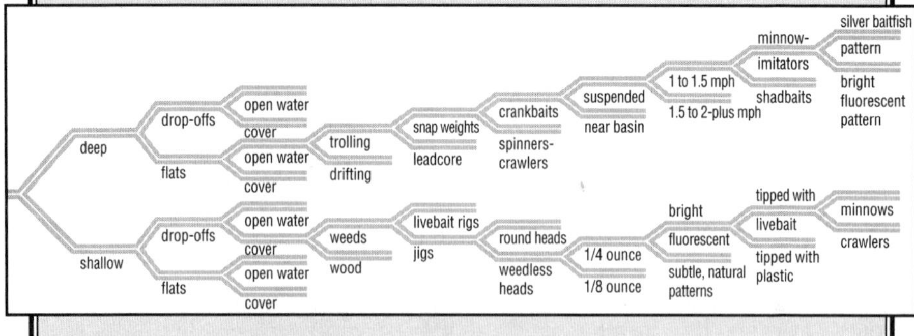

decisions were involved in deciding on that plan. Based on experience, you chose a basic area of the lake, a type of structure, a general depth range, a general presentation, and a type of livebait. Small leeches dictated small hooks and light line. The presentation dictated boat control—in this case, backtrolling. And backtrolling necessitated a slow presentation speed. Backtrolling tends to work best along drop-off edges, so you probably scouted drop-off edges with your depthfinder while probing different depths for the presence of fish.

This basic game plan set a flurry of actions and reactions cascading into motion. Once you contacted fish—or failed to contact them—other decisions needed to be made. Either you left the area, changed depth levels or type of cover, switched presentations, or fine-tuned a productive presentation.

These triggered even more choices: if you switched presentations, you were likely to try a different speed, such as spinner-rigging a nightcrawler (faster speed) behind a three-way rig or bottom bouncer, vertically jigging a jig-and-minnow (slow speed), vertically jigging a jigging spoon (more aggressive presentation), or something much faster, like trolling a crankbait.

Or, if your livebait rigging was productive, you may have elected to refine it by lengthening the snell, downsizing the hook, adding a colored float for attraction, keeping the bait slightly off bottom, switching to a colored hook, adding a colored bead, slowing down or speeding up, or switching to lighter line.

Say you switched to a spinner rig. That set a new series of choices into motion: trolling speed, sinker type and size, blade type and size, blade color, bead color and number, snell length, and hook size.

All these decisions without even switching spots! A simple change in presentation style set into motion a series of decisions and consequences that called for even further actions and reactions. Changing locations to another lake area, such as a weedbed, might require an entirely different presentation—maybe using a weedless jig tipped with a crawler, a minnow, or a plastic tail. If so, what size and color tail? How heavy a jighead? Was heavier line required to withstand the abuse of ripping weeds?

Considering how many choices an angler makes during a fishing day, most of those decisions are good, even though the opportunities for wrong choices are almost limitless. Opportunities are ample to be observant, to react, and to fine-tune—to respond a little better than the rest of the crowd.

Assembling a successful fishing pattern involves a series of choices. The average angler takes the process only so far. "We fished livebait rigs with leeches along the drop-offs of midlake humps, concentrating on fingers at the 25-foot level." Impressive? Compare that to a more refined and defined approach: "We began by livebait rigging jumbo leeches on 10-foot 4-pound snells, using #8 hooks and 1/4-ounce slipsinkers, lifting, pausing, then momentarily touching bottom without dragging and snagging as we backtrolled the 22- to 28-foot level along the edges of a series of midlake humps. We tempted a few walleyes at the base of the drop-off, where it changes to soft bottom at 32 feet, by spotting fish on our electronics, then hovering above them and sticking the bait in their faces.

Assembling a successful fishing pattern involves a series of choices. The average angler takes the process only so far.

"Once the wind came up, however, the fish seemed to come predominantly from small rocky patches at the inside corners of fingers along the north and northwest corners of the humps. They became more active, moving up onto humps to feed on perch. We switched to faster-moving #3 orange-chartreuse crawler harnesses

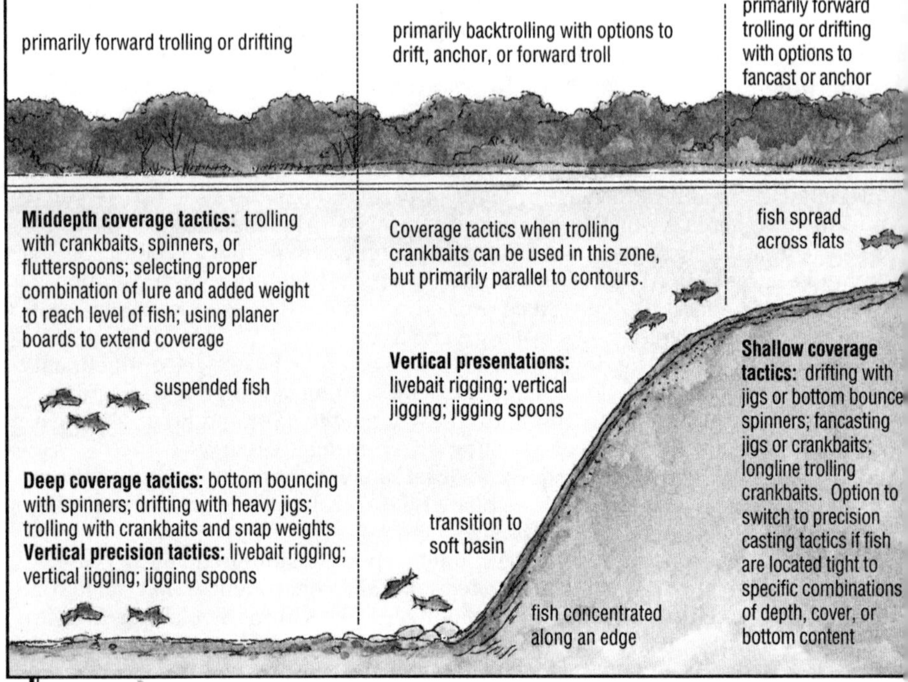

with Indiana blades and bottom bouncers to quickly work through groups of fish, triggering aggressive bites with a faster approach that worked more areas and caught more fish. We also tied into a few larger ones."

Both anglers did basically the same thing, but the second angler paid attention to subtleties and refined his approach throughout the day. Both left the dock in the morning with the same tackle, but angler number two aggressively sifted through the clues. Both caught fish. If this were a tournament, however, which angler would you bet on?

Certain basic principles apply in all conditions, but choice of presentation generally is a matter of edges versus flats, finesse versus covering water, and cover versus open water.

EDGES VERSUS FLATS

Distinct edges focus fish activity along precise, definable paths. Be it a drop-off, channel edge, weedline, or timberline, a distinct edge acts like a wall. Fish relating to the edge tend to tuck up tight to and along it. Presentations should therefore be parallel to the edge. Precision casting, drifting, backtrolling, or forward trolling places lures or lure-livebait combos exactly along or parallel to the path.

On irregular or indistinct edges, fish are more likely to spread out, particularly into adjacent cover or across areas of a gradual change in bottom, rather than

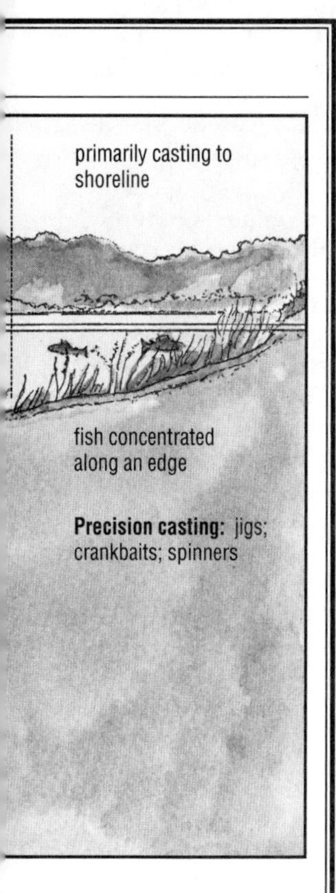

focusing along a line. Presentations should penetrate or span the general transition. A series of drifts or trolling passes along general depth levels or fancasting across areas of transition are more appropriate.

When fish are spread across flats, whether those are shallow food shelves or deep basins, they aren't focused along any distinctive wall-like edge. Tactics designed to cover large areas quickly are best: forward trolling with planer boards, a series of drift passes, or fancasting.

PRECISION VERSUS COVERAGE

Precision methods generally are slow and meticulous, geared to strain limited areas and to tempt fish to bite. Hovering or backtrolling with livebait rigs or jigs are precision tactics. Casting slipbobbers baited with livebait or casting and lift-dropping jigs toward targets like points, humps, or distinct areas of cover puts your offerings in likely spots long enough to provoke responses.

Coverage tactics sacrifice precision for working large areas quickly—longline trolling shallow flats with diving crankbaits, open water trolling crankbaits or spinners with planer boards, or a series of rapid drifts with bottom bouncers-spinners-crawlers along windswept shorelines. Many trolling tactics can closely regulate lure depth over even large areas. Still, they're more like a shotgun pattern aimed at a big target rather than a precise rifle shot directed at a discrete bull's-eye.

In between are presentations that offer varying degrees of precision and coverage. A bottom bouncer backtrolled along a dropoff typically provides more speed and coverage than a livebait rig, for example, though it may consequently be less precise. Casting and lift-dropping a jig to tempt biters is more precise than casting and ripping a jigging spoon to provoke strikes, although the jig requires more time to cover the same area. In general, livebait presentations tend to lean toward precision and finesse to entice bites, while artificials cover more area at increased speed to trigger strikes. Livebait-lure combos fall in between those two extremes. Each basic presentation offers its own unique blend of precision and coverage that must be matched to walleye location and behavior.

COVER VERSUS OPEN WATER

Cover like weeds, wood, boulders, and manmade structures attracts and holds predators and prey. Walleyes often relate to cover, if it's not too thick to prevent fish penetration and movement. Some cover, like rock, is relatively snag-free unless your lure becomes wedged between tiny cracks. Other cover, like weeds or wood, may require lure modifications—weedless jigs, for example—to permit penetrating and working the cover effectively without frequent snagging.

Fish position and aggressiveness determine fishing approach for walleyes in cover. Active fish along outer edges, near open pockets or lanes, or rising above cover are relatively easy to reach with a variety of presentations. But when they penetrate down into cover and are reluctant to bite, slow, meticulous, probing techniques like weedless jigs or slipbobbers and livebait may be necessary to elicit strikes. As weedgrowth changes throughout the year, so do the areas and patterns that fish use.

If walleye anglers have a common weakness, it's their reluctance to probe cover with snag-resistant techniques. They're more comfortable covering deep open water areas where they can spot fish on electronics, determine their depth and orientation to structure, and employ a variety of traditional methods without excess snagging and frustration. Yet in many environments, cover plays an important part in a walleye's life, at least part of the year, and it must be dealt with.

Fish suspended in open water or using traditional deep structure—drop-offs, points, humps—are easier to locate than fish in cover. They're visible on sonar, instead of having to be searched for with hook and line. Also, open water offers fewer restrictions in presentation because of fewer snags. In fact, almost any walleye presentation at times can be productive in open water: livebait rigging, vertical jigging with jigs, jigging spoons, or bladebaits, bottom bouncing with spinners-crawlers, trolling for suspended fish with crankbaits, flutterspoons, or spinner-crawler harnesses, and drifting and casting. This is classic walleye fishing at its best.

Just because fish can be easily reached doesn't make them easy to catch, however. You need to evaluate their position and mood in relation to structure—or lack of it—and to match presentation to their degree of aggressiveness.

POSITION AND MOOD

Walleye position and mood can run the gamut from easy-to-reach aggressive fish in open water, which will strike anything put near them, to hard-to-reach unwilling biters buried in weed or woodcover, to just about any fish in between. Walleyes can remain in the same area all day, but their position in relation to cover or other surroundings may change slightly based on feeding mood and aggressiveness. Thus you never can be sure of what you'll face until you probe likely areas and evaluate fish response.

Mood Determines Position

Fish mood determines fish position relative to structure, which in turn determines bait choices.

In general, walleyes holding along edges of cover are relatively aggressive. Those patrolling just outside the edges of cover in search of meals are quite catchable. Fish resting a few feet within the edge, meanwhile, may be less willing to chase a bait. They're all referred to as *edge fish*. Different edge techniques apply to different cover conditions and fish responses. Aggressive biters fall to parallel presentations like livebait rigs, while less aggressive walleyes may require probing into the edge and down toward bottom with jigs. If the cover's too thick for an exposed hook, switch to a weedless version. Fine-tune as required.

Walleyes that penetrate far up into weed- or wood-cover tend to be inactive when they're not feeding aggressively. Yet as they move out to the edges of open pockets or lanes, they typically become more aggressive. Where cover is uniformly thick, the most active fish often are above the tops of the cover. Longline trolling a Rapala Minnow above weed tops at night is a great pattern for active fish, while probing down into the weed clumps with a jig may catch less active walleyes during the day.

Out in open water, away from cover, walleyes often display varying degrees of aggressiveness. For example, fish you spot on electronics a few feet off bottom are probably a bit more aggressive than those lying belly to bottom—but that's only a generalization. Suspended walleyes may be in any attitude, from attack mode to ignoring your best efforts. No rule of thumb exists, except that fish rising higher in the water column during the day usually are becoming more active.

With no obvious indicator of fish activity, you should begin with a technique tailored to the area . . . then move through a spectrum of presentations that offer different combinations of speed and attraction.

With no obvious indicator of fish activity, you should begin with a technique tailored to the area—an edge or a flat, with or without cover—then move through a spectrum of presentations that offer different combinations of speed and attraction.

THE ONE-TWO PUNCH

Theory must be put into practice. Once you understand how certain conditions suggest corresponding presentations, you can begin responding with likely options. At the very least, inappropriate techniques can be eliminated.

We'll call this process the one-two punch, but the truth is, it's more like a 1-2-3-4-5-6 repertoire of punches that match the many positions and moods of the fish. The trick is to carry several prerigged rods that can cover a range of speeds and depths. Then, when your instincts tell you to switch presentations, simply reel up, switch rods, and drop another line without wasting time digging through tackle boxes and re-rigging lines. The easier switching is, the more likely you'll be to do it.

Example #1—The example we discussed earlier incorporated livebait rigging leeches on a midlake hump. Livebait rigging was an obvious first choice, because it's a precision method for fishing vertically along the edge of a drop-off. Drop-offs form vertical walls that tend to stack fish in limited areas. Once the tactic was established as productive, the approach was fine-tuned with long, light-weight snells.

The angler was also prepared to use a spinner snell to present livebait in tandem with a bottom bouncer. This aggressive technique covered water quicker, using increased speed as a trigger. Once this presentation showed that it worked, the angler fine-tuned blade size and color to increase his catch.

Fine-tuning Presentations

Frosting on the cake. Tinsel on the tree. Spinner blade color and size. It's easy for a spectator to see the surface, the final touches on a masterpiece of creativity and productivity. But it's harder to visualize all the effort and talent that go into constructing the foundation and framework supporting the end result. And even harder to construct the recipe from scratch unless you're a talented chef. Most folks would prefer a quick microwave meal, but it's seldom that easy.

Basic correct systems catch fish; refinements catch more and bigger fish. This example traces decisions several steps beyond the 10 described earlier.

Note several differences: first, we start branching out of *either/or* choices into areas with more options, such as spinner size, color, shape, line length, snap weight and size, and the combination of line length, trolling speed,

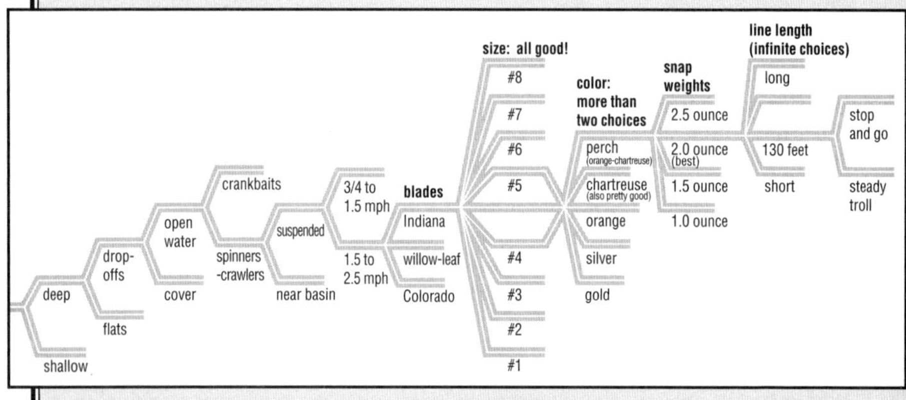

Livebait rigs in tandem with spinners are an excellent one-two punch for drop-offs in summer. Had the angler been rigged for any condition, he might have carried additional rods baited with heavy jigs or jigging spoons for vertical jigging, and a trolling rod teamed with a crankbait and snap weights to troll a lure along the drop-off edge and adjacent open basin. A 1-2-3-4 punch that could be fine-tuned once the most productive tactics were determined.

Example #2—Let's put our angler on a river stretch below a power dam in late spring. His basic strategy here is to fish current breaks formed by obstructions that divert the flow in 6 to 25 feet of water. We know from experience that this is an excellent starting strategy. Now he must actually fish to determine what refinements work best.

His first lure is a jig-and-minnow vertically jigged while he slips downstream along visible current breaks, lifting and dropping the jig slightly off bottom. Need a more aggressive tactic to trigger strikes? How about a jigging spoon, snapped up and fluttered down in the same area? Need a slower and more meticulous presentation? Try a three-way rig baited with a live minnow, fished at anchor or while hovering, to appeal more to nonaggressive walleyes. Three rods rigged for these weight, and boat control to reach the correct depth while imparting a productive lure action. Whew! A mouthful . . . and a mindful.

Fact is, a good angler subconsciously makes the first half of those decisions in perhaps a few minutes. At some point, however, choices cease being so obvious, and it becomes necessary to physically work through the options to progress further. Each step is still a step, but no one could equate the last few steps necessary to reach the top of Mt. Everest with the leisurely stroll at the beginning of the expedition. It becomes progressively harder to reach the next level of refinement. But that's what must be done.

Don't become too enamored with the trimmings until you have a system in place to incorporate them. Frosting's nice. Ever eat a whole bowlful? Quickly loses its appeal without the cake. So does a perch-pattern spinner harness fished in the wrong location.

options pretty well cover the basics and can be fine-tuned from there.

Unless, of course, high water has pushed walleyes into flooded cover like brush or fallen trees. Such conditions call for a weedless jig, spinnerbait, or even a slipbobber rig to penetrate shoreline current breaks. For walleyes atop wing dams, midriver shoals, or rock points, casting a diving crankbait across the tops of the rocks might be a better option. You don't know till you try, but at least you're prepared to experiment with a range of presentation styles. You'll do whatever it takes.

Let's see, that'd be a 1-2-3-4-5-6-7 punch. Water level, the location of current breaks, plus fish position and mood determine what produces best.

Example #3—Reservoir walleyes along main lake points in summer. In this scenario, walleyes may be up shallow under mudlines, relating to drop-offs at the ends of prominent points, cruising atop points, or spread out along adjacent shoreline. They're probably also relating to wind. They may be down the drop-off edge, at the bases of prominent points (if they're not too deep), or suspended off the edge. That's a depth range from inches to over 50 feet of water.

No way you can do it all with one lure. But with your several prerigged rods and your willingness to change lures and experiment throughout the day, you can match the position and mood of walleyes from precision-finesse tactics to aggressive coverage.

For shallow fish, cast a jig or diving crankbait to shore or drift or forward troll a bottom bouncer-spinner-crawler through shallow water parallel to shore. Shoreline fish call for the same bouncer-spinner tactics. Or try longline trolling diving crankbaits, using planer boards to run the baits up shallow to avoid spooking fish with your boat. For aggressive fish atop sprawling points, cast if they're shallow (less than 5 feet) or troll some of the previous options for walleyes from about 5 to 20 feet deep.

Tips of points and down their drop-off edges are classic wall-like formations that stack fish. These are excellent opportunities for vertical finesse tactics like livebait rigging, jigging, or jigging spoons. If the fish don't respond, consider contour trolling diving crankbaits tight along the edges of prominent structures and the shoreline drop-offs between them. Add snap weights to reach deeper than 20 feet. Planer boards are optional.

For fish suspended in open water outside prominent points, use similar crankbait-trolling tactics, adding planer boards to cut a wide swath through open water. Experiment with depth, speed, crankbait style, and color pattern.

How many punches was that? A whole buncha' punches thrown in differing combinations.

Each of these examples has described a different structural condition and called for a different adaptation to match fish position and mood. But the principle was the same in all cases: choice of presentation was dictated by local condition. If necessary, use a spectrum of presentations. Once you're in the ball park, fine-tune with color, size, and shape.

REACT AND ADAPT TO BUILD SUCCESS

Imagine a quarterback or golfer who didn't compensate for wind. Or a pitcher whose curveball wasn't working but who decided to throw it anyway. Or a hunter who hunted all day where the game used to be. Doesn't matter how sharp your knife is if you bring it to a gunfight; doesn't matter how good a jig fisherman you are if the fish are suspended and hitting trolled crankbaits.

Presentation Spectrum

Different presentations have inherent blends of characteristics. Some cover water quickly, while others strain small spots where fish concentrate along edges or within distinct spots. Some extract fish from cover; others excel in open water. Tactics for triggering strikes typically incorporate higher speeds, while those used to entice bites from fussy fish often call for livebait presented at slow crawl.

Some presentations are limited in scope and are applied strictly to certain speed ranges and small areas: slipbobbers fished in and around cover at minimal speed, for example. Others require minimal speed to make lures work properly, like trolled spinners or crankbaits.

Method	Precision vs. Coverage	Cover vs. Open Water	Mood Appeal
livebait rigging	precision	open water	passive
vertical jigging	precision	both	all
casting jigs	both	both	all
jigging spoons	coverage	both	aggressive
three-way rigs-livebait	precision	open water	passive
bottom bouncers-spinners	coverage	open water	aggressive
crankbait trolling	coverage	open water	all
crankbait casting	coverage	open water	all
suspended spinner trolling	coverage	open water	passive
slipbobbers-livebait	precision	cover	passive

And no amount of talent and skill can catch fish that aren't there.

Situations above the water are easy for you to recognize and adapt to. The underwater world, however, remains pretty much of a mystery. We are visually oriented creatures prone to go through the motions without adapting whenever we can't see what we're facing. The common perception in fishing failure is that the fish aren't biting, not that we're fishing incorrectly. Thus a veteran angler may continue fishing the same way all day quite unsuccessfully, while a beginner with no preconceived notions may switch lures or baits and chance upon something that works.

Use your experience to select likely lake areas, presentations, and boat control. Start simple, and don't worry at first about fine-tuning with things like snell length or spinner color. If your initial presentation doesn't work, switch to another. When you hit on something that does work, begin fine-tuning. Don't add the tinsel until you set up the tree. Once you're on the right track, fishing with an effective method, you can use refinements to catch more and bigger fish.

Still others work at a wide range of speeds, such as jigs, which excel everywhere from motionless to subtle hopping to snapjigging.

Prerig several rods with systems appropriate to the lake, river, or reservoir you plan to fish. We suggest one precision-finesse system, one coverage system, and perhaps a third with characteristics of each. Then fish several likely areas to judge fish response. Once you determine that a certain presentation is working, begin fine-tuning it with modifications in sight (profile, color, flash, action), sound (vibration), or scent (livebait), or try refinements in the system itself, like switching to lighter line, smaller hooks, added weight to achieve better depth or control. Try speeding up or slowing down your coverage. But don't place too much faith in little things like color pattern or scent until you have the basic system in place. Appropriate systems catch fish; after that, refinements catch more and bigger fish.

Good, Bad, Ugly

MATCHING TACTICS TO FISH LOCATION, POSITION, AND ACTIVITY

Most anglers, like people in general, prefer simple choices and options, instead of complex patterns and intriguing decisions. Thus wouldn't it be nice if all the walleyes in a lake inhabited the same depth on the same type of structure, biting on the same thing? All you'd need is one kind of bait or lure, one rod, and a treasure map with a big X indicating walleye location. You'd simply go out after a leisurely breakfast, dip into the pot of gold, and be back in time for an afternoon nap.

Such easy pickin's, however, might get kind of boring after catching the first 10,000 or so fish. Fortunately, Mother Nature in her infinite wisdom has made the aquatic puzzle significantly more complex and varied—particularly during the summer season.

The warmwater environment of summer typically offers fish many habitat and feeding options. Every element of the food chain is in high gear, from the lowliest plankton to the largest predator. With such abundance, walleyes and other gamefish don't need to expend much energy chasing food. Rather, they time or match their activities to periods of peak feeding opportunity.

Because summer is a time of relative environmental stability, fish behave predictably for long periods.

Because summer is a time of relative environmental stability, fish behave predictably for long periods. Their activity is triggered chiefly by changing weather or light levels. Brief but intense feeding periods are the rule, but not all fish feed at the same time.

For example, walleyes enjoy an advantage in vision over prey during low-light periods, as well as throughout the night. Thus they may remain fairly inactive through long periods of the day, then burst into sudden activity when easy opportunities arrive with dusk. Similarly, when wind cuts light penetration and roils the water, disorienting schools of baitfish, walleyes may quickly zero in on the foodfest, picking up telltale vibrations of vulnerable forage via their highly sensitive lateral lines.

While the combination of habitat options varies from lake to lake, they share this simultaneity of multiple patterns, ranging from shallow to deep, from structure to open water. Different groups typically become active at different times, with light levels being the chief factor. As a general rule, the deepest groups become most active at midday. Fishing deep structure, trolling open water or basins, or fishing the deep edges of cover thus becomes a high-percentage tactic for the most active fish. At the opposite extreme, the shallowest groups of walleyes typically become most active during windy conditions, on dark days, during low-light conditions, or at night. That's when fishing shallow, either by casting or longline trolling, tends to excel. Probing weeds, fishing timber or brush, working inlets, trolling shallow flats, and trying other shallow options offer good potential opportunities for walleyes.

While these are usually sensible tactics, there are always exceptions. The darker and more fertile the water, for example, in prairie lakes or farm country waters, the shallower that walleyes are likely to live. In such waters, it's common to catch fish by flippin' jigs or casting crankbaits in less than 5 feet of water, even on calm, sunny days. And in clear reservoirs, walleyes inhabiting deep water during calm conditions may immediately move up into inches of water when sudden winds generate mudlines along shore, creating brief but superb feeding opportunities. Same thing for deep Canadian lakes, where walleyes move shallow to forage atop rock reefs when the time is ripe. Walleyes—and good anglers—automatically react to changing conditions.

There are many ways to catch walleyes during summer, though not all ways are equally good on all waters, nor are they equally productive throughout the day. Location and type of forage, presence or absence of cover, water clarity and structural layout combine to determine where walleyes may be. Once you get a handle on the different patterns, the quicker and better you react to changing weather and light levels, and the more fish you'll catch. This often demands extreme versatility—you need to be able to fish effectively from the shallowest cover to the deepest structure. The better you apply your experience and skills, the more consistent your catch.

So, in the end, you have many options, many choices, and a plethora of potential results ranging from ecstatic excitement to bite-free blues. No way you're gonna win all the time. But if you're a sharp angler, the empty-net syndrome shouldn't strike too often. Most of the time, action will fall somewhere in the middle, with the high side of average a realistic goal. Or course, the more experienced and versatile you become, the higher you raise the bar, with your typical day on the water marked by more successes than failures, more significants than cigars.

The following presentations and patterns are successful walleye patterns from a wide range of waters. Some can be considered good, strong, or classic fishing patterns that make perfect sense on a variety of waters. Others might at first appear odd or even bad choices until you consider all the environmental factors involved. Still others seem to fly in the face of all logic and are downright ugly—until you start catching fish on them. At that point, if they work, swallow your pride and set the hook. Whatever works, works. Anything goes for walleyes.

This chapter, and the following two, examine examples from each group—the good, the bad, and the ugly—and show how the correct combination of elements is assembled to produce fish-catching patterns. Remember, presentations don't have to be pretty to catch fish. Beauty's only skin deep, and during tough times, you sometimes must get downright ugly and do whatever it takes to catch fish.

Let's begin with "The Good"—things that logically maximize odds or match the mood of the fish.

DEAD IN THE WATER

A dead stick is:
   1. *what your dog chases.*
   2. *the fishing rod your partner stepped on.*
   3. *your unemployed brother-in-law.*
   4. *none of the above.*

The correct answer is *4, none of the above.* In fishing jargon, a dead stick is a second or third rod you're legally allowed to fish with in most (but not all) states and provinces. Most folks, not being ambidextrous, put the second or third rod in a rod holder in hope that a fish may grab on.

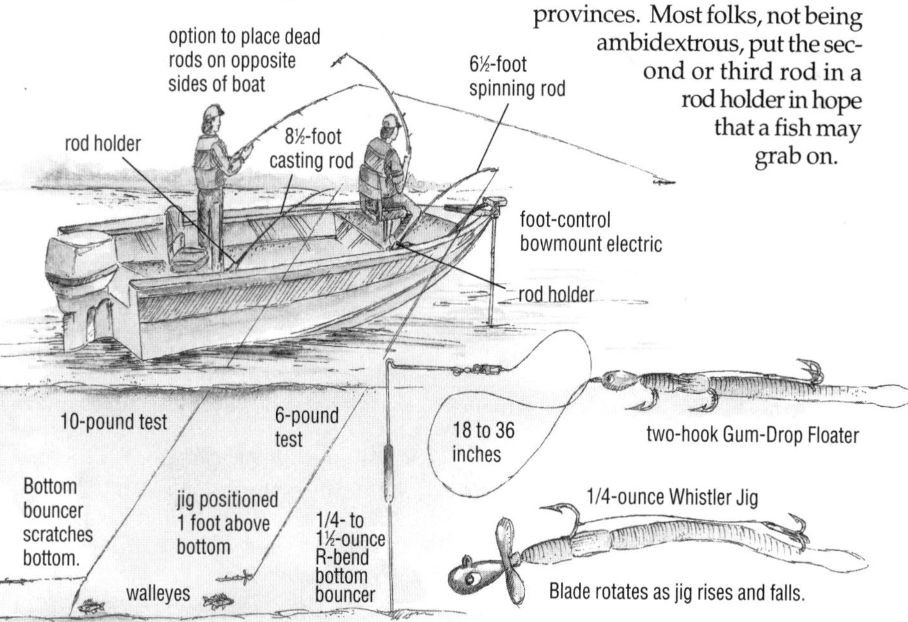

Many people don't view deadsticking as an important or even legitimate technique. Whaddaya mean, bonus or suicidal fish don't count? They sure do. Deadsticking is, in fact, a legitimate and important system, not just a use for a rod you're tired of holding.

DEAD OR ALIVE?

Have you ever seen a walleye angler operating a bowmount trolling motor while holding a rod in each hand? These are often called live sticks. Some tournament anglers are coordinated enough to make two-fisted angling an art form. Have you ever tried jigging two rods at the same time for an hour or two? Some anglers find that when they set one of the rods in a holder and leave it alone, they catch a fish on it. The second live stick became effective only when transformed into a dead stick. This is particularly true any time walleyes prefer a bait presented in a natural manner instead of in the pattern imparted by retrieving or jigging.

Using a dead stick also allows you to cast a lure on one rod while drifting or trolling another, thereby combining the best of both worlds—simultaneously checking shallow and deep water or presenting a variety of lures.

Using a dead stick also allows you to cast a lure on one rod while drifting or trolling another, thereby combining the best of both worlds—simultaneously checking shallow and deep water or presenting a variety of lures. Even if you're not catching fish on the cast, you can often see walleyes following your lure or bait to the boat. When they notice the natural-appearing bait on the dead rod, they grab the free meal.

DEADLY DOUBLE

Professional walleye angler Tom Johnson uses two dead stick combinations that are particularly deadly on walleyes. One incorporates a 1/4- to 1½-ounce bottom bouncer with an R-bend to the angled wire arm. He experiences fewer line tangles with this style of bouncer while obtaining the rocking motion a fixed-arm bouncer imparts to the bait. Even subtle changes in speed and direction trigger fish.

"Tie a snell to the bouncer with a Northland Gum-Drop Floater—a single-hook version for a leech or minnow, a double-hook model for a nightcrawler. If the crawler's tail is being bitten off by fish that hold, then drop the bait, I tie a stinger hook behind the second hook of the floater, for a total of three. A small, lightweight treble like a #12 Eagle Claw #L754 Featherlite minimizes any loss of bait action.

"Use 10-pound-test Trilene Ultra Thin on both the main line and the leader—it's heavy enough not to break too quickly when snagged, allowing a little time to move the boat back to the snag, grasp the line, and try to pull it free. Also, deadsticking provides surprisingly big walleyes, and 10-pound line provides a little cushion when a hooked big fish suddenly pulls against the drag while the rod's in the holder. Use about 18 to 30 inches of leader, because anything longer tends to tangle on tight turns."

Use a long, medium-action rod to prevent tangling lines on tight turns, to impart a natural pulsing motion to the livebait every time the bouncer touches and hangs, and to avoid spooking fish when they bite. A rod must give sufficiently to let the fish grasp the bait without feeling resistance and spooking. Using rods that are too stiff alerts the fish, and it often drops the bait. Johnson's favorite combo for this approach is an 8- or 8½-foot, medium-heavy Eagle Claw Crosswings casting rod with an Abu-Garcia 5500 C-3 reel.

His second-favorite dead stick tactic involves spinning equipment and lighter line to present a jig—an often-overlooked technique. "Spool 6-pound test on a spinning reel and 6½-foot spinning rod, and attach a 1/8- or 1/4-ounce Whistler Jig," Johnson says. "A propeller near the eye spins easily as the boat moves, imparting flash, vibration, and action. Keep the bait fairly vertical. Don't fish the jig on bottom. Keep it about 1 foot above bottom, letting it rise and fall, flash and spin, as the boat rocks in waves." Johnson's favorite jig colors are chartreuse, gold, and silver.

The Whistler's single hook is designed to be fished with a minnow, leech, or half crawler. But the hook is long enough for adding a plastic or Power Bait Grub, which often adds to the productivity of the jig and livebait. When using a half crawler, thread the broken end on first, with a small piece protruding past the end of the hook. When fishing a whole crawler, add a small stinger hook to the jig and insert the stinger near the crawler's tail. Use light line like 6-pound test, with a small, lightweight treble—#12, #14, or even #16.

Dead stick walleyes aren't accidental fish. Deadsticking is a deadly tactic that at times can outproduce more aggressive tactics, and at the very least, can add to your catch. Just watch for the rod to bend, then slowly and gingerly take it out of the rod holder, and gently sweep forward to make sure the walleye gets the point. The 'eyes will do the rest.

DOUBLE VISION—
THOSE RASCALLY RIVER RIGS

Popular on the Iowa section of the Mississippi River, the Dubuque Rig is a one-line, two-lure presentation incorporating a heavy jig to maintain bottom contact in strong current, plus a trailer hook with livebait or a plastic tail that dances in current. Walleye pro Chris Gilman used it in a classic manner to win a PWT tournament at Dubuque, where he fished along the front face of a closing dam, lifting the jig on and off bottom while brushing the front (upcurrent) face of the rocks with the trailer, then trolling upstream along the adjacent shoreline.

Walleye pro Mark Martin finished second in the same event, combining the heavy-weight two-leader principle of handlining the swift Detroit and St. Clair Rivers in Michigan with rod-and-reel trolling to ply the strong springtime current. Rather than handlining a 1- to 1½-pound weight, however, he used a 5-ounce drop-weight on heavy casting tackle to maintain

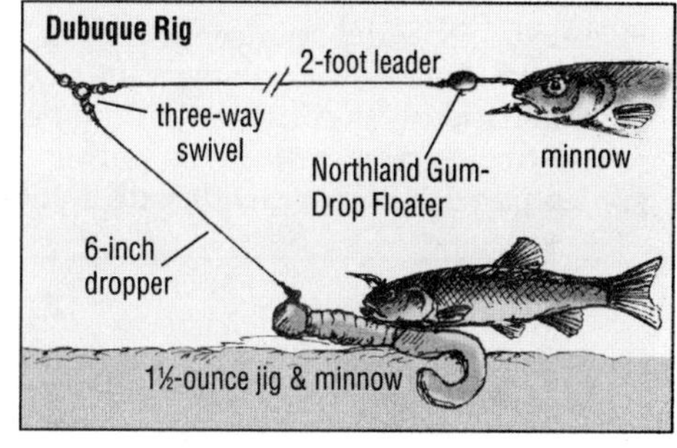

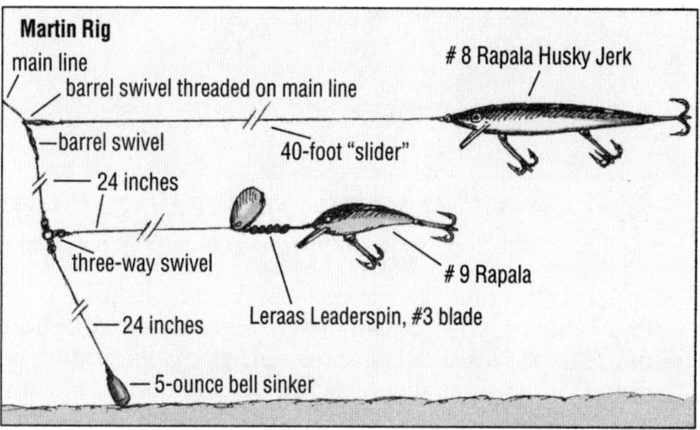

bottom contact while trolling slowly upstream with his kicker outboard. His 20/8 FireLine enabled him to pull the rig free from snags and minimize cutoffs from zebra mussels.

Martin simultaneously trolled two crankbaits on individual leaders. He presented the lower Rapala on a classic three-way rig, sometimes adding a 6-inch Leraas Tackle Leaderspin ahead of the crankbait to deflect snags and prevent fouling with floating debris. He trolled the upper lure, a Rapala Husky Jerk, in a unique fashion—on a 40-foot "slider" held 2 feet above the lower lure by an in-line barrel swivel.

At the beginning of his trolling passes, Martin fed out the long line and dropback lure behind the boat, then lowered the weight and three-way rig into the water. Water resistance caused the long leader to slide down the main line until the two barrel swivels made contact, positioning the dropback lure 40 feet behind the swivels, near bottom. While lifting the sinker on and off bottom, he used his TR-1 AutoPilot to slowly troll contours along the current-deflecting tips of small shoreline points. When a strike occurred on the long leader, he reeled up until the swivels were within reach, then grasped this line and hand-over-handed the fish for the last 40 feet.

Martin claimed that the extreme difference in leader lengths caused the lure on the long line to swing farther out to the sides on turns, covering a different path than the front lure. Establishing the proper combination of leader length, weight, and trolling speed was critical to handle the strong current and to trigger strikes from reluctant fish. Best colors were chartreuse, gold, or orange for added visibility in dirty water.

During the same event, several contestants trolled Bellevue Rigs—two in-line crankbaits attached nose to tail by a 1- to 2-foot leader. Presented on either three-way rigs or bottom bouncers, Bellevue Rigs offer a double shot at fish while creating the illusion of schooling baitfish.

Refinements in presentation can pay big dividends. In some cases, finding ways to present more lures or baits effectively within a limited area, not just by spreading them far and wide with planer boards, can vastly improve your catch.

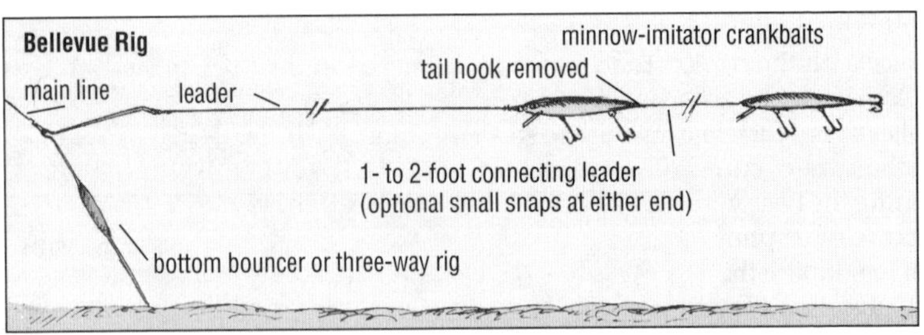

CASTAWAY TACTICS FOR
TAILWATER WALLEYES

Vertical jigging has always been the classic approach for river walleyes in winter, particularly in tailwaters, where the fish concentrate in deep holes or along main channel breaks. When feeding time rolls around, walleyes slip up the dropoff to the top of the hole or across the breakline onto adjacent flats. Perfect conditions for vertical jigging.

With ever-increasing pressure, the first few drifts of the morning usually produce fish. But after an hour or two of vertical jigging, the bigger fish seem to shut off, leaving only the smaller cigars. On some days, especially bright, sunny ones with high pressure following cold fronts, vertical jigging produces few decent fish at all.

Glenn Marshall, former In-Fisherman PWT pro and Mississippi River veteran from Rochester, Minnesota, several years ago experienced morning success on his first two or three drifts, followed by big fish shutting off. "I knew they were still there," Marshall says, "because I was marking fish on electronics and occasionally would foul-hook one. That's when I realized the fish were responding to fishing pressure.

"With the water clear in winter and bright sunlight penetrating the water more as the day wore on," Marshall recalls, "I realized that fish were reacting to the boat passing directly over them." To combat the situation, Marshall experimented with dragging the jig well behind the boat, both down- and upstream. Same result, with a few more jigs lost to snags. Wrong answer. Then livebait rigging with Lindy Rigs produced a few fish, but that still wasn't the optimal solution.

These presentations all involved positioning the boat over the fish. What about positioning the boat over the deep hole or river channel, casting up onto the flat, and then working the jig or Lindy Rig across it and down the break? That was the answer.

In a crowd, boat positioning turned out to be the major key to successful presentation. Too close to the break for too long, and you either spook the fish out of the area or shut them down. Too far from the break, and you lose control and feel of the jig.

THE MARSHALL PLAN

Start by positioning the boat with the bow facing the current, perhaps 5 to 10 feet from where the base of the break meets the deeper channel. This provides ample opportunity to work the first 5 to 10 feet atop the break, down the drop-off, and onto the flat at the bottom of the break—all in one cast.

Cast perpendicularly to the break and leave your spinning reel bail open, allowing the jig to drop straight down instead of swinging it pendulum-style toward the boat. Count the lure down—*one thousand, two thousand*—to determine how deep you're working.

When the jig reaches bottom and your line goes slack, engage your reel and allow it to rest motionless a few seconds. This sometimes triggers strikes. Keep your rod tip pointed at the jig. Then tighten slack and pop the rod tip up to 11 o'clock. The jig simultaneously glides toward the boat and quarters across the flat in the current. Allow the jig to come to a rest for a few seconds, then repeat the sequence.

After three or four pops, the jig begins working its way down the drop-off. You'll notice the lure sinking more than previously. When this happens, shorten the distance of your pops by half to work the break more slowly and effectively.

When your jig reaches the bottom of the break, work it back to the boat in traditional lift-drop fashion until it's almost directly downstream from the boat. Then reel in and repeat. Vary your retrieve by shortening hops or aggressively ripping the jig. Let the fish determine the most productive action.

Castaway 'Eyes

Active river walleyes, particularly larger walleyes, may at times move shallower than most anglers think. Shallow fish, however, are prone to spooking by boat traffic or overhead presentations. Casting a jig to the fish alleviates much of the spooking.

Position your boat 5 to 10 feet off the base of the break, using your trolling motor to hover in current. Cast onto the flat, allowing your jig to reach bottom. Subsequent hops and pauses quarter the lure downstream across, down the drop-off, and behind the boat. Once you thoroughly cover an area, slide slightly downstream and repeat the process.

In winter, shallow eddy areas and shoreline flats sometimes freeze over at night, preventing the early morning brigade from fishing them immediately. Later, sun melts and opens the canopy, allowing you to reach previously untouched fish with a subtle long-distance cast.

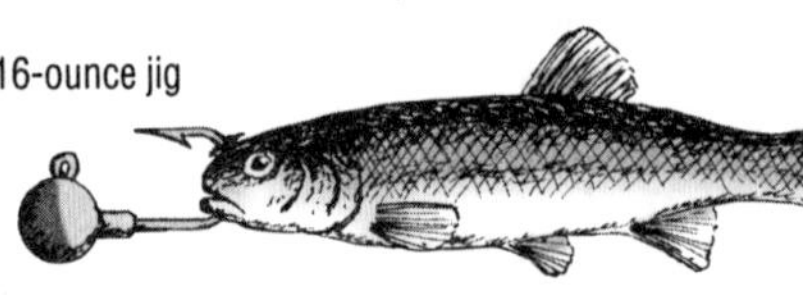

When casting, try to avoid adding a stinger hook to minimize snagging, unless one is necessary to hook reluctant biters. Stingers typically are more effective for vertical jigging.

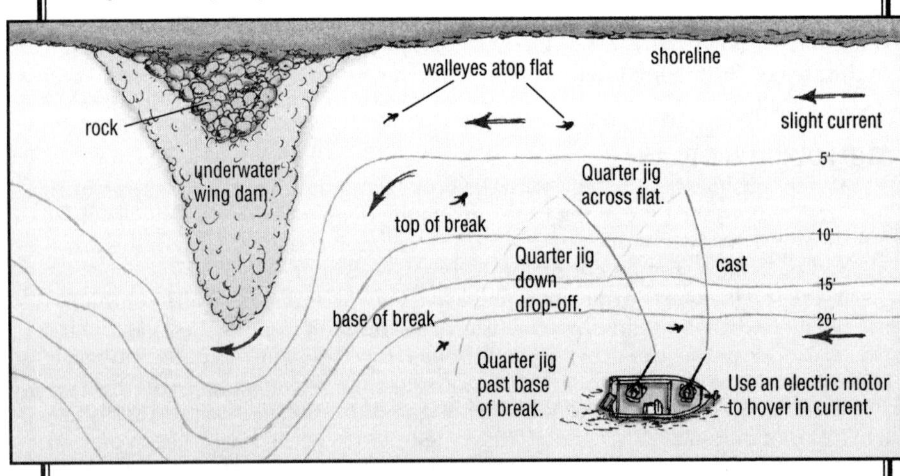

Use your electric motor to maintain the boat in one position until you've thoroughly worked the area. Then slip downstream 5 to 10 feet, hover, and repeat the process. But don't beat a dead horse; keep moving until you locate fish. Where there's one, there should be more. Go back and rework areas that were hot earlier and have now been undisturbed for a few hours. Often they become recharged with more fish.

Use a 6- to 7-foot, high-modulus graphite spinning rod with a moderately fast tip. Four- to 6-pound, high-visibility monofilament like Berkley Trilene XT Solar is a must, because most hits appear only as slight twitches in the line rather than being felt. High-vis line also allows you to work the break better. And polarized sunglasses make the line easier to watch.

The lighter the jig, the better it is for working shallow water atop flats, within eddies, or near the front faces of wing dams. Remember, pressured fish are likely to have been bombarded by 3/8- to as heavy as 1-ounce jigs. Where current is slack or slight, 1/16- to 1/4- ounce jigs tipped with minnows usually do the trick. Marshall's confidence colors are chartreuse, glow, and gold. You may prefer orange or pink. Whatever works.

As with all presentations, casting light jigs in river current takes practice. Once you learn it, though, the results are amazing—especially all those 6- to 10-pounders you've been missing.

TUMBLING PLASTICS WITH THE CURRENT

The old *Outer Limits* television show comes to mind, with its intro proclaiming you are about to lose control of your TV set: "We control the horizontal. We control the vertical." After that, you just sat back for the next hour and took a wild ride wherever "they" decided to take you. You trusted that something good would come out of the deal/ordeal, even though, quite frankly, nobody likes giving up that much control—unless you enjoy entrusting your fate and survival to questionable dynamics, like roller coasters or bungee jumping.

Here we offer a similar prospect for veteran river anglers who take pride in their ability to control lures and interpret light bites and bottom changes. Take it on faith when we ask you to give up control, sacrifice sensation, abandon your livebait, and go with the flow. Stay with us at least long enough to experiment with tumbling plastics for walleyes in current—an unexpected deviation from traditional river walleye tactics.

TUMBLING, NOT FUMBLING

Larry Erickson finished first in the amateur division of a major spring Mississippi River walleye tournament by using lightweight jigs and plastic worms—no livebait. While many considered his victory an aberration from accepted walleye methods, it left many others wondering exactly what he'd done to outdistance the field under such difficult conditions. The essence of his formula:

plastics + light jigs + slow movement = coldwater river walleyes

The formula works best in current, but it has potential in lakes and reservoirs as well. In rivers, however, walleyes tend to feed more aggressively, because current allows a smaller window of opportunity for them to examine passing food. If something passes by with the current in a natural fashion, a walleye's likely to pounce on it—even plastic. In lakes, jigs tipped with livebait may be more productive.

While many types of plastic tails have the potential to work, PWT pro Bill Koval, like Erickson, prefers Guido Ringworms or similar tails with ribbed bodies for

Gettin' Drastic with Plastic

The most common way to tumble lightweight plastic jigworms is to anchor in light to moderate current, cast almost directly upstream, and wait. Eventually the lure descends to bottom, where it skips and tumbles naturally. The proper weight enables the jig to dance downstream, neither lodging nor floating.

The more directly you cast upstream (**Cast 1**), the more natural the tumble downcurrent. Retrieve line occasionally to minimize slack and maximize feel. Set the hook at any sign of resistance.

Progressively, the more you cast cross-current (**Casts 2** and **3**), the more line bow occurs by the end of the retrieve, complicating feel and control and potentially reducing your effectiveness.

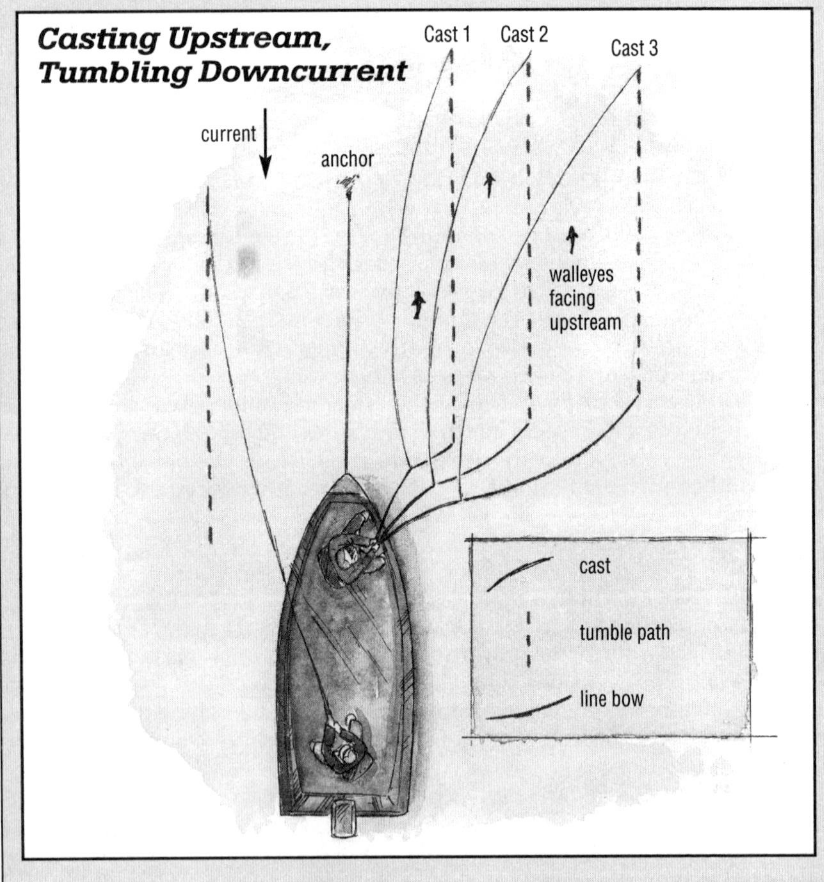

several reasons. First, Ringworms are flexible, so current gives them a lifelike action. Even if the jig-and-worm combo momentarily comes to rest along bottom, the tail continues to wiggle in the current—with luck, in a walleye's face. Second, Koval and Erickson believe the ribs or rings retain air bubbles and liquid

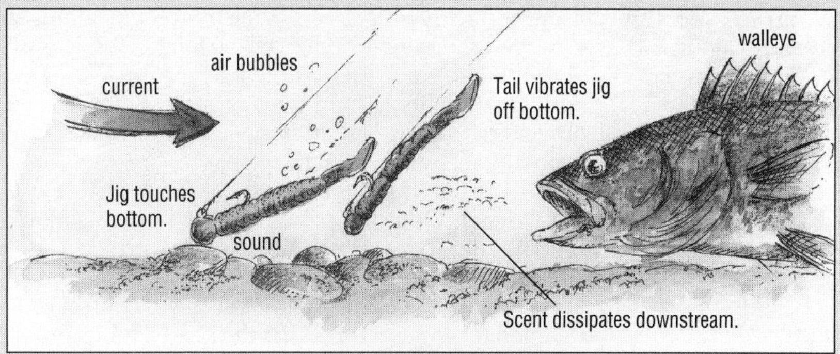

The jig contacting bottom makes noise. The plastic tail vibrates and undulates. Air bubbles rise and pop, creating visual and sound clues. Scent dissipates off the plastic. The combo tumbles helplessly downstream until . . . gulp!

scent. As the jig tumbles across bottom, tiny air bubbles disperse sound and a scent trail. The extra attraction often equals or outproduces livebait, and there's no dipping into icy minnow buckets to numb your fingers in cold weather. If you can catch as many or more walleyes without livebait, there's no reason to use it when plastics are more durable and convenient. Plus you always have something on your jighead; no bare hooks, the victim of bait-stealing light biters or small fish.

Erickson strongly believes that the weight of the jighead is critical to triggering walleyes. He normally uses lightweight heads ranging from as light as 1/16- to 1/4-ounce, with a surprisingly light 3/32-ounce size being his favorite. Whether he's fishing a channel edge, wing dam, basin flat, or eddy, the best jighead size allows the combo to roll and travel with the current, ticking bottom only occasionally. If you feel the jig dragging, bouncing, and occasionally hanging up, immediately downsize the jig. The setup should create a free-tumbling effect, much like an injured minnow pushed along bottom by the current—an easy, natural meal.

Natural flotation of the plastic tail, combined with the occasional slight drag of the jighead across bottom, should send the jigworm wriggling and wiggling tail up, tail downstream, hook point up, most of the time, minimizing snags. It's easiest to fish in shallow to moderate depths, perhaps 4 to 15 feet, but it can be fished below 20 feet if the proper conditions exist.

Match tail color to water clarity: brighter in dark water, more natural in clearer water. Start with chartreuse-lime, orange, motor oil, or electric blue. Keep changing colors until the walleyes tell you what they want. If action slows, downsize the plastic, or try other colors. Preference can change by the hour or remain constant all day. Most of the time, Koval and Erickson prefer about a 4-inch worm, though they go up to 6 inches for big or aggressive fish, and smaller when times are tough.

Line size is important to balance the system and to allow free movement of the lightweight jigworm combo. Four- to 6-pound is best. They use 6-pound-test FireLine at air temperatures above 34°F and Trilene Pro Select monofilament under colder conditions. FireLine is more sensitive but retains more water and freezes faster when the weather's cold.

FEEL IT, WORK IT, BELIEVE IT

The system performs best anywhere that light to moderate current moves the jigworm across bottom naturally: midriver flats, across the tips of wing dams and points, and along and over flooded shoreline woodcover. So long as the jig is light enough to caress bottom without dragging, it will tumble over some snags, even with an open hook, light wire jighead. If you snag up, however, a strong pull may straighten the hook, especially if you switch to slightly heavier line for working flooded snags. If snags are really bad, switch to a weedless jighead. Otherwise, put up with the occasional lost lure in order to maintain finesse and control.

The system performs best anywhere that light to moderate current moves the jigworm across bottom naturally: midriver flats, across the tips of wing dams and points, and along and over flooded shoreline woodcover.

We alluded to a sacrifice in feel with this system, and that's true to a point. But some sense of control can be retained by anticipating what the lure is doing and noting any changes in behavior that reveal a possible strike.

Slip your boat along with the current, using your electric motor to maintain a vertical line to the lure, much as in traditional jigging. Often it's more productive and revolutionary to anchor or hover in place as you pitch your jig upstream. Then follow it back downcurrent, holding your rod tip high while feeling for subtle changes and occasionally reeling slowly to pick up slack or drag the jig back to the boat. We're talking *sloooooooooooow*—no hopping. This may mean taking up to several minutes to retrieve one cast. It takes patience, persistence, and concentration to work at such slow speeds, but they're critical to success.

Expect some bow in your line. Try to minimize it, but not so much that you affect the natural tumbling of the jig in current. Pick up slack, and watch the line carefully to detect any slight change indicating a pickup. You probably won't feel a strike. If you think you've been hit, set the hook with a solid sweep. Don't be bashful. Current always causes a bow in the line, so your set must first straighten it out, then bury the hook.

CONFIDENCE

Confidence has no substitute, especially after you toss away all accepted ideas and do everything against the traditional grain. But in this instance, the revolutionary approach is something walleyes see seldom, if ever. The nonbait is a lifelike imitation moving downcurrent naturally. After many years of river fishing, Erickson no longer uses livebait on rivers; Koval, almost never. That's confidence born of experience.

The system can be described as a modified steelhead drift using bass baits for walleyes—something weird that deserves a try. And if you try it, you just may like it. Tumbling numerous walleyes amidst a host of boats that are catching few to none with traditional tactics should be enough to convince anyone—if, that is, you let them in on the secret.

CASTING STICKS & WORKING QUICK

"In 1974, while casting to rock reefs on a Canadian Shield lake," says In-Fisherman editor Matt Straw, "I discovered a new walleye killer—the Rebel Suspending Deep Wee R. When the lure smacked a rock at about 7 feet, I paused it. The bait hovered, not floating up like all the other crankbaits of the day. Suspending at the spot where it clicked the rock, the Wee R waited until a curious walleye could find it, stalk it, and devour it.

"Those early suspending baits outproduced every other option we tried on the reefs during the ensuing week up on the Shield. The classic options for Canadian walleyes in those days included drifting with spinner rigs dressed with nightcrawlers and weighted with anything from a split shot to Dan Gapen's Bait Walker, or trolling with lures like Helin's Flatfish or floating Rapalas weighted with one or two split shot on the line, and trolled deeper with three-way rigs. Jigs-and-minnows or plastic grubs worked, too, but nothing outproduced the tight wobbling Wee R on rock points and reefs. I couldn't wait to see what innovations might follow this breakthrough idea."

It was a long wait—about a quarter of a century, in fact. Yawning apathetically, 1970s America was unconcerned and unprepared for neutrally buoyant fishing lures.

Well, we're ready now. Suspending baits are all the rage. Huge lure companies and workbench manufacturers alike are churning out "jerks" and making a small fortune selling them. But, as so often happens, in our haste to try new and different things, old standbys get forgotten. Doctoring floating baits to suspend or nearly suspend and using sinking minnows along with the new wave of suspending baits combine to form a potent three-pronged attack for walleyes all season long. We call them *slashbaits*.

Slashin' the flats early puts more baits in front of more fish.

When seasons open in most states and provinces, walleyes are shallow, following their ancient postspawn routines. Still expanding out and away from the big bang (spawning), ravenous from the double-dip energy deficit created by winter stress and the rigors of spawning, walleyes roam the agreeable shallow flats. They're willing to bite because the water remains cool in the 2- to 8-foot depths in spring; cool though it may be, a shallow flat is warmer than deeper flats, drawing baitfish by the billions; it's agreeable on those flats because perch are staging or beginning to spawn there. Walleyes'll bite with authority, so why play cat and mouse? Stroke 'em with slashbaits.

SLASHBAITS

The term *slashbait* refers to all kinds of nonfloating minnowbaits, including doctored floating baits (lures drilled, filled, or altered in some way to suspend or to fish deeper). The concept is to slash and burn the flats, rippin', jerkin', 'n smokin' away at those hungry walleyes, in depths and corners that can't be trolled efficiently, at speeds that jig fishermen alternately dream of and scoff at.

Jigs are just fine—for numbers. But for finding walleyes, at least sometimes, nothing beats a little slash-n-burn. And for trophies, it's the odds-on thing. Sort through a few thousand walleyes to get an 8 with jigs. On good water, with slashbaits, sort through 100 or so to find a 10.

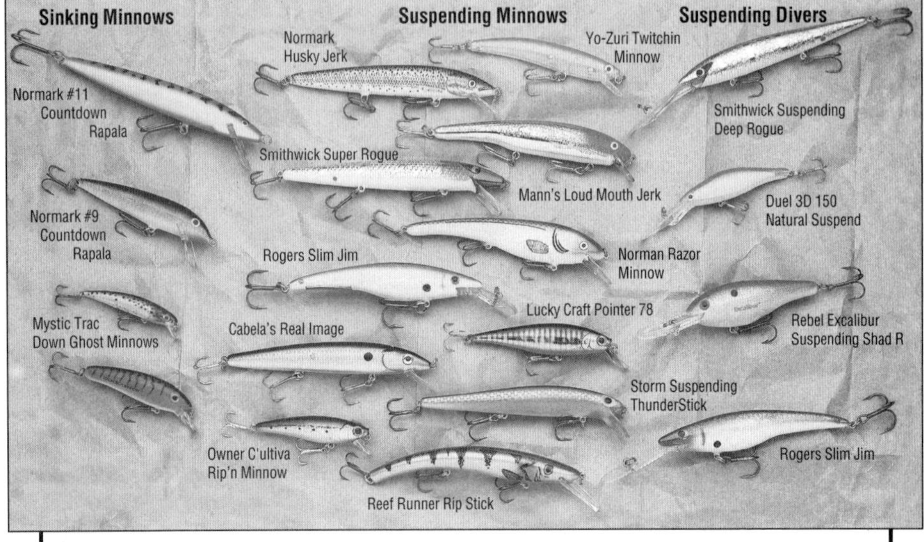

Here's the deal: it's May. You know where the walleyes spawn and how they disperse. Get on the trail somewhere between that spawning habitat and classic summer haunts in the main lake. Flats that consistently produce can be anywhere from right outside the mouth of a spawning creek to miles down the shoreline. Lake spawners may remain near the flats where they spawned, or they may be across the lake on shallow rocks. How do you find them quickly in depths under 5 feet? Slash away.

Longline trolling with minnowbaits is a mainstay this time of year. Trolling locates walleyes quickly but becomes tedious, even impossible, in most lakes from the 5-foot contour to the bank, right where the most overlooked walleyes position to feed. Difficult, too, to get lures into tight corners along productive emerging weedlines.

Somewhere along the postspawn walleye trail, find the biggest shallow flats. The best flats have a slow taper from about 12 feet up to the bank, not the sharp drops we associate with walleyes during the remainder of the year. Get upwind, drop the bowmount trolling motor at about 8 feet, and start pitchin' sinking or suspending minnows, fancasting from the bank out to the 10-foot contour. Most days, it's possible to move quickly. Aggressive walleyes slam baits moving much faster than most folks realize at this time of year.

SLASHTRIX

Slashing things up right involves an arsenal of sinking, suspending, and doctored baits. Straw's first choice, right from the get-go on opening day, is a suspending bait. According to Al Lindner, "Nothing this productive has hit the market in a long, long time. Jerkbaits trigger bigger walleyes, and more of them in less time than any other technique, whether the walleyes are scattered or concentrated. Name another lure that catches a bigger variety of fish in a wider range of conditions. From cold to warm water, and especially during transitions between

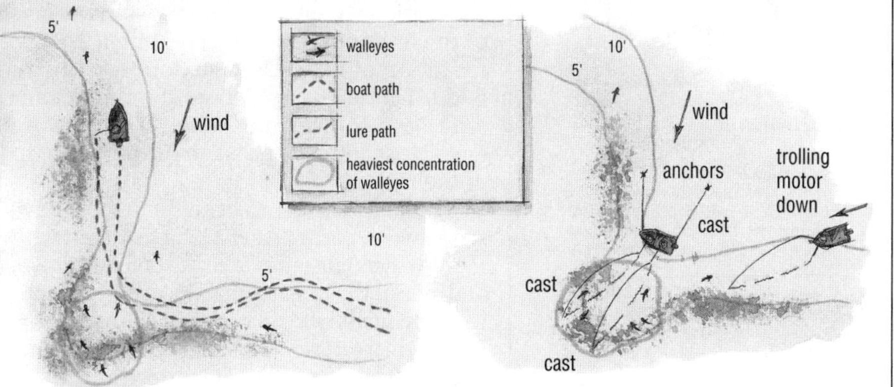

Trolling—Trolling past an inside turn (or cup) in the weedline, hugging the edge tight as possible, only intersects the outer fringe of this shallow concentration of walleyes. A bite on several passes through a spot like this suggests that casting is required.

Controlled Casting—Anchoring and casting with the wind at your back covers this tight, difficult concentration point much more thoroughly. Controlled drifting or cruising slowly with the trolling motor while casting from the bow covers more water.

those phases, jerks trigger shallow walleyes better than any other hard-body bait."

The trick with the new suspending baits is making them dance. Rapala Husky Jerks, Smithwick Super Rogues, Lucky Craft Pointers, Mann's Loud Mouth Jerks, and other suspenders work best with a slow to moderately quick, erratic, stop-and-go action. The pause is the trigger. A walleye tends to commit when the bait stops and hangs in front of its face without rising or sinking. At the end of a long cast (the longer, the better with slashbaits), monofilament stretches, dulling the action. Braided polyethylene lines (superlines) are much better choices for this activity.

Start with a medium-light-action 7-foot spinning rod. Add a midsized reel, such as the Daiwa 1600 or Shimano 2000 series spinning models. Use mono backing, and tie it to a 100- to 150-yard length of 14-pound-test fused braid, such as Berkley FireLine or SpiderWire Fusion, with back-to-back uni-knots. Standard braids, such as Innovative Textiles Power Pro or Suffix HercuLine, are thinner and cast even farther in the same pound-tests, and using 20-pound versions of these products is feasible.

Braids have no memory, so coils and line slap won't reduce casting distance. Some of the problems associated with braids, such as wind knots and tangles, can be alleviated by soaking the line with Blakemore Reel Magic or WD-40 before spooling it on. But while braids in the same pound-tests are much thinner than mono, braids are opaque. Light passes through mono and fluorocarbon, creating stealthier options for leader material, along with the stretch factor. Mono stretches, braids don't, so a mono leader provides a modicum of shock resistance for all the various knots being used. Along with a soft rod tip, mono leaders also keep big fish from ripping free.

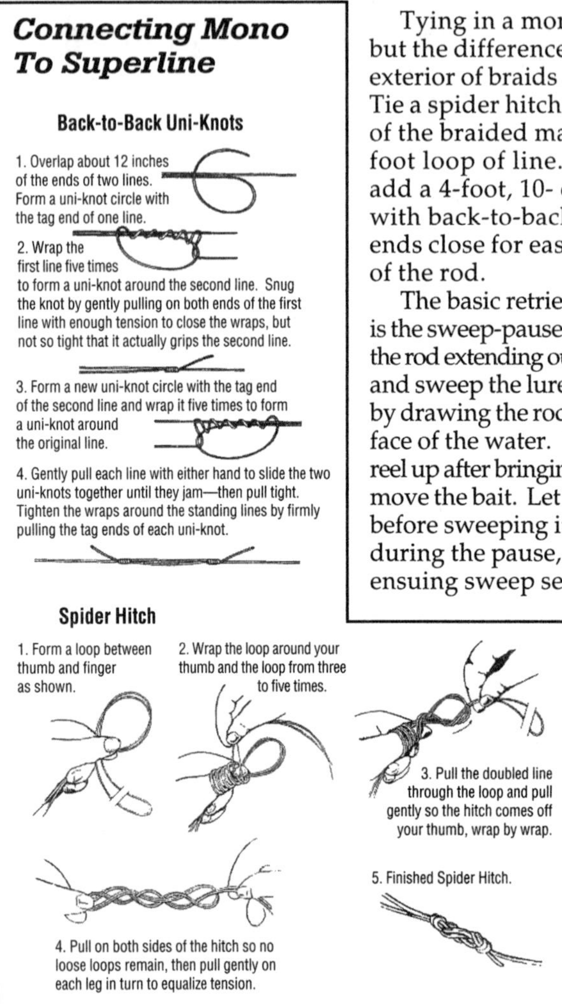

Tying in a mono leader is a wise choice, but the difference in diameter and the slick exterior of braids can lead to slipping knots. Tie a spider hitch or Bimini twist in the end of the braided main line, creating a 2- or 3-foot loop of line. Use the doubled line to add a 4-foot, 10- or 12-pound mono leader with back-to-back uni-knots. Trim the tag ends close for easy passage through the tip of the rod.

The basic retrieve to begin with most days is the sweep-pause. After a long cast, start with the rod extending out in front, tip pointing down, and sweep the lure down to its running depth by drawing the rod tip back just above the surface of the water. When retrieving slack line, reel up after bringing the rod tip forward. Don't move the bait. Let it sit for 5 seconds or longer before sweeping it again. Most strikes occur during the pause, and they aren't felt, so the ensuing sweep sets the hook. Play with the strength of the sweep and the length of the pause. Some days walleyes won't commit to the lure until it sits still for 20 seconds or longer. In most cases, the wobble attracts and the pause triggers.

Really active walleyes respond better to a snap-snap-pause-snap retrieve. Starting from the same position, rod tip pointing down, snap the rod tip back 6 to 12 inches, push the rod tip back to the starting point while retrieving, and snap it again. The lure, if tuned correctly, should dance from side to side, almost like walkin' the dog with a Zara Spook, only underwater. Braids are critical for this technique—the lack of stretch provides a much sharper snap at longer distances. Here again, the flash attracts; the pause triggers.

Most days, use a twitch-twitch-pause-sweep-pause-twitch. The twitch, if done properly, causes the bait to move side to side, but at a slower pace. The pauses can be anywhere from 5 to 20 seconds, depending on what the walleyes want. The sweep is just fast enough to make the bait wobble; the slight vibration is easily felt with braided line.

The longer 7-foot rod makes longer casts, longer sweeps, and more powerful sweepsets. Long casts are critical because walleyes tend to follow these baits. The farther the lure travels on the cast, the better, creating more room for triggering fish before they slip into the shadow of the boat.

Larger suspending baits dig deeper than floating models, sometimes 2 feet deeper than corresponding sizes of floating minnows, making them poor choices for casting to 2- to 3-foot depths, where walleyes can stack up even during the day in spring, when the wind is blowing in on a spot. Smaller suspending baits (C'ultiva-Owner Rip'N'Minnow or smaller Excalibur Ghost Minnows) and sinking minnows (Countdown Rapala) tend to work better in really thin water.

Don't be afraid to work minnow-style suspending baits in 12- to 15-foot depths. Walleyes come up for them, especially in spring and fall. In darker waters, deep-suspending divers can get right in their faces at those depths. Lures like the Rebel Excalibur Suspending Shad R, the Smithwick Suspending Deep Rogue, and the Rogers Slim Jim take deeper fish with the same tactics, and they serve as excellent stop-and-go trolling tools as well.

OTHER SLASHBAITS

Whenever walleyes respond best to a steady retrieve, such as in cold water, sinking or countdown baits excel. Wide, erratic, wobbling lures can intimidate walleyes in cold water. Something with less action or a subtle wobble tends to produce more strikes in water temperatures below 48°F, though fairly quick retrieves often work better than most anglers realize. These baits are prime for covering 4- to 7-foot depths in tight corners along weedlines, where trolling can't reach them. Larger models can be worked effectively to about 10 feet.

Hold your rod tip high in shallow water, low in deep water. Vary the retrieve speed to slightly modify the running depth of countdown lures like the #5, #7, #9, and #11 Countdown Rapala. On limp 8-pound mono, a #5 or #7 can be pitched to a lipped shoreline or worked over a bar 2 to 5 feet deep at the right speed with the

right rod angle. The #9 works well in water ranging from about 4 to 7 feet deep, the #11 down to 10 feet. Worked correctly, these lures can outproduce longline trolling at night when fish are concentrated in hard-to-reach spots.

"For me, achieving absolute neutral buoyancy has never been the key to catching walleyes at night," *In-Fisherman* Editor In Chief Doug Stange says. "Depth control is critical, not the ability to suspend a bait or work a lure. In my mind, the best lures barely float at rest. Speed, action, and depth control are more important than the ability to suspend. Something that wobbles right at a slow, steady pace allows walleyes to zero in at night.

"A Rapala Husky Jerk, for example, doesn't have quite the wobble that a well-doctored #13 Husky Rap (now out of production) has on a straight retrieve. The Husky Jerk also dives deeper, which gets you into trouble with sandgrass and rocks in those 3- to 5-foot depths that are so key when fishing from shore. Similarly, whenever a straight retrieve

Reaping the rewards of slashbait mastery.

is critical, I wouldn't count out the old countdown-style lures."

Stange doctors the #13 Husky Rapala by drilling two holes deep enough to add five 3/0 Water Gremlin round shot. He drills the holes in the side of the lure about halfway between the head and tail of the lure, but slightly closer to the head. Then he covers the holes with epoxy. He also reduces the buoyancy of injected-plastic minnows by heating a sewing needle, poking a hole in the lure, injecting about 2 to 4 cc of water (depending on the make and size of the lure) with a hypodermic needle, and then using the heated needle to melt the hole shut.

Though it took 25 years to reinvent the wheel on suspending baits, slashbait tactics have been with us for a long time and continue to produce hot early-season walleye action. The key is applying them in the right times and places. Wherever walleyes gather, some of them will be occupying hot spots too shallow or corners too tight for you to troll through.

Heavy concentrations may require a slash mentality, too. Where trolling may produce four or five fish, slashtrix can pull double-digit numbers of 'eyes from a small spot. No time lost reeling in and turning around or working unproductive water. This is the major alternative to searching with slo-mo jigging.

Chapter 8

Bad to the Bone

PATTERNS THAT APPEAR TO GO AGAINST THE GRAIN

We've looked at logical fishing patterns; now let's consider some that seemingly go against the grain of traditional wisdom and experience. Here's the important lesson: keep an open mind. Should tradition fail, experiment by showing the fish something different. Sometimes stepping a bit outside your comfort zone puts you in touch with walleyes.

Walleye anglers have long been programmed to fish slowly in cold water, theorizing that cold-blooded fish simply won't respond to faster presentations. This chapter is largely devoted to debunking that myth. And to really kicking the motor into high gear in summer!

FAST MOVES, FRIGID WATER

Walleyes, rivers, and cold, late winter flows, mixed thoroughly, create a captivating recipe, one that enthralls thousands of fishermen every year. Big fish migrate upstream together to hold in predictable wintering areas, staging months before they eventually spawn. Anglers traditionally fish them with jigs-and-minnows.

Like Tevya in *Fiddler On The Roof*, you may do something mostly because it's *always been done that way*. Slow, precise jigging is (was?) best because walleyes are lethargic in cold water. Their metabolism slows. They eat less and need to be teased into striking. Right?

Is this merely a mind-set, a tradition passed on through generations? Tradition totes a hefty load of mythological baggage. Well, maybe not myths. But half truths. Yes, walleyes' metabolism slows. But it doesn't stop. Yes, they may eat less. But when they get hungry, *they get just as hungry*. Force them to react quickly, and active fish will slam a lure in the coldest water.

A high-velocity lure triggers a reaction in cold water that can't be duplicated with a jig crawling along on bottom. Walleyes aren't crippled in cold water—they aren't moving like it's *The Night of the Living Dead* down there. They scrutinize slow-moving baits. They take them with suspicion. With livebait, you feed them line and wait for them to gulp the bait. But about half the time, they drop it, or you misjudge and set early.

> *A high-velocity lure triggers a reaction in cold water that can't be duplicated with a jig crawling along on bottom.*

They can't drop a crankbait flying by at 2 to 4 mph (not usually, anyway). Ever try to spit a live crab out of your mouth? Must be what it's like to try spitting out a tandem of trebles. If you're doing everything right, once you trigger a fish, that fish is yours. Even with livebait like minnows or crawlers on spinner rigs, the added velocity of a high-speed troll creates automatic tension on the fish. A bite quickly loads the rod, making it difficult for the fish to drop the bait. And walleyes don't nibble at high-speed presentations—they wolf 'em.

"Speed increases your capacity to search," Al Lindner says. "Segments of hard-fished rivers hold unpressured walleyes. Walleyes will winter in unlikely backwaters and channels. But most fishermen stick with classic spots, because they feel they don't have time to explore. They're limited by their own perception of what they can and can't do in cold water.

"High-speed trolling frees them from that limitation. It quickly works better in a lot of situations that we traditionally approached with jigs or livebait rigs. For years, we thought jigs were the mainstay approach for walleyes in any situation. It takes time not only to alter that perception but also to try something else long and hard enough to be able to say with integrity, *Maybe another mainstay tactic works*."

While experiments the past few years proved that speed works in cold water, the results weren't that surprising. We suspected long ago that the old adage, "Slow in the cold" was a barrier. The jigging spoon breakthrough of the mid-1980s provided essential clues. Jigging spoons are aggressive baits. You rip them off bottom, snap them up to achieve optimal triggering capacity. Over subsequent years, jigging spoons sometimes outfished jigs in cold water.

Blades, which can be worked even more aggressively on the uptake, became the subject of experimentation under the ice. They worked just fine in frigid water.

We're not saying go out and fly around all day at 4 mph. Some days, walleyes respond better to normal or even slower than normal trolling speeds. Most days,

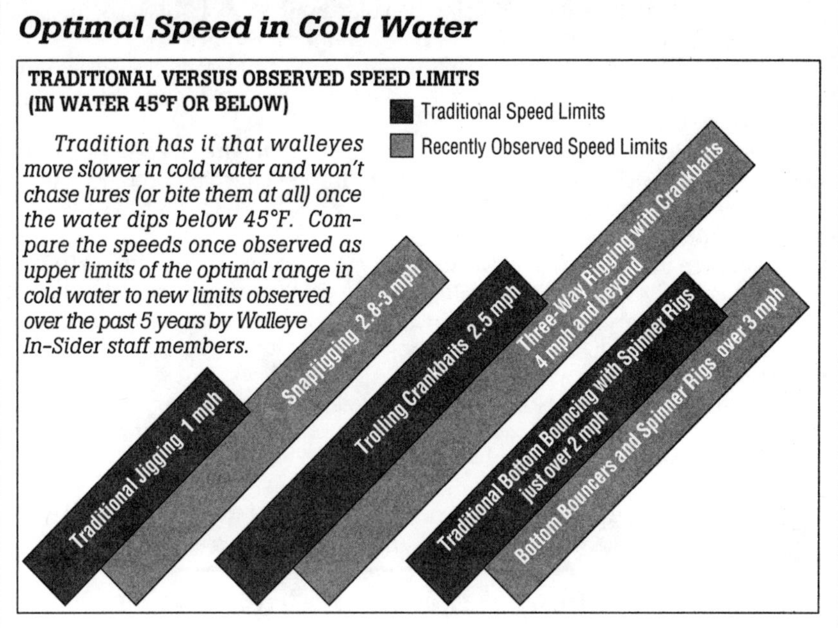

you can return and glean a few neutral fish by jigging in productive areas you discovered while trolling. But unless you try speeds of 2 mph or better, you won't know how effective re-fishing those spots can be.

TECHNIQUE

River walleyes stack below barrier areas, such as dams, downstream of narrow stretches where current increases, and in deep holes miles from the next adequate staging area upstream.

Consider starting by trolling rather than jigging. Some situations call for flatlining, others for leadcore, others for combinations. Most situations are best approached with the more versatile three-way rig or a basic bottom-bouncer rig at this time of year.

"I seldom leave the boat ramp without two rods rigged to troll three-way rigs," Al says. "I find myself relying on them all year. I rarely start with jigs anymore. I can determine faster which structures and which parts of these structures fish are using with three-ways and minnowbaits. I know sooner if active fish are up and biting. I don't waste time covering unproductive water. The first rod I pick up on any river this time of year is a three-way rod."

Fact is, crankbaits and cold water *do go together*. That's no longer an issue. What continues to be controversial is speed.

"You aren't going to be able to make fish chase a lure down in cold water," walleye pro Keith Kavajecz emphasizes. "I think the important thing to differentiate is lure speed versus pulling speed. When you snap a crankbait forward, you excite fish, but a subsequent pause or slowing of the lure's progress triggers more strikes.

"That's why handheld rods produce more strikes in calm weather. Pumping the rod is usually more effective than a steady troll. A board rod—or any rod in a holder—does better on a windy day when waves sweep you forward, then stall you out. But I still think slower is better as water temperatures drop."

This minirevolution isn't just about three-ways and crankbaits, however. Lures may well be the best way to go on many occasions, but livebait's effectiveness can never be overruled entirely.

Bottom bouncers and three-way rigs are probably the most versatile trolling rigs for rivers. Leadcore tactics and flatline trolling are effective techniques where bottom is even or fish are restricted to spots easily reached by lures traveling along the same plane.

But walleyes in rivers during February and March are usually within 1 to 2 feet of bottom. The heavier the current, the closer to bottom they'll be. With bouncers and three-ways, you know a lure or spinner rig is tracking bottom no matter how much the depth changes. The bait or lure never travels through dead water in a fish-holding area.

What's the cutoff—at what temperature do spinner rigs become ineffective? Probably 32°F. In other words, it works until water is no longer water. If you can troll a rig under the ice, it probably will continue to be effective.

Why?

Why not? That's the point. Change your perceptions about speed and cold water.

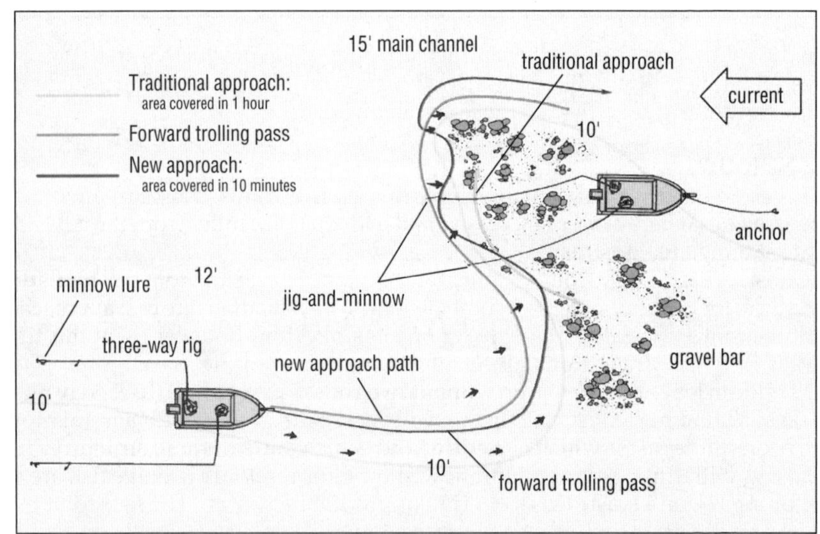

Coldwater Trolling in Rivers: A Gravel Bar

Water temperature: 36°F. *The traditional approach: anchor and jig the edge of the bar. It works. But you have to reposition the boat three or four times, crawl the jigs slowly along the slope, and retie after snagging. Time elapsed: 1 hour.*

A new approach: using three-way rigs, forward troll with 3-ounce weights and minnowbaits, zigzagging the downstream slope of the bar. In 10 minutes or less, you know if active fish are present and where the main concentration of fish are holding. Troll upstream on the first pass to ensure better control. Add a stall or hovering tactic to the scheme, letting the lure work in place, but don't neglect trolling downstream, too. Speed may be the pivotal trigger on any given day, even at these temperatures.

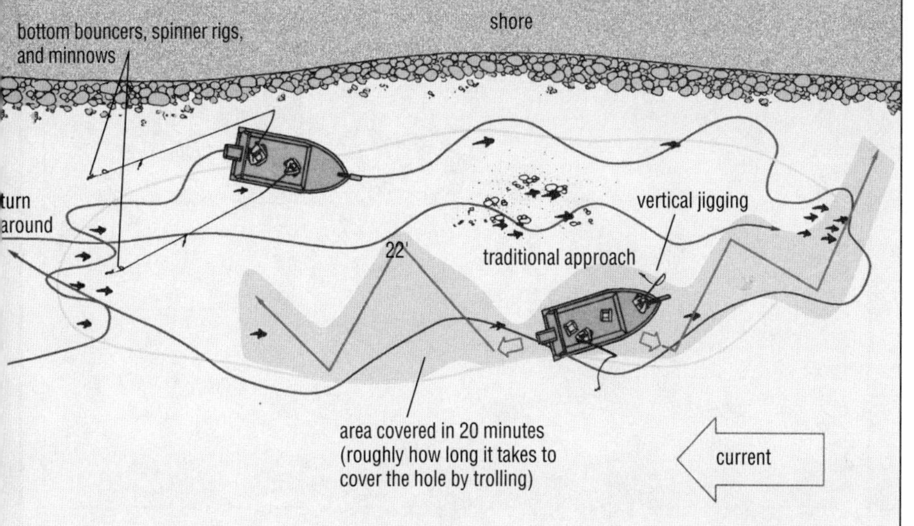

Water temperature: 38°F. Traditional technique: use the bowmount trolling motor to slip downstream or move slowly upstream, quartering at angles to the current. An efficient but time-consuming technique. Time elapsed to cover the entire hole: 1½ hours.

A new approach: troll upstream with bottom bouncers, spinner rigs, and livebait, or with three-way rigs and hardbaits. Use 2- to 3-ounce weights to get down quickly and to maintain lines at a 45-degree angle to the transom. Weights should never be more than 2 feet below the main line because walleyes are never more than 2 feet off bottom. Cover the shoreline side of the hole first, then troll downstream along the midriver side. Then turn around and zigzag up the middle of the hole. Covering the area should take less than 20 minutes.

FAST-BREAK SAUGER

Life's full of contradictions. Take fall fishing, for example. Traditional wisdom suggests that cooling water temperatures in fall demand slower presentations to match the slowing metabolisms of fish. Yet experience shows that walleyes and saugers, their close cousins, often go on feeding binges in fall, evidently to prepare for the coming winter. Selecting the right presentation makes a difference. Fast or slow—how to know?

Faced with such decisions, it's often best to play percentages, probably starting with classic slow presentations like livebait rigging and jigging. But keep an open mind and an open tackle box should the classics fail. As Sherlock Holmes was fond of saying, "When you eliminate the impossible, whatever remains, no matter how improbable, must be the truth." That remains true when it comes to speeding up instead of slowing down to catch fish, no matter how cold the water and how late the season.

Mississippi River sauger along the Minnesota-Wisconsin border are an example of why exceptional fishing sometimes requires exceptional techniques. In fall, when sauger stack in heavy numbers along the lower end of Lake Pepin—a large,

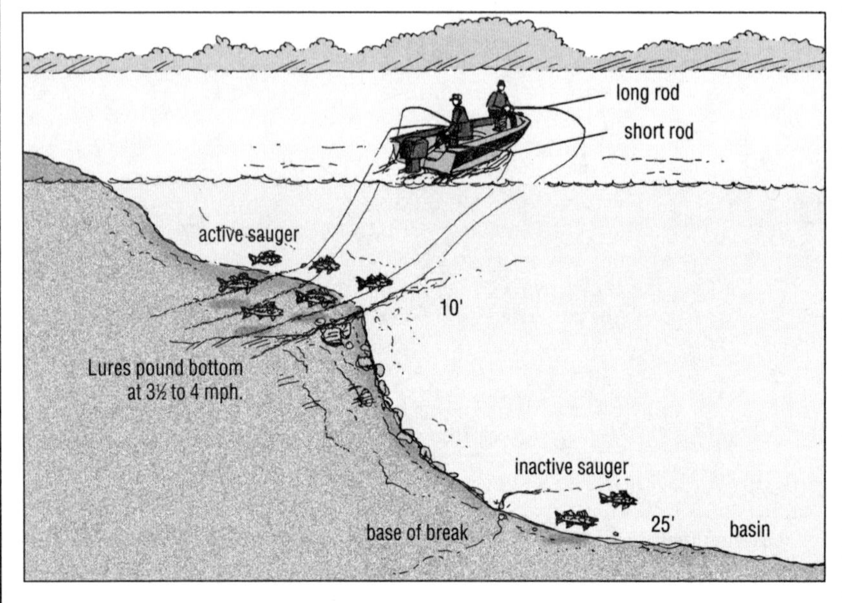

fairly shallow impoundment with dispersed current—they line up along classic shoreline points that drop rapidly from 10 to about 25 feet.

Inactive fish often lie at the base of the breakline where the hard-bottomed drop-off meets the basin of the lake—places perfect for livebait rigging and jigging. When sauger are shallower and perhaps more active along the top of the break, however, they often prefer faster-moving lures and may ignore presentations moving at slow speeds. If slow doesn't produce, pop on a crankbait and pick up the pace.

How fast is fast? Try 3½ to 4 mph, even in cold water following the fall Turnover. Sauger that ignore a lure moving at 2 mph may slam the same bait banging and bashing bottom at 3½ to 4 mph. Contact trolling.

That's right, pound bottom—the more disturbance, the better. Be too obnoxious to ignore. Whether they strike out of self-defense or a feeding instinct, they nevertheless open their mouths and attack. Increased speed equals more coverage, more strikes, and more fish in the boat.

To troll at such high speed, cranks must be tuned to run true at increased pace. Just because a crankbait runs straight at 2 mph doesn't necessarily mean it won't peel off to the side or spin in circles at 4 mph. Your best bet is to tune your cranks carefully by lowering them into the water on a short line and supertuning them to run at 5 or 6 mph, well above typical trolling speeds. Use pliers to bend the eyelet slightly left or right until your baits run deep and straight at high speeds. Now you're set for trolling.

Professional walleye angler Scott Fairbairn likes Cordell Wally Divers and unusually deep-diving #7 and #8 Rapala Shad Raps for slam-dancing bottom at high speeds for sauger. The durable, plastic-bodied Wally Diver withstands the punishment of continual bottom contact, but the more fragile, balsa-bodied Shad Rap is an unexpected choice. Scott feels the low eyelet position on the Shad Rap's diving bill makes it easier to supertune than many other lures as well as less likely to be knocked out of whack during relentless pounding while trolling hard bottom.

Use fairly stout but not overly large diameter monofilament—12- or 14-pound test—to withstand the punishment of trolling without substantially reducing the lure's diving depth. Fairbairn often prefers running three colors (30 yards) of leadcore ahead of a 50-foot mono leader to make his lures run a little deeper and to consistently pound bottom better than mono. Running depth seldom varies more than a few inches with leadcore.

Once fish are hooked—you'll know immediately by the sudden whack and bend of the rod at such speeds—be prepared to slow the boat immediately to prevent ripping out hooks.

Hang on tight, or pop your rods into a holder. Once fish are hooked—you'll know immediately by the sudden whack and bend of the rod at such speeds—be prepared to slow the boat immediately to prevent ripping out hooks. Slow down too quickly, and you feed the fish slack, so it can shake loose from the lure. Don't slow down sufficiently, and you often rip the trebles out of the fish's mouth. Experience is the best teacher.

The high speeds necessary to trigger sauger under these conditions pretty much prevent the use of in-line planer boards to spread lines to the sides of the boat; the rapid pace simply pulls them back behind the transom. If you wish to run four lines, use one 6- to 6½-foot rod off each side of the boat and another, longer 7½- to 8-foot rod off each gunwale. This setup spreads lines far enough to the sides to minimize tangles.

To prevent crossing lines, avoid excessively sharp turns. Properly executed, the system works well enough to extend your coverage laterally and perhaps depthwise. With crankbaits diving at different depths, you can cover a breakline with the equivalent of a high-speed blanket. Fish hardly have a chance.

Does high-speed trolling in cold water work for sauger everywhere? You tell us. It's worth a try on other large, dirty water systems like the Tennessee, Ohio, Missouri, and Arkansas rivers, where fall and winter concentrations of sauger reach huge numbers. High-speed crankin' also triggers sauger following summer cold fronts, when slower methods get ignored. Reaction strikes? Perhaps. If it triggers a reaction, it's worth the effort.

When conventional methods fail, speed may prevail. Keep the option open next time the bite's off, and get crankin' for fall sauger success. The best defense is a good offense, and running the fast break along fast breaks breaks down even the best tight-lipped defense a sauger can muster.

COUNTERCURRENT CRANKIN'

Traditional wisdom suggests that effective crankbait trolling in rivers should be executed while moving upstream. Moving into current allows diving lures to achieve action with little forward speed—even when hovering or just barely moving upstream. The force of the current supplies the necessary water resistance to wiggle the lure. When trolling against current, it's possible with little effort to slide the boat side to side in the current to cover a larger area. You can also slow the boat to hover over hot spots, letting lures wobble enticingly in front of neutral walleyes. These aspects of boat control enhance fishing effectiveness.

But what about trolling with the current, counter to tradition? Usually when

you first try it, trolling crankbaits downstream appears to be a recipe for disaster. Lines may tangle; the boat goes out of control; strange things happen. Often, however, one of those strange things is catching a fair number of fish.

Trolling crankbaits downstream works when done correctly. But several rules must be kept in mind. First, trolling downstream doesn't lend itself to multiple-rod spreads and to covering wide expanses of river channel. Even if running more than one rod per angler is legal, don't try.

Second, instinct tells us to travel a lot faster than the surface current to make cranks wobble. Wrong. The fastest water is on top and in the middle of the channel, with slower water near bottom and shorelines because of friction against the basin or surrounding shore. In theory, moving at the same speed as surface current should wobble crankbaits near bottom. Yet in practice, this doesn't happen. To start and maintain a crankbait diving, move slightly faster than surface current, but not by much—just enough to maintain control often is fast enough.

Last, make sure the bait touches or even pounds bottom. Making contact with bottom while trolling downstream is more important than while trolling upstream. Why? The bait, even though it's wiggling wildly, moves much slower while trolling up- than downstream, so fish have a larger window of opportunity to attack. When moving downstream, you bounce the lure along bottom, making pauses, so walleyes get more opportunity to respond.

When should countercurrent cranking be used? We've all spent countless hours on rivers lined up in a boat parade, trolling against the current through areas that occasionally produce fish. Heavy boat traffic usually results in lures being presented in the same manner and direction, and it screams for a different approach. Amidst groups of boats trolling the right way, moving the wrong way often succeeds.

Trolling downstream shouldn't be reserved for heavy traffic areas, however. When you're alone and trolling upstream, rather than running downstream and resetting lines for another upcurrent trolling pass, simply turn around and troll downstream. You may encounter something different. And you won't be violating one of the primary tenets of fishing—*If your line isn't in the water, you won't catch fish.*

Suppose you're prospecting for walleye hot spots in an unfamiliar river. A particular stretch looks promising. You can vertically jig the stretch or troll crankbaits upstream. Three-way rigs may work. But to find fish fast, you decide to start at the top of the area and troll downstream. If the fish are there, they'll let you know. If not, you'll move on. Use countercurrent cranking as a search method.

Diving lures with significant but not exaggerated action generally make the best downriver trolling baits for walleyes. Shad Raps, for example, have a slightly more pronounced wobble than subtle minnow-imitators like Rapala Minnows, so they're excellent candidates. Select proper lure size and action to reach and rustle bottom,

Contrary to Ordinary

Water flowing against the basin and shorelines of a river creates friction along the point of contact, slowing current slightly, compared to current speed in portions at the center and surface of the river. To troll a lure downstream near bottom in the area of reduced flow, it's not necessary to overpower downriver current. Just increase your speed to move slightly faster than surface flow. This is sufficient to wobble a modest wiggler like a Shad Rap. More aggressive wobblers require more speed, perhaps moving downstream too quickly to trigger walleyes, particularly in cold water.

When trolling downstream, crankbaits must contact bottom, even pound it. This ensures that lures run through the area of reduced current where fish are holding. It also instills an erratic action to help trigger strikes.

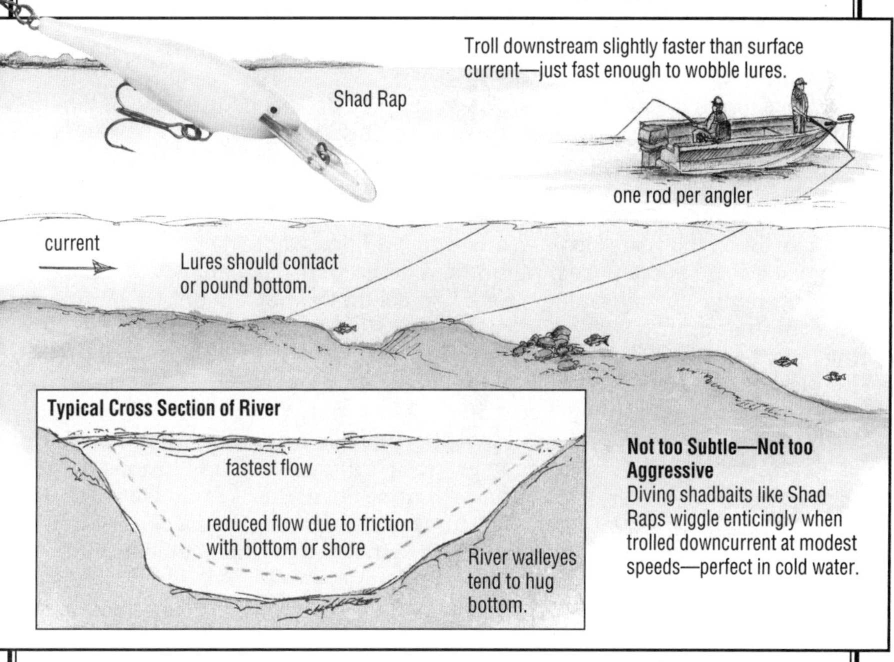

simultaneously sending out sufficient vibration to alert fish to the lure's approach.

Countercurrent cranking excels during some periods and is more of a trick-up-your-sleeve during others. In late winter and spring, walleyes and sauger make predictable movements upstream to traditional spawning grounds. At this time, traditional upstream cranking tends to be best. But once the spawn is complete and fish begin slowly dispersing downstream toward their summer haunts, downstream trolling increases in effectiveness. Remember, downstream walleye migration occurs not only after the spawn, but also any time current is reduced or water levels fall. Sometimes going the wrong way can be the right way to catch walleyes.

SPEED LIMITS FOR WALLEYES

Al and Jim Lindner were rigging up to troll with wire line using a three-way swivel rig and a blue-back #13 Rapala. Surface temperature 33°F.

No way was this gonna fly.

On this big river system, walleyes were 20 to 40 feet down. Nearby anglers were drifting and jigging, occasionally boating walleyes over 8 pounds. Traditional tactics. All and Jim trolled around them in figure-eights and circles, kicking the motor in and out of gear to stay within a reasonable facsimile of walleye speeds.

The rods snapped down on fish after fish as they trolled *downcurrent*, moving at speeds considered breakneck even for warmer conditions. The tactics outproduced jigs in water that would have frozen if it hadn't been flowing.

So what are walleye speeds? Drifting, trolling, jigging, rigging. How fast is too fast? What's the speed limit?

Faster than you may think, especially by the time July arrives.

SPEED SENSE

Editors Dave Csanda, Matt Straw, and Doug Stange sat down to talk speed for walleyes.

"Boils down to speed ranges," Csanda opened. "Each lure presentation has an optimal range. Certain lures work best at certain speeds."

"Probably," Doug agreed. "But most walleye fishermen are grooved into the slow side of those speed ranges. Five, 6, even 8 mph—almost up on plane—is effective at times.

"During all the years I lived in Iowa, the tradition was to move slow. Walleyes equaled slow. People were programmed to accept that equation.

"Suddenly," he continued, "for reasons I don't know, people fishing those surrounding prairie lakes in Iowa, Minnesota, and South Dakota began moving quite fast and catching lots of fish. Even at the beginning of the season (early May) they were trolling 3, 4, 5 mph—keeping it up and moving faster as the season progressed. And they were catching lots more fish than guys running at traditional speeds. But that's still not as fast as I'm going to propose trolling in some situations.

"Start fast, not slow, and let the fish tell you when to slow down."
—Doug Stange

"What will come out of this?" Doug waxed rhetorical. "Perhaps nothing more than a change of perspective. Start fast, not slow, and let the fish tell you when to slow down.

"An hour passes with Ole and Sven, the quintessential Minnesota Norwegians, trolling for walleyes on opening day," Doug continued, telling a story. "'Nothing's happening. Finally Sven looks up at Ole and says, 'Ole, you sure ve're moving?' Ole, startled, looks up, looks around, looks down at his motor, 'Oh, gosh darn it, Sven, forgot to put the motor in gear.' "

Doug, smiling: "Ole and Sven should be starting fast and finding the fastest speed they can get away with."

"If you're trying to locate fish," Csanda added, " true, you're better off starting fast when you're on the hunt, especially in shallow lakes and flowages where walleyes use every square acre. The only way to cover enough water is by moving fast. But 7 mph?"

"That's pushing the outer edge of the envelope," Straw added. "I mean way out. They don't even push it that far on Erie."

"That's because they don't need to," Stange countered. "Thousands of active

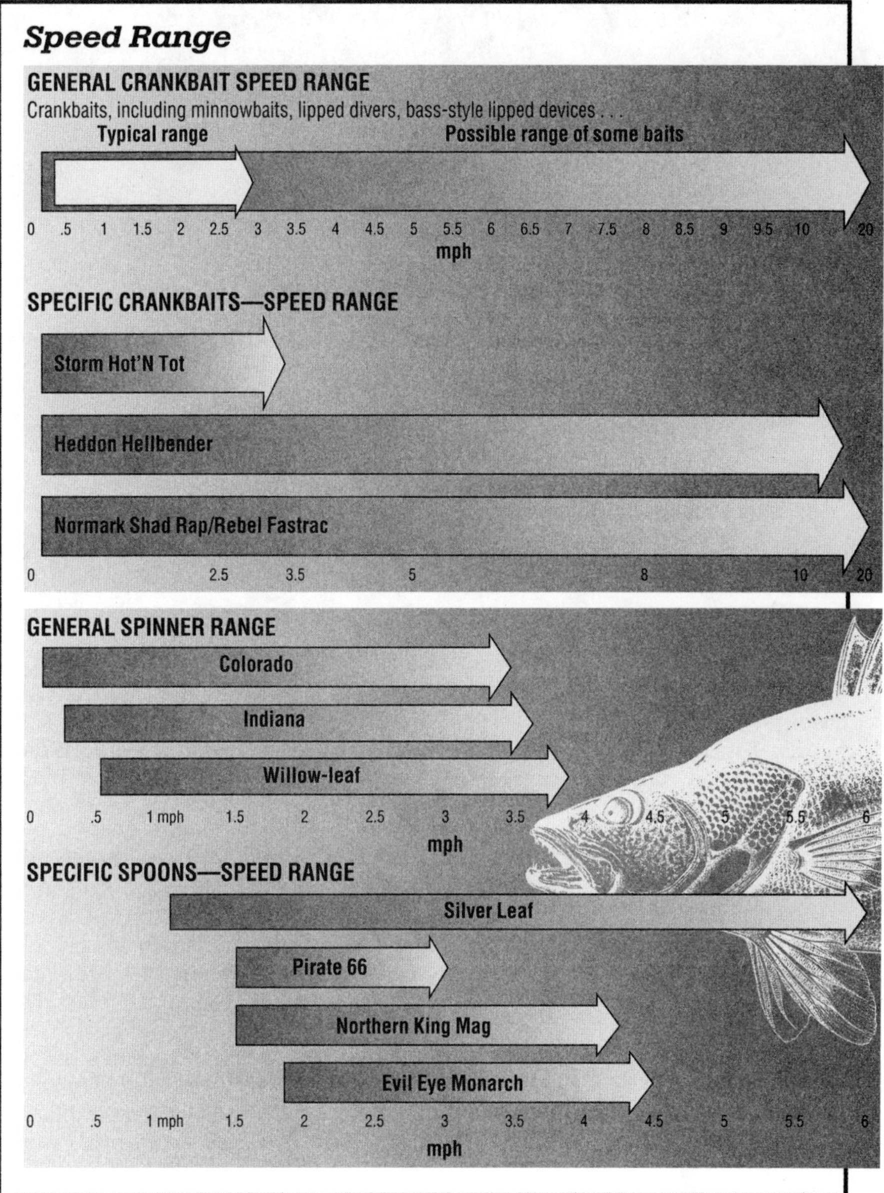

fish are under you and thousands of neutral fish, too. In lots of lakes, though, particularly in the Walleye Belt, years of fishing pressure have thinned populations, educating the remaining fish.

"Tell you what a few of us used to do," he continued. "Along about July on those tough lakes, not one walleye could be scratched on leeches or crawlers with conventional trolling methods. When you're not catching anything anyway, you may as well try something else.

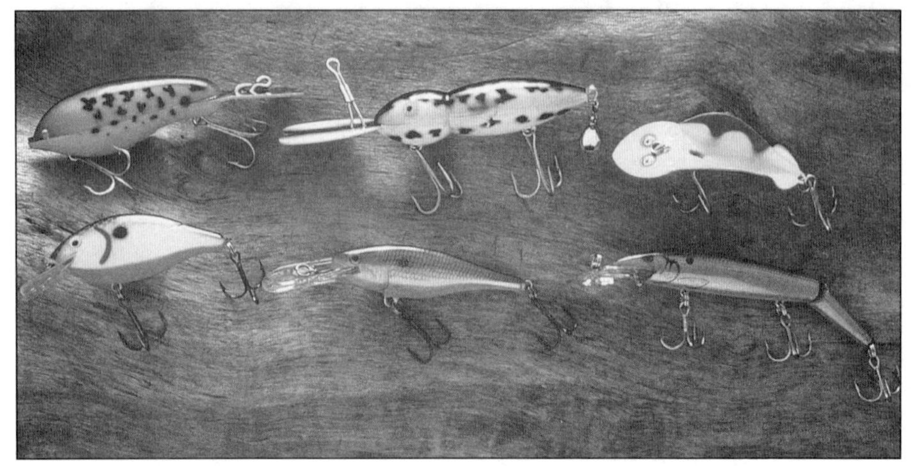

Traditionals–Arbogast Mud-Bug, Heddon Hellbender, Spoonplug. Moderns–Luhr Jensen Speed Trap, Normark Shad Rap, Rebel Fastrac.

"May sound desperate to most fishermen today, but it wasn't quite so desperate back in the 1970s, because many more good fishermen were schooled then in Buck Perry's trolling tactics. Structure fishermen were used to cruising along, using Spoonplugs to maintain depth and speed control. And it's possible to go fast with a Spoonplug or Heddon Hellbender, or move right along with a Arbogast Mud-Bug.

"Six, 8 mph? Occasionally. We used those lures because they were the only ones that handled those speeds. We'd speed troll for a day and scratch fish by racing across a point and along the sides of a bar, buzzing a weedline, strafing a hump, sailing down a rocky breakline. A good day might be three, maybe four fish. But good fish, 4 pounds or better, on bodies of water where traditional tactics were firing blanks.

"At times, classic walleye lakes and reservoirs are like Lake Erie on a smaller scale. Schooled fish are feeding competitively, a situation where they'll respond to a bait moving faster than you ever dreamed of pulling a walleye lure," he added.

SPEED LIMITS

We once polled the great poobahs of walleye angling and received the following consensus: *Don't waste time trolling faster than 3.5 mph.* David Frey is one of the fiercest Lake Erie trollers around. "Nobody I know runs 4 to 6 mph. Believe me," Frey asserted. "I've tried going very fast. I suppose walleyes can be caught at 4 mph, but never consistently.

"Strange things start happening at 3 mph," Frey said. "Hot'N Tots are effective to 2, maybe 2.5 mph. Go much faster, and they start doing a half moon. Dipsy Divers begin blinking out at 3 mph. Most spoons lose their effectiveness at 3 mph. A thin spoon starts spinning in circles between 2 and 3 mph and no longer resembles a baitfish."

John Oravec, charter captain on Lake Ontario and longtime *In-Fisherman* contributor, disagreed slightly with Frey's assessment on Dipsys. "Depends on your rigging, but you can chug Dipsys up to 4.6 mph (4 knots)," Oravec said. "But the fastest I've been moving when I connected with a walleye was 3.5 mph."

Such disagreements beg the question: just how much of a professional's perceptions about tools like Dipsys, built on thousands of hours of perfecting deadly techniques, are biased by their belief that *walleyes = slow*? Are such perceptions models of reality?

Will lures trolled at 2 mph trigger more walleyes over the long haul? Probably. Does that mean walleyes can't be caught at higher speeds? No. But that's the perception. Even with log books full of data, are perceptions always accurate, or might they be more accurately characterized as barriers?

Oravec spends most of his time chasing salmon and trout. The fastest he trolls for them is slightly over 4.5 mph. "At that point, lure choice is limited. Few presentations can move that fast and still resemble something a fish wants to eat or even try to kill. It would be like biting into the Tasmanian Devil as he buzzbaits overland in his vortex mode. Not an appealing prospect."

But that, Stange explained, is the point. "Most lures aren't made to travel at those speeds. But some are—the Heddon Hellbender and Buck Perry's Spoonplug, to name two. People ogle them and say, 'They aren't walleye plugs.' And they're right. Cast and retrieve those lures, and they don't appeal to walleyes. But using Perry's system, where speed and depth control are the principal priorities, those lures catch walleyes at over 5 mph. Sometimes. In the right situation. I'm not suggesting always trolling that fast."

Perceptions. Is an *effective range of speeds*, even one offered by a successful professional, a useful model of reality or a set of barriers bracketed by the limitations of certain equipment?

Back to Lake Erie for a moment. Professionals who sharpened their canines on that particular body of water troll faster than pros elsewhere. "We call it the Lake Erie Troll," said Don Nagel, Jr., from Avon, Ohio. "The basic 1.65 to 2.75 mph trolling speed so common here is rare at other tournament sites. On outside turns, lures travel over 4 mph. During short, intense feeding periods that last a half hour or less, trolling at 4 mph can be productive.

"In fact, we often start the day near that trolling speed. The bigger boats used here are going fast, anyway. We have to work at slowing down by dropping plates or dragging bags. The most efficient method is to start fast and let the fish tell us how far to scale down, because losing 1 mph demands a chore of one kind or another."

But Erie is a fish factory. It's possible to troll all summer at 1 mph (.87 knot) and catch lots of fish. But go to nearby Pymatuning or the reservoirs of the Allegheny River, and walleye fishermen, especially in the heat of summer, may become desperate.

"Now there we go again, using that word *desperate*," Stange said. "Very fast isn't desperate; it's just another tactic that happens to have been lost over the last decade. Sometimes, you're going to trigger something while covering water fast with a lure that maintains its equilibrium at speeds over 4 mph. Carp can catch lures moving that fast. Bullheads can. Walleyes can, too."

VIBRATION

"A common perception is that speed and depth control are the two most important variables in angling presentations," Stange said. "But during the last decade, I've come to believe in three vital variables. The missing one's vibration."

Each lure, each blade style, each blade size, and each livebait gives off a vibration pattern. Walleyes sense vibrations with their lateral line and inner ears. Lower frequencies within about the 1 to 200 cycle-per-second (Hz) range can only be felt. Those in the 600 to 13,000 Hz range, depending on the species of fish in question, can probably only be heard. Apparently, overlap occurs between approximately 20 and 200 Hz levels.

So it seems that all lures, blades, and baits produce low-frequency vibrations that fish can distinguish with their lateral lines and that many lures produce higher-frequency vibrations fish can hear, including the clatter of rattle chambers and hooks. Most lures do both.

Is it important to hit that overlap button? Maybe. Some days. The point is, vibration plays a large part in the lives of predators. Certain signals from wounded or fleeing prey trigger predators into striking, because the same vibrations led to success in the past. Perhaps certain other vibrations produce curiosity; perhaps others evoke a response similar to anger or irritation.

Speed plays a large part in vibration. The faster a lure moves, the faster it vibrates, up to the point when it begins to gyrate out of control. Lures that stay in control at high speeds are perhaps more likely to push that overlap button. That can be either good or bad. But those lures most certainly will be felt and heard by any fish in the vicinity.

"Vibration is equally as important as speed and depth."
—Doug Stange

"The object of speed trolling on tough lakes was to trigger walleyes unresponsive to typical tactics," Stange explained. "And we didn't only catch walleyes. Pike, bass, muskie, even catfish were regulars at Speedy's Bar & Grill.

"But remember, speed and depth aren't the only primary factors," he continued. "Vibration is equally as important as speed and depth."

"Perry called it *sound*," Csanda pointed out.

"But he put it into a second group of variables," Stange said. "At times, vibration overrules speed. Different baits give off different patterns of sound and vibration. Some days it takes a particular pattern to push that button that says 'dinnertime' to a fish."

SPEED ARSENAL

As Stange says, Spoonplugs and Hellbenders can scoot. More recent designs also track well at high speed—lures like the Normark Shad Rap, the Luhr-Jensen Speed Trap, the Rebel Fastrac, and the Storm ThunderStick. Of course, no lure type always comes out of the box capable of running that fast, but these baits do, or they can be tuned for fast running.

Lanny West, former marketing director for PRADCO, said the Fastrac was filmed running true at 20 mph. "It reaches optimum depth at 2.3 mph (2 knots)," West reported. "Fishing line, because of its surface area, creates resistance and bows, pulling a lure up at higher speeds. But the Fastrac continues to track true at high speeds. That's what it was designed for. The maximum speed we recommend is about 8 mph (7 knots)."

"I suppose the Shad Rap has a limit," answered Craig Webber of Normark, "but I haven't seen one. We've had them over 10 mph, and they continue to run true. The same generally holds for Rapalas. They work both ultraslow and ultrafast."

Level-wind reels, minimum-stretch lines, and 5½- to 6-foot, medium-action rods are the ticket for high-speed trolling with lures. Wire, either braided or single-strand, No Bo, and superlines are good line options. The rod must be soft

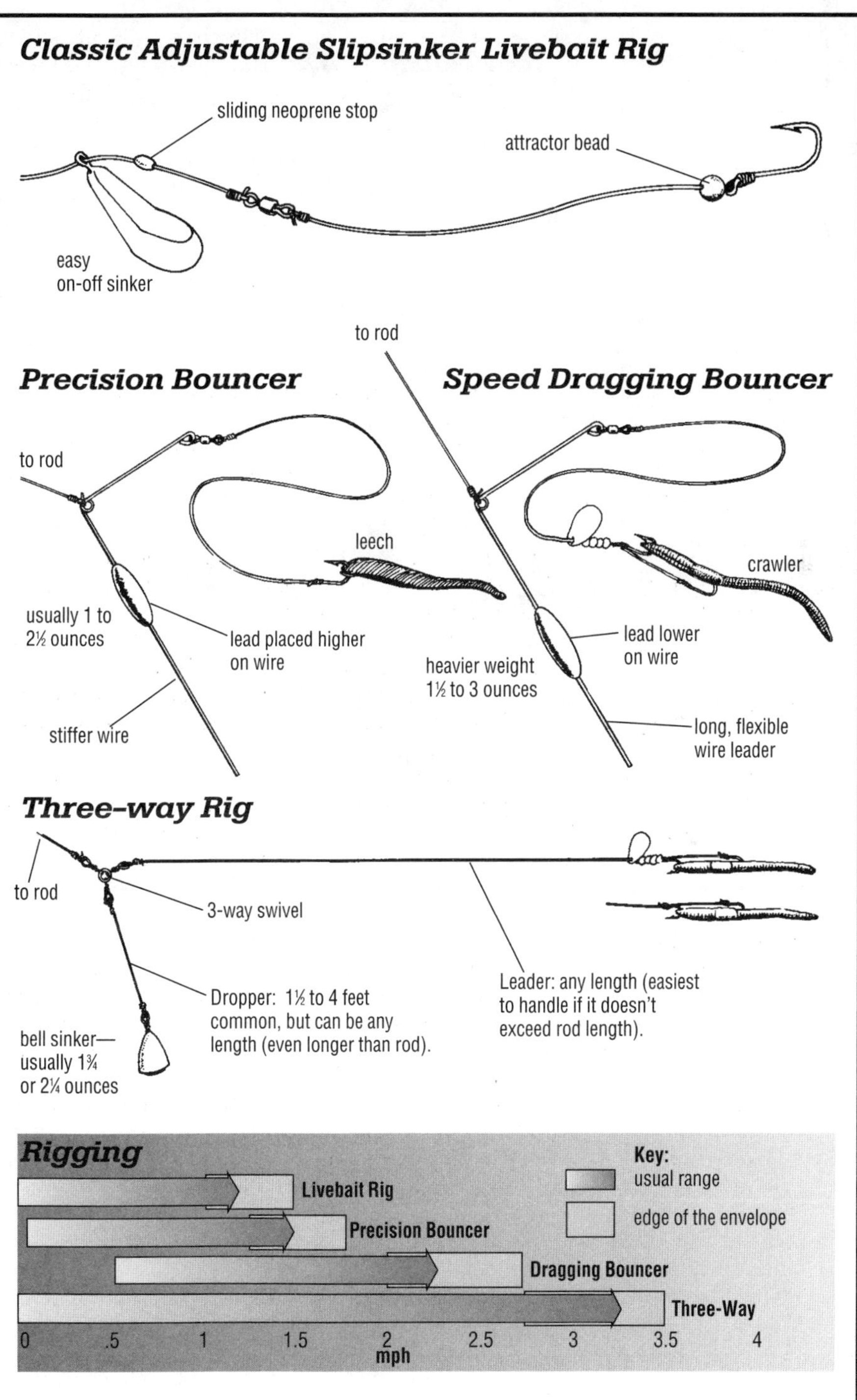

Classic Adjustable Slipsinker Livebait Rig
sliding neoprene stop
attractor bead
easy on-off sinker

to rod

Precision Bouncer
Speed Dragging Bouncer
to rod
leech
crawler
usually 1 to 2½ ounces
lead placed higher on wire
lead lower on wire
heavier weight 1½ to 3 ounces
stiffer wire
long, flexible wire leader

Three-way Rig
to rod
3-way swivel
Dropper: 1½ to 4 feet common, but can be any length (even longer than rod).
Leader: any length (easiest to handle if it doesn't exceed rod length).
bell sinker— usually 1¾ or 2¼ ounces

Rigging
Key:
usual range
edge of the envelope
Livebait Rig
Precision Bouncer
Dragging Bouncer
Three-Way
0   .5   1   1.5   2   2.5   3   3.5   4
mph

Move Along Quickly

Al Lindner is the classic example of a great fisherman who often pushes the edge of the speed envelope with his presentations. "Take livebait rigging, for example," In-Fisherman Contributing Editor Dave Csanda observes.

"Used to be the man moved so fast that if you were in the boat with him, you had to use a 1-ounce slipsinker to even stay in touch with bottom."

Al's point is to move along quickly, searching for active fish. Today, Al uses a precision bottom bouncer when he wants to move along more quickly with a livebait. And when he reaches the edge of the envelope with a precision bouncer, he switches to a heavier bouncer and a spinner rig.

The livebait rig works best from about 0 to a maximum of 1 mph, the precision bouncer at about 1 mph, a heavier bouncer and a spinner rig up to about 2.5 mph. Beyond that?

Lindner: "I'm big into three-way rigging these days. It may be the most versatile rigging of all. Lets you move slowly with livebait, but with enough weight, it also allows you to move at least 3 mph with a spinner rig."

enough to protect the connections on impact with a fish, yet sturdy enough to stand up to the pull of a lure traveling at hat-on-backwards speed.

Spoons, thought to be a high-speed option by many, almost disappear from the charts after 5 mph. Many thin spoons start to spin out at 2.5 mph. Heavier trolling spoons, like the Silver Leaf and Evil Eye Monarch, hang in there to between 4.4 and 5 mph.

"Every so often I read about a walleye tournament angler who likes to troll directly with or against swells," Oravec commented. "If you're surging with the waves at 2.8 mph, you're spinning most spoons. A better strategy is to cut the waves at a 30-degree angle."

Surging affects any presentation. It speeds and slows lures, spoons, and baitrigs, which can be good or bad. "Always watch your lure in the water to see how speed changes affect it," Oravec suggested.

What about bait options at higher speeds? Will walleyes respond to Super Leech, able to circumnavigate small lakes at a single bound, or wiggle?

Gary Roach offered us his opinion. "You can go 2 mph with a spinner rig, but you need 4 ounces of weight to do it," he replied. "But if you want to go heavier, you can. As long as you can keep it on 'em, there's no reason you can't go as fast as you would with a crankbait."

What if you want to go 6 mph?

"Get serious."

We changed the subject to blade types. We concluded that a Colorado blade starts turning when it's barely moving, an Indiana blade gets going at less than .5 mph, and wil-low-leaf blades revolve at about .5 mph.

We concluded that a Colorado blade starts turning when it's barely moving, an Indiana blade gets going at less than .5 mph, and willow-leaf blades revolve at about .5 mph.

Blades keep turning at speeds beyond that, but their vibration patterns change.

Speed and vibration are linked. If a certain vibration pattern is required to trigger a fish, the presentation has to move at that speed. If you concentrate only on lure type, size, and color, you may be missing fish by passing in and out of their optimal speed range.

Which brings us to speed-measuring equipment. Moor Electronics, Eagle Claw, and several other companies market devices for measuring surface speed. Some anglers depend on the speed indicators built into their Liquid Crystal Display units. Few of these devices yield the same readouts. Side by side on the same dash, one reads 2.4, while another reads 2.8. It depends on how they're mounted and the flow dynamics at the point where each device enters the water.

Nonetheless, what the device reads when you're catching fish is the reading to keep as a point of reference.

Keith Kavajecz, noted walleye professional, told us, "I put a crankbait in the water and start moving. When it starts to wiggle and dive, I start trolling. For the most part, I don't troll fast. I usually can pull bigger fish from the pack by going 1 to 1.5 mph. A lot of lures like Hot'N Tots lose their random, erratic flash off to the side at higher speed.

"I troll at my maximum of 3 mph during warm, stable, summer conditions when fish are really on the feed and willing to chase. That's not a minnow-lure bite; it's a high-action, erratic crankbait bite. When they want something faster, I pump the rod. That creates a stop-and-go that seems to trigger more fish than a steady speed."

OUTER LIMITS

Stange agreed with Kavajecz about erratic motion. Erratic lures, he said, often trigger more strikes. "Bass fishermen call it *deflection*," he added. "Lures have to deflect off an object, or deflect to the side during a speed change, or have their own built-in deflection pattern."

But Stange disagreed with the entire planet on the speed issue.

"Most predators can move at least 12 mph in bursts," Stange said. "Why? Escape speed? From what? From pike, bass, and walleyes. And if they can escape at that speed, they can attack other things at speeds close to that."

Salmon, as Oravec quickly pointed out, can cruise at speeds of over 30 mph. Does that mean we should troll that fast?

"The speed trolling popular in a few areas years ago is no strange phenomenon," Stange said. "It works almost anywhere under certain conditions. Ultra-fast trolling never was popular and never will be. The point isn't to engender a bum's rush on Spoonplugs and high-speed equipment. The point is to alter perceptions, to get fishermen questioning the speed equation—pushing the outer edge of the speed envelope with every type of presentation, whether rigging or jigging or speed trolling with vibrating baits.

"Sometime this year, whether you're a pro in a tournament or on a weekend jaunt, you're going to hit a wall; you'll cull and cull, looking for—needing—a 6-pound fish; you'll become desperate (there's that word again) for just one fish for dinner. That's the time to grab a Shad Rap and push the edge of this speed envelope; bounce a bait like a Mad Shad along bottom at the edge of a bar where fish that have never seen it are holding. Surprise!"

BIG *AND* FAST?

"Look at those guys; they're flying," said pro walleye angler Dave Kidd to his partner, pointing toward a competitor's boat. They'd been bouncing around in the other boat's wake all morning and had yet to see the other competitors net a fish. Although the speed indicator on Kidd's graph read 2.8 mph, the other boat continued to pass them as if they were standing still.

The weather was a walleye angler's nightmare. A cold front had blown through during early morning, leaving a flat, calm lake full of inactive fish. Or so Kidd thought.

Meanwhile, the seemingly misguided duo continued to troll laps around the entire field as Kidd continued his jovial ribbing. Come weigh-in time, however, the other team providing the comic relief for the day bested the entire field, claiming first place by several pounds. Trolling up to 6 mph with baits twice the size of the predominant forage paid off for them—after a cold front, no less.

OLD HABITS DIE HARD

Most walleye anglers still believe that walleyes always prefer slow-moving, subtle presentations, regardless of season. Traditionally, our baits are a proper size for walleyes. And trolling speeds are well within accepted limits—slow in cold water, slower than slow after cold fronts, and a little faster during summer.

As a result, we usually spend a large part of each summer picking away at the few reservoir 'eyes we're fortunate enough to catch out of the seemingly count-

less arches scrolling across our sonar screens. If our summer trolling speed ever rises above 3.5 mph, we plead temporary insanity and slow the boat down to a rate at which a walleye can actually be caught. No doubt many of these fish would readily bite a slower presentation earlier in the season, but in warmer water, the rules are different.

Fact is, the tactics used by walleye anglers today haven't changed so much as they have expanded upon the foundation laid by the pioneers, evolving as new frontiers get explored. For dedicated walleye chasers targeting fish in shad-based reservoirs throughout the Midwest and Mideast, the frontier today is speed trolling with large crankbaits.

Trolling large crankbaits at high speed can help you make more frequent catches of larger walleyes as well as of many smaller specimens. But how fast is fast and how large is large?

Kidd made the speed with large-bait connection for walleyes on a summer trolling trip for muskies. After several unsuccessful passes over a flat loaded with fish, he decided to search for greener pastures. Leaving lines in the water, he kicked the boat speed to 5 mph and motored up the shore to a weedline that had been productive in the past. About halfway there, the rod, which was towing a Bagley Monster Shad, started to buck under the strain of a fish. With his reel spooled with 25-pound test, Kidd quickly boated not the small muskie he expected but a 6-pound walleye.

A fluke? Can walleyes be caught on muskie-sized baits at ludicrous speeds? Actually, this is a common occurrence among trollers from the natural lakes of New York to the reservoirs of Kentucky and beyond. Many regional chapters of Muskies Inc. are awarding prizes for the largest walleye caught during a muskie tournament.

Most walleye anglers in the region use small baits throughout the year: the C.C. Shad, Big O, and the Storm Hot'N Tot are popular and work well when walleyes are keying on forage that size. But as shad grow, bait choice should progressively become larger.

MATCH THE HATCH?

During summer, masses of small juvenile shad, along with a smattering of holdover adult shad huddle in pods across the many flats of a reservoir. Suspending around and below them are loose schools of walleyes, primarily fish from the same or closely related year class. Remnant populations of larger walleyes from earlier year classes roam the water, too, seeking out pods of bait. Walleyes, young and old, gorge on the abundant bait.

Competing with such massive schools of forage fish can be frustrating. You need to show the fish something similar to what they're feeding on, yet different enough to attract their attention.

"Traditional summer presentations, such as small crankbaits trolled at standard speeds, give a walleye too much time to examine and inspect a bait," says Elmer Heyob, Jr., an exceptional angler and fishery biologist with the Ohio Division of Wildlife. "In the warm water of summer, fish are active and feeding heavily. Small walleyes and saugeyes readily give chase to a big bait. Anglers should take advantage of a big walleye's appetite for a substantially larger meal and a younger walleye's aggressive nature."

LARGE IS RELATIVE

Large baits, such as the Bagley Monster Shad, Bagley DB O6, and Rapala Super Shad Rap, match the size of adult shad. Considering that these baits don't necessarily represent a large meal for a big walleye or saugeye, you realize that large is more often in the mind of the angler than the fish.

A walleye can and will eat prey roughly one-third of its own size. This explains what that 17-inch walleye was doing

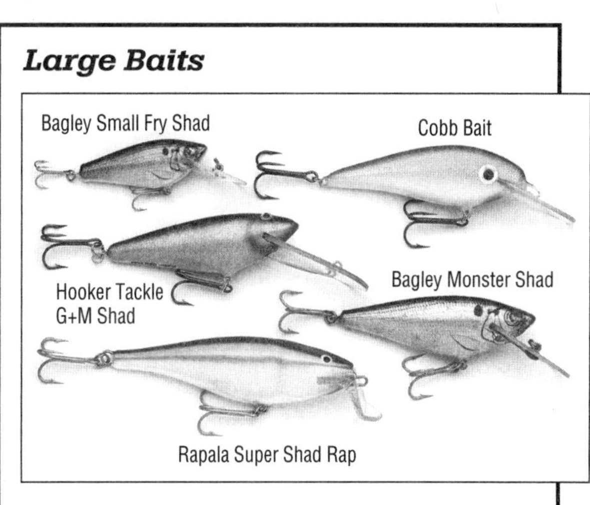

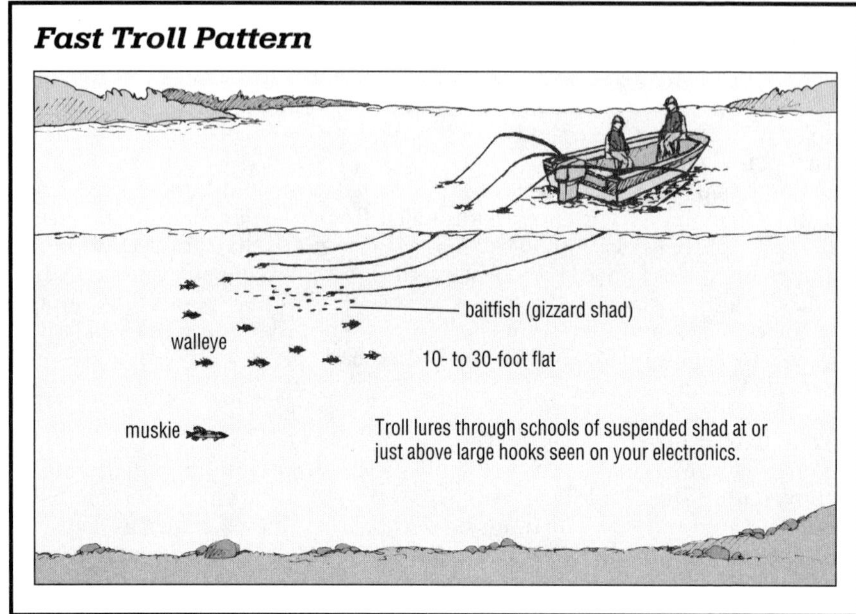

with that 6-inch bait. Remember that walleye you boated last summer that left a mess of half-digested shad all over your boat? How big were the shad? Chances are they were bigger than the crankbait you caught the walleye on.

FAST MAY BE FASTER THAN YOU THINK

A bait used in a fast presentation creates an immediate reaction that says *grab it before it gets away or another fish gets it.*

"Impulse strikes happen all the time," says PWT touring pro Mark Brumbaugh. "I've had many fish hit a lure as I reel in to check or change bait. Add the reel retrieve speed to the trolling speed, and you realize that the lure's moving at a pretty good clip."

Rather than using traditional baits, try trolling larger lures substantially faster. Move up to heavier line, at least 12- to 14-pound test, and rods and reels capable of withstanding the pull of these large, deep-diving baits trolled at fast speeds.

Once you locate walleyes, note their depth. Typically they'll be from 10 to 30 feet deep, depending on water clarity and temperature, over the large flats that are common in reservoirs. Run your baits slightly higher than the majority of the hooks on your screen. Perhaps the best approach is to troll lures close to or even through pods of bait spread across the flat, often relating to a thermocline.

Set your first line so the lure runs just above the baitfish. Then gradually run each lure deeper, with the last lure running below the school. Next, kick up your boat's speed to 4 mph. Experiment with speed, going up to 7 or 8 mph if that speed doesn't exceed the running capability of your bait. Change baits, colors, lead length, and depth until you get bit. Once you identify a pattern, set up each line with the hot lure to intercept active fish at that depth.

Looking beyond what most anglers believe about walleyes frees us from the limits that hold too many of us captive. Revving up summer trolling with larger baits and faster speeds is but one way to break free.

Mark Romanack

'Eyeote Ugly

THERE IS NO JUSTICE IN WALLEYE FISHING

In keeping with our Good, Bad, Ugly theme, let's now examine several patterns that absolutely shouldn't work, but that under the right circumstances do. They fly in the face of traditional wisdom—yet may catch fish when classic systems fail.

An old proverb states that beauty is only skin deep but that ugly goes clear to the bone. Thousands of years ago, the first anglers employed carved bones as primitive fishhooks. Apparently, some things never go out of style.

GIVE A RIP FOR WALLEYES

Certain things in my fishing career jerked the slack out of my line. My first exposure to ripjigging was one of them. You think you've got it all figured out, then you're completely embarrassed by somebody using a weird technique you've never even heard of.

—Al Lindner

The ripjigging or snapjigging technique developed by legendary Minnesota fishing guide Dick "the Griz" Grzywinski is an amazingly productive system that breaks just about every rule in walleye fishing. The best advice for anyone who wants to learn to ripjig is to start with the basic principles of jig fishing—and then do just the opposite.

- Standard jig trolling procedure is to backtroll very slowly. Ripjigging involves trolling forward at two or three times the normal jig trolling speed.
- Standard jig trolling strategy is to keep your line as close to vertical as possible. When ripjigging, toss your lure far behind the boat.
- In standard jig trolling, you twitch the jig lightly. In ripjigging, you jerk it violently.
- Ordinarily, you keep your jig bumping bottom, twitching it and allowing it to settle back. But in ripjigging, you keep the jig off bottom, almost never allowing it to touch.
- In jig trolling, you usually twitch the jig, then keep your line taut as it sinks. In ripjigging, you intentionally throw slack into the line while the jig sinks.
- The usual way to detect a jig strike is to feel for a subtle tap as the jig sinks. In ripjigging, you often don't feel the tap; the fish is hooked on the next snap of the rod.

The Legendary Griz.

Always forward troll into the wind, either directly or at an angle. "I see lots of guys trying to backtroll and ripjig," Grzywinski chuckles. "That may work on calm water, but not on a windy day. The waves go right over their heads when they backtroll that fast."

On choppy water, the Griz clips a drift sock to his bow eye on a 3-foot rope. The drift sock stabilizes the bow, so the wind doesn't swing it around when he trolls forward. With the short rope, the sock trails back under the boat but won't foul in the motor. It's a slick system. Not only do you stay dry, but you also enjoy a much smoother ride.

Ironically, ripjigging is much harder for an accomplished jig fisherman to learn than for a novice. "Women often seem to do better at it than men," Grzywinski notes. Fewer preconceived notions to overcome.

Many first ripjigging attempts are disasters. You can be sitting right next to the Griz, observing his every move and trying to duplicate it, and he's still likely to do the ten-to-one number on you.

Novice ripjiggers typically don't throw enough slack into the line, so their jig doesn't have the necessary erratic action. For long-time jig fishermen, it's difficult to break the habit of keeping the line taut while the jig sinks. Snap your rod forward with a sidearm motion, then immediately drop it back to the starting position before snapping again. This puts your arm in position for a strong hookset. Again, it's easy for a novice but unnatural for a veteran jigger.

The other difficult part of ripjigging is gauging the right amount of line. "Ya got to learn how far back to toss the jig for different depths of water," the Griz explains. The idea is to keep your jig as close to bottom as possible without making bottom contact. As a rule, line length should be 4 to 5 times the water depth, although you may need a little more on a windy day to make up for line bow. The only sure way to determine the right amount of line, however, is to experiment. If you're picking up weeds or debris, shorten up.

EQUIPMENT

The Griz swears by his own hand-tied chicken feather jigs. "Takes me an hour to tie one," he grumbles. "But it's worth the trouble. The wiggling feathers drive the fish crazy. If the fish are bitin', ya don't even need a minnow, just a plain jig. White or chartreuse—it doesn't make much difference. When it's windy, I like 1/4-ounce; otherwise, I use 1/8-ounce."

On a trip to North Dakota's Lake Sakakawea a few years back, Grzywinski made a believer of some local guides by badly outfishing them with an unbaited "Griz Jig." When one of them didn't show up the next day, a friend explained, "He's out to the farm catching chickens."

Another of Grzywinski's favorites is the Northland Fire-Ball jig, which he tips with a fathead minnow hooked through the eyes. "Fire-Balls are easy for my customers to use," he notes. Many of your favorite jigs will probably work.

A few of the Griz's famous chicken jigs, which work so well for ripjigging. Similar jigs, particularly hair jigs, work, too.

Grzywinski prefers a 7-foot, fast-tip spinning rod for ripjigging. The long rod helps him snap the jig with less effort and makes it easy to take up slack when setting the hook. He spools up with 8- to 10-pound Trilene XT. Lighter or softer line won't stand up to the violent jerking. Even tough line should be changed frequently because sometimes the rod tip frays it.

WHEN AND WHERE

Primarily a warmwater technique, ripjigging can be effective well into fall. When water temperatures drop below 50°F, however, walleyes may refuse to chase a fast-moving jig.

Prime ripjigging water is less than 15 feet deep, with long, subtle breaklines, but it's possible to ripjig in water as deep as 25 feet. "Most people think structure is absent where I do my ripjigging," Grzywinski says. "But I'm usually following a gradual break. I see guys weaving back and forth along the break, but I keep my boat at a precise depth—exactly where the fish are.

"In the large, often windswept lakes I fish, lots of times I find walleyes around

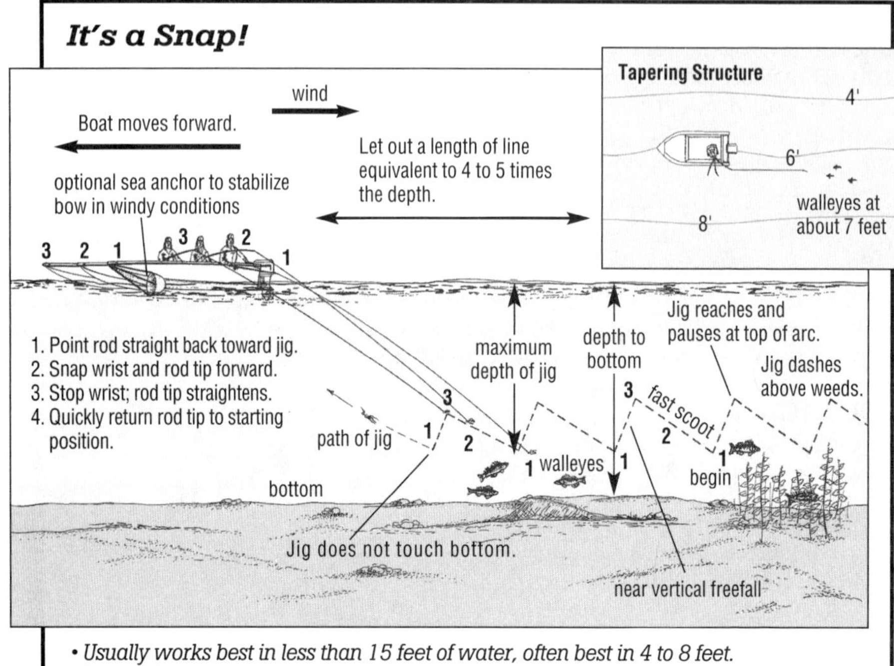

7 feet, even on calm, sunny days. Walleyes are programmed to feed shallow. A lot more fish are shallow than people think, and the shallow ones are the biters."

Bottom where Grzywinski does most of his ripjigging is sandy, sometimes with light weedgrowth. But you can also ripjig over rock reefs or weedbeds, particularly cabbage or coontail. Just run the jig right over the weed tops and rip it hard when you feel it catch a weed. "Walleyes come right out of the weeds and blast it," Griz explains. "They think it's a minnow trying to get away.

"Time of day doesn't seem to matter. I catch 'em all day long. Sometimes the best bite is at midday."

WHY IT WORKS

Ripjigging has an unparalleled triggering effect on walleyes. Like most predatory fish, walleyes focus on baitfish swimming abnormally while ignoring an entire school swimming in unison. So it's not surprising that they find an erratically darting jig hard to resist. Their propensity for picking out the odd baitfish also explains the technique's effectiveness in late summer and early fall, when the glut of young-of-the-year forage fish slows walleye action in most waters.

Standard walleye-fishing advice is to keep bait on bottom, but when you're ripjigging, work the jig higher. Walleyes' eyes are positioned high on their heads, which explains their responsiveness to a jig dancing above more than to one dragged below.

Another advantage to ripjigging is that it requires trolling at a fairly rapid clip, so you cover more water than you would with other jigging or livebait techniques.

"Took me years to get a real feel for it," Al Lindner recalls. "But it's a technique you should have in your arsenal, because it triggers walleyes when they won't hit any other presentation. Ripjigging proved to me that a lack of success doesn't necessarily mean the fish aren't biting. It means you just haven't found the right technique to make them bite."

SHORTLINE TROLLING FOR NIGHTTIME WALLEYES

The standard formula for taking nighttime walleyes on flats is longline trolling with long, slim, minnow-shaped crankbaits. The idea behind using a long line is that in relatively shallow water, walleyes spook easily, and having at least 100 feet of line behind the boat gives them a chance to settle down after being disturbed by a boat.

When walleyes are in an active feeding mode, this technique is effective. But on many occasions, the fish are unaggressive, hugging bottom, or positioned below the tops of coontail. After several nights in which standard longline trolling couldn't buy a walleye bite, researcher Bruce Carlson experimented with a new

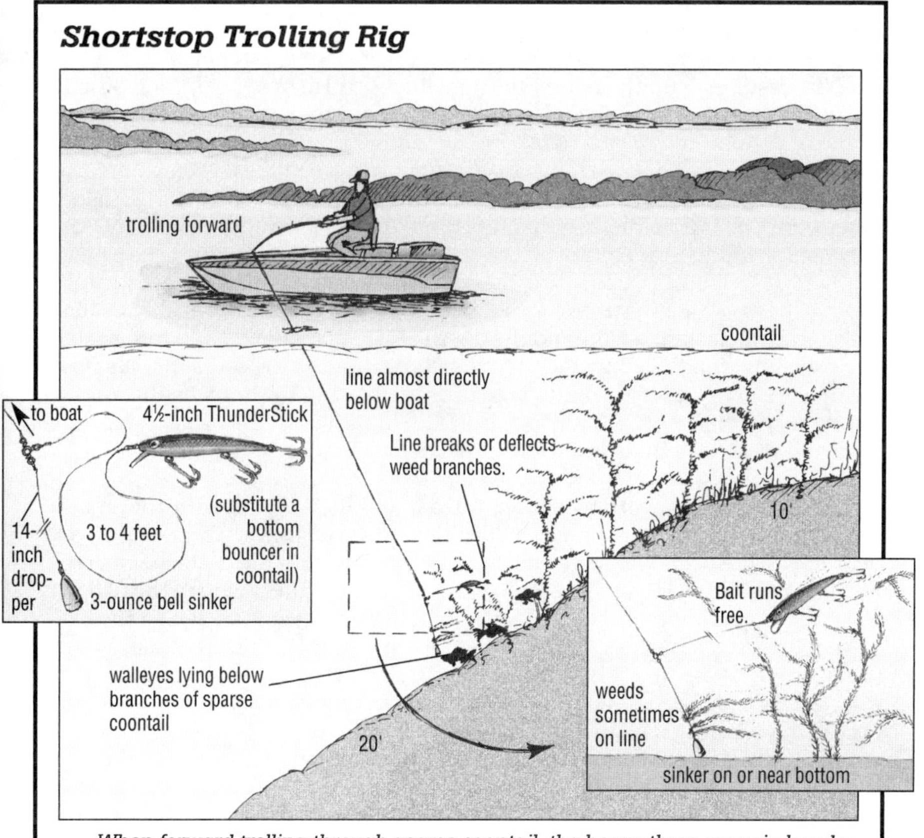

When forward trolling through sparse coontail, the heavy three–way rig breaks or deflects weed branches, allowing the crankbait to run free and rustling walleyes from beneath the weeds.

technique that has proven considerably more effective than longline trolling when fish aren't aggressively biting.

The most important element of shortline trolling is overcoming the belief that your crankbait must be far away from the boat. With this technique, the bait is located almost directly below the motor. The basic setup consists of a three-way rig with a 3-ounce bell sinker on a 14-inch dropper line and a 3- to 4-foot leader.

To date, a 4½-inch ThunderStick has proven to be the most effective bait for catching fish and not getting hung up. In areas with weeds, especially chara (sandgrass), but also coontail, using a wire bottom bouncer instead of a drop sinker on a leader greatly reduces fouling in weeds. It's not uncommon to troll through a 100-yard bed of lightly to moderately dense coontail and emerge with no weeds on either the bottom bouncer or the bait. In dense beds of chara, a bell sinker becomes quickly covered with a wad of weeds, but weeds don't seem to adversely affect the fish-catching ability of this rig.

Basic to the success of this technique is precision. The presentation has been tested principally on weedy lakes at depths of 14 to 18 feet, where a variation in bottom type and vegetation is present within a 2- to 5-foot depth range. Use a standard baitcasting outfit, and release the rig with the reel in free spool. As soon as the sinker touches bottom, engage the antireverse. Keep the sinker on or within a few inches of bottom, and release or take up line according to feel or graph readings.

Shortline trolling also is effective on structure or weedlines when you're making numerous turns over a small area. Hitting all the important areas with longline trolling is impossible, but this shortline trolling technique allows the same accuracy as Lindy Rigs with livebait.

Over clean bottoms, use of the rig is straightforward, but its effectiveness in coontail beds came as a surprise. The lack of constant fouling probably is due to the short, almost vertical line and the depth at which the sinker and lure are usually traveling (that is, below the first branching point of the coontail). It's possible to feel the rig going through the weeds, displacing the branches of coontail, but rarely do the hooks actually catch on it. This offers access to fish lying at the base of the coontail that won't rise to strike the standard presentation of a bait trolled just above the tops of the weeds.

Why do fish bite an artificial bait trolled almost directly beneath your motor? For many years, anglers assumed that fish close to a boat and motor passing directly overhead were negatively affected and needed time to settle down before striking a bait. This obviously is not the case, at least at night. Some of the fish may be spooked, but apparently even more of them are triggered by seeing the bait.

In retrospect, it may be that the sound of a smoothly running outboard motor really doesn't scare fish. This theory is supported by 40-year-old research, which revealed no negative effect during stillfishing when a motor was run continuously above livebaits. The shadow of the boat going overhead may be more significant as a spooking factor—certainly it's an important consideration in daytime. But experienced night-fishermen know that fish are spooked less by boats at night, which probably accounts for many boatside strikes at night. Fish located under coontail are probably less affected by the presence of a boat than are fish in open water.

We haven't tried this technique extensively in daylight. We're not confident that it would be effective during the day in clear water lakes at depths shallower than 15 feet, although we've used this technique on walleyes in 20 to 24 feet of water in clear lakes. But the lake used in the initial nighttime experiment had a Secchi disk reading of 27 feet during the testing period. Such deep water clarity wasn't a negative factor for night-fishing. This technique may be effective during the day in turbid water or near mudlines in reservoirs.

Whether or not a motor passing directly overhead serves as an attractant to walleyes hasn't been seriously considered. It's certainly a factor in muskie fishing; in some waters, such as Lake St. Clair in Michigan, most experienced trollers keep at least one bait in the wash of the propeller.

This technique is still in the early stages of development but has already earned a solid place in the walleye trolling repertoire. When the fish are actively biting, we still rely on longline trolling most of the time. But when we see most fish hugging bottom, we consider turning to shortline trolling, confident that it often outproduces longline trolling.

WOOD 'EYE? COULD 'EYE?

As population centers grew from small towns into major cities, the need for electricity and the desire to put large numbers of people to work led the U. S. Corps of Engineers and the Tennessee Valley Authority to dam great rivers for generating hydroelectric power. The resulting dams created large bodies of water like Laurel River Lake, Lake Cumberland, Old Hickory Lake, Norris Lake, Center Hill Lake, and many others.

Formation of these impoundments drastically changed the habitat and migratory patterns of the great southern river walleye. Popular belief held that many populations were pushed to extinction. Was this because local anglers lost their favorite river fishing spots when the rivers were impounded? Or was it that they lacked the knowledge, equipment, and opportunity to locate and catch walleyes in such large bodies of water?

Add the proper number of adhesive SuspenDots to make a ThunderStick or other minnow-imitating crankbait descend and hover at a productive depth.

Obviously, local anglers had fished for and continued to fish for native southern-strain walleyes in known spots during spring spawning runs, but during the rest of the year, the walleyes seemed to be gone. Surely some were destroyed, but the survivors adapted to reservoir habitat and continued to grow to gigantic proportions exceeding those of most northern walleyes.

Experience indicates that good populations of large fish are still vulnerable to anyone armed with a modicum of walleye tackle and savvy. Potential world-record fish swim within easy reach of anglers who are just becoming aware of open water walleye fishing year-round in mild climates.

QUESTIONS NEEDING ANSWERS

Many walleye systems developed on northern waters apply equally well to southern impoundments. Jigs, crankbaits, spinner rigs, livebait rigs, and slip-bobbers can all be used to great success. Fishing the gin-clear water, extreme depths, and mountainous topography of many southern reservoirs, however,

Threading the Needle

No needles in this haystack. Them's big walleyes in there amongst the trees. You just gotta find a way to get 'em out. Here's how.

Move into the timber with an electric motor and visually establish open lanes through which you can retrieve a crankbait 20 to 25 feet deep, between and above deep flooded timber. Once you establish open lanes, mark the trees with colored chalk as a visual reference. Move the boat to one end of a path (**A**) and lower a weighted Storm Suspending ThunderStick into the strike zone or to just above the tops of deep flooded trees. Adjust how deep the lure will sink by adding or eliminating adhesive Storm SuspenDots as needed. A perfectly weighted lure will suspend in or just above the zone of walleye use.

Once the lure reaches the proper

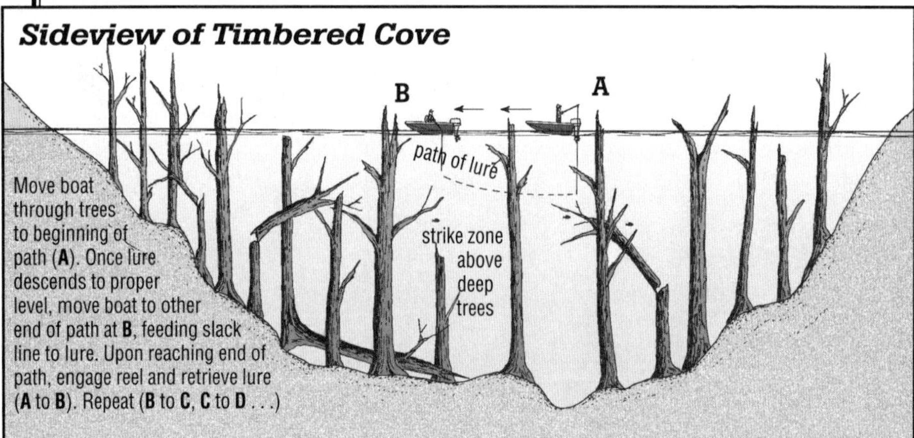

requires adjustments in strategy. Unique questions have arisen:

- Where do the majority of walleyes spend most of their time after spawning is over?
- Which areas of reservoirs should you concentrate on? Are there particular structures that hold fish better than others?
- Are there any special or new techniques to fine-tune success?

Fortunately, there's a single answer to all of the above: wood.

In many southern reservoirs, miles of standing timber are located along points and within coves. Flooded hemlock, pine, oak, and maple trees form major structure within these areas. Fishing standing timber in clear water is one of the toughest challenges imaginable. Casting crankbaits, even vertical jigging with spoons, is frustrating because of the number of hang-ups and lost tackle. Add the spooking factors of gin-clear water and wary walleyes, and you wonder if fish were even there in the first place.

John Williams, district biologist with the Kentucky Game & Fish Department, implemented a telemetry study designed to track walleyes in Laurel Lake, Kentucky.

level, slowly move your boat to the other end of the path (**B**), feeding slack line to the lure. Upon reaching the other end, engage your reel and begin slowly retrieving the lure. Experiment with steady retrieves, stop-and-go motion, or even vertically jigging beneath the boat. The lure will descend into the strike zone and hover there each time you give slack line.

Once you finish one leg of a path, continue down other doglegs and bends (**C**, **D**, **E**) using a similar method. Remember, establish your route ahead of time to avoid snags. If you just cast ahead of the boat, you'll snag often.

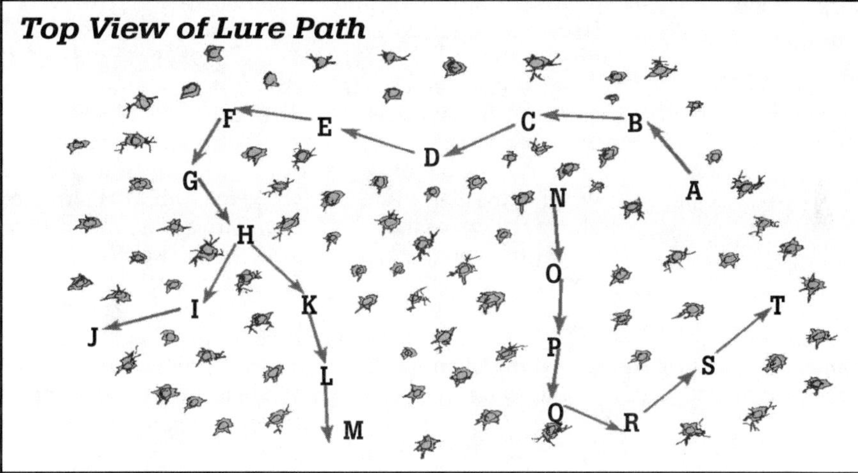

Walleyes may be deep inside timber, not just along outer edges. Weave through the maze of timber, selecting paths where you can fish the lure not only between standing trees but also above the tops of deep treetops and wedged tangles.

His goal was to find seasonal patterns, preferred depth levels, locational patterns, as well as many biological data on these mountain reservoir walleyes. Between his telemetry study and input from anglers like Kentucky walleye pro Rick Markesbery, the seasonal locations and techniques for catching these fish were uncovered.

Williams' tracking study of walleyes weighing between 2 and 14 pounds revealed that 75 percent of the fish studied stayed in timber most of the time. One 14-pound walleye tended to leave the timber, move 300 to 400 yards and occasionally perhaps up to 1/2 mile to the closest points, then proceeded back to the timber again. Its movement occurred at dusk. The fish always returned to the same pine tree; hemlock and pine appear to be the walleyes' preferred flooded timber cover in Laurel Lake.

Most timbered coves hold a tremendous number of threadfin and gizzard shad, which usually suspend in open water just outside the deep timber edge. During summer, when water temperatures commonly reach 73 to 74°F, walleyes occupy a depth of 20 to 25 feet. This depth often contains a large amount of fallen timber. Treetops have broken and fallen into and against nearby standing timber, forming a wedged mass of tangled wood. Where this condition exists, an artificial lake bottom forms, similar to a summer thermocline, with walleyes suspending in and around the submerged wood. During cooler fall and winter conditions, walleyes often drop as deep as 40 to 80 feet.

So how to catch 'em?

STORM'N THE TIMBER

After considerable experimentation, Markesbery developed a system he calls Storm'n the Timber, which encompasses several aspects to catch suspended wary walleyes in clear water timbered coves. Everything in the system must come together properly for it to work, so don't cut corners.

> *Markesbery developed a system he calls Storm'n the Timber, which encompasses several aspects to catch suspended wary walleyes in clear water timbered coves.*

First, be extremely quiet when approaching potential areas. Use an electric trolling motor to ease into the wood. Use your depthfinder not only to mark the presence of fish but also to look for tangled masses of submerged wood, underwater treetops, fallen trees, or any other form of woodcover that might snag your lure in the top 25 feet of water. You're looking for areas between standing trees where you can maneuver your boat, with enough open water above the submerged wood to be able to fish a lure above the top of the wood. Ease through a timber field, and you'll find pockets that meet these criteria and paths you can follow through the flooded forest.

For example, one path may be 20 yards long and a boat length wide, then angle off for another 10 yards, whereupon you can zigzag to another path 30 yards long, lying in another direction. This lane of open water between and above the woodcover is where you should fish. Instead of trying to visualize and remember these confusing paths, simply use a piece of red chalk to mark the trees as you pass them, clearly indicating the path you want your boat or your lure to follow. Carefully cast diving crankbaits along and through these paths, running them just above the submerged wood.

Even better, attach enough Storm SuspenDots to a Suspending ThunderStick minnow-imitator to make the lure sink to a depth just above any submerged wood or down into the strike zone. These tiny dots of adhesive lead tape can sink a minnow-imitating crankbait to a certain depth and cause it to suspend there. Experiment until you find the number of SuspenDots needed to take your bait to the desired level. Add several dots along the belly of the lure, lower it over the side, and let it sink. Count the number of feet the lure descends until it stops sinking. Readjust with more or fewer Dots until you get it right.

Once your lure is tuned for running at the proper depth, move to one end of your path and drop the lure over the side. Here's the weird part: once the lure sinks to the correct level, use your electric motor to slowly move to the other end of a straight path while feeding slack line to the hovering lure. Once you reach the other end of the path, stop the boat, engage your reel, and slowly retrieve the lure to the boat. Seems like a lot of work, but it's far easier and more effective than trying to cast between trees. This technique allows you to look down into the water to make sure you won't snag anything before you retrieve. When you reach a bend in your path, repeat the process of lowering the lure, moving the boat, then retrieving the lure. Continue following the path until you run out of fishable water. Then move on.

Markesbery uses heavy 12- to 20-pound-test Berkley Trilene XT for battling big walleyes in timber. Imagine the fight involved in trying to bring a big fish to the surface while trying to keep it out of the trees! Get it up as fast as you can, and then fight it near the surface. If you don't, you'll be wrapped around several trees in no time. Use a heavy casting rod, even a muskie rod if necessary.

Once you get the hang of the system, try casting the lure down well-known paths, or use a vertical jigging approach between trees. Markesbery's had thrashing attacks on lures jigged a few times, then allowed to flutter downward. He prefers glitter silver, glitter fire-tiger, and Tennessee shad patterns on crankbaits for these conditions. It's important to learn the pattern, develop confidence in your lure selection, and then hang on tight.

Southern walleyes are obviously catchable on more traditional presentations, as evidenced by the large numbers of incidental walleyes caught by bass, crappie, and striper anglers using a variety of techniques. Try vertical jigging with jigs or jigging spoons in timber, on main points, humps, or deep channel edges. You'll catch lots of walleyes on spinner rigs with nightcrawlers fished behind bottom bouncers. And livebait rigs with leeches, crawlers, or minnows are as yet almost unfished on most southern walleye impoundments. Try 'em all. But for a real twist, try Storm'n the Timber to turn wood 'eyes into could 'eyes.

THINGS THAT GO THUMP IN THE BITE

Thump . . . thump . . . thump—impact tremors growing louder and closer. Alert, the beast is on the prowl. Tyrannosaurus, king of the predators? Nope. A thumper jig—big, mean, and nasty—has its sights set on old marble eyes. Like a doomed moth drawn to an irresistible flame, the walleye instinctively turns, facing the approaching Thumpasaurus, lateral line and inner ear tingling. A profile appears out of the murk, rising, falling, resting. Closer now, vague shape and color become discernible form—a big meal, vulnerable to attack. Another jump, a plummet, and *whack*. The fish engulfs the lure.

The main differences between a thumper and a bumper are bulk and weight. Standard walleye jigs run up to 3/8-, maybe 1/2-ounce, and generally are dressed with plastic bodies balanced to match their heads—fine meals for fish of all sizes. Where bumpers leave off, thumpers kick in—3/4-ounce, perhaps a full ounce of lead, with correspondingly larger and bulkier bodies. Use 'em when extra-deep water or strong current demands additional weight to reach, hug, and work bottom.

Avoid jigheads with wide, flat bottoms, which resist sinking and cause jigs to plane. Better designs are either round, oblong, or banana-shaped to cut water and current, drop deep, and stay there. On the best deep water versions, hook eyes poke from the top of the heads rather than forward from the noses. Those with eyes at the noses tend to skip over snags better, however, and work well at medium depths.

Designs sold predominantly as striper or saltwater jigs have bucktail dressings and stout hooks and border on being too large for walleyes. Those designed for walleyes have moderately large hooks that penetrate the fish's mouth without excessive hooksetting force. Note differences in design and select head styles to match conditions.

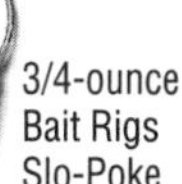

Pulling Thumper Rigs

Thumper Rigs used for the pulling technique are simple three-way rigs consisting of a Jumbo Jig on the dropper, plus a trailing bait. These jigs are heavier than most anglers consider using, ranging from 5/8 ounce up to 2½ ounces, depending on current strength. Saric and Campbell use 1-ounce Lindy Fuzz-E-Grubs on their droppers. Trailing baits typically are one of two choices. First and most common is a minnow-imitating crankbait, like a #10 Rebel Minnow or a #7 Rapala in blue-silver, chartreuse-silver, or shad. A crankbait typically produces the biggest sauger, but only when fish are active.

The second trailer option, used for less aggressive fish, is a simple bead and hook. Place a red or chartreuse bead 4 to 8 inches above the hook and tip the hook with a minnow. Add a Fuzz-E-Grub body to provide a bigger profile—a transitional tactic for fish that won't bite a larger crankbait, yet are active.

"Dropper and trailer lengths can vary. We commonly refer to them as a 123, or a 95," Campbell explains. "A 123 indicates a 12-inch dropper to the jig, and 3 feet back to our trailer. A 95 is a 9-inch dropper with a 5-foot trailer. We start the day with thumpers rigged several ways, both length-wise and baitwise," Campbell continues. "Sauger may hover over bottom at a certain depth, or right down on it. Changing dropper and trailer lengths covers the water column. To keep the trailer at the level of the fish, only the fish can tell us."

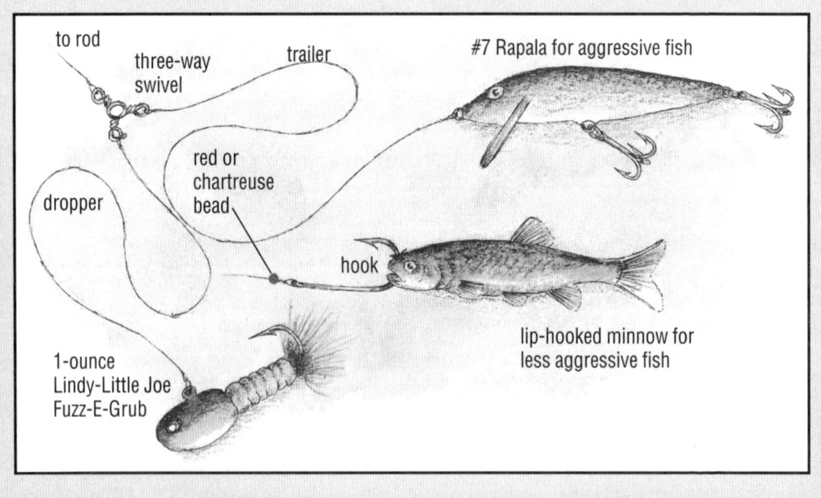

While thumpers can catch small walleyes, they excel for larger fish, for whom their big profiles suggest bigger meals. Fish 'em plain, dress 'em with fatheads or shiner minnows hooked up through the jaw and out the top of the head, or for really big sows, larger chubs create megameals. Thumpers have the weight needed to present large minnows in deep water or current. Smaller jigs are inadequate under extreme conditions.

Heavy weight takes thumpers out of the range of most shallow water or casting situations. They're more effective for deep vertical presentations like backtrolling, drifting, and even forward trolling. Professional tournament anglers like Ted Takasaki and John Campbell use them to troll slowly upstream against current, lifting and dropping the jig to impart a different look to their presentation. Against the current is against the grain in most circumstances, but when normal doesn't produce, abnormal is worth checking.

Most anglers, however, find thumpers best for vertical jigging below 30 feet in lakes or reservoirs. Don't be afraid to try 40 feet or deeper, either. Thumpers plumb the depths. Use standard lift-drop-pause jigging motions. Medium-action rods and 8- or 10-pound-test line should suffice, too, unless you're more comfortable with a slightly beefier combo. After all, a thumper puts quite a bend in a rod, even before a walleye's attached. And for deep water success, you should be able to rear back and slam the hook home, removing line stretch and burying the hook.

Thumping isn't finesse fishing. It's banging on walleyes' doors, huffing and puffing, threatening to knock them down. It's daring fish to bite, and daring to be daring. It's not for the timid. Hang on tight, expect to be soundly jerked at any moment, and be prepared to jerk back with equal gusto.

A BIG NUTHIN' AT NIGHT

If opposites attract, then fishing structure for walleyes has its antistructural counterpart in the web of aquatic life. The opposite of something with a distinct shape and substance must be something shapeless, unseen, unknown. The closest parallel we see in the walleye world is fishing for walleyes that are either suspended over or roaming across open basins. If we take this one step further, we'll be exploring the ultimate anti-pattern—fishin' in the middle of a big nuthin' at night.

Who would do such a thing? A small group of ninja night fighters battles stealthy walleyes that appear nightly like ghosts out of the inky darkness, far from the traditional arena of daytime patterns and presentations. These 'eyes are not just out of the blue; they come out of the infinite blackness, slashing and attacking their hapless prey, then silently disappearing back into the void come dawn's early light.

These 'eyes are not just out of the blue; they come out of the infinite blackness, slashing and attacking their hapless prey, then silently disappearing back into the void come dawn's early light.

"Night-fishing is a common occurrence on Lake Mille Lacs," says former guide Joe Fellegy, the acknowledged sage of all things historical about mid-Minnesota's premier walleye fishery. "But it's chiefly practiced on shallow structure, either by longline trolling minnow-imitating crankbaits along shallow rock points or by anchoring and casting lighted slip-bobbers and leeches atop shallow rock reefs poking toward the surface. In recent years, more anglers have begun night-fishing the edges of deep midlake mudflats, soaking their leeches in deep water along twists and turns in the drop-off at the 20- to 30-foot range. But this new breed of midlake basin anglers has rocked the boat of traditional fishing logic—especially at night."

"The past few seasons, a handful of launches and a growing number of anglers in small boats have been fishing the soft basin areas lying outside the glacially deposited areas of table-top flat humps locally referred to as *mudflats*," says Mike Gannon, a launch driver and fishing guide. That in itself isn't unusual, considering that anglers in many areas now troll such areas for suspended fish. "The big

difference ," Gannon continues, "is that we do it at night, using lighted bobbers and livebait, far from structure of any kind. Baitfish, more than bottom changes, key the areas of best productivity.

"We started fishing this way by probing the edges of the flats at night, then began exploring off the edges, drifting across the adjacent basin. We found that soft-bottomed areas where insects or baitfish were present also attracted walleyes. We had a hard time catching any walleyes there during the day, but when we started fishing for them at night, we found the pattern consistent, easy, and lots of fun.

"Basically, we begin at the edge of one of the larger mudflats. Then we scout the adjacent open basin with our depthfinders, looking for the presence of baitfish. Wherever we spot schools of fish, we toss out the anchor, then set our slipbobbers to dangle a small fluorescent orange or chartreuse jighead, baited with a leech, just above bottom. Or we use a split shot, a red hook, and a chartreuse bead, also with a leech. Then the whole guide party tosses out their bobbers and starts fishing. Sometimes it's necessary to pick up and move a few times to get in on the hot action. But generally, if we anchor within 50 to 100 yards of a school of baitfish, we find walleyes."

Does the same thing work with insect hatches—say, during mayfly or fishfly hatches in early summer, which can make daytime fishing notoriously difficult? "It seems that where insects are hatching out of the basin, baitfish generally are there, too," Gannon says. "The two seem to go together. And, yes, the night bite remains consistent throughout. The pattern lasts until late October, well past the time when insect hatches end. We still catch nice midlake 'eyes at times when a hot night bite also kicked in on shallow rocks in fall, when ciscoes moved up shallow to spawn. No one expected the pattern to last so late in the year.

"We fished mostly within 1/4 mile or so of one of the big mudflats, at around 32 to 36 feet, because we were successful there and usually didn't have to move much. But when activity tended to slack off in an area after a few weeks, we found similar conditions sometimes as far as a mile or more out into the midbasin, usually in the deepest water in the area. Peak activity seemed to occur between about 11 p.m. and 1 a.m., which is when our guide parties typically conclude. I've stayed out later, though, and anglers in small boats often remain out all night, doing the same thing. Calm nights seem best; wind either makes bobbers jerk up and down too much or causes walleyes to feed more during the day.

"We had a television crew come up to investigate the pattern. They felt launches were using lights to attract walleyes at night, which is illegal in Minnesota. Well, we weren't shining lights in the water, just using a few lights on the boat to help anglers bait up and fish. Sure, some light trickled down into the water and attracted insects. But I can't say we ever saw walleyes in the water near the surface. And we caught all of our fish right near bottom."

THE LIGHT BRIGADE

Can lights be used to attract walleyes at night where it's legal? Yes. In southern states, crappie anglers shining floating lights down into the water at night often attract walleyes into the glow. And the lights of shoreline docks and seawalls trigger inshore walleye movements after dark. Yet few folks specifically use lights to trigger walleye activity.

"But it's definitely worth trying," says Captain Jim Fofrich, Sr., former president of the Lake Erie Charter Boat Association and a veteran Lake Erie guide. "As far back as the '50s, we drifted the open Western Basin at night, towing a Coleman lantern on a floating inner tube a short distance behind the boat. We'd tie it upright and set up a slow drift. Little by little, the light penetrating the water would attract plankton and insects, then minnows. Pretty soon, the glow of walleye eyes slashed into the outer perimeter of the lantern's glow. All we did was cast weight-forward spinners baited with nightcrawlers, pitching out into the darkness and retrieving along the outer edge of the glow. We caught lots of walleyes far from structure, just beneath the surface.

"With the gin-clear water we have nowadays, due to the filtering effect of zebra mussels, I see a lot more opportunity for anglers to apply the night-light bite pattern on the shallow, generally less than 40-foot Western Basin, and perhaps in the deeper Central Basin as well. Also in other areas of the Great Lakes. Or wherever daytime fishing conditions make walleye fishing difficult. Darkness is a great equalizer for cold front conditions, clear water, or fussy walleyes. Catching walleyes by the light of a lantern may be one solution."

You don't bring a knife to a gunfight, but you do bring a fillet knife to a night fight when ninja walleyes are on the prowl. And a lantern, if it's legal. If not, a lighted slipbobber does just fine, and not just on structure but also out in the great beyond. And don't worry about looking weird out beneath the stars. Anybody out there doing the same thing is just as crazy—or enlightened—as you.

THE FALL BASIN BITE

Among walleye anglers, few things are as eagerly anticipated as fantastic fall fishing along the edges of deep, classic structure. All summer, you've dealt with fragmented populations, different patterns, cover, suspension, boat traffic, weather changes, brief flurries of activity followed by long hours of trolling practice, and myriad other environmental nasties that complicate life on the water.

But after fall Turnover, walleyes have assembled into larger groups, dropped deeper, and set up on drop-offs and points, just as they're supposed to. Perfect conditions for livebait rigging and jigging. Well, most of the time, but perhaps not all the time or under all conditions.

Don't doubt or abandon fall's classic, deep structure strategy. But have you ever considered that some of those walleyes, perhaps some of the largest, might be out

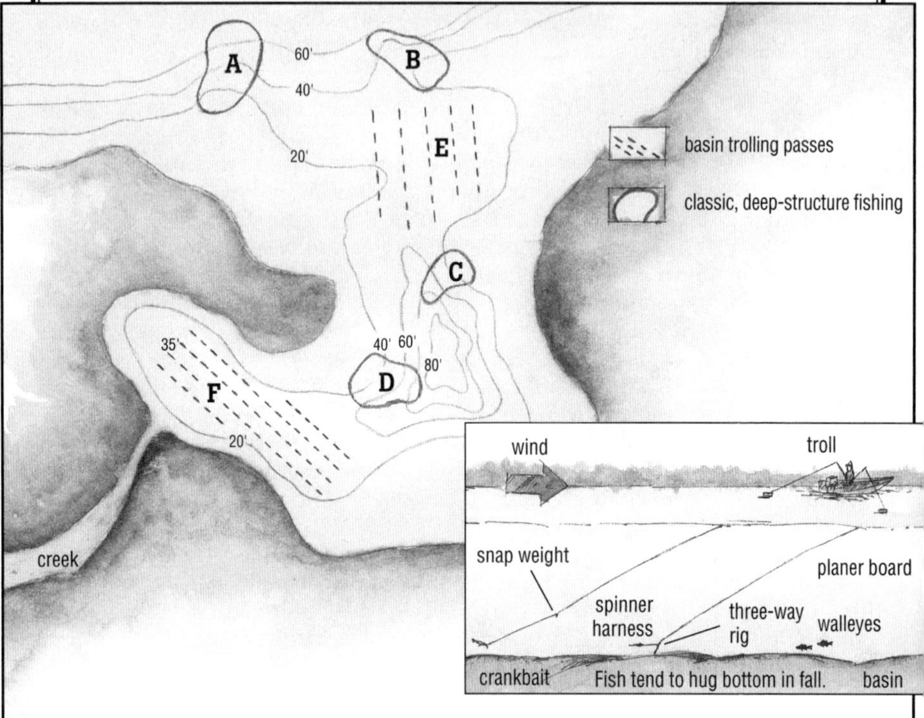

Classic fall walleye fishing calls for fishing the edges of deep, fast-dropping structures meeting deep water, such as **Areas A, B, C,** and **D**, chiefly with vertical tactics like livebait rigging, jigging, jigging spoons, or bladebaits. Saturate prominent drop-off areas along major structures, search for changes that concentrate fish, and whale on schools of big walleyes.

Basin trolling, however, is the wild card, an often-unknown alternative. In this case, **Points B** and **C** both drop off to deep water, with a moderately deep basin between them, slightly less than 40 feet deep. Could walleyes be here, cruising across the expanse, rather than tight to structure? Won't know till you try.

Area F is another modestly deep basin area lying just off a river inlet where fish move shallow at night in fall. Where do they go during the day, given a lack of shallow structure or cover to hold them and such a fast drop-off to deep water? Somewhere in the great beyond, most likely somewhere nearby, and most likely fairly tight to bottom, given the coldwater conditions. Go get 'em!

The same principles apply in shallow, featureless prairie or farm-country waters and in expansive bays of the Great Lakes. A flat expanse of basin hosting readily available forage, providing it isn't too deep, can be flat-out fantastic.

past the edges of that beautiful structure, roaming across the basin?

Probably didn't want to hear that. Why complicate a straightforward situation? Well, we didn't create the condition, but we've identified it in enough circumstances to warrant discussing it. At the very least, should the ugly situation arise when big fall walleyes are absent from expected structural edges, you have another option to explore, another environmental cranny to discover.

THE BASIN OPTION

Over the years, we've broken through misconceptions associated with fishing for suspended walleyes so that it's now become a common, accepted tactic in many areas and is being explored in others. Now let's take it a step further. After fall Turnover, when the lower layers of the water become reoxygenated and temperature is generally consistent from top to bottom, what barriers prevent suspended fish from dropping straight down? Or prevent fish on structure from dropping down and moving out across the adjacent soft basin? None.

Why would they move unless food is present—typically ciscoes, shad, smelt, or some other wandering, pelagic baitfish? Even perch drop to the edges of deep structure and spread across relatively shallow, 30- to 40-foot adjacent basins in fall. Shiners may, too. So conditions may exist where walleyes don't simply intercept baitfish along structural edges but may actively hunt them across adjacent expanses of flat bottom.

Where is such behavior likely to occur? Well, probably not across a basin that's 100 or 200 feet deep, such as in deep reservoirs or the chasm areas of the Great Lakes. But if we look at bays and shallow sections of the Great Lakes for guideposts, we can find basin areas where walleyes are likely to congregate in fall.

As water cools in autumn, several species of Great Lakes baitfish move into shallower areas. Not shallow, as in 5 to 10 feet during the day, but shallower, as in 30 to 50 feet. Large bays like Saginaw, the Bays de Noc, Quinte, the Western Basin of Erie, and the eastern outlet of Ontario share similar characteristics: each sees an inshore movement of baitfish with big walleyes close on their tails.

Areas formerly too warm or too shallow to attract many big walleyes in summer now host growing populations of post-Turnover walleyes while the water continues to cool. Suspended fish, or fish close to bottom—basically basin fish— roam and follow their forage across such basins, setting the stage for open water trolling with planer boards, snap weights, and either crankbaits or spinner rigs.

Now why doesn't this also occur on the similar, but shallower, basins of inland lakes? No reason it can't, if the forage is present to attract fish. In many cases, it does occur—in reverse. Instead of moving shallower, the fish actually move deeper, toward similar environments. Because the concept flies in the face of traditional inland walleye fishing, it remains mostly unexplored and untapped.

Next time you're crossing an open, 30- to 50-foot-deep basin area of your favorite walleye lake, moving from one area of classic structure to another, slow down a bit and watch your electronics. See any baitfish out there? Any signs of big fish? Unlike summer, when fish suspend high in the water column, in fall they tend to tuck tighter to bottom, making them less obvious.

If you see signs of life out there in the great beyond, particularly if it's within a few hundred yards of classic areas that typically attract walleyes, consider exploring that basin's potential. What do you have to lose? Certainly not your image, because no one else will be out there to see you. The potential gain, however, is tapping into a previously unrecognized segment of the fall walleye population.

In years past, anglers viewed the large open portions of inland lakes as vast wastelands too large to explore. Yet anyone who's spent any time fishing walleyes on the Great Lakes now sees these inland basins as mere drops in the bucket—a handful of square miles, instead of the Great Lakes' hundreds. Fishable territory, accessible through trolling techniques developed for open water.

THE TROLLING SETUP

Trolling with planer boards and snap weights takes multiple lures down and out to the sides, a deadly system for intercepting suspended fish. In this case, however, we're primarily fishing tight to bottom, so a little fine-tuning is in order.

Whether you're using crankbaits or spinners, add sufficient weight to the line about 50 feet ahead of the lure to take it near bottom at a typical trolling speed of about 2 mph, using perhaps 100 to 150 feet of 10-pound monofilament line. If anything, err a bit on the heavy side; you can always shorten your line to reduce depth. Then experiment a bit with longer or shorter lines until you detect the bait bumping bottom, signaled through the telltale, momentary relaxation of the rod tip. Now reel up a few cranks, set the rod in a holder, and let out a similar rig on the other side of the boat. Use a similar weight and line length, and you're in position to troll just above bottom.

Or, if you prefer an easier setup, remove the snap weight and add either a three-way rig or bottom bouncer, probably between 2 and 3 ounces, perhaps 5 feet ahead of your lure. Bouncers skip and tightly hug bottom at modest speeds, so they work best with spinner rigs. Three-ways offer more latitude. By adjusting the length of the leader or the dropper, you can run cranks, spinner harnesses, or flutterspoons just above the basin. Spoons and spinners run almost directly behind the three-way swivel; cranks dive beneath it. Adjust to match conditions. Done properly, the system will skip across bottom, making occasional contact without dragging.

Additional lures and more lines expand coverage, so once a line is rigged and running at the target depth, snap on a planer board and let out enough additional line to sweep it and your lure out to the side of the boat. Then engage the reel and set the rod in a holder. Repeat on the other side, typically setting out two to four lines.

Now troll, typically downwind to minimize tangles, using systematic passes to cover the basin areas where fish appear on electronics. Generally, weaving in S patterns to vary depth and speed isn't necessary, because depth and speed already are fine-tuned to the bottom zone. To keep baits in the bottom zone, experiment with speed, compensating by lengthening or decreasing the amount of your line.

Strikes appear as sudden bobs, plunges, or dropbacks of the planer boards. Watch 'em continually to detect tiny hooked fish or fouled weeds. Significant fish, however, should be readily evident. Grab the rod out of a holder, reel slowly, progressively detach first the board, then the weight, and finally net that big hawg over the transom. Pop the hook out, take a picture, toss the fish back, and return for another pass.

While planer boards extend lateral coverage and allow you to present multiple lures, they're not essential for basin trolling. Fact is, when tightly related to bottom, walleyes aren't prone to spook beneath the passage of an overhead boat, like suspended fish. Because of this, using a handheld rod with a heavy bottom bouncer or three-way rig to present a spinner rig is not only adequate but appropriate. Several ounces of weight are sufficient to maintain frequent bottom contact and skip across bottom at a quicker pace than livebait rigging. This tactic expands your

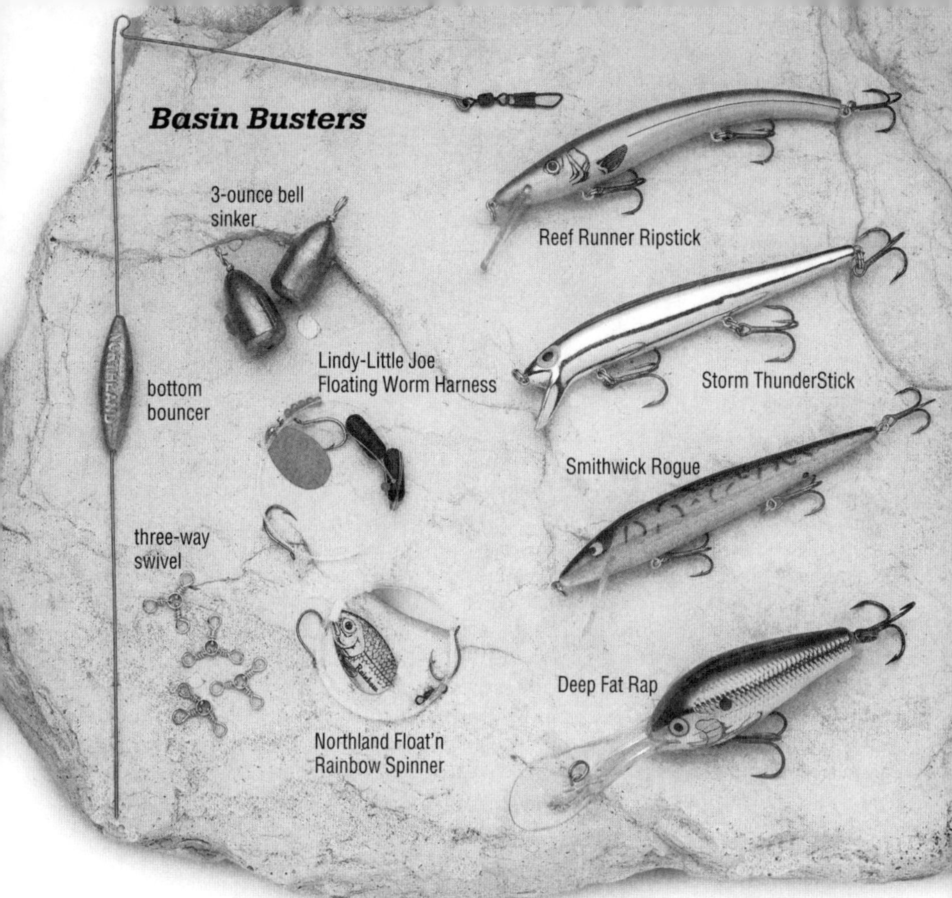

Any minnow-imitator in the 4½ to 6-inch range is a good candidate for basin walleyes. Typically, shallow runners offer a more subtle action better suited for cold water. Deep divers, though, typically offer more wobble and may be able to dive deep enough to reach the fish zone on unweighted lines. Otherwise, pinch a snap weight onto the line 50 feet ahead of the lure. Same for spinner harnesses. Use two-hook versions for crawlers, single-hook models for minnows.

For closer, more precise, tight-to-bottom trolling, switch to either a bottom bouncer and spinner or a three-way rig with a crankbait, spinner, or flutterspoon. Vary the dropper length to position the bait just off bottom. Remember, crankbaits dive below the level of the swivel, while spinners and spoons swim along at about the same level.

coverage with speed rather than with multiple lines. Pump the rod occasionally to add a surge-pause triggering action. If you see suspended fish on your depthfinder, quickly reel up a few cranks to place your lure at the matching depth.

BASIN OPPORTUNITIES

Basins aren't all deep, nor are they all featureless. During recent Octobers, anglers have discovered waves of huge walleyes at the mouth of the Winnipeg River where it meets Manitoba's vast Lake Winnipeg. The biggest fish sometimes relate to modest rock humps surrounded by the flat basin and have been caught by anglers long-line trolling Shad Raps in about 15 feet of water. Deep or shallow, the principle's the same: troll until you encounter pockets of fish, then repeat successful combinations.

Bays of the Great Lakes are the most proven trolling grounds for basin walleyes, but they're far from the only candidates. In inland lakes, shallower basins of major bays can function like their own individual mini-basins, collecting fish that either drop down off structure or roam the basin. In some cases, shallow, shoreline flats may attract fish at night, but lack of cover or structure may send walleyes dropping down across the adjacent basin during daylight. Or fish spooked off the edges of deep structure by fishing pressure may move out over the adjacent flat. For these and other reasons, big walleyes can and do occasionally make use of flat, moderately deep, 30- to 50-foot basin areas in fall, and not just on the Great Lakes. Waters you already fish may be ripe for exploration, and the results can be surprising.

ANYTHING GOES

Good . . . bad . . . ugly—whatever works. You're not out there to look pretty; you're out there to catch fish. Give 'em what they want, whether classic, drastic, or something in between.

Walleye anglers tend to have preconceived notions. We instinctively favor livebait presentations and fishing slowly. We tend to use small baits and light lines and avoid wood snags if at all possible. We desperately cling to the edges of structure instead of also exploring flats, shorelines, weeds, basins, and other possibilities for suspended fish.

These high-percentage principles fit many situations. But they're not universal. Habitat, forage, and seasonal needs determine walleyes' location and behavior. Weather, time of day, and other factors determine the fish's moods and whereabouts. Once you begin to get a handle on the interaction of these factors, select and fine-tune presentations to match the conditions, even when they go against the traditional grain. Beauty's in the 'eye of the beholder, and we'd all rather be holding big 'eyes.

Head to Head and 'Eye to 'Eye

HOW TOURNAMENTS SHAPE THE WORLD OF WALLEYES

Barely 30 years ago, walleye tournaments typically consisted of a handful of anglers tossing five bucks into a hat for a one-day fish-off. Then Honest John Lundquist made his mark in walleye history by arranging the first major walleye event on the Missouri River below the dam at Pierre, South Dakota. Approximately 120 two-angler teams participated, and competitive walleye fishing was born.

Buoyed by initial success, the Honest John tournament became an annual event. Three years later, however, spring rain and snow turned the Missouri River into mud. Not a single fish was caught by the full field of anglers. The tourney was then moved above the dam to Lake Oahe, where it evolved into the South Dakota Governor's Cup. Honest John went back to selling cars—with a name like Honest John, that was probably a pretty good career move.

Minnesota anglers, meanwhile, began fishing walleye events, too. Early Mille Lacs tournaments hosted by Burger Brothers Sporting Goods and other retailers began in the mid to late '70s. Large fields of anglers participated in partner competitions, even though boats and motors at the time were inadequate to tackle such huge bodies of water.

"I fished from a 16-foot Starcraft with a 25-hp outboard," recalls Mike McClelland. "Then guys went to 35s, even twin 35s. That was big-time in those days."

"I began with a 60-hp outboard and a Starcraft aluminum boat," says Jim Randash, another veteran of the early years. "Nowadays, big water and unlimited boundaries have taken me away from that style of boat, even though that's what I prefer to use. I need a bigger boat to compete."

"I had the seventh Lund Tyee ever built," notes McClelland. "That boat changed the way big reservoirs were fished. We could run the lake with high-horsepower engines and expect to make it back alive. Tyees were the forerunners of modern walleye boats."

By the late '70s, local tournaments began appearing in most eastern and midwestern states. But Mille Lacs and the Dakota reservoirs remained the hot spots of early tournament fever.

"Those early days were magic. Kind of fun," Randash reminisces. "Often they were big-fish tournaments. A boat, motor, and trailer were awarded for first place, and not much for second or third. Nowadays, the pressure is greater. Draw-for-partner pro-am events with big money on the line are more stressful."

"I enjoyed the old days," McClelland agrees. "Tournaments were held on new waters—new challenges for everyone. Exploring new places was a thrill."

In 1984, the Manion Walleye Circuit brought together talented walleye anglers in a traveling road show. It drew top walleye guides and anglers into competition, then encountered financial difficulty and fizzled. Sponsors recognized an important future for competitive walleye fishing, however, and with strong financial support from Mercury Marine, they formed the Manufacturers' Walleye Council (MWC).

"Over the next three years," says former Executive Director Jim Kalkofen, now executive director of the In-Fisherman PWT, "the MWC sanctioned tournaments and standardized entry fees and rules, bringing them together into a uniform circuit."

The MWC clearly became the premier partners' walleye competition, eventually changing its name to the Masters Walleye Circuit. The MWC triggered angler interest and became the foundation upon which many walleye anglers built national reputations and careers.

"I fished the early MWC years partnered with the legendary Bob Propst, Sr.," says McClelland. "Back then, anglers discovered bottom bouncers, and Propst began using sea anchors to enhance boat control in wind. He was the first to do that."

"People think I got the idea from saltwater fishermen," explains Propst. "Actually, I got it from the sailing crowd. Tournaments quickly spread the word. Soon, everyone in the Dakotas was draggin' bags."

Six-angler partner events flourished on Lake Erie in the 1980s, when the fishery rebounded from previous low levels. Big boats and big water led to big teams casting weight-forward spinners. Anglers drifted in 27-foot Sport-Crafts, totaling the length of their biggest fish in "inch tournaments." The fishing was so good that catch-and-release was not considered necessary.

As competitive fields increased, tournaments began to outgrow many waters. The largest tournaments targeted big waters, often taking advantage of rebounding Great Lakes fisheries or Dakota reservoirs as host sites. "Only so many places exist that can host large walleye tourneys," says Kalkofen. Smaller waters continued to host a variety of big-fish derbies, club tournaments, and weekend competitions.

Attempts at live-release walleye tournaments began in the 1980s, sometimes successfully, sometimes not. The PWT circuit entered the ring in 1989 with the theme "Better Walleye Fishing Through Live Release Competition," spearheading research into the care and live release of walleyes, which proved more difficult to release than bass.

The PWT circuit entered the ring in 1989 with the theme "Better Walleye Fishing Through Live Release Competition," spearheading research into the care and live release of walleyes, which proved more difficult to release than bass.

Early PWT tournaments were pro-to-pro, draw-for-daily-partner tournaments. Eventually, they evolved into today's pro-am format, enabling larger numbers of anglers to participate. Additional partner and pro-am circuits have entered the game on a national level.

Walleye tournaments encourage anglers to try non-traditional tactics, paving the way to discovering and catching shallow water and suspended walleyes. What today seems commonplace was simply conjecture a few years ago, until competitive anglers unlocked the secrets and refined new tactics for catching fish. Competition spurs new ideas, better equipment, and improved walleye fishing. Every walleye angler wins— even those who will never fish in a competitive event.

WALLEYE FISHING COMES OF AGE

In the early days of walleye tournaments, few circuits existed, and turnouts were small compared to those today. Even the professional circuits experienced growing pains. Today, circuits operate in more than a dozen states and provinces, along with several major professional circuits and many large team circuits. Many local events have grown large. Some western states offer Governor's Cup walleye tournaments drawing hundreds of teams.

Pro-am competitions have changed, too. When major pro-ams began, a pro was anyone who had a boat and the cash to pay the entry fee. Today, potential pros are carefully screened, and only the best are invited. It's become more difficult for a walleye tournament regular to turn pro. But that's good for tournament angling, because it maintains a high level of competition. It's also good for television viewers, amateurs, sponsors, and the fishing industry as a whole.

According to Jim Kalkofen, only a few openings each year are available for new pros hoping to compete on the circuit. "We look at things like their time on the water, how well they've competed in other tournaments, and how they will represent the sport. PWT pros are ambassadors of the walleye movement. We not only look at their overall angling experience but at how they present the sport to other anglers. We want the best anglers to represent their sponsors and the PWT."

Smaller walleye tournaments provide potential pros with the steps to climb. But finishing well is not enough. "An angler's résumé for entering the PWT should look just like the résumé he would send to a potential sponsor," Kalkofen says. "Things like appearances at marinas and sporting goods stores, along with seminars at sport shows, help promote the walleye movement. State, local, and regional tournaments allow an angler to build a résumé that will help him make it to the top of the walleye world, if he so desires."

Harvest Tournaments?

Research shows that delayed mortality can be high among walleyes released during warm weather. This has prompted tournament participants, directors, and biologists to take a hard look at walleye tournaments. Decisions regarding tournament management are not arbitrary or haphazard.

Most catch-and-release events are scheduled during coolwater times of the year to minimize the number of fish that might die, using local fisheries department guidelines to limit takes to a level not harmful to the fishery. All attempts are made to maintain fish in good condition and return as many healthy fish to the water as possible. Nonreleaseable fish are cleaned and donated to local civic organizations or similar outlets. Events scheduled during the warm summer months are instead typically harvest events that make no pretense of releasing the bulk of the catch. Where waters are not able to sustain the desired level of harvest, summer walleye tournaments generally are not allowed.

Some people seem to have no problem with fishing for food but don't understand fishing that calls

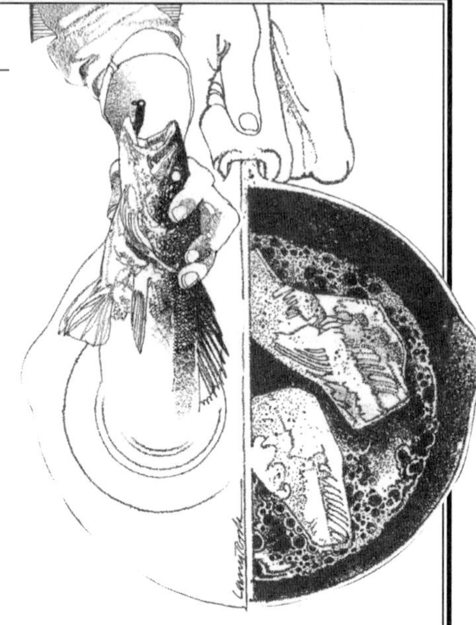

for release of every fish that's caught. Antifishing activists have capitalized on this, labeling catch-and-release a form of harassment. While biologists contend that it's important to send a message about the value of releasing most top-of-the-line predators like bass, walleyes, and pike, they agree about the danger of overselling catch-and-release. Some argue that the growth in antifishing activity should be countered by sending a message that some fish should be harvested for the table.

The fishing industry is pleased by the proliferation of small walleye tournaments. Sponsors have a lot to gain by following smaller events closely. Bruce DeShano of Off Shore Tackle says that small tourney circuits help sponsors sort out up-and-coming anglers from wannabes. "Every major tackle manufacturer gets many requests from anglers seeking sponsorship," he explains.

"When we look at a résumé, we choose anglers who have shown they can compete at various levels. We want to see a track record. Without state and regional tournaments, we have little to go on. These tourneys give anglers a chance to prove themselves and build a résumé. And they help us choose the right people to represent our products."

Doug Burns, who fished the PWT as a pro for the first time in 1997, agrees. "Winning and finishing well in state and local tournaments not only gave me more confidence in my ability," he explains, "but more importantly, it gave my résumé validity."

Walleye events across North America are in a continual state of flux. Tournament walleye fishing today is where tournament bass fishing was two decades ago. But tournament walleye fishing is growing up much faster.

Many anglers have wondered how their fishing ability compares with others. Small walleye circuits are the way to find out.

Becoming a walleye pro isn't going to become any easier. But state, local, and regional tournaments are made for the weekend angler. To test your skills against the pros, a small event nearby is the best place to start.

ON THE TRAIL AGAIN

In 1989, the PWT held its first tournament. The following year, the PWT circuit began hosting walleye tournaments all across walleye country, and by 2000, cash and prizes exceeded $10,000,000, with an additional $1,600,000 paid out in 2001.

Since the PWT's beginning, pro anglers have garnered respectable purses. Five-time PWT winner Ron Seelhoff has amassed nearly $500,000 in career winnings, including placing first in two successive PWT Championships. In 2000, the first two-time PWT amateur winner, Bill Needles from Necedah, Wisconsin, won back-to-back tournaments, claiming two Lund boats, Mercury outboards, and Eagle trailers.

PWT amateurs sign up with high expectations of learning from the pros. Amateurs fish with a different pro each day (luck of the draw), and both contestants work together to weigh in the day's catch in their respective pro-am divisions. Learning boat positioning tactics, rigging and trolling tricks, and the fine points of electronics and GPS usage are just a few of the benefits to amateur participants. Many amateurs discover they enjoy the excitement of tournament fishing and take their experiences and enthusiasm home to local events. They may also return home with significant prizes and new friendships; some even step into the ranks as rookie pros.

The PWT has been a learning experience for everyone involved. An original goal was to create the best-possible release scenario for walleyes. (Previous tournaments were mainly harvest events.) Cooperation among sites, hosts, tournament planners, boat manufacturers, and anglers was needed to successfully accomplish this goal. Releasing most tournament-caught walleyes and encouraging others to do so on a voluntary basis make sense for many fisheries countrywide.

In 2001, the top 30 places received checks or prizes. Payouts were based on a full field of 135 pros and amateurs at each event. The top pro earned $50,000, while the amateur took home a Lund/Mercury boat package valued at $12,500. Other significant prizes include Bass Pro Shops big-fish prizes of $16,000 per tournament. The biggest fish each day was worth approximately $2,000. The Storm Heavyweight award went to the heaviest one-day weight, with $500 going to the pro and a tackle box of Storm lures to the amateur. The T-H Marine live-release award went to the highest-placing pro who released the most walleyes of those brought to the stage. The Coleman Cool Under Pressure award of $1,000 was awarded to the pro who advanced the most places from start to finish of the event. The highest advancing amateur received $600.

The PWT tour is split into two divisions of three tournaments each. Amateurs may fish in just one tournament or all six. Pros may fish either the East or West Division (three tournaments) or both divisions. Seeding is based upon the previous year's performance, with qualified pros invited to fish. In 2001, pro registration was $1,075 per tournament; the amateur fee, $575.

Upon acceptance, contestants receive PWT confirmations. Lodging information is handled by host communities. Entry blanks are available from PWT headquarters at 218/829-0620 or *www.in-fisherman.com*.

In recent seasons, the PWT Championship has featured the drama and excitement of an indoor weigh-in held in conjunction with a huge sport, fishing, and boat show in an adjacent exhibit hall. Spectators tell us how much they learn by attending and visiting with pro anglers at tournaments. Anglers who accompany the pros during the championship tournament days as observers learn by being in the boat with pros competing for a $100,000 first prize.

CLASSIC EVENTS

Six thousand excited fans rise to their feet, applauding feverishly. Camera flashes penetrate the darkness as a slow procession begins. Spotlights careen and trumpets blare, the action simulcast to big screens throughout the arena and exhibit hall. Flag in hand, surrounded by family, the PWT champion takes the traditional victory ride.

"The event has the pageantry of a pro wrestling match minus the chair throwing," wrote Natasha Kassulke of the *Wisconsin State Journal* after witnessing her first arena PWT Championship weigh-in.

The origins of indoor tournament weigh-ins stretches back to Ray Scott, the legendary founder of the Bass Angler's Sportsman Society (B.A.S.S.), who brought his traveling road show into the Montgomery, Alabama, Civic Center in 1981 for BASS Masters Classic XI.

Over the past two decades, the Classic has evolved into a fishing extravaganza, drawing upward of 30,000 fans to weigh-ins. All the glitz and glimmer—the fireworks, laser light shows, and country western acts—that jazz up indoor weigh-ins also can be traced to Scott, the ultimate fishing promoter.

In this same twenty-year period, fishing tournaments in the US have grown to over 50,000 events annually, yet fewer than a handful have followed Scott's arena scenario. Why? The answer may lie in the degree of difficulty and expense of moving weigh-ins indoors.

While a staff of 25 is adequate for a well-run outdoor PWT event, upwards of 150 people are needed to conduct a PWT Championship event and sport show. The Missouri River at Bismarck, North Dakota, has been a frequent PWT site and is a good example.

Each day, 45 observers and media are placed in the pros' boats; 20 volunteers man the

shuttling of vehicles and trailers at the landing 18 miles downriver from the arena; another 14 patrol the 80 miles of tournament waters, ready to assist contestants in distress; and another 12 clean, maneuver, and hitch the pros' boats to Dodge trucks prior to their trip into the arena. An additional 40 or so volunteers and technicians assist with the weigh-in, big-screen presentation, sport show, press room, sponsor functions, and banquets.

Off-site weigh-ins also present fish-handling challenges. Fish are transported from the landing to the arena for weighing and are then returned to the water. The smaller tournament fields (currently 46 anglers for the BASS Masters Classic and 44 for the PWT Championship) normally associated with these events lead to high-percentage releases.

Both organizations work closely with state fisheries departments to minimize negative effects on fisheries. Over the course of five indoor PWT events, release percentages have exceeded 94 percent; with the easier-to-release bass species, successful releases typically are higher.

Rental expenses for arenas, exhibit halls, and big-screen technical crews can total tens of thousands of dollars, a cost often shared with the host community and the tournament organization. The benefits to the community can be significant.

These high-profile, multiday events, with their accompanying high purses (both the BASS Masters Classic and the PWT Championship pay first-place winners $100,000), draw fans into the host communities, along with members of the national press. Sponsors, sport show exhibitors, family, friends, and fans fill lodging facilities and generate revenues for the host community.

The resulting media coverage, including television shows that air to national audiences of millions, can direct a steady stream of anglers and visitors to the host city for months and even years.

The resulting media coverage, including television shows that air to national audiences of millions, can direct a steady stream of anglers and visitors to the host city for months and even years. Sport shows are a natural tie-in, giving tournament sponsors and the fishing and marine industry an opportunity to showcase new products to a highly qualified, targeted audience. Many dedicated fishing fans often travel long distances to attend and participate in "Classic Week" activities.

In 2000, the BASS Masters Classic was held in Chicago's Soldiers Field. The fishing industry's ICAST trade show ran at nearby McCormick Place concurrent with the BASS Masters Classic Outdoor Show.

The PWT, besides frequently hosting a sport show in Bismarck, North Dakota, is also closely aligned with a longstanding Chamber of Commerce event called

Making the Transition from Amateur to Pro

When asked the difference between fishing the PWT as an amateur or a pro, 1997 Exide Rookie of the Year (and pro) Terry Carr says, "As a pro, I need four of everything."

Carr fished as an amateur in 1996, winning Mariner Top Amateur honors. That award, worth $4,000, enticed him to fish as a rookie pro in 1997. He placed 17th, 30th, 31st, and 90th—only one fish out of the money in two tournaments.

Moving to the pro ranks required maintaining a good relationship with his employer, Pella Corporation, where he worked as a chop-saw operator. His requests for leaves of absence to fish the PWT totaled 28 days in 1997.

The most valuable lesson Carr learned during his rookie year was to have confidence in what he learned in practice. The second-most valuable lesson was not to worry about anybody else.

In only one season, Carr realized that the game's really between him and the walleyes.

"The transition was easier after a year in the amateur ranks," Carr says. "Anyone interested in becoming a pro needs to fish as an amateur." After 12 days of fishing with 12 different pros and observing them closely, Carr became aware that they made daily and hourly decisions.

An amateur isn't pressured to make the same decisions, but by watching the pros, Carr weighed the consequences of every move they made. He says it was helpful to observe a range of pros, then imagine what he would do in the same situation. After Carr's amateur season, he had gained the necessary confidence to make decisions and trust his instincts.

Carr admits that in his first season as a pro, he tallied twice as many sleepless nights as he had as an amateur. Being a pro also more than doubled the cost of his equipment. But by learning to cover water in five practice days, he gained confidence—the key difference between an amateur and a pro.

"Folk Fest," which annually attracts thousands to the area for a host of functions. This event complements the championship venue and gives visiting fans an even fuller slate of entertainment.

The "PWT Experience," a family-oriented event featuring fish-fighting machines, casting demonstrations, and games for all ages, attracts many families. NPAA members help staff it, and after each weigh-in, competing pros appear at the sport show to mingle with fans and to sign autographs. On day-one, the first 500 kids to enter the arena receive sponsor-provided tackle packs. On day-two, it's 500 Plano tackle boxes. On the final day, the first 500 kids receive a Silstar rod and reel.

The charged environment of an arena event can't be duplicated elsewhere, but the degree of difficulty in conducting these tournaments is likely to limit their number. With a few breaks, however, maybe we're seeing the World Wrestling Federation of the future. Move over, Vince McMahon!

THE BASS-WALLEYE GAP

Want to see a serious walleye pro go bananas? Bring up the subject of bass fishing. First, he'll reflect on good old days, when 5-pounders sucked up spinnerbaits like 6-year-olds inhale M&Ms. Then he'll realize it's been 10 years since that happened. He's been too busy fishing and promoting walleye tackle to fish for bass. His mind calls up television shows with Roland Martin, Bill Dance, Jimmy Houston. And those quicken his pulse like nothing else.

Why? Money. Bass pros cruise in overdrive because of their perceived image. As a rule, they make lots of money. Walleye pros don't, despite the fact that most walleye guys would crawl over broken glass in a Wal-Mart parking lot to please a sponsor.

Daryl Christensen, far from unknown in the walleye industry, once chatted with a bass pro at a sports show.

"I'm glad last year's over," the bass pro confided. "Barely survived."

Christensen's eyes narrowed, and a look of compassion filled his face. "Gee, anything I can do to help? I'd be happy to . . . "

"Yeah, only netted $80,000 in '93," the bass pro continued. "A third of '92."

"Eh-eighty thousand?" Christensen stuttered. "I'd like to have a bad year like that."

Image is everything in this crazy world of advertising, marketing, and promotion. An ounce of image is worth a pound of performance. That's why bass pros come as close to celebrity status as any single-species angler can get.

"Not because bass are the superior species or because they require greater angling skill to catch," explains Mike McClelland, one of the few walleye pros who makes a living from fishing. "It's largely because bass fishing and bass articles are year-long events. Walleyes have a 3- to 6-month competitive window; the rest of the year, other fishing topics take priority, even in the Walleye Belt. This severely limits a walleye pro's exposure, which in turn determines his earning power."

Some bass anglers have achieved public fame because of a unique chapter in the history of competitive angling. Early on, manufacturers invested in the images of top winners. It seemed to pay off in much the same way that a race car driver promotes, say, STP. But the days of celebrity endorsement contracts, even in the bass world, are largely over for two reasons.

First, manufacturers can get advertising and promotion practically free if they avoid costly image building. Initially, the fishing industry gave bass pros a valuable image that is now considered inflated. "It isn't the job of a national sales manager to create a cushy job for a fishing nut," McClelland says. "It's the fishing nut's job to maximize profits by cutting costs any way he can. I can't begrudge a manufacturer for conducting better business. Whining won't help. Coming up with better ways to get the word out might help. A good start is to give them more bang for their buck."

Most bass guys with endorsement contracts are committed to only a handful of days a year of outside promotions. "Cushy," McClelland

puts it. "You don't see them arranging outdoor writer get-togethers at exotic destinations, investing $80,000 in a high-tech, multimedia event, or spending a week on a Rainy Lake houseboat with Wal-Mart or Kmart buyers."

Second, the "Bass Road Map" has shown tackle companies how to profit from previous mistakes. By the time the walleye tournament scene unfolded, bass manufacturers were already avoiding paying pros large sums of money to endorse their products. "The key to narrowing the bass-walleye gap is to move out of promotions and into advertising," McClelland says. "People understand advertising, and it's always a much larger slice of the pie. Everyone in promotion constantly asks the impossible question: 'What did we get for our investment?' If the pro can't respond in dollars and cents, he's in trouble. At the bare minimum, he must be able to take credit for increased sales, at least in his geographic area.

"Walleye pros must create a promotional vehicle to get into the advertising side of the ledger. It doesn't have to be television, video, radio, or the printed word, but all of these help."

Pro success is impossible without seeing the Big Picture, the multifaceted full circle of promotion that always brings us back to image. A common misperception views walleye anglers as less sophisticated than bass anglers. Walleye pros are often cast as dirty fingernailed livebait trollers and bass pros as sage casting machines.

"The current walleye generation are definitely the Rodney Dangerfields of fishing professionals," claims Daryl Christensen. "Fact is, 50 million anglers nationwide are responsible for nearly $100 billion in economic output—the equivalent of one million jobs. The walleye industry contributes more than its fair share. Where would fishing magazines and advertisers be today without the tremendous growth in the walleye market?"

Growing the walleye industry is part of the answer to improving opportunities for walleye pros. When a walleye pro wins a tournament and takes home a check that matches the top payout of, say a Megabucks bass tourney, then perhaps the public and manufacturers will place both pros on the same economic pedestal. But for that to happen, enough walleye anglers must be willing to shell out a $1,000 to $1,500 entry fee to fish a tournament. Then the winnings—and the fame, prestige, and image—will follow.

A wider field of sponsorship would help, too. "I just don't understand why sponsors outside the fishing industry don't get into the game," Christensen muses. "What's more wholesome than a walleye tournament—all-American contestants the viewing public can identify with?"

But we can't compare walleye pros to bass pros—or apples to oranges—without going bananas.

THE WALLEYE MEDIA

In the early 1980s, Lindy-Little Joe sponsored a tagging program in Lake Erie during which anglers who caught specially tagged walleyes were awarded up to a whopping $500,000 dollars. Cult singing favorite Pat Dailey wrote and recorded "Big Money Walleye," which urged that one special fish to take a bite of his worm so he could "Go fishin' for the rest of my life." He captured the dream of anglers everywhere: hit the big time, give up workin', go fishin'. Walleye pros didn't have many opportunities back then, but the times certainly have been a-changin'.

Walleyes have hit the big time. Walleyes and professional walleye anglers are charting new territory:

• more fishing tackle designed specifically for walleye fishing.

The National Professional Anglers Association (NPAA) is a nonprofit organization of tournament anglers and supporting industry sponsors dedicated to the advancement of professionalism among tournament fishermen and to the growth of the fishing industry. It was formed to identify, recognize, honor, and promote professional fishermen and to assist anglers seeking a career in the fishing industry. The board of directors is composed of influential members of the walleye fishing community.

Many professional walleye anglers belong to the NPAA, which offers a quarterly newsletter, insurance discounts, a legal fund, and a wealth of advice for those at the professional level. Plus the latest updates on walleye tournament schedules across North America. Contact them at: NPAA, PO Box 7048, Pierre, SD 57601; 605/223-2136; e-mail: *anglers@dakota2k.net*; website: *www.ProAnglers.org*.

- more boats, motors, and related equipment designed for walleye fishing.
- more professional walleye anglers appearing in ads, endorsing products, and giving seminars at sport shows.
- tackle companies sponsoring a walleye pro staff or placing walleye anglers on their national promotional team.
- more walleye articles in fishing magazines, triggering more opportunities for anglers to write or be featured in articles.
- increasing opportunities for anglers to earn a living related to the walleye market.

At In-Fisherman, we recognized the potential interest in the walleye market early on. In addition to regular walleye features appearing in *In-Fisherman* magazine and on In-Fisherman Television and Radio, we targeted a healthy portion of our efforts toward educating walleye anglers through a growing number of specialty media outlets, such as:

- The *Walleye Guide*—our annual walleye special publication, published since 1983.

- The *Walleye In-Sider*—our bimonthly "walleyes only" magazine.

- In-Fisherman Books and Videos—beginning with the printed word and evolving into an extensive series of educational walleye videotapes.

- The In-Fisherman PWT—since 1990, the leader in professional walleye fishing competition, evolving into a $1,000,000 circuit of pro-am competition, educating contestants and those who read our analysis of the results.

- In-Fisherman Walleye

Television—a thirteen-week walleye series, featuring PWT coverage and a variety of walleye fishing tactics.

Yes, walleyes now have their own media—make that multimedia. In 1980, the walleye media consisted mostly of a few articles in national and regional magazines. Today, it's a multimedia, print, and electronic barrage offering a wealth of information to the average angler. And it's growing. When walleye stocking programs trigger interest in new areas, the local press sees the trend and devotes a growing amount of coverage. National media coverage fuels the fire. Tackle is purchased. Anglers catch fish on it. More exposure. More information to help you catch fish.

A growing number of walleye pros featured in magazines and on TV have realized that it takes work to make a living in the fishing business. They don't just talk tournament strategy. They talk career strategy—acquiring and justifying sponsorships, promoting products. This, too, is part of the Big Picture.

Tournament winnings open doors, not retirement accounts. To go fishin' for the rest of your life, be prepared to work hard and spend a lot of time talking, writing, and communicating fishing. The expanding walleye media can help.

Major Walleye Tournament Organizations

PRO-AM CIRCUITS

Professional Walleye Trail, 218/829-0620.

RCL Walleye Series, 270/362-5259.

TEAM CIRCUITS

Cabela's Sportsman's Quest, 308/254-4179.
Chain Walleye Series, 815/675-6447.
Colorado Walleye Association, 303/469-5640.
Iowa Walleye Tournament Trail, 515/565-3389.
Kansas Walleye Association, 785/379-5158.
Masters Walleye Circuit, 612/833-1522.
Michigan Walleye Tour, 517/895-8223.
Montana Walleye Circuit, 406/265-8523.
Nebraska Walleye Association, 308/384-9626.
Northern Wisconsin Walleye Trail,
   715/356-9855.
USFA Team Walleye Tournament Trail
   Illinois, 309/527-6328.
   Iowa, 972-713-6207.
   Lake Erie, 330/537-8602.
   Michigan, 616/744-1441.
   Minnesota, 320/679-5609.

USFA Team Walleye Tournament Trail (cont.)
   New York, 518/296-8901.
   North Dakota, 701/224-0667.
   Ohio, 937/390-1294.
   Pennsylvania, 724/295-2358.
   South Dakota, 320/598-7774.
   Texas, 806/376-5236.
   Wisconsin, 320/598/7774.
Walleye Angler's Trail, 319/588-0374.
Walleye Pro Team Tournaments, 612/432-3388.
West Michigan Walleye Club, 616/455-2391.
World Walleye Association
   Minnesota, 320/679-5609, 920/924-2100.
   South Dakota, 605/622-7151.
   Wisconsin/Illinois, 708/425-0996.
   Wisconsin/U.P., 920/824-5375.
   Wyoming Walleye Circuit, 307/857-6924.

MAJOR INDEPENDENTS

Leech Lake Mercury Walleye Classic,
   800/833-1118.
Mercury Nationals, 920/929-5688.
Montana Governor's Cup, 406/228-2222.
North Dakota Governor's Cup, 701/463-2781.
Oregon Governor's Cup, 541/567-8419.
"Shut up & Fish" Walleye Tournament,
   308/778-5879.

South Dakota Governor's Cup, 605/224-1138.
Tracker Marine Legends Tournament,
   417/873-5618.
Vanity Cup, 306/862-9801.
Washington Governor's Cup, 509/935-4148.
Wave Wackers, 612/924-0931.

(courtesy of NPAA; events and contacts subject to change)

Chapter 11

Competition Breeds Excellence

Tournament Savvy

PROS' POINTERS FOR ANGLING SUCCESS

So much water, so little time—a challenge facing tournament pros and weekend walleye warriors alike. If finding big walleyes fast and trying to figure out what makes them bite were easy, everyone would show up at weigh-ins and launch ramps every day with limits of big walleyes. But even the pros get skunked once in a while. With this proven four-step plan, however, you can simplify the task and improve your odds.

STEP ONE: INFORMATION

This is the Information Age, a fact no less true where fishing is concerned. Tap the best sources to learn as much as you can, as fast as you can. The best walleye sleuths begin the process long before they arrive at their fishing destination. Attend sports shows and contact guides and resort owners in regions you plan to visit. Ask probing questions about traditional patterns, seasonal migrations, and presentations. Before you depart for your trip, make phone calls to resorts, marinas, bait shops, chambers of commerce, guides, the outdoor writer at the local newspaper, and the nearest state or provincial fisheries office. They can help make your trip successful.

Whether you plan on fishing a lake, river, or reservoir, the critical questions are the same: where are the biggest schools of active walleyes, how deep are they holding, and what do you need to do to catch them?

Whether you plan on fishing a lake, river, or reservoir, the critical questions are the same: where are the biggest schools of active walleyes, how deep are they holding, and what do you need to do to catch them? Add to the equation what you know about walleye behavior, the time of year, a detailed hydrographic map. Circle likely spots. Then organize and group those spots according to where you plan on launching.

Get the results and summaries of tournaments conducted on that body of water at the same time of year. What method worked and where? What were the winning weights? After all, you might catch a limit of walleyes, but you want to catch the right fish—ones heavy enough to win or big enough for bragging rights.

Once you arrive at your destination, visit bait shops for the last-minute word. Stop by launch ramps to chat with fishermen. Be genuine and be friendly. Glance inside boats to see what's tied on lines. Ask to see fish in livewells. Most anglers are proud of their catch and are excited to share their experience. Offer tips of your own, too.

STEP TWO: ANALYZE, THEN PLAN A STRATEGY

By now, you've collected data and eliminated unproductive water. Eighty percent of the fish in the lake are in twenty percent of the water. Evaluate what you've learned, and write out a game plan. "First I'm going to do this, then I'll try that, and I'll go there," and so on. Have several locations and key tactics ready. Keep in mind that you're writing your plan on paper, not chiseling it in stone. Stay flexible, and adjust to new information.

Finally, take a look at the water. If you're just out for a good time, launch near where your scouting reports indicate the biggest schools of walleyes are located. If you're preparing for competition, launch at the tournament site and systematically run to spots from the closest to the farthest way. The closer to the scales you find active schools of big fish, the better.

Use electronics to look for walleyes and baitfish. Find the spots you circled on your map. Crisscross those spots with your boat, and use electronics to visualize what's below. You can cover far more water with a sonar unit than you can with a rod and reel. Fishing every spot takes time, and time is precious. If you're marking walleyes on the screen, note how—and if—they're relating to structure. Are they tightly schooled and belly to bottom? Then maybe a slow, natural, and precise presentation like jigging or Lindy rigging is the key. Are they dispersed over flats or suspended over open water? Perhaps trolling will work.

As you travel from spot to spot, look for humps and other structure not appearing on your map. Fish only where you mark fish or on spots that are known producers. If you see others catching fish when you're not, determine what they're doing and why it's working. Differences often are subtle. Fish are always biting. It's your job to figure out where and how.

Use GPS. Save waypoints of productive fishing spots. Also mark a safe route: the sun may be shining during prefishing, but the launch site may be fogged in on opening day. Update your map with what you've learned. Cross out spots if the fish that were there last week are gone. Focus your attack. Identify the area of water with the highest concentration of potential spots, areas where you can spend the most time fishing and the least time running.

STEP THREE: TEST YOUR STRATEGY

You've found the mother lode when you find a spot with a combination of good structure and fish relating to it. Trolling has always been a great search tactic because a lot of water can be covered in a short time. Choose crankbaits that sift the water column from top to bottom. Fine-tune tactics often. Try different sizes, shapes, and colors. Do the same when jigging or rigging. Use different colors, with or without plastic, and try different types of livebait.

Keep moving. Even if you're catching fish, you still may need several backup spots, and the fish just a mile away may average an additional 2 pounds. If you're marking walleyes that won't bite no matter what you do, try a different spot and return later. The walleyes are always active somewhere.

STEP FOUR: DEFINE AND REFINE

If fun is your only mission, mission accomplished!—You've found active fish, and you know what it takes to make them bite. But if you've been practicing for a tournament, your work has just begun. Begin refining successful presentations, trying different trolling depths and speeds, various crankbait actions and color patterns, the most productive combinations of snell construction and livebait.

Analyze what you've learned. Plan a step-by-step strategy that includes at least five or six spots and two or three presentations. When you started, your boat was probably crammed with all the equipment you own. Now sort out only the tackle you need. Stick to what you've learned in prefishing, rather than experimenting during competition.

Finally, put fresh line on your reels. Sharpen hooks. Retie knots. Get a good night's rest, and sleep well, knowing that you started with little or no knowledge of the tournament waters, and that now you have a proven plan to catch fish.

OFF-WATER RESEARCH SPELLS
ON-WATER SUCCESS

There's an old saying, "Luck is preparation meeting opportunity." An example of this is the approach Jim Randash used to win the 1996 In-Fisherman Professional Trail Championship at Bismarck, North Dakota.

Randash is a firm believer in doing his homework before venturing onto a body of water. The first thing he does is locate the best topographical map he can find. Preparing for the 1996 championship tournament, this South Dakota pro procured the original Corps of Engineers survey map of the Missouri River system in North and South Dakota, a map drawn in 1932 before construction of the Oahe Dam.

Randash's next step was to identify various lake features using different colors. "I colored the main river channel and feeder creeks, then marked the present lake elevation. Finally, I colored underwater humps and shallow areas (possible food shelves). Once colored, the reservoir came alive. The process of coloring also helped teach me the lake and river system."

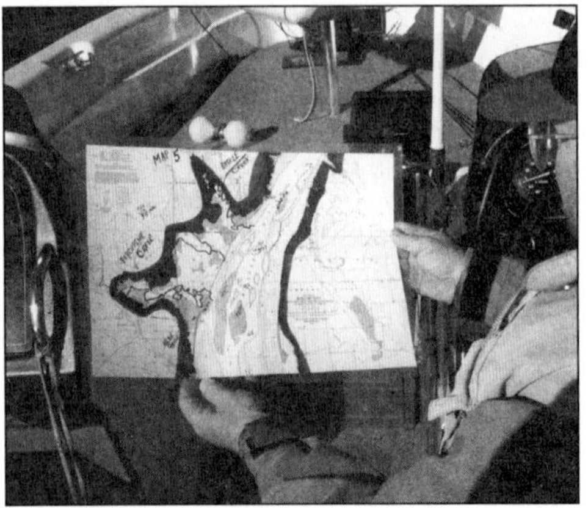

Marking potential fishing areas helped Jim Randash prepare a winning strategy for the 1996 In-Fisherman Professional Walleye Trail Championship.

While preparing his map for the PWT Championship, Randash identified approximately 25 areas he felt had potential to produce walleyes during the tournament. Many were intersections of feeder creeks with the main river channel. During practice, Randash's electronics showed fish on almost all 25 spots, but he only caught walleyes where he also found baitfish. On just such a spot, Randash caught a five-fish limit to jump to lead on day-one of the tournament.

On day-two and day-three, strong winds made fishing difficult on the open water locations Randash had identified during practice. He needed to change his game plan.

During practice, he had noticed that the falling water level was moving the walleyes out of shallow backwater areas. Going back to his map, he noted a narrow opening to a large bay and decided that this necked-down area would concentrate walleyes migrating from the bay, allowing him to intercept them on their way to deeper water. Best of all, the area was out of the wind. Randash caught a limit of walleyes from this spot on day-two and day-three.

Randash's victory in the PWT Championship is an example of how valuable off-the-water preparation can be. Even if you don't fish tournaments, taking the time to color and study a map can make your time on the water more productive.

Randash feels the best maps of western reservoirs like Lake Oahe are the original Corps of Engineers survey maps. Unfortunately, these are becoming more and more difficult to locate. If a survey map isn't available, get a commercial map from a local tackle store. These maps may lack detail and require you to spend more time examining areas with electronics. Once your homework is done, however, you'll not only have some idea of where to start looking for fish but a much better understanding of the reservoir system you're fishing. This will enhance your ability to interpret how weather and changing water levels may affect fish behavior and location. You have the opportunity to get lucky if you come prepared.

THANKS FOR THE MEMORIES, BUT . . .

"Don't fish memories"—an invaluable lesson soon learned by anglers pursuing a professional fishing career. Known hot spots and past experiences on a body of water are great springboards for good tournament performance, but they've also spelled the end of many tournament-fishing careers. Memories and tips are good starting points—something to help build a successful game plan. But they're no substitutes for a thorough effort during the practice period preceding a tournament.

Fish activity during the few days before a tournament has more of a bearing on strategy than memories of past fishing days, so invest significant effort during the practice period preceding tournament events. Don't expect to coast into an event on even a familiar body of water, because fish location and behavior may not be in sync with your preconceived notions.

Change is normal. Rarely during the course of a competitive fishing event do conditions remain the same. Weather shifts. Boating and fishing pressure increase. Winners react successfully to change. After every tournament, you hear one story from the winners, and a whole lot of "I shoulda coulda woulda won, but . . . the weather changed . . . my fish moved . . . the crowd moved in on my spot . . . or I had 'em on, but . . ." Some of these are legitimate reasons; others are only excuses for not having checked during practice for conditions that might change.

The average recreational angler falls victim to miscellaneous obstacles, too: sudden weather changes, increases in weekend fishing and boating traffic. Some, like cold fronts, are obvious. Others may be so subtle that they're easy to miss. Either way, the end result forces a change in fish location, fish behavior, and productive fishing patterns.

Consistent anglers like 2001 PWT champion Mike Gofron successfully react to changing conditions.

"On the Fox Chain of Lakes in northern Illinois, weekend boating traffic not only bothers anglers but greatly affects summer fishing patterns," says 1999 PWT Angler of the Year Mike Gofron, a veteran angler on the Chain, a summer playground for heavy recreational boat traffic just north of Chicago.

"During the week, the water tends to clear. One set of patterns may apply for Saturday morning fishing. But once the boat traffic increases, conditions change. By Sunday, the water is so roiled and muddied by boat traffic that fish shift position—typically shallower—and different patterns apply. It's a predictable change. This popular chain of small lakes never develops a typical summer thermocline, because the relentless boat traffic keeps the water stirred sufficiently to prevent stratification.

"Then toss in weather—a less predictable change, though one that can be reacted to. After several days of rain, which increase current flow between lakes, for example, walleyes on the Fox Chain relate heavily to bridge areas and narrows, drawn by the feeding opportunity associated with flowing water. During sunny afternoons, fish might bite in just a couple feet of water, right in the wakes of passing boats.

"And then consider unpredictable changes. One November, when we thought we had the fish wired on some deeper patterns typical of fall fishing, the walleyes suddenly disappeared from traditional spots. An unusual warming trend drew them shallow, to feed on mayflies that began hatching in 1 to 2 feet of water, near shallow mud-bottomed areas.

"Mayflies in November? That's not supposed to happen. But no one told the walleyes. They simply reacted, shifting shallow, following the new-found food opportunity. Only by checking other possibilities when traditional patterns fail do you discover what's happening today."

Every fishing trip provides a unique challenge. Weekend anglers tend to think about what's happening today. Successful tournament fishermen do the same,

Two-fisted Ted Takasaki tackles walleyes.

but they also consider the possibilities for tomorrow should the wind blow, water levels change . . . or mayflies hatch in November. They anticipate what might happen when conditions change and how to adjust to them.

VISUAL 'EYES

Walleye anglers aren't Supermen, able to use X-ray vision to find walleyes. We can, however, do the next best thing by combining tools of the trade with new technology. In addition, we need to go one step further, using the data gathered from observation to develop a three-dimensional picture of every subtle feature of the structure below our boat. Whether we plan to jig, rig, or troll, it's critical to know what's down there.

At what depths do the breaks occur? Where are the turns? Does the structure reach all the way into deep water? What is bottom made of—mud, sand, gravel, or boulders? Where are the forage-rich transitions?

Every weed patch must be explored. How big is it? Is it large enough to hold a limit or just one or two fish? Are the weeds green and healthy or turning brown? Every brushpile needs to be checked. How dense is the cover? How close does it lie to the nearest drop-off?

When all this is known, we have a "mind map" of the entire area. That, coupled with our understanding of the walleyes' seasonal behavior, can be used to analyze where fish are most likely to be. All it takes is some mental conditioning—think of it as the "Zen" of fishing. We will travel mentally over every inch of the structure, combing it for fish.

We call the process "Visual 'Eyes." Attention to detail and ability to concentrate often mean the difference between a full livewell and no fish. For example, during three days of fishing, Ted Takasaki used the technique to put a Fuzz-E-Grub precisely at the tip of one particular branch of a fallen tree that reached into a 10-foot hole on a creek off the Missouri River. From it, he plucked the winning weight in the 1998 PWT Championship.

Start simply. Obtain hydrographic maps of your targeted waters. Compare what you see on paper with what you observe on the shoreline after you launch. Imagine what extends out into the lake, river, or reservoir beyond what you can see above water. Sharp-breaking hills are likely to create sharp breaks. Long sloping banks probably extend below the surface. The farther apart contour lines are spaced on the map, the slower the break; the closer the lines, the steeper the break.

When checking a point, align the boat at a right angle to shore and slowly travel outward. Watch your sonar to see at which depths the breaks to deep water occur. Mark them with buoys. Next, watch your GPS as you motor slowly around the point over each breakline, noting twists and turns. If you don't have GPS, use buoys to mark them. Few points are regularly shaped, and often the overlooked, small spot-on-the-spot serves as a contact point that holds fish. Mark other features that you see, such as cover.

The same process can be used to map river channels. Note the depth at which a midlake hump tops out; find the breaks and examine the shape of the hump. Note its position relative to deeper water and to the channel.

You now have a map with visible surface reference points on your GPS screen. Additional details will come when you lower a bait over the side. Whether you're jigging with a Fuzz-E-Grub, rigging with a No-Snagg sinker, or pulling bottom bouncers and spinners, the weights telegraph information about the kind and location of cover. Probing the depths indicates where bottom changes from hard to soft and registers minor depth changes that don't appear relevant on sonar.

After concentrating so intensely for so long, you begin to notice even more about the area. Your awareness becomes heightened. And you begin to actually "visual 'eyes" the bait as it travels over a spot. Now you're primed to sense whatever can help locate fish. Feel any subtle changes through your rod that might indicate a bite. Watch your line angle and where your bait is relative to the position of the boat. Your boat may be in 20 feet of water, while your bait is in 10.

You now have enough data to imagine the underwater world. Presto, the water is gone. The boat is floating on thin air. Train your mind to clearly see what lies below. With recent breakthroughs in underwater cameras like the Aqua-Vu, you can check to see how right you were and fine-tune your ability to visual 'eyes.

HOCUS FOCUS

The silence was deafening, save for the steady drone of the kicker motor and the occasional lap of half-footers against the hull. His partner wondered whether or not this guy appreciated his presence in his boat, even during prefishing. Conversation was limited to a few short answers to probing questions.

Finally, a breakthrough. "I'm not ignoring you or trying to be rude," Sam Anderson said, with a rare glance away from his planer boards. "I'm like this on the water. I focus on my presentation, looking for little things that might need changes or tweaks."

By the time they rounded the breakwall on their way to the dock at day's end, the conversation became enthusiastic for the rest of their time together.

Good professional walleye tournament anglers share the ability to concentrate or focus on a single goal. Few do this better than the touring pros on the In-Fisherman PWT.

"The ability to focus is paramount to a professional angler's success," says Anderson, who once juggled the roles of full-time college student and professional competitor.

In his early years as a pro, able to be away from school only for a limited time, Anderson often cut his prefishing short while still developing a program—an edge of sorts. That program, which consists of seven mental exercises, begins long before an event takes place. Anderson shares his formula for success:

(1) Imagery—"Several months before an event, I begin going through hundreds of scenarios to identify possible patterns," Anderson explains. "I recognize these possibilities from past experiences at that particular location,

In-Fisherman Professional Walleye Trail pro Sam Anderson describes the mental aspects of competitive angling.

common characteristics of the type of water in question, and as the event draws near, present conditions. Once I consider these factors, I begin to think about odd-ball patterns, ones that my competition might not think about. Something that few other anglers are willing to try could give me an edge."

(2) Focusing—Perhaps one of the hardest aspects of competitive angling, as well as of life itself, is being able to concentrate on a single goal. "If a pro can't focus all his strength and emotion toward a single goal, his success is severely limited," Anderson says. "On the trail, it's impossible to win tournaments while worrying about other aspects of life. On the water, I think only about the task at hand. Troubles of life must be left at home, or at least at the dock. With this mind-set, it's possible to put together a game plan and use practice time to its full potential."

On the trail, it's impossible to win tournaments while worrying about other aspects of life.

(3) Visualization—Anderson visualizes what and where his baits are doing under or behind the boat. While trolling, he stands at the transom on constant vigil, while he visualizes his spread of lures set at various depths.

"Say I'm contour trolling along a point. I use my electronics to search for subtle changes in bottom composition. While looking back at my lines, I visualize my baits as they approach these areas. I visualize where the fish are holding and how they view my baits."

This mental exercise keeps an angler's mind sharp in anticipation of the slightest hint of a bite. In short, if you expect a bite, more often than not, you'll get bit.

(4) Zooming In—The smallest mistake or omission can bring the fishing machine to a screeching halt. Subtleties such as line diameter and color, as well as hook sharpness, play an important role in a pro's success or failure. "Fine details like sharpening hooks often are overlooked by even the best anglers," Anderson says, while working on the trebles of a Storm ThunderStick. "Simply put, if hooks aren't razor sharp, fish are missed."

(5) Zooming Out—By focusing on the little things and creating mental pictures of what's going on in the watery world below, you can easily lose sight of the big picture. "Take time to look at the present situation. On any body of water, seasonal migrations and environmental conditions often point in the direction of fish," Anderson says. "Consider whether a particular season is early or late this year. For instance, if you're looking for walleyes in their pre-summer locations, but a mild winter and early spring have made the water 10°F warmer than at the same time last year, you may need to focus on summer locations and presentations."

Water clarity also affects walleye location or at least their activity. These things may sound elementary to most anglers, but more often than not, this is where we make most of our mistakes.

(6) Defocus—Once you've reached the dock at the end of the day and made the next day's preparations, relax and let your mind rest. "Now's the time to contact family back home," Anderson says. "Eat dinner with friends and fellow anglers. Have some fun."

(7) Refocus—After a good night's rest, a pro awakens to another day. His mind re-engages, and his focus is once again singular. "Focus is necessary to be successful on the pro circuit. Lose your focus, and you lose fish. Also money."

Focusing builds confidence in your presentation, your execution, and in yourself. This may not actually be magic, but the results seem like it.

DISSECTING RESERVOIRS

Reservoir fishing is relatively simple if you concentrate on a few key ingredients. Steve Bissett, two-time PWT winner, has fished reservoirs for many years and knows the keys to the Reservoir Kingdom.

First, avoid the common but curable reservoir rut. Because conditions change almost daily on reservoirs, you need to be versatile. "Too many anglers return to a spot that produced fish the previous day," Bissett says. "Then, if that doesn't work, they fish the same depth at a similar spot. That usually doesn't produce. From my experience, the fish don't completely abandon the immediate area but instead move shallower or deeper, depending on forage conditions. Now, if walleyes are shallow, you can't mark them with sonar, so it's necessary to fish the 1- to 5-foot zone before eliminating it as a consideration."

If that fails, Bissett moves deep—deeper than most anglers would consider walleye water. "I can't count the times that I caught a dozen or more fish from one spot in 40 to 50 feet of water, while nearby boats worked middepths and only landed a few fish," he said. "This is a relatively easy pattern, too, considering how simple it is to mark fish with electronics before wetting a line."

Once he finds fish, Bissett reaches for a hefty bottom bouncer, teaming it with a Lindy Rig or a spinner rig, if the fish are in the mood for a faster offering. If walleyes are really stacked up—say, off the end of a long point or the edge of a hump—he hovers over them and vertically jigs.

Steve Bissett follows the bite.

As a rule, use just enough weight to maintain solid bottom contact. A 45-degree trolling line angle is critical for successful angling down deep. At these depths, slower Lindy rigging requires less bouncer weight (1½ ounces) than spinner rigging (up to 3 ounces).

Next, get cranking. "If you want to catch fish as fast as tuna crews working a frenzied school," Bissett says, "you must master the crankbait game. Leeches and crawlers are fine for numbers. And jigs-and-minnows are tough to beat in the spring. But when I want to catch big fish, and lots of them, I get out the cranks."

Part of the reason crankbaits are catching on in impoundments, particularly in the Dakotas and Montana, is the way that they resemble the forage base—typically the smelt and ciscoes that big fish are accustomed to feeding on. "I've seen it time and again," Bissett says. "Bigger, older fish know what brought them in, and they aggressively tune in to the frequency of a good vibrating bait."

For Bissett, this means hooking up a Shad Rap in a fluorescent fire-tiger pattern (for muddy water) or deep-diving ThunderSticks and natural metallic-hue Rattlin' Rogues (for clear water). Recent PWT events on Lake Oahe substantiate the hardware connection: two were won with crankbaits, and about 50 percent of the contestants trolled artificials at least part of the time.

"Leadcore leaders remain popular for getting crankbaits into the fish zone, but don't forget the pseudosuspended bite," cautions Bissett. "Tie on a #7 Shad Rap," he says, "and work the zone near to but not along the breakline. Depending on the fish's mood, time of day, and forage availability, walleyes will be anywhere from 10 feet to several hundred yards off a key structural feature."

Which leads to Bissett's favorite reservoir hot spot: "I always look for a large flat—50 yards to a quarter-mile long—extending from a point. I like a slow-tapering food shelf because it attracts baitfish all year, year in and year out." Flats like Oahe's Moose and Akaska are prime examples. "I'll bet 10,000 fish are taken off Moose some years. You can fish this flat any which way you want—Lindy rigging, jigs, trolling cranks with boards along the breakline. And Moose offers a lot of micropoints to sort through."

As for the best time of day, Bissett agrees with many pros that 10 a.m. to 2 p.m. is usually most productive. On flat, calm water, however, he tends to fish a little deeper. Should he find a pod of fish, he works that same zone in other areas, so long as prevailing winds remain constant (which they probably won't).

And speaking of wind, Bissett loves to backtroll when fish are bunched tight to the beach. "The shallow zone is made to order for backing over and slipping back on top of the fish," he says. "With my 90-horse Merc tiller, I can comb any turn, cup, finger, or pocket." Interestingly, while nearly every pro relies heavily on an electric bowmount trolling motor for this type of presentation, the last time Bissett fished with one was back during his bassin' days in the early 1970s. For walleyes, it's strictly backtrolling.

Won't this spook fish if the wind isn't howling and the lake isn't choppy? "Not a chance," Bissett says. "I used to guide on south-central Minnesota's Green Lake, which is as clear as most walleye waters get. I remember watching fish hit right underneath my rod tip. Heck, your boat will spook fish before your motor does."

Indeed, Bissett knows the true art of backtrolling livebait. He deftly works a leech on a relatively short line but with a fairly long snell—5 feet or more—close to his boat. "I change speeds often," he says. "That's the key. Allow the bait to sink when you slide the motor into neutral. Then when you motor forward or backward, water resistance will lift the bait upward. That kind of triggering action doesn't happen often, considering the way most guys work livebait with a bowmount electric."

And most guys don't catch fish like Bissett does, either. But you can come close if you practice his pointers until they become second nature.

POINT HOPPING FOR BIG LAKE WALLEYES

Time is valuable. As it is, we have little enough time on this earth, much less have it to waste on petty stuff like work, when we could be spending it on the water, doing something significant. Every diehard angler, from the most ardent pro to the most aspiring novice, wishes for more time to fish.

Now for the bad news: we only have so much time, no matter who we are. How is it, then, that some anglers regularly outfish the competition, or at least their local counterparts? Especially when they have the same or, in some cases, even less available time to fish?

When it comes to fishing tournaments, time is money. Efficient time management may provide the key to winning, or at least to bringing home a healthy check. The better we make use of our available time, the more fish we catch. Thus the concept of quality time—time invested wisely, making every second count, in the search for big walleyes.

Running around at high speed all over the lake may look cool, but having a line in the water is necessary in order to catch fish. Time spent moving and hunting must be balanced with time spent effectively fishing in prime spots to maximize your odds of catching walleyes—quality time, not just total time on the water.

HIGH-PERCENTAGE POINTS

Even beginning anglers realize that a point or other prominent structure sticking out into a lake has potential for attracting walleyes. But some anglers make the mistake of fishing points only because they're a shape. Wrong. For a point to produce, it must be seasonally appropriate. It must lie in the proper section of the lake. Example: A deep point 40 miles from a walleye spawning area won't attract fish in early spring, no matter how

Pros like Daryl Christensen know that quality time produces fish. Don't waste it.

good it looks. Similarly, a point lying well beneath the summer thermocline may attract no walleyes in summer, but it can be a great spot in fall.

A productive point also must have the proper bottom content, cover, forage, or some other characteristic to attract and hold walleyes, even for a short time, while swimming down the lake. If the area is conducive to feeding, however, chances are the walleyes will stay awhile.

So fishing points is a good idea, most of the time. Some anglers take the concept even farther, fishing only the tips of points—the extreme outer ends, which historically are known to hold fish. Well, this can be a good strategy, a meek attempt, or a bum deal, depending on conditions.

Say you pull onto a huge reservoir, swivel your head, peer down the lake in either direction, and see a hundred points. Wow! Are you gonna fish 'em all to determine which ones hold fish?

Time management. Proceed point to point, investing a little time running the tip with your electronics, determining if walleyes or forage fish are present, how deep they are, how they're oriented to the drop-off, and what kind of bottom they're using. If you see fish, stop and fish awhile, matching your presentation to the type of area.

Example: match livebait rigs to drop-offs; jigs to weededges; crankbaits to rock flats. If you don't catch anything in 10 or 15 minutes, move on. You run the risk of missing something subtle that may hold a few walleyes, instead trying to find a significant concentration elsewhere down the lake. But the clock's tickin', and you gotta keep movin'.

Now, let's look at the opposite extreme. Say you're not under the gun and have the luxury of lots of fishing time. Or you're fishing a familiar lake where you have plenty of time to nitpick down along the edges of drop-offs to either side of the tip of the point, looking for those little twists and turns, bottom changes, weed patches, or other intricacies that hold big fish even in heavily fished waters. You're searching for those minispots the point hoppers missed because they fished only the tips of points and left too quickly.

Judgment call. Do you maximize mobility and coverage by scanning for fish life with electronics, hit primary spots quickly, and then move on to the next prospective area? Or do you fish fewer areas, using saturation and extraction techniques to locate subtle irregularities that hold fish on heavily fished lakes? Time management—you make the call.

Natural lakes often have a primary breakline that focuses significant fish activity at that depth, all around the lake. Water clarity may cause weedgrowth to end at that depth. That's a general clue for how deep to fish on points all around the lake.

Large reservoirs with significant water fluctuation, broken by periods of stable water, display distinct breaklines formed by wind-generated shoreline erosion during periods of stability. Thus a particular depth may tend to be hot all around the lake.

Proceed point to point, scan or fish at that level, and move on to the next point if you fail to catch fish. If you catch some, fish until they stop bitin'. Then decide if staying is worthwhile to extract another fish from the fringe of the area. Or should you head on down to the next similar spot? Decisions, decisions. Correct decisions win tournaments. Incorrect decisions shoulda/coulda won tournaments.

Some points, based on their shape, bottom content, lake orientation, or other features just seem to regularly attract lots of fish, especially those that often bear the brunt of a prevailing wind. Others that look good to us for some reason may not attract fish, or seldom draw walleyes.

We can't always explain why. Don't have to. Let the fish tell you which ones are best. When you find a good location, however, make it a permanent spot on your route. Check it coming and going, even if for only a few minutes. But don't waste all day on it if the fish don't respond.

Time management. Quality time. Point hopping. Return on investment. Sounds more like playing the stock market than a lazy day on the water. Not a lazy day, in fact, but more of an intense, focused, strategic hunt for roving walleyes. Determine an investment strategy based on the local market, and jump in.

Clock's tickin'.

PLAYING THE WIND

"The Wind is your ally. The Wind is your friend. Can't wait for that ol' Wind to start blowin' again."—Anonymous

Perhaps Anonymous has never been miles offshore on the Great Lakes in 7- to 9-foot seas. Or trapped in a cove by huge rollers movin' up the lake, 50 miles up the reservoir from the launch site, wind straight into your face, should you dare venture toward home. Or paddling home (upwind, of course!) the last day of a canoe camping trip, with miles to go before you sleep. At times like these, the wind is friend to nobody.

But in lesser degrees, based on personal preference, experience, fortitude, and seaworthiness of craft, wind is indeed good. Particularly when it comes to making walleyes bite.

Wind may cool off the air temperature, but it also raises the degree of walleye action, triggering intense feeding in the shallows. How? Why? Picture a school of minnows roaming the shoreline atop a rock reef or along a shallow weedline, the entire school perfectly coordinated, twisting, turning, swimming along like one big silvery shimmer. Fin-eye coordination to the max.

Minnows have large eyes compared to the sizes of their small bodies, all the better to see you with, friend or foe. In clear water or sunny conditions, when one minnow turns left, all the other minnows turn left, too, reacting like a network of creatures operating off a single brain cell. Should a walleye or other predator approach, all the minnows burst to attention and flee, easily evading teeth and jaws before they ever come close to chomping.

In light to modest wind, minnows and baitfish enjoy a feeding advantage over vulnerable insects and plankton, which are unable to evade attack. Now, however, add wind pouring into the shallows. Wind riffles the surface, roils and darkens the turbulent waters. Suddenly, baitfish and minnows can't see well or perhaps at all. They become disoriented, less able to function as a unit. In low light and darkness, wind, dark or dirty water, vulnerable minnows are at a considerable disadvantage. Stragglers become separated from the crowd, distinct targets for predators able to navigate amidst the gloom and roar of waves rather than individual glimmers amid the shimmering mass.

Walleyes are efficient and versatile predators, able to feed using a combination of sight, sound, lateral line (vibration and water displacement detection), taste, touch, and smell. Basically, when walleyes decide to eat, baitfish don't have much of a chance .

Thus the sudden movement of walleyes from deep, clear water up to reservoir shorelines when wind-churned mudlines begin to develop along eroded shale banks. Thus the sudden activation of walleyes moving atop a rock reef as wind builds to a sufficient degree to toss and boss the local minnow community. Thus the movement of walleyes out to weededges, or up to the tops of the weeds from former hiding places beneath the greenery. And thus the general principle of fishing the windy side of the lake, within reason (meaning safety and efficiency), for active walleyes.

The sudden onset of significant wind can trigger walleye activity within minutes, turning a tough outing into a sudden smorgasbord of fish activity. Constant wind can lead to greater activity, in general, along the windy side of the lake, or along the sides of structures that bear the brunt of the wind, such as the upwind side of a shallow rock reef.

In spring, constant wind from one direction stacks the warmest surface water along one side of the lake, increasing fish activity there. Constant wind can shift water from one large section of a lake, through a narrows, to another section, generating current that draws walleyes to the downcurrent entrance. When wind subsides, the water flows back in the other direction, creating a reverse attraction at the opposite entrance to the narrows.

In the walleye game, wind is indeed a good thing, within reason. It greatly increases shallow fish activity. As long as the water isn't so deep or cold that finesse presentation and holding baits motionless are required, wind even improves activity for livebait rigging and vertical jigging middepth structure. Retain control and efficiency, and you're set for action.

In extreme conditions, less windy areas become more appropriate fishing choices. In fact, even the calm side of the lake begins to look mighty attractive, although the fish there may not be as aggressive. At least you can fish there effectively and safely. Too much of a good thing is a good thing to avoid. Especially when that thing is excess wind.

WHEN THE GOIN' GETS ROUGH, HANG TOUGH

Ferocious winds, 5- and 6-foot waves, and bone-jarring rides. Why even bother? Can walleyes be caught under those conditions? Yes, especially if you read the wind correctly and use it to your advantage.

Successful tournament anglers learn to deal with the worst from Mother Nature. This includes unrelenting winds that punish you and your equipment to the breaking point. PWT anglers have learned that if they use their heads and exercise caution, tremendous catches can be made under even the toughest conditions.

Unlike a fisherman, a walleye has nothing to lose and everything to gain when Mother Nature lets loose. Walleyes sometimes react positively to pounding waves and can turn on with ferocity. This seems to hold true on natural walleye lakes like Mille Lacs in central Minnesota, to reservoirs like Oahe in South Dakota, as well as on the Great Lakes.

Using the situation to your advantage takes preparation and appropriate equipment. Bigger boats have opened up fishing in areas previously thought unsafe and unfishable. To get there safely and smoothly, most walleye pros rely on 19- to 20-foot boats to fish effectively.

Beyond a length of 20 feet, a boat's ability to stay on a precise trolling run or hold on a minute breakline or point is greatly diminished. Even with today's powerful electric trolling motors, the weight and size of the boat can become too much to handle. Nineteen to 20 feet is a good compromise between safety and effectiveness.

On Lake Oahe in South Dakota, heavy north winds bring waves that seem to stand straight up and down. Just getting to the fish can be a challenge. The first necessity is to keep a cool head. If you have any doubt, don't go. But if you're going, here are a few tips for navigating high seas:

• Try to run on the calm side of the lake, even if you have to run out of your way. Take your time in the rough stuff and make up time on flat water. Conditions are more civil on the lee side of a lake.

• Don't run on plane when you're in the rough stuff; take it easy, and you'll get there soon enough. Keep the bow up, and let the boat's hull smooth out the ride. If the waves are too high to run straight into them, take them at an angle, and work back and forth to get to where you're going.

• Heavy winds can bring walleyes up shallow. On reservoirs like Oahe, waves pounding into a shoreline can create a mudline that attracts shiners and other

baitfish, which in turn attract walleyes. When walleyes move shallow, they are there to chow down, which makes them vulnerable.

• Walleyes that make a move shallow in heavy waves often fall for a properly presented crankbait. Choose one that runs deep enough to occasionally tick bottom. If snagging is a problem, choose a bait that runs close to but just above obstructions. The Shad Rap is a good choice for trolling shallow water structure. It imitates a shad or shiner and is available in sizes that cover the shallow fish zone. Other good choices include the CC Shad and Storm Junior ThunderStick.

• Always forward troll with the wind. Going against the wind will keep you busy hanging on to what little boat control you may have left. When trolling into the waves, you'll find that the wind constantly grabs the bow, trying to turn you back in the direction you came from.

• On natural lakes like Mille Lacs in Minnesota and Winnebago in Wisconsin, heavy winds pull walleyes onto shallow rocky reefs, bars, points, and shorelines. Current pushes baitfish into shallow areas, where they become an easy target for hungry walleyes. Trolling crankbaits can cover water quickly and efficiently.

• If the fish are bunched up in specific areas, drop an anchor and cast to the spot. To anchor in a big wind, use a 28-pound anchor and rope at least 150 feet long. The extra rope length places the anchor at the best angle for grabbing and also serves as a shock absorber that holds the anchor where you dropped it.

• Sea anchors or drift socks can slow a boat to a crawl, even when gusty winds are blowing the tops off the waves. In early spring and late fall, when walleye metabolism may be slowing down, the dead-slow presentation of a jig or livebait rig may be needed. In that case, placing a medium-sized drift sock off the transom and a big one off the bow can slow you down to a productive drift speed that walleyes may find more agreeable. Use the drift socks to control speed and the main motor or kicker to keep you positioned, especially if you're trying to follow a breakline.

• On the Great Lakes, where walleyes spend a good deal of time suspended, a heavy wind can bring fish right to the surface. High-riding schools of baitfish become easy targets in heavy seas, and walleyes can actually be seen breaking the surface as they chase down dinner. The next time you're working open water and your fish disappear, try running a bait just under the surface. You probably won't mark fish riding that high in open water; the only way to find them is to run a bait right in their faces.

• If you're chasing mudline fish when hard-pounding waves turn the water to chocolate, move. The same applies to lakes like Erie, where a heavy wind can shut down the bite completely. The exceptions seem to be natural lakes like Mille Lacs, where the shoreline is mostly rock and sand. Here, the water never gets too muddy for active walleyes, no matter how hard the wind blows.

GOOD FISHING IN BAD WEATHER

Ninety degrees, sunny skies, and flat, calm conditions greeted the PWT Championship field as they headed out onto Big Traverse Bay, Lake of the Woods, Minnesota, on day-two of the 1994 finale. Catches matched the great conditions: five walleyes topping 10 pounds, including Reggie Thiel's 12.12-pound whopper.

As contestants mingled around the weigh-in site, a forecast of severe weather began to circulate for the final day. Perry Good, an Eagan, Minnesota, pro who once trained as a meteorologist, responded to the forecast: "If the weather gets nasty, I think I can win. If we get the big blow and the severe weather, I believe my fish will hold and I'll have an advantage."

Perry Good. Bad weather.

Good had spent the first two days of the competition meticulously scouring an unmapped deep water hump that he discovered during practice. Going into the final day in second place, he felt he could still squeeze a winning catch off this tiny one-boat spot even if the bite turned off.

Stiff westerly winds, severe thunderstorms, and a tornado swept across Big Traverse basin the next morning, becoming so severe at one point that tournament officials instructed the field to return to shore. One- to two-fish baskets replaced the limit catches of the previous day—an obvious response to the radical change in weather. But by adapting his presentations to the weather conditions, Perry Good managed to scrounge a $50,000 Championship catch.

GOOD OBSERVATIONS

Weather conditions often determine walleye location, dictate presentation, and ultimately measure success, yet weather is probably one of the least understood elements of the fishing equation. Perry Good's unique background in meteorology, coupled with his angling skills, suggest the following observations.

When severe weather systems roll in, walleyes typically become less aggressive, calling for a less aggressive presentation. On that final day of the 1994 Championship, Good changed from his previous day's combination of a bottom bouncer, 5-foot leader, and leech, to a slipsinker Northland Roach Rig and leech. He shortened his leader so he could slow his presentation and hovered over the school of walleyes that now huddled together deeper on one small corner of the hump.

Good always considers wind direction when formulating his plan. For example, with a west wind, which often accompanies high pressure, he typically searches out the eastern shore, or shallow reefs where waves are crashing, to take advantage of the roiled water. To locate aggressive walleyes, he begins with a fast presentation like trolling a Shad Rap.

With an east wind, which often ushers in low pressure, however, Good generally heads to the western shore, where he uses a finesse livebait presentation such as a slipbobber or Roach Rig to locate nonaggressive walleyes.

During a PWT pro-am on Saginaw Bay, Michigan, Good was onto a hot bite of big suspended walleyes. He plied the 6-foot level with a spinner-and-crawler behind in-line trolling boards. When a low-pressure system arrived overnight, Good adjusted his presentation by eliminating the boards and downsizing his spinner blades for more precise presentations to walleyes now positioned near bottom.

He also switched from four to two rods so that he and his partner could hold the rods and detect subtle bites while quartering the waves, which slowed down their boat. These adjustments advanced Good into second place, despite distinct changes in weather and fish aggressiveness.

When fishing on a system that includes a river, Perry often heads toward the river when severe weather moves in. He believes that river walleyes are less susceptible to varying conditions, tending to hold their position and to remain more catchable than their lake counterparts.

Good's experience in both fishing and meteorology enables him to read the skies for advancing weather conditions and provides subtle clues to changes in walleye behavior that call for adjusting presentations. While most anglers lack textbook weather training, they nevertheless develop an instinct for how changing weather may affect fishing. Trust those instincts. Don't continue fishing the same way when conditions change. By applying Good's advice, you should be able to adapt when a weather system moves in, turning bad weather into good fishing.

PREPARATION + PRECAUTION = ORGANIZATION + EFFECTIVENESS

"Here I am, on the road again. Here I am, up on the stage. There I go, playin' the star again. There I go, turn the page."—Bob Seger

Bob Seger could have been referring to the life of an PWT pro during tournament season, instead of a rock star in the chorus of his rock 'n' roll classic, "Turn the Page."

Fishing competitively as a PWT touring pro surely isn't so glamorous as being a rock star, but it's certainly as demanding, perhaps even more so, when planning, packing, traveling, and lodging are considered. At least rock stars have roadies to handle the physical tasks of packing and transporting the wares of their profession, agents to book their gigs, and assistants to make lodging reservations and travel plans. Whether you're a full-time fishing pro or a weekend angler, these tasks come with the territory.

Successful trips begin with planning. Once gear is stowed and the journey begun, they build momentum. The more successful we are at constructing and executing these plans, and safely reaching our destination, the more successful our trip will be. Touring pros have travel secrets that allow them to focus exclusively on fishing once they reach their destination.

"My neighbors think I load and unload my truck for a living," says Ross Grothe, Apple Valley, Minnesota, referring to his habit of packing and unpacking gear. Grothe takes his time on the road seriously. "I concentrate on time management," he says. "My time behind the wheel is thinking time." Grothe carries a pocket tape recorder in his truck. If an addressable issue pops into his head, he records it for future action. He also uses his tape recorder on the water, storing information like water

PWT pro Sam Anderson checks his rig for potential problems before they become inconveniences —or worse.

temperature and clarity, successful lures and presentations under certain conditions, and lists of work to be done on gear and boat when he gets off the water.

Mark Brumbaugh, 1995 PWT champion, manages a farm operation along with his competitive fishing. As a result, he carries his cellular phone wherever he goes. "From the tractor, to the truck, to the boat, I can address business as it happens, while giving my sponsors, my business associates, and my family the ability to contact me."

Brumbaugh and Grothe keep their gear locked in Dee Zee tool boxes in their trucks. The boxes keep gear organized so that time isn't wasted searching. Dee Zee boxes are waterproof and dustproof, so contents stay dry and clean. And they're heavy enough not to be easily toted off by thieves.

Adding a different twist to road organization is Ted Takasaki, who stores his gear in Flambeau Stow-N-Go's. "They're modular, so they can be neatly stacked and organized," Takasaki says. He organizes the contents by category, with tools in one box, electrical items such as extension cords, battery chargers, and three-way plugs in another. The box labeled "Road Emergencies" contains jumper cables, flare kits, and other when-you-need-'em, you-need-'em supplies.

Takasaki once kept a checklist, but now he's confident that he knows that when all his Stow-N-Glos are loaded, he has everything he needs to fish a tournament. And when he returns home, unpacking and stacking is that much easier.

Professional Walleye Tournament winner Tommy Skarlis keeps all his maps—road, topographical, and Fishing Hot Spots—in a file cabinet. There's a file folder for every state, lake, and river. "When I leaves for a PWT event on Mille Lacs, for instance, I grab the file folders marked "Minnesota" and "Lake Mille Lacs." This system is especially convenient if I have more than one map for a given body of water."

Once everything is packed and it's time to zoom off to your destination, keep this last and most important tip in mind: safety first. Sam Anderson offers this advice: "Before leaving the driveway, I thoroughly inspect my rig—the coupler-trailer hitch connection, tie-down straps, air pressure in the tires on both trailer and tow vehicle, wire connections, even the winch strap that connects to the bow eye on the boat." Anderson also checks his rig every 100 miles or so, realizing that this seemingly small task can save time and money by avoiding potential disaster.

Whether you're a touring pro or just an average Joe, planning and packing are the foundation of a successful trip. Now is the time to get organized for summer travel. Then, if you've remembered everything and prepared properly, the only other thing you need to seize that trophy—whether it's a fish or a tournament plaque—is a little luck.

THE TIGER WOODS OF WALLEYE TOURNAMENTS

Ron Seelhoff, winner of two consecutive PWT Championships (1999 and 2000) and runner-up the previous two seasons and 2001, has enjoyed unprecedented success in recent years. We asked him to shed a little light on how he does it.

Question: If there's such a thing as a Tiger Woods of competitive walleye fishing, you're it. What's makes you so much better than everyone else? Or are you simply luckier than most?

Seelhoff: Walleye pros seem to compete on different levels. There's a reason why some finish in the top 10 and others don't. I'd like to think I'm among that elite group of versatile anglers. Everything has come together for me in recent seasons. I've been blessed, or lucky, or whatever you want to call it, and able to reach my full potential.

I just go fishin' instead of worrying about it. It's important to get into a rhythm that often just comes to me while I'm fishing. I start by trying different things, and when something works, I simply keep repeating and refining the procedure. I think basic fishing fundamentals, along with natural skills, are a major part of being able to get into a rhythm.

Question: What's your foundation in competitive angling?

Seelhoff: I have a love for the outdoors, with fishing the reason for being there. I like the challenge of it all. I also strive to tip the odds in my favor. While we're vulnerable to Mother Nature and will always have our ups and downs, we need to make better decisions when conditions change. Watching and learning from guys like Gary Parsons and Keith Kavajecz are important, too.

Question: What's your strong suit?

Seelhoff: I'm a pretty good troller. Sometimes I just saturate a zone, putting in the hours. But the trolling game has a lot of aspects that some pros don't consider. For example, fish in different bodies of water respond to different presentations.

Question: Explain.

Seelhoff: In Lake Erie, the fish seem to like big baits with erratic actions that displace a lot of water. In contrast, walleyes in lakes Oahe and Sakakawea prefer smaller baits like Shad Raps with tighter wobbles that can bounce off rocks and keep on ticking. Try the opposite tactic, and you're out of luck. Then consider the million refinements possible to this scenario.

Question: What do you say to those on the tournament scene who call trolling-oriented tournaments "troll-a-thons"?

Seelhoff: Trolling's a science. I mentally picture my baits underwater, how they're working and how to take my boat alongside a reef and work around it. I visualize what's going on down there. Many anglers don't see the need to be versatile. If they began applying themselves to the trolling game, they'd be four or five years behind. They don't have the confidence or the knowledge of how to work crankbaits. In fact, they hate it. It isn't jiggin' and it isn't riggin', and they don't want to change.

Question: Your skill at visualizing a spread of crankbaits and positioning trolling passes has been likened to dusting crops.

Seelhoff: I'm a crop-dusting pilot by trade. Anyone who works hard to master what he does, whether it's teaching, flying a plane, or fishing, must dedicate the time to gain experience needed to become an expert. Once you reach that level, performing those skill should feel almost second nature.

Take trolling, for example. I can only tell people what to try so they may possibly catch a fish while trolling. Boat control is critical. So is boat speed, because it dictates crankbait speed. It takes time and practice to be good at watching the depth so you can position your bait precisely. Sometimes a particular lure triggers more strikes. Finding a specific depth at which fish seem to be holding is key, too. But I have no set guidelines. I just have to figure it out.

I like trolling, but some people, even pro anglers, simply don't like to troll and probably never will like it, so they'll probably never be any good at it.

Question: So what does it take to win the trolling game? Is it necessary to memorize lots of depths for a bunch of baits and learn complicated formulas?

Seelhoff: I don't own a crankbait chart. I know my baits by feel. Basically, it's necessary to do everything the same. Repetition. The look of your rod—how far it's bent over. The movement of the tip. The sound of your motor. What's different about going with the waves instead of against them? Getting a bait to work the way you visualize it involves many details. The starting point is perception—seeing those baits down there, how they perform under different conditions, and how changing conditions affect them. The process is more mental than mechanical. It's impossible to skip that part and jump into a neat formula. Doesn't work that way.

> *I don't own a crankbait chart.*
> *I know my baits by feel.*
> –Ron Seelhoff

Question: You're one of the foremost proponents of trolling crankbaits with leadcore line. Why do you like it so much?

Seelhoff: I always tote along leadcore rigs, because they're deadly when I know the depth of the fish and a lure they like. I can bounce the bait, raise up a color or two, and get it right in the fish's face. But the flip side is that skill is needed to orchestrate a symphony of baits with leadcore.

For instance, if you get snagged and have to stop the boat, all lines sink into the rocks—things are hurry, hurry, hurry. And if you hook a good fish, you either have to take him out to deep water or fight him gingerly with the motor running. Sounds easy, but it's also frustrating and complicated. Besides, leadcore rigs are big and bulky. They need to be balanced. My 9-foot rods are just Kmart specials, but they have the right bend and the right feel. I'm able to reel up a few colors when I see fish off bottom, so it's worth the hassle.

Question: During practice before tournaments, some pro anglers work with friends and other pros to learn what, when, and where walleyes are biting. You primarily fish alone, although acquiring information about the body of water is critical for both recreational and tournament anglers.

Seelhoff: To survive in this business, you need good friends that you can trust to give you honest answers. I have friends, even other pro anglers, I feel comfortable asking questions of and giving them honest answers in return. General information, like is the bite fast or slow? Big or small fish? Sometimes the answer is, "Sorry, I just can't give you that information," but at least it's an honest answer.

Question: You're incredibly effective on the water. But no one has ever accused you of being fancy.

Seelhoff: Good! True, I don't own too many fancy rods and reels. In fact, most of mine weren't expensive, and I've been using them for so long that they're like old friends. But I also have great sponsors that provide me with the tools I need to use my skills. I'd have a hard time making it in this business without Lund boats,

Mercury outboard motors, Rapala crankbaits, Stren line, and Gamakatsu hooks.

Question: You rarely seem to lose your composure under pressure, even when you lose a big fish, experience equipment problems, or get crowded by other anglers.

Seelhoff: I try never to panic. Making the right decision at the right time often is the turning point, especially in competitive fishing. The decision always is somewhat of a gamble, but it's necessary.

Question: What's it like fishing with a different pro-am partner each day when big money is on the line?

Seelhoff: I make a point of getting to know my amateur partners the first two hours of each day to get a feel for who they are and what their angling capabilities are. Most pros immediately start fishing when they reach their destination. I don't hesitate to yawn, tell a joke, pour a cup of coffee, and maybe take a couple of sips before reaching for a rod. It relieves any tension.

Question: Jim Courts coached South Dakota high school athletes for over 35 years. He preached "mind over body," which he said meant that no matter the competition, provided you had developed good fundamentals, strategies, and tactics, you controlled 90 percent of how you performed. Many talented competitors fail to achieve greatness because they don't use their minds to visualize possible scenarios, to make good decisions, and most important, to stay focused and in control of the situation.

Seelhoff: Good point. Many anglers second-guess their decisions and worry about what everyone else is doing. It's better to just go fishing and keep trying your best—don't give up.

Question: What does the future hold for Ron Seelhoff?

Seelhoff: To be honest, it's a tough grind. But I'm ready for the challenge and thankful for the opportunity.

Competition Breeds Excellence

So You Wanna Be a Walleye Pro?

EXPERIENCE IS THE BEST TEACHER

Typical PWT pros have fished for walleyes for many years, accumulating a repertoire of time-tested, fish-catching tactics and presentations. They look for patterns and similarities to bodies of water where they've successfully caught walleyes during a particular time of year. Pros at the top year after year find winning bites in a short time. Finding the right pattern early enough is critical to success.

Being adaptable to all types of water—reservoirs, rivers, natural lakes, and the Great Lakes—is important for consistency and success on the circuit. Pros' physical skills, such as two-fisted jigging, multiple-rod trolling, boat control, livebait rigging, and jigging, must be above average. These are achieved through time and effort on the water.

Seasoned pros should have good equipment, competitive boats, and good motors. They develop networks of sponsors who support their efforts to showcase sponsors' products. The best possible equipment isn't absolutely mandatory, but it increases the pros' likelihood of better catches and reduces the chance of equipment failure.

Positive mental attitudes and clear, calculated tournament strategies go a long way toward effective decisions on the water. Time-management skills are always a bonus, because the clock is the enemy. In the PWT pro-am format, pros must remain calm and professional in order to maximize the effectiveness of the amateurs they're paired with, in addition to teaching their amateur partners new techniques and tactics.

True pros pay close attention to such details as sharp hooks, fresh line, and slight changes in wind and weather. They know that one fish can make or break their chance for success during a single tournament or the entire season.

AMATEURS PAR EXCELLENCE

Local hot walleye sticks who wants to participate in PWT tournaments on their home waters have many advantages. First, they've fished these waters for years. They know seasonal locations and walleye migration. This gives them tremendous advantages, especially when the circuit selects a new lake that the touring pros haven't fished.

On diverse bodies of water like Lake Winnebago, Saginaw Bay, and Mille Lacs, with many different bites, local fishermen have an advantage. They have extensive networks of friends pulling for their hometown heroes and offering information to help locate winning schools of big walleyes.

Hot sticks should consider the following challenges when they enter as pros. Several hot spots have produced big fish over the previous years. Although local pros know these spots well, and know they can produce tremendously during the tournament, more often than not they fish "yesterday's memories." Fish old hot spots during practice, but keep an open mind to emerging patterns and new spots.

Obtaining better equipment can be addressed slowly over time. If aspiring pros intend to fish professional walleye tournaments, the time to begin acquiring good equipment is right now, little by little. Manufacturers won't sponsor pros until they've used their products successfully and have established credentials within the industry.

Aspiring pros need to work on expanding their tactics and multiple-rod presentations, since where legal, all major walleye tournaments allow multiple rods. Boat control is a skill to be worked on well before the tournament. Most recreational fishermen don't fish often when conditions are poor. Touring pros have to go out in bad weather and still maintain good boat control.

The last aspects to consider are managing time and establishing solid tournament strategies. Once prefishing is over, planning the tournament day on paper helps to manage time for increased chances of success. A simple plan might include fishing spot #1 with a particular presentation until 10:00 a.m., then on to spot #2 until 12:30. With a limit, go to a big-fish pattern. With no limit, go on to spot #3 with a different presentation. The more tournaments you fish, the more concise and detailed your plans and strategies will become.

The fun in fishing tournaments comes from the camaraderie and friendships formed and the skill of learning how to catch walleyes consistently, day after day, under all conditions. That's what makes pros pros.

MAINTAINING A PROFESSIONAL IMAGE

Professional anglers are always in the public eye. On the water, they stand out. Members of the National Professional Anglers Association (NPAA) wear their pro numbers emblazoned on their boat or outboard and usually wear clothing emblazoned with the logos of their sponsors. At restaurants and gas stations, fans approach with questions and seek autographs.

When they tow their boats, their vehicles and boats are proudly lettered and tell the world who is driving. When they step out, their shirts and jackets tell the same story. "They're sharp" is a phrase often heard. From "sharp," an entire culture has developed.

Pros represent not only themselves but all others. At any turn, they might meet their next sponsor. Pro anglers not only must fish the part, they must also look the part. When they don't, they hear about it from PWT directors, sponsors, or their fellow anglers.

"Sharp Angler" is a description that covers the pros' response to fans, to each daily fishing partner (amateurs), and to their boats and tow vehicles. It should also describe their ethics on the water.

Sharp Angler was spawned from within the ranks. It was jump-started when the PWT offered Sharp Angler awards of $500 at tournaments in the early 1990s. When considering candidates for this award, the review committee took into account each pro's attire, boat cleanliness, stage presence, and working relationship with daily amateurs and the public. Once the pros understood the criteria, they developed a collective commitment to become Sharp Anglers.

Among the goals listed in the NPAA yearbook is "being dedicated to the advancement of professionalism among tournament fishermen and the growth of the fishing industry." President Mike McClelland says, "When founding the NPAA, the goal was not only to help the sport grow but also to develop professionalism among competitors."

Northland Tackle President, PWT tournament winner, and regular championship qualifier John Peterson talks about the image of the anglers who represent his company: "The profile of the angler is extremely important. To be on our team, a pro must portray a positive image and be a role model. Pro fishermen are not fishing bums. We love the fishery, the sport, the outdoors, the competition, the environment, the resource, the catch-and-release aspect of fishing, and we want to prove what we believe in. We can only do that by example. Neat dress and equipment are essential; so are a pro's actions."

Northland works with 15 Elite Pro staff representatives, about 25 Regional Pro staffers, and many other affiliated anglers. "Their image is our image," Peterson says.

Peterson credits the PWT for bringing walleye anglers to their current level. "At every meeting in those early years, the directors admonished us to be professionals, look like professionals, and speak like professionals." He reminds all team members that the public is constantly watching, so they must always act responsibly.

Pure Fishing's Jim George, says, "I have noticed a more professional attitude emerging in the pro walleye ranks, and this is reflected in the overall growth of the sport." He knows how vital professional anglers are in conveying fishing and product information. "At Pure Fishing, we look for individuals who are honest, responsible, and proud to wear our colors. And that means looking sharp," he says.

He advises pro anglers to be aware of how visible they are and to become spokesmen for the entire fishing and marine industry. If they compete in tournaments, they should represent all tournament contestants. "As our promoters, we want clean-cut people who are good anglers."

Pam Behnke, pro team manager for Mercury Outboards, deals with anglers throughout the United States. She advises her team members to become involved in habitat restoration, resources improvement, fishing club participation, and youth fishing programs. "Practice what you preach and give back to the sport with your time and enthusiasm," she says.

Behnke's advice: "Always dress neatly and keep hats fresh and clean. Even consider a change from fishing clothes to weigh-in/stage clothes for high-profile events. Communicate with the public wherever and whenever, and be positive—about fishing, about even the weather."

In-Fisherman television producer Mike Simpson, who has filmed anglers for two decades, has noticed increased professionalism in the way pros dress: "I seldom see casual clothes except maybe during a hot prefishing day," he says. From his vantage point behind the camera, Simpson knows that someone is always watching.

According to industry leaders, being a professional angler means being a sharp angler.

DEVELOPING AND MARKETING COMMUNICATION SKILLS

Anglers breaking into the pro ranks may think/wish/hope that all they need do to build a career is to go fishing and do well in tournaments. That's seldom the case. Most won't last long living strictly off tournament winnings—they're a real low-cal diet. Additional sustenance generally is required in the form of sponsor dollars or deals, speaking fees, guiding, writing articles, or other sources of income.

Building credibility with potential sponsors, sport show promoters, and the public generally requires making many public appearances. While aspiring pros may want to leap directly to the main stage at major sport shows—and this can happen following a major championship tournament win—more likely they'll need to build up slowly by fine-tuning communication skills and credibility. A number of avenues are open to foster this approach, some traditional, others less so.

Seminars at fishing clubs provide exposure for sponsors and build name recognition regionally.

Most clubs have limited budgets, so don't expect to get rich by following this path alone. It's one of many stepping stones to credibility and success.

You can also build name recognition through in-store promotions at local sporting goods stores or regional chains. Once again, exposure puts a few bucks in your pocket. Build a local reputation by calling the local newspaper's sports or outdoor writer and offering to take him fishing. You won't make any money, but you may receive follow-up exposure in the paper, which is like planting seeds for the future. Newspaper clippings add to your résumé.

Contact a regional outdoors publication and offer to take a writer or editor fishing. If you feel competent, suggest ideas for articles you'd consider submitting. Recognize that if you elect to pursue writing, you'll need to make more than a token effort, plus provide good photographs to support your submissions. Expect to be turned down at first, but you have to start somewhere—if you don't make a cast, you can't get bit.

Through some combination of persistence, exposure, talent, and luck, you'll start to build a reputation . . .

Through some combination of persistence, exposure, talent, and luck, you'll start to build a reputation, and perhaps you'll land sponsor dollars and a request to represent a certain sponsor at shows that could range from weekend shopping-mall promotions to major sport shows in large cities. Appearances build a track record and put you in touch with the right people—manufacturers, media, sponsors, and sport show promoters. Submit résumés and offer to perform speaking engagements. Keep casting. Don't be dissuaded by initial low-frequency bites.

Eventually, you may be able to arrange for major stage performances, which tend to pay a bit better, though not necessarily. Some promoters would like to see your sponsors pick up the cost, figuring that they're providing the stage and the audience for you and your benefactors. Most promoters, however, recognize that you'll require a little cash. The bigger your reputation, the more people you'll attract, and the more funding you can request for each performance.

At this point, keep fine-tuning the process, making more contacts and perhaps triggering more appearances. These are ways to generate income during the winter sport show season, when fishing and tournament activity often enter a lull. Talk to anglers, promote your sponsors, work the system to garner new sponsors and contacts—all traditional and logical steps.

Now comes the intriguing part. You get a phone call from someone who likes to fish but isn't in a fishing-related business. Instead, he is, or represents, a contractor, landscaper, equipment manufacturer, salesman, or an unrelated business that employs numerous males who are at least somewhat outdoor oriented. He's seen you at a seminar or in-store promotion and has an idea that you just might make a good speaker at a monthly association meeting—particularly the one just before walleye season opens. Naturally, everyone at that meeting won't be a diehard angler, but some will be. Even the golfers are likely to be respectful and will listen to you, provided you don't talk too long, become too technical, and manage to weave in a few interesting or funny stories related to their business. Adjust your presentation accordingly.

Voilà!—a nontraditional opportunity. You've employed the communications skills you've honed by talking to fishermen into a windfall. And if you do a good job, word of mouth or a review of your performance in the next association bulletin may trigger another bite from someone else. And who knows where it'll go from there?

The point is, to be successful in this business, you need to be a good communicator, not only a good angler. If you're a good communicator, opportunities will arise, albeit not always from expected sources. Talk may be cheap, but it helps to pay the bills, bit by bit. Just as in tournaments, every bite counts.

NO SUCH THING AS AN OFF SEASON

"Boy, would I like to have your life! Being a pro fisherman must be the best job in the world. All you have to do is fish all the time."

Granted, being able to make a living doing what one loves is great, but being a professional walleye fisherman isn't only about fishing tournaments a few months of the year and then taking the rest of the year off. What most people don't realize is that making a living at the profession is hard work, and doing it right means no off season.

What is a professional fisherman? Many anglers fish tournaments. Some even arrange with various companies to get equipment and tackle free or at reduced prices. But to be a professional—to be able to make a living in the fishing game— takes money. It's possible to win some by doing well on tournament circuits, but even the hottest sticks on the trail rarely make enough from tournaments to carry them through the winter.

Pros supplement their income in several ways, such as giving seminars in the winter months and selling articles and photographs to magazines. Those help, but to truly survive as a professional fisherman demands finding sponsors willing to pay a retainer in exchange for promotional work. And they're not easy to find.

Successful sponsorship isn't a one-win situation anymore; you can't simply win a major tournament and expect companies to offer you money. It takes longevity— doing well over time—before you're recognized in magazines and on TV.

The real work begins when the tournament season ends. If you disappear from October until April, you won't survive in the fishing industry. Your off-season job is getting to know the people who make sponsorship decisions. You must show these people that you can give them opportunities that will gain their company more exposure with the fishing public, thereby increasing their sales.

Good photos that can be used for magazine articles and advertising are important. A company can always use a fine shot of a trophy fish with a company lure hanging out of its mouth or the company logo on the angler's cap and shirt. October and November are great months for photos. On many bodies of water, good numbers of big fish are taken in the fall. Because of colder water temperatures, fish look better and stay healthy longer before being released.

Investing the time and money in good photos and good video is important. They're also important in putting together a professional seminar to present at sport shows and to fishing clubs during the winter. A professional seminar helps a pro grow in the industry.

Fishing is only part of a professional angler's full-time job.

From January through March, attend a major sport show every weekend—it isn't difficult. If you do your leg work over the summer, you'll be booked to present seminars at some of them. But even if you aren't speaking, attend the bigger shows, introduce yourself to the shows' promoters, and visit with tackle representatives. If you can impress a company representative, either by helping at the company booth or by putting on a good seminar, that representative will become a valuable ally while you're working toward a sponsorship.

There's no off season for the professional walleye fisherman.

Stay in contact with potential and actual sponsors. Let them know what you're doing via written reports. More important, find out what their plans are for the upcoming year. Be aware of new products they plan to promote, and work with them to get the word out. This is where you, as a professional angler, can be a big help. You know if a product catches fish, because you spent all last season fishing with it. Let the company know they have a hot product and how you can help promote it.

There's no off season for the professional walleye fisherman. The time that you spend not fishing should be spent getting to know the industry, how it works, and the people who make it tick. Conduct yourself as a professional, both on the tournament trail and during the so-called off season. You're representing a big industry, and companies are more likely to deal with you if they think of you as a professional.

KEEP YOUR 'EYES ON THE ROAD

"You can't draw flies in your own hometown, but 500 miles from home, you're an expert."—Anonymous

The places walleye pros are most in demand as seminar speakers from January through April are not warm southerly destinations like Key West, Padre Island, or the Bahamas. Instead, they spend many midwinter weekends on the way to, coming back from, or wrapped within the chilly embrace of towns like Cleveland, Chicago, Detroit, Milwaukee, and St. Paul, aspiring to warmer cities like Harrisburg, Cincinnati, Nashville, Indianapolis, and Omaha, along the lower fringe of the Walleye Belt. Canceled flights, long drives in snow and darkness, and sore throats are all part of the charm of so-called fishing for a living in the North Country.

Twenty years ago, few walleye speakers were doing weekend seminars at sports shows. Al Lindner, Gary Roach, Mike McClelland, and a few others were the only walleye anglers out pounding the pavement on a national level. Today, the roster of frequent walleye fliers has expanded manyfold, bringing firsthand walleye fishing information to auditoriums throughout the country.

From the Speaker's Perspective—What's the walleye seminar market like? Breaking into the seminar business isn't easy. Walleye pros compete for the prime speaking slots that major sport show promoters make available. They also boost their résumés and sponsor performance reports

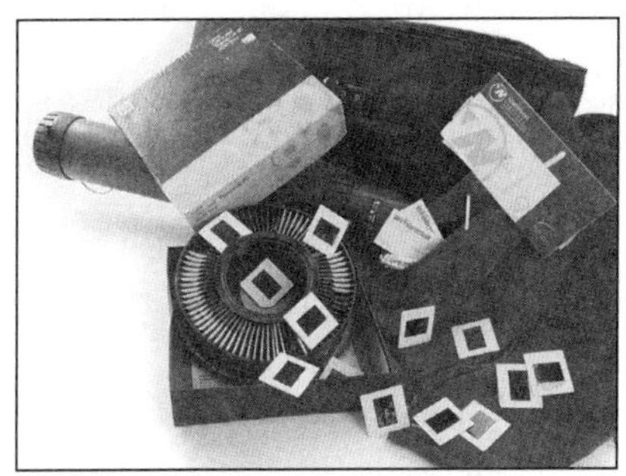

Have slides. Will travel.

by manning sponsor booths at large shows and by speaking at smaller outdoor shows, marine dealerships, sporting goods stores, and fishing clubs.

Promoters seldom chase a prospect down and beg to put him on stage, however. It often takes a big tournament win, followed by persistent contacts with sport show promoters, including a résumé and references, to earn a contracted appearance. Fortunately, veteran promoters in the North Country realize that walleye speakers draw crowds, and crowds spend money with exhibitors and concessionaires. Gary Parsons, Keith Kavajecz, Ted Takasaki, Gary Roach, Mike McClelland, and other well-known PWT gurus zigzag the nation in a frenzy, maintaining a punishing schedule.

Seminar speakers need to take their responsibilities seriously. The promoter is counting on his speakers to be knowledgeable, educational, and friendly, giving his customers something of value in return for their ticket stub. Attendees expect to learn something new about how to catch fish. Most walleye speakers come prepared with slide presentations detailing various aspects of walleye fishing. Some go high-tech, with the latest audiovisual aids. Others develop fine discussions or question-and-answer sessions with only a few rods, reels, and lures as props. It all depends on the performer-presenter.

Today's video age, however, has reduced the attention span of a typical audience member to about the length of a Fuzz-E-Grub body. That's a concentration level best measured in seconds, not minutes. Blackboards and standard slide shows are on the verge of being eclipsed by more sophisticated communications.

Blackboards and standard slide shows are on the verge of being eclipsed by more sophisticated communications.

A few guys have forsaken their chalk and blackboards, progressed through the slide show stage, and graduated into multimedia programs. A leading example is the duo of Gary Parsons and Keith Kavajecz, producers of a next-generation audiovisual extravaganza. "We approach walleye fishing from a professional viewpoint, and it doesn't stop when we leave the water," says Kavajecz, who drew upon his extensive computer programming background to create a slick multimedia package. "To compete, we must take advantage of every possible medium." So multimedia is the buzzword, as long as it transcends mediocrity.

For starters, there's the video projector designed for computer output ($12,000). Then there's the video computer that feeds information to a laser disc, telling it which frames to overlay on the screen for video effect. A sophisticated sound system works off a wireless microphone and CD-ROM to create every imaginable audio special effect—from the *doink* of a jig hitting the water to crickets chirping under a golden sunset. Naturally, a handful of software programs are needed to run the show. And don't forget the copyrighted music that sets the mood and tempo. All told, it cost the P-K boys about $40,000 to get into big-time multimedia, and that doesn't include the four months of full-time experimenting and tweaking that Kavajecz spent breaking this new ground.

Is it worth it? "Say you're trying to describe crankbait action," Kavajecz counters. "You want to explain the roll and wobble of a ThunderStick. What good does it do to wriggle a 4½-inch bait in front of the crowd when most of them can't see it, let along visualize its action? You need a close-up on a big screen."

"Besides, close-ups, bars, graphs, and 3-D illustrations simplify the more complicated aspects of advanced fishing techniques," adds Parsons. "Multimedia's invaluable.

"Want to take the fear out of GPS? Animation is ideal. Remember, electronics can't be photographed or videographed easily, so we animate to show a waypoint, explain an icon. Toss in appropriate background music, and it's fun instead of intimidating. Keep images changing constantly, and you can bring your mother-in-law to a one-hour seminar. Time flies."

Whichever approach you choose, you must hold the interest of an audience for 45 or 50 minutes and then perhaps answer questions without trying to cram sponsors' product down people's throats. Soft selling appropriate products is fine, even encouraged, tastefully fulfilling sponsor obligations with a slide or brief mention. Audiences can and do recognize the difference and don't appreciate being force-fed sponsors' products. A little humor is useful, too, but a good speaker fills the hour with more than jokes and fishing stories.

From the Audience's Perspective—Anglers flock to winter sport show seminars to learn what's new, what's hot, and what's not for walleyes. When an angling authority appears on stage, the audience eagerly awaits some gem of information that will make a difference in their fishing success. They expect a live performance from a real live human being, often accompanied by slides of big fish and notable tackle and equipment, explanations of how and where fish are caught, perhaps some hands-on tackle demonstrations after the slide show, usually followed by a question-and-answer session. Someone notable is right there in person and can answer questions on a variety of angling topics, not just the seminar subject.

Seminar crowds have grown more sophisticated. They appreciate a well thought out and personable presentation on current angling topics. They recognize the flaws in a one-size-fits-all performance that's been repeated too many times, creaks with dated material, or is not pertinent to local waters and anglers. Anglers cringe at too-frequent and too-obvious sponsor deluges and are embarrassed by someone who tries to get by simply with stories and jokes. And they walk out when faced by a barrage of ego from the stage—no one likes being talked down to.

Seminars provide an opportunity for speakers and walleye pros to mix and mingle with fishermen across the country, read the local pulse of angling interest, become better acquainted with regional fishing opportunities and tackle, introduce their sponsors' products at a grassroots level, and better understand the kinds of questions fishermen want answered. Local fishermen reap the benefit of having top walleye anglers share their experiences and answer questions, face to face. Everyone wins.

PROS WHO GUIDE

Each workday begins in the same way: handshakes and introductions, small talk, maybe a bite of breakfast. Then it's into the boat and tallyho and after fish they go, led by an angler who does this for a living.

One day it might be Lake Erie, as a professional contestant in a PWT tournament. Next Tuesday it might be the Chippewa Flowage in Wisconsin or an inland lake in Michigan, as a professional fishing guide. In both roles, the pro angler faces the expectations of not only family and fans but partners who are amateur tournament entrants one day and guided clients the next.

After a week on home waters, the experienced guide has the bite dialed in. But the next tour stop beckons, so a 19-hour drive puts him on unfamiliar

Mark Martin, a pro's pro.

water, and the process begins again—searching, testing presentations, sorting out a game plan.

If he's lucky, he'll finish in the upper echelon and cash a check, then drive home powered by satisfaction and caffeine to go head-to-head against local guides who never left and still have the local bite dialed in.

Mark Martin, from Twin Lake, Michigan, has been living this dual life for as long as he can remember. One of the most consistent producers of fish in PWT history, he claims that the pressure and his approach to it are the same whether he's guiding or fishing a big-money tournament.

But for Jeff Taege of Rhinelander, Wisconsin, there's a perceptible difference in demeanor and approach, based on the situation. "I'm a Jekyll and Hyde," he admits. "When I'm guiding, I try to be personable, tell jokes, and carry on a conversation. But when I'm tournament fishing, I try to be as focused as I can be, unless maybe I get an early limit. If I'm carrying on a conversation with my amateur during a tournament, 10 or 15 minutes can go by, and I suddenly notice I'm not tightly following the contour.

"When I'm guiding, I don't want my clients to feel like they've put in a day's work. But I hope that during a tournament, my amateurs are as exhausted as I am at the end of the day, because our whole focus is putting fish in the boat." Interestingly, Martin considers the dual demands of guiding and fishing tournaments as complementary.

"I think my guiding gives me an advantage," Martin says. "In my night-fishing"—he's famous for guiding customers to huge walleyes after dark—"I have to feel the boat. I don't rely on the directional arrow on my electric motor. I do everything by feel—watching the graph, following contours.

"I'm constantly practicing for tournaments with my boat control. Whether vertical fishing, following a breakline, or controlled drifting a piece of structure, the guy with the better boat control catches more fish. I can feel my boat starting to get away from me before it actually goes off course."

The concept works for touch and feel with a rod and reel, too. "For sure it helps with bite detection," Martin says. "Especially when I'm in night mode, I have to rely totally on feel, and a lot of times the reaction time must be split-second. I work on my ability to know when it's a bite, a rock, or a weed."

Martin doesn't even begrudge his fellow PWT pros the opportunity to prefish prior to the weeklong closed period before each event. "We're allowed four or five days of practice," he says. "Something big always changes, anyway, like the weather, so I see guys running all over during the tournament, going back to spots that produced three weeks ago. I don't have those misconceptions."

For Taege, rewards come his way during guiding days, because clients seek him out to learn his tournament-won secrets.

"I'd say a fourth of the people I take out," he says, "are as interested in learning how to fish as they are in how many fish we can catch that day. I have people tell me they want to learn how to troll, or fish weeds, or fish deep structure, or whatever."

The teaching is a constant, no matter which hats these guys don. As guides, they're often expected to show clients how to fish. As pros in the PWT pro-am format, they're looked upon as superguides by the amateurs who draw them as partners for a day.

"When my amateur partner tells me he's hardly ever fished before," Martin reveals, "I'm actually happy about that. It doesn't bother me a bit, because by the end of the day, he'll have all my bad habits. You can tell him how to hold the rod, how to do this and that, and he listens. Pretty soon he gets involved and may end up catching more fish than I do—and that's what I'm hoping for, because we're in it together."

A pro who guides has a rigorous lifestyle, with highs and lows, sunny days, and driving rainstorms. But the rewards win out, if you're cut from the right cloth.

"I'm thankful every day that I'm able to do what I do," Taege says. "I'm not a millionaire, and I'm not living in a mansion, but I'm happy. It kind of makes me wish summer was twelve months long, so I could fish tournaments half the time and guide the rest of it."

GUIDE ETIQUETTE

- Always be on time. Anglers have driven a long way and invested time and money to fish. They're not interested in hearing about your truck not starting, power failures, or any other excuses. Clients should be offered extra fishing hours, discounts, or free trips to make up for late starts that are your fault.

- Deposit refunds must be made promptly when a trip is canceled because of you. Weather or water conditions unsafe for boating also call for a prompt refund.

- Never cancel a trip without notifying the client as far in advance as possible. Offer to try to find another guide.

- Before smoking, ask if it will bother the client. Save any drinking of alcohol until after the trip. You are responsible for the safety of those who hire you.

Teamwork begins at home, jells on the water, and reaps big rewards by the end of a fishing day.

- Treat the client's equipment as if it were your own. Replace anything you break.

- Be glad when your client points out something you're doing wrong. This gives you the chance to save the trip and send away a happy customer.

- The guide never wimps out first. No matter how cold, windy, or wet it gets, you must be prepared to go out. If being on the water is safe, you must go. Some anglers are willing to fish no matter how tough the conditions. After driving long distances, staying in motels, eating in restaurants, and using up vacation time, the client deserves your best effort. If the weather is really miserable, offer clients the option of a refund. But if they want to go, go.

- Don't hog the fish. If you're catching fish but your clients aren't, try to determine why. If they don't catch their share, they won't be back.

- Answer questions. Clients are paying to find out why a spot is good, why a certain lure is the best choice, or why you're fishing a bait a certain way.

WALLEYE CIRCUITRY

Are you up to the grueling schedule of today's walleye pros? With the proliferation of national tournament circuits and increased competition for sponsorship dollars, some guys are busier than a kite in a thunderstorm.

Is such a frantic schedule necessary? Keith Kavajecz, walleye pro from Chilton, Wisconsin, says it isn't unless you want to soar in the world of professional fishing. He insists that to maximize exposure and promotional value, fishing the PWT and other pro-am circuits is the only way to fly. Master's Walleye Circuit (MWC) partner competitions are more family oriented and serve as a farm system for pro-am competition, just as Red Man bass events complement the B.A.S.S. circuit.

"There are lots of sacrifices," says the full-time walleye pro. "But if you add it all up, I believe the pluses outnumber the minuses. Actually, I consider it a dream job." Kavajecz ought to know, having quit a cushy job with a giant electronics corporation to go full-time on the walleye circuits.

So what's it like to crisscross the walleye circuit? Here's an inside look at the summer lifestyle of a pro. You decide if it's worth it.

The season begins early. Actually, it hardly ends, considering the seminar tour and continual clamor from sponsors requesting fishing clinics and last-minute, in-store promotions. But what's it like to fish more than one tournament circuit? Circle April on the calendar. Then flip ahead to September. That's six months of hectic, hardcore competitive angling, with maybe a week off here, five days there, another week here.

"It's pretty grueling," Kavajecz says. "In a typical summer, I'm home only ten days between April 20 and mid-August. It's hard on the body. You'd be surprised at the kind of shape you need to be in to stay with the pack these days. I remember taking off three weeks, then fishing a big-money tournament. Man, I ached all over for days. I didn't realize the muscles I'd developed until I aggravated one.

"Back, neck, and legs have to get accustomed to the pounding that choppy waters dish out. To anticipate waves and work the electric trolling motor takes coordination and balance. We hunt down fish with a clock ticking against us—no time to waste between spots. To win, it's necessary to run full-bore regardless of the waves. Heck, at Lake Oahe, Gary Parsons once made a 110-mile journey to work over a school of fish—and that was only in one direction. You just do it."

Another demanding aspect of the walleye circuitry is the never-ending maintenance. "Bolts unbolt, screws unscrew, nuts loosen. A simple mechanical failure, like an untimely frayed wire or loose bracket, can cost thousands of dollars in winnings. Today's walleye pros have to function like the pit crew at an Indy 500 race—identify the source of a problem and repair it without delay.

"We tote along back-ups for indispensables like a spare trolling motor and an extra GPS. But it's the little things that drive us crazy. It helps to carry the right tools. For example, every year for Christmas, I ask my wife and kids for a new cordless tool. I can't get enough impact wrenches and battery-powered gizmos and gadgets."

What's a little nut tightening or wire crimping? "A lot, if it costs you sleep," Kavajecz says. "Like I said, it's grueling. I need my rest. Nighttime is for recharging the batteries, not fiddling with equipment into the wee hours."

One precaution for eliminating this bugaboo is a detail that Kavajecz and Parsons have worked out with their boat sponsor: two boats apiece per year. "That's right—I switch boats midway through the summer circuit," Kavajecz confesses. "That may sound extravagant, but worked out on paper, it's not frivolous."

Perhaps. Consider that the average angler's rig probably travels no more than a couple of thousand miles in a given summer. Kavajecz's trailer racks up 30,000 miles, and his boat takes about 99 million waves.

"Don't forget that tournament fishing is like an Iditarod or Enduro race—it's a far cry from recreational fishing. I bet my boat averages twelve seasons of abuse in one summer. Besides, because we do a lot of photography, our rigs need to look showroom-shiny."

So today's double-circuit pros have their work cut out for them. "It goes with the turf," Kavajecz says. Instead of complaining, he counts his blessings: "I get to fish the best walleye waters in the world with the best equipment available. I'm even asked to help design better tackle. What more could a guy ask for?"

How about less time spent away from home? "That's the one sacrifice I will never get used to," Kavajecz admits. "It's tough. I have three young boys, and I hate missing their baseball games. I can't enjoy lawn work or gardening like the guy next door. And I don't have time to visit with my neighbors and relatives."

Understandably, everyone in the Kavajecz household has had to adjust. Days on the calendar are circled months in advance. Scheduling is an art and a science. "The good part is that when I'm home, my attention is undivided. I try to make it seem like a continuous weekend, quality time to make up for the lack of quantity. I think it's a good life."

Perhaps for Kavajecz. But anyone short on stamina and long on impatience would easily become frazzled. The double circuit, considered a boon to walleye pros, could easily become a short circuit.

JUST BETWEEN YOU AND ME

Do you confide intimate thoughts to family members? Have you shared the coordinates of that out-of-the-way Lake Mille Lacs mudflat that never fails? What about that little hump in Saginaw Bay you've kept under wraps, despite all of the interviews? Then there's the bait you catch most of your fish on but can't share with a soul, especially your top sponsor. More to the point, what have you said in confidence about "that other guy"? Well, go ahead, cup your hands around your mouth so nobody can read your lips. Whisper it. Just between you and me.

Say you just won a tournament, and you spill your guts to a newspaper reporter; it's just "between the two of you." Next thing you know, headlines feature every juicy tidbit. Big mistake. When something's off the record, it must remain off the record.

Fact is, this kind of exchange has gone on between anglers ever since the first caveman speared his first Friday night fish fry. You can't risk telling your own mother about this morning's catch.

Fortunately, In-Fisherman's editors and cameramen have a reputation with PWT contestants for being able to draw the line between what's reportable and what should remain forever buried in the bottom of the tackle box. But what happens if some reporter starts asking questions of unsuspecting family

members who've never been exposed to the wiles of extracting fishing information from any and all available sources?

Picture this scenario: No more "C'mon, did you really catch those fish on an XYZ crankbait?" type of questions. No, siree—from now on, it's going to be more like "So, Mrs. Walleye Pro, what does your husband say about his buddy edging him out for Angler of the Year?" Or "You know, your husband told me the name of that trophy walleye lake where I was supposed to meet him this weekend, but it seems to have slipped my mind." Or "He said it would be OK to let me into the garage to pick out a couple of lures to try while he's out of town . . . Did he say where he left his marked lake maps for this weekend's tournament? Did he leave me any GPS coordinates? Don't worry, I'll just copy them off his GPS screen."

Just between you and me: if the words leave your mouth, they're public knowledge.

PRO TO PRO, WHAT DO YOU KNOW?

Whether they like it or not, today's pros are forced to share information and rely on input from others. Not on the water during actual competition, but during practice or evening bull sessions, when friends compare notes. Everyone does it, even Mr. Walleye, Gary Roach: "There's just too much water to comb in big-water tournaments and too little time to do it," he says. "With only five days of pre-fishing, give-and-take is as much a part of the game as livebait rigging."

Unwritten rules on networking have evolved, and it pays to decipher the code, but you won't find it in any book or manual. With this in mind, let's take a look at how some pros sift through tournament information.

"When it comes to gathering information, I see three distinct tiers," Keith Kavajecz says. "First is the intimate level, like Gary Parsons and me. We share everything."

Even specific spots?

"Yup, right down to GPS coordinates. The only stipulation is that if one of us happens to find a smaller spot that's really hot during the tournament, he gets to fish it first."

The next tier, according to Kavajecz, includes a handful of guys who have access to "walleye demographics"—techniques that are working and the numbers and sizes of fish that Parsons and Kavajecz are catching.

"The single most valuable clue in a tournament isn't always where or what, but how big. For example, what good would it do for us to beat up on 3-pounders if others are whaling on 4- or 5-pounders? I mean, automatically we'd be out of the running. So we kind of have an agreement with four or five guys we trust and who trust us."

Swappin' strategies at the weigh-in.

Within this tier, the information exchanged is more like "We caught 20 fish averaging 6 pounds in open water at 15 feet with cranks" than "Fish fire-tiger ThunderSticks 18 feet down just north of Dead Man's Reef."

The composition of the second tier may change from year to year. "Trust must build," Kavajecz explains. "If it's ever violated, there's no second chance. This may sound cold blooded, but one bad piece of information outweighs ten pieces of good information. At this level, the information isn't specific enough to win a tournament, but misleading tips can hurt by wasting valuable time."

As for the third tier—friends—the overriding rule of thumb is honesty. "This level is sort of relegated to how many fish we're catching—we're doing great or we're hurting," says Kavajecz. "This last level is pretty informal.

"Now, things may change if I'm really doing well in a tournament. If I notice someone struggling, I may show him the baits that are producing. Still, we try to stay consistent—not gouging guys for information when we're out to lunch and not disappearing when times are good."

> *"At this level, the information isn't specific enough to win a tournament, but misleading tips can hurt by wasting valuable time."*
> *–Keith Kavajecz*

Gary Roach: "I used to tell a few guys everything, but I think I might have been doing them an injustice, not forcing them to use their heads. Now I prefer pointing them in the right direction with the basics they need. If it's a lake tournament, I won't share my number-one or number-two spot, but I'll probably let a few friends in on numbers three, four, and so on. If they're ahead of me with a chance of winning, I may even give a good friend my number-one spot." As for ethics, Roach agrees with Kavajecz's rule of "one strike, and you're out."

Another interesting perspective comes from Scott Fairbairn, a fishery biologist turned walleye pro who's a relative newcomer to the professional scene. Early on, Fairbairn learned the value of choosing the right partner.

"I like to work with two types of professionals," Fairbairn says. "First, the obvious inner circle. Two's about right, three's usually a crowd. This has to be a special commitment. Heck, you end up spending more time with this guy during the tournament season than with anyone, including your spouse. And your partner has to be as good as you. If he's not, he can't push you. That's why I think Parsons and Kavajecz have become so successful in recent years—they're equally proficient, and they seem to be maturing at the same pace.

"You must have total trust in your partner, too. Parsons, for instance, knows that Kavajecz will always find fish, and vice versa. It doesn't matter who's on the finding end, just that it gets done. This kind of relationship will work so long as both benefit equally."

The second type of relationship is nearly as special in Fairbairn's book. He remembers well the time he was hopelessly lost on Winnebago and turned to Mike McClelland for help. "He gave me insights on a few key spots," Fairbairn recalls. "I said, 'OK, I won't infringe on you.' He said, 'Just don't pile in on me if you see me on a spot; leave me be. Otherwise, go ahead and fish the spot.' I hope that if McClelland ever needs a tip, I can return the favor."

A final thought. In the short run, sharing information may not appear wise. After all, the competition is keen enough; put more boats on a spot, and odds plummet. But the long run is another story: networking probably benefits the giver as much as the receiver, because as the field of contestants grows, so do the earnings, including each slice of the pie.

THROUGH THE EYES OF BILL KOEHNE, AN AMATEUR TURNED PRO

Through the Eyes of an Amateur—An In-Fisherman PWT entry form sat on the coffee table, enticing me. I'd always considered myself a decent angler. And the chance to pitch jigs with Hall of Famers and learn more about my home waters was just too tempting. In the mail it went.

My first tournament will always stick in my mind. I was impressed by how the professionals made walleye fishing so much more than just fishing. It was like fishing with my dad, being taught all over again.

Bill Koehne eyes a career in professional fishing.

A day spent with John Peterson, when we proceeded to hammer walleyes on jigs and spinner rigs, taught me that minor variations in presentation make all the difference. No wonder Peterson jigged himself to victory the following year at Baudette, Minnesota.

Chris Gilman provided another lesson as he zipped to victory, trolling Junior ThunderSticks at higher than conventional speeds. On that day, a new crankbait won a home in my tackle box, and walleye fishing for me would never be the same.

Originally, my goals were to learn more about walleyes and the presentations that catch 'em, but that was only the beginning. With the various pros using different boats, tackle, and equipment, I had the opportunity to test products to determine which ones I felt were superior. Purchasing a Champion Fishunter boat was easier after having the opportunity to fish from many different models. The same with rods, reels, and other weapons necessary for a proper walleye arsenal.

Traveling, prefishing, and just plain sharing philosophies with so many PWT anglers and staff helped round out what the tournament trail and pro fishing is all about.

Tom Bruno explained the differences between being a tournament angler and a pro. Being a tournament angler is challenging enough. Becoming a pro is a feat in itself, trying to reach the top and being able to earn a living—lofty and challenging goals.

A conscious decision, a commitment, and a business game plan are needed in order to become successful. These include lots of hard work and promotion during the nonfishing season—many calls, letters, appearances, and weekends away from home.

I've found stepping from amateur to tournament angler exciting and rewarding, although the experience becomes humbling when the fish don't cooperate. But even on tough days, I always learn something new. Sometimes only wisdom learned from years of competition is the key ingredient to winning. Other times, it may be a small but critical piece of information.

Through the Eyes of a First-Year Pro—Once my first PWT pro season had drawn to a close, I found that some of my preparations had been on the money and that a few unexpected developments had arisen. I found that when I fished as an amateur, the pros were open to discussing tactics, presentations, and locations. When I turned pro, however, information suddenly became harder to acquire. Being a pro elevated me to the level of fellow competitor, and only trusted comrades are privy to inside information after that.

Groups known as *networks* or *teams* develop over the years. Within these networks, a limited number of members share the information critical to success. A good team whose members share knowledge gained in prefishing is tough for an individual to compete against. I struggled during the first year to form a network, to make valuable links for the future.

A special code of ethics is required and strictly enforced within these groups. If you're taken into someone's confidence and information is shared, you never spread that information without the group's approval.

Bruce DeShano, owner of Off Shore Tackle, cautions that it's important to spend several years as an amateur to gain fishing experience. Investing several years as a pro, making contacts, and becoming acknowledged and accepted by your peers are necessary before you can expect exceptional results. Even then, winning is never guaranteed. Years of fishing in themselves don't secure a top-10 finish.

To pursue this goal with reasonable expectations, you need to expect disappointments along the way. A number of years must be spent gaining enough wisdom, developing relationships, and learning the industry just to have the chance to fish on a professional level.

No one said it would be simple or easy. But it's exciting and fun. With a little risk, a love of walleye fishing, a good start as an amateur, and a pro season under my belt, my dream of tournament fishing is coming true. I've seen it through the eyes of an amateur and now through the eyes of an aspiring pro.

FISHIN' FOR A LIVIN'?

When it comes to making a living, what a fishing pro does off the water is more important than what he does on the water. When competing for a first-place purse of $50,000 in a PWT tournament, the pro may disagree somewhat. But most tackle and marine manufacturers agree.

"No matter what happens on the water, how many tournaments are won or records set, the bottom line is still selling product," according to Jim Morton, former promotions manager for Storm Lures.

Morton agreed that a pro's performance on the water, successes and accolades, are important because they provide credibility with the public. Success on the water also creates a bond between a pro and the companies he represents. "No matter how good the product, it must end up in the hands of consumers," Morton emphasizes. "This is the goal of advertising programs, public relations efforts, and careful packaging, distribution, and pricing. The pro must help move products into the hands of the public."

ADVICE FOR DEALING WITH SPONSORS AND MEDIA

1. Know how to speak to sport show crowds as well as to fishermen on the water and at fishing club meetings.

2. Don't call sponsors unless you have important news. They have limited staff. FAX or mail them a letter instead.

3. Keep sponsors informed. Let them know what's happening, what you're doing. Send them frequent news clippings of promotions and tournament wins. Let them know how their product is being used. Report big news immediately.

4. Never phone on Monday morning.

5. Know the sponsor's goals and product lines thoroughly.

6. Don't get caught with the wrong product.

7. Be loyal to sponsors. It's important for long-term relationships and for marketing yourself through ads, brochures, and catalog photos.

Asking for a sponsorship is like interviewing for a job.

8. Don't compare your sponsor contracts with those of other pros. The contract between a sponsor and pro outlines the minimum expected.

9. When contacting a sponsor for support, don't tell him what your contract with another sponsor contains.

Stren's former Field Promotions Manager, D.D. Fuller, adds that pros should mull over the following:

1. There are three levels of corporate sponsorship:
   a. Products (the starting point)
   b. Tournament staff
   c. National team

2. Each level varies by individual pro and company and from year to year. Sometimes contingencies are built into the pro package.

3. Receiving product is like receiving money, because it costs money to manufacture product.

4. Asking for a sponsorship is like interviewing for a job.

5. Pro staffers are important because they create awareness of a product and demonstrate the innovative uses and the tournament-tested tough conditions a product withstands.

6. Sponsors need to know that the pro can communicate.

Fuller says, "A fishing pro can only go so far on fishing ability—then it becomes a business. Image is vital. Someone's always watching. Be a professional to be recognized as a professional." He adds that money exists outside the fishing industry for potential sponsorships. The door is wide open.

Industry veteran Mike Finé says, "A good sponsor is a good partner. Product knowledge is vital." Pros should promote products that are key to the tactics they use most. "Become known for your expertise," Finé says. "Always exhibit a positive mental attitude. Get to know local reps and the distribution systems used by the companies you represent. Calling on dealers is always beneficial, too."

Dave Csanda, *Walleye In-Sider* editor, encourages pros to get into print in the most influential walleye magazine in the country. How? Simple. Call with innovations, new uses for products, tips, and top spots to fish at a particular time of the year. Make it easy for editors to work with you. Don't wait for them to call you.

He also says that all magazines are not the same. Get to know them, their editorial needs, their formats. Then remember that magazines have deadlines a couple of months in advance of appearing in print.

Wade Bourne of Clarksville, Tennessee, one of the many freelancers in the industry, reminds pros that they're in the public relations business. In order to do their jobs adequately, they should make it easy for writers to do their jobs. His advice:

1. Be reliable. Call a writer when the fish are active, and then take him to the best spots.

2. Be ready to do a story whenever a writer calls.

3. Always consider new angles and fresh approaches.

4. Develop new uses for the products you represent.

5. Convey only a concept to the outdoor writer. He will prepare the story.

6. Do not mention sponsors just for hype—it isn't part of the business.

7. Mention sponsors when they're a legitimate part of the tactic or action—such reminders will usually get used.

8. Each editor treats a story differently, so the final article may be edited. That's the way the business works.

Mike Simpson, In-Fisherman Television Director, says he needs to know about good bites and new or unusual patterns. He reminds the pros that TV gives visibility to small products used as parts of specific techniques.

Many writers and pros with many sponsors, and all PWT sponsors have offered the following to would-be pros seeking sponsorship. "We're always looking for new ways to help sponsors and influence the industry," says pro Gary Parsons of his promotional efforts with partner Keith Kavajecz. The key to being a full-time pro is full-time promotional work within the industry. Al Lindner says not "good luck" but "good work" make a successful fisherman or pro. That message is heard often. Fishin' for a livin' is more than just fishin'. It's hard work, full-time, all year long, not just on the water.

There are more full-time pros in the walleye industry than ever before. A few dozen depend on their fishing and promotional activities for a living. Another few dozen are full-time fishermen, supplementing their income by guiding, running tackle companies, custom boat-rigging companies, resorts, and their own companies. How many will be full-timers in five or ten years? Time and performance will tell.

FIRST AND FOREMOST

Winning isn't everything, but it sure beats second place," says 1997 PWT Championship winner Rick LaCourse. For many championship winners, victories changed most aspects of their jobs and fishing.

For 1994 winner Perry Good—"It took fishing and my career to a new level." Mark Brumbaugh, the 1995 winner—"Before winning, I never thought of pro fishing as a job."

Good and Brumbaugh won PWT tournaments the year after their championships. They both gained a winning attitude by stepping into the winner's circle. Good says, "Personally, I have more confidence in myself. Since my championship win, I've only missed the money a few times."

"Once having won, I enter every event with an attitude of winning,"

Mark Brumbaugh

Brumbaugh says. "I'm not fishing for second anymore."

Nineteen ninety-six winner Randash admits the money is nice, and the exposure via the media is exciting. Not only has he been the star of PWT television shows, but he also began doing a segment for KOTA-TV in Rapid City—a 20-minute fishing lesson every other week for a year.

"I can't believe the number of outdoor writers who contacted me," Randash says. He expanded on those relationships and continued to work with his many sponsors, who increased their retainers, product, and pricing. Randash is a certified estate planner, primarily servicing ranchers and farmers. He works with clients during the winter and concentrates on fishing during the summer, when his clients are busy. "I fish full-time during the PWT season and work with my clients full-time the rest of the year," he says.

Jim Randash

Good and Brumbaugh received press, publicity, and TV exposure after winning. "It took my career to a new level," Good says. He went into fishing full-time in spring 1995. Although he realized his planned income, he still works closely with his sponsors to sell their products and create a better position for himself. His speaking engagements and appearances have increased. Good garnered several nonindustry sponsors since his championship win, and these pay the bills and help defray entry fees and other expenses, making tournament winnings even sweeter.

Brumbaugh still farms 300 acres, but in August of 1996, he quit his third job as building supervisor for a plastics plant. "Fishing, for me, is a business, and I'm treating it like a business," he says. "But I still enjoy the fun of competitive fishing."

His sponsors all significantly increased their commitments for equipment and retainers, and several new sponsors were signed. "Sponsors realize that the more I win, the more people know me. That continues to surprise me," Brumbaugh says. He increased the number of seminars he does by fifteen per year, conducts a half-dozen in-store promotions annually, writes a syndicated column, fishes with outdoor writers, and works with In-Fisherman editors and TV producers for segments and articles. He sees no end to these publicity efforts.

Perry Good

Earning top PWT honors in 1998 on the PWT tour were pro In-Fisherman Angler of the Year Scott Fairbairn, and Mariner Top Amateur Charlie Christofferson. Fairbairn won thirteen times as much money in 1998 ($64,600) as during his first three years on the tour. Christofferson earned $19,495 en route to being named Mariner Top Amateur.

Since becoming Angler of the Year, Fairbairn's fourth quarter report to sponsors outpaced all his prior media work. He has fished the tour since 1995 and graduated with a fisheries and wildlife biology degree from the University of Minnesota in 1996. His wife received her doctor of veterinary medicine degree in 1998, and the couple moved to Walker, Minnesota, on the shores of Leech Lake.

Fairbairn says he now receives a better response when contacting new sponsors. "I think my recommendations now carry more weight than they did in the past, and credibility is extremely important," Fairbairn says. Even though he won the 1998 Angler of the Year, he feels a solid public relations package is still vitally important. He warns other pros that it's a mistake not to attend industry shows. He says that meeting prospective sponsors is important and that shows help him determine whom to contact at companies he plans to pursue. "This professional fishing business involves 70 hours each week and 50,000 miles per year on the road," he says.

Christofferson observed PWT tournaments from the stands on several occasions and envisioned winning the Mariner Top Amateur award someday, though not his first year. At the championship, he confessed to being on a high all week, signing autographs, riding in the beam of a spotlight in the civic center, talking with his heroes, and enjoying every minute of the thrilling experience.

On the 1998 tour, Christofferson learned three important lessons:

1. Never quit.
2. Don't let your intensity dip, because every bite is critical.
3. Adapt to conditions. Figure out how and why the pros do what they do.

"The PWT provides an exceptional learning experience," he says. "And I've met so many fine people." He developed a good relationship with his hometown (Park Rapids, Minnesota) chamber of commerce and works their sport show booths. He's beginning his sponsorship quest locally. "I never thought my success would generate so much excitement for others, but it has," he says.

The PWT provides a format in which pros and amateur anglers alike can excel. Those attaining championship victories say doing so has changed their lives.

SPONSORS OUTSIDE THE FISHING INDUSTRY

Professional walleye anglers are recognized for reaching a wide range of outdoor folks with a positive recreational fishing message. This is why a growing number of PWT pros are promoting companies outside the traditional marine and fishing industries.

One such pro is Scott Fairbairn of St. Paul, Minnesota. In 1997, his boat became a floating billboard for North Star Ice, because the company, with 4,000 outlets in Minnesota, wanted to sell more ice, and Scott offered to help. North Star Ice became Fairbairn's biggest sponsor.

Fairbairn says, "Ice is a natural sponsor because fishermen use lots of ice. Besides, every angler is a potential customer for ice." Throughout April, Fairbairn appeared at grocery stores on Fridays and Saturdays, primarily to meet young people while their parents shopped. His boat was parked in front of the store, and he conducted a series of 10-minute miniseminars from the North Star boat.

In-store specials on ice were run. Posters were displayed in advance, and the huge inflatable North Star penguin, Sir Windchill, was present. Fairbairn gave away Berkley line, Blue Fox jigs, and other prizes to youngsters.

He also fishes with key buyers and customers during prefishing days at PWT tournaments. He says, "This has opened the door for other grocery products as sponsors."

Grand Rapids, Minnesota, pros Scott and Marty Glorvigen also work the grocery isles, but for Coca-Cola. They also work the airwaves with *Pros Pointers*, a fishing tips television series seen throughout North and South Dakota, Minnesota, and Wisconsin. Their 60-second show airs during the sports-news hour for fifteen weeks each year. This turnkey operation for distributors has expanded since 1997, based upon its successful first year in the Duluth market. "Coke sold additional cases in 1996, so continuing the fishing tie-in made sense," Marty says.

Coke's campaign has run point-of-purchase displays in over 5,000 grocery stores and supported their effort with ads featuring Marty and Scott. A special sweepstakes featured their rig—a Lund-Yamaha—along with other sponsors' products, like Northland and MinnKota.

Walleye pros provide credibility on TV and at store displays. Even better, according to Marty, "We create a sale." He says big companies like Coke don't need consumer awareness—they need sales. Local distributors solidly backed the Glorvigens. Coke is their largest nonindustry sponsor, but it took them four years to land it.

Marty says the Coke connection gives them a chance to approach other nontraditional sponsors. It also opens the door for other pros to work with nontraditional sponsors.

Another nontraditional sponsor is Pepsi. Gary Gray of Oshkosh, Wisconsin, has worked with Pepsi for years. He's associated with the local distributor and is available to fish with key personnel. He works in-store promotions and displays the Pepsi logo on his vehicle and on his shirt.

"I've had basically the same six local sponsors and several major sponsors since I began fishing," Gray says.

One of his local sponsors is Chief Equipment, a farm implement dealer. Chief's billboard on Gray's Dodge truck is important to them. Even though the company doesn't demand much more than visibility through a respected angler, Gray keeps them informed regularly regarding the PWT and his promotional schedule. He also makes himself available to take people fishing for Chief.

Former PWT Champion Dave Hanson of Bemidji, Minnesota, became affiliated with another local sponsor, Bemidji Woolen Mills. In addition to wearing their clothing on tour, Hanson attended clothing shows from Las Vegas to the Midwest with his sponsors. "More time means more money, and my goal is to make enough money to be a full-time pro, and to maybe move farther from my machine shop."

Three-time PWT winner and former championship winner Perry Good of Apple Valley, Minnesota, established a relationship with three sponsors outside the industry: Minnesota companies 3M and Jiffy Lube and Thru-Way Fasteners of Buffalo, New York. Sponsors expect Good to show their key customers and employees the best possible fishing day on the water.

The owner of Thru-Way Fasteners contacted Good after reading about him and a boat problem he faced. Good says, "A niche exists for touring PWT anglers to become the official pro for companies who deal with customers and clients from all over the world. When their clients come to Minnesota, many of them want to fish instead of golf. I can do that."

Anglers with nontraditional sponsorships share several things in common: (1) they've performed well enough to gain credibility with fishermen; (2) they present a professional image and communicate it through seminars and articles; and (3) they've taken the time to contact potential nonindustry sponsors, to provide a professional résumé, and to follow up with convincing evidence that the sponsors' trust and dollars should be invested in them.

Many fishermen feel they have steps 1 and 2 well in hand. But many are waiting for step number 3—sponsors—to jump into their boats. Don't wait for the phone to ring, expecting someone to call and offer you big bucks to go fishing. Contact potential companies whose products you may be able to promote. Find the appropriate marketing person. Introduce yourself. Send a résumé and a proposal. Follow up with details. Show them how you can help increase sales.

If you don't make a few casts, you won't get bit. And even on the best of waters, you need to make a lots of casts and land numerous small fry before hooking a whopper.

THE HIGH COST OF 'CRAWLERS

Ah, the glamorous life of a professional walleye angler! On the road, on the water, on the fish. On guard! Sounds like you have it made, but the real side to riding the walleye wave is moolah. Dough. Dollars. The high price of crawlers, gas, equipment, lodging— even the occasional meal. Can you believe some guys expect to eat every day?

"Product sponsorship is nice," one pro says, "but you can't eat reels." Sure, many pros receive a modicum of free equipment, discounts on others, delayed billings, and other incentives that help keep 'em afloat. But you still gotta eat, gas up the boat, maintain and replace equipment, and put livebait on the hook. Even cutting every possible corner, you'll find that life on the road to walleyes demands a considerable investment. And then when you win, the IRS wants its cut. Where was Uncle Sam last year when you were looking for a tax break? Probably out fly-fishin' for trout.

Reggie Thiel, Walker, Minnesota, former PWT Rookie of the Year and Big Fish record holder, provides a list of expenses he incurred while fishing one PWT season. Like many PWT contestants, Reggie

Fortunately for Reggie, he's a skinny guy who doesn't eat much—unless it's on the house.

Event	Lodging	Travel & Mileage	Meals	Entry Fees	Other*	Total
The Price of Fame						
Erie	$213.10	$269.38	$135.97	$640.00	$128.50	$1,386.95
Oahe	146.39	188.81	123.14	640.00	111.01	1,209.35
Winnebago	222.50	207.15	62.50	640.00	35.99	1,168.14
Saginaw Bay	421.95	408.16	130.12	640.00	128.46	1,728.69
Lake of the Woods						
Prefishing	68.79	137.92			27.19	233.90
Championship	43.80	352.41	66.43		50.62	513.26
Total	$1,116.53	$1,563.83	$518.16	$2,560.00	$481.77	$6,240.29

*Boat gas, oil, bait, licenses, miscellaneous supplies.

cut costs a bit by sharing motel rooms or cabins with other contestants—decent lodging, but not the Ritz—sharing some prefishing costs like carpooling when feasible, and doing some of his own cooking where conditions allowed.

His expense summary is typical of the realistic, no-frills cost of plying walleye tournament circuit waters. Note that the totals do not reflect the amount of vacation time used or time off work for travel, prefishing, and tournament competition, nor the initial investment in boat, trailer, motors, rods, reels, and miscellaneous tackle.

The road to professional walleye fishing may not be easy, but it's challenging. Congratulations to those new pros who take the plunge and to the sponsors who help make it all work. Now if we can only entice some food sponsors, livebait suppliers, perhaps a motel chain . . . Then walleye pros will really have it made.

INSURANCE GOTCHA' COVERED?

Most boat owners insure their boats through their homeowner's policy. That works for many, but as you become involved in competitive events, seminar-show-tournament circuits, clinics and open houses at boat dealerships, and active guiding, more appropriate boat insurance becomes extremely important.

According to Todd and Steve Grams, touring PWT pro anglers and vice presidents of Greater Insurance in Wisconsin, recreational anglers may be adequately covered by their homeowner's or even standard boat owner's policy, but they should "beware the gray area between *recreational* and *commercial* policies."

Coverage generally stops when a recreational angler engages in any of the following:

- fishing tournaments, even small tournaments
- guiding
- becoming involved in angling-related pursuits for profit or gain.

These activities are usually cited in the exclusions section of the policy, which policy owners seldom read. "This problem needs to be addressed," Grams notes.

His advice as an insurance agent is to contact your agent to determine if your specific activities are covered. If the agent assures you that you're covered for such activities, request confirmation in writing, and attach the letter to your policy.

Every walleye angler has tackle boxes, rods, reels, and way too much gear. Insurance companies consider this personal property, which usually is covered under your homeowner's policy. When engaging in some of the professional activities listed here, many insurance companies consider tackle tools of the trade, according to the Grams brothers. Tools of the trade are not covered under your homeowner's insurance.

Even when tackle is covered, the amount is usually limited. Consider carrying a special rider to cover it. Or request a letter stating exactly what is covered and for how much. In either case, make sure your tackle is covered.

Insurance—What It Costs

PACKAGE 1: $625 ($750 SOUTHERN STATES)

ITEM	INSURANCE LIMIT	DEDUCTIBLE
boat, engines, & equipment	up to $35,000 ACV*	$500
trailer—physical damage	up to $2,500 ACV*	$250
fishing gear & personal effects	$1,000	$250
nonemergency towing and assistance	$300	0
professional angler's liability	$500,000 CSL**	0
medical payments	$1,000	$100
tournament fee reimbursement	$1,000	0

PACKAGE 2: $800 ($950 SOUTHERN STATES)

ITEM	INSURANCE LIMIT	DEDUCTIBLE
boat, engines, & equipment	up to $45,000 ACV*	$1,000
trailer—physical damage	up to $3,500 ACV*	$500
fishing gear & personal effects	$5,000	$250
nonemergency towing and assistance	$300	0
professional angler's liability	$500,000 CSL**	0
medical payments	$1,000	$100
tournament fee reimbursement	$1,000	0

*ACV: Actual Cash Value   **CSL: Combined Single Limit

Document what you own. Make a photo or video record along with an inventory list. Pictures of your tackle box trays will help explain the number of crankbaits (and their cost) should they ever disappear. Itemize your gear with dates purchased, amount paid, and model numbers, and update this list regularly.

Don't forget the gear in your boat—compass, tools, flare kits, life jackets, electronics, nets, spare tire, and batteries. This document, should you ever need it, will simplify your life and drastically reduce your paperwork. It also will jog your memory so you can claim all your losses.

The Gramses researched a solid policy for anglers who participate in for-profit fishing activities and arrived at the following basic policy for National Professional Anglers Association (NPAA) members. Their chart shows what is covered and for what amounts.

The 2001 policy premium for NPAA members ranged from $625 to $800 for this amount of coverage. Additional fishing gear and personal effects coverage costs an extra $30 per $1,000 of equipment. This plan was developed from a commercial policy specifically designed for activities and equipment not covered by homeowners' policies and for people who want to avoid gray areas. Similar policies are available for non-NPAA members at an additional cost. Most policies (including this one) do not cover anyone acting under the influence of alcohol.

Steve says, "When comparison shopping or determining if your homeowner's policy adequately covers you, be honest with your agent. Tell him about tournaments you fish, any guiding you do, and seminar and speaking engagements."

REALITY BITES

You love to fish and are good at it? Talent alone won't ensure success. Nor will a bankroll and access to the best equipment. It takes a combination of skill, desire, determination, sacrifice, experience, and endurance to reach the upper echelons of competition in any sport, just as it does to become a big fish in a world full of flashing teeth and jaws. Fishing for a living is more than just fishing—it's survival of the fittest. To remain afloat, you must find your place in the boat and hold on tight. There's only so much room.

Most folks who fish for a living are guides. Basically, their job is to take other people fishing, though many also fish while they work. Tournament anglers, meanwhile, fish to win prize money, but few survive on winnings alone. Sponsors foot much of the bill for tournament fishermen who've earned public recognition. But sponsors also expect something in return for their investment: seminars, in-store promos, working with outdoor writers.

Outdoor writers, by the way, don't write their articles in a boat. There's a lot of office or home time on the computer, producing stories that foot the bill by outdoing other writers competing for the same editorial space. So, outdoor writing isn't all working outdoors.

A lot of people, from tackle sales representatives to resort operators, make a living in some way related to sportfishing. But almost no one gets paid just to fish, tournaments or otherwise. Not something you want to say to a wide-eyed little kid filled with hero worship who wants someday to be a professional fisherman, as well as a firefighter, astronaut, and doctor. But it's something that an adult who seeks a place in the fishing business while supporting a family should consider before taking the plunge.

Do you have what it takes to become a top walleye pro, bass pro, or all-around fishing hotshot? Many do have the calling. Some enjoy a brief moment in the limelight. Others linger on the periphery, longing for but never quite entering the spotlight, yet basking in the glow of the sport they love.

Those who reach the top and enjoy years in the fishing business are good at what they do and extremely determined to make it work. They may be superb competitive anglers, but again, that's only a part of the equation for success. They must acquire, satisfy, and keep sponsors, aggressively converting some measure of fame into sponsorship dollars instead of waiting for sponsors to come to them. They must prove that they can truly affect the market by generating awareness and increasing sales of sponsors' products. They must be innovative, creating new opportunities for promotions and products. They must garner public trust as spokesmen with reputations for excellence. And yes, they must be fierce competitors on the water, more than able to hold their own against a hungry pack of wannabes.

Reach for the stars. Anything is possible. Never lose sight of the majesty of the sport and how fortunate we are to live in a country where people can actually make a living from an activity they love. But be realistic, too. Realize you have to keep facing upstream while swimming hard.

Chapter 13

'Eyes On The Future

Walleyes Aren't Bass

PERSPECTIVES AND PREDICTIONS

In-Fisherman founder Al Lindner, one of the world's best anglers and perhaps one of its most obsessed, has seen innumerable changes during his fishing career—breakthroughs, inventions, innovations, new lures, new techniques. So who better to ask about the future of walleye fishing?

"Walleyes aren't bass," Lindner says, "and most people who like fishing for walleyes also like to eat them. To make people feel bad about harvesting walleyes sends the wrong message. Selective harvest is an important aspect of walleye fishing.

"Novice anglers should feel okay about keeping or releasing trophy fish," Lindner says. "Although they may decide to keep a particular fish, they may also, from that point on, decide to release most big fish they catch. To sustain a healthy population of trophy-sized walleyes, promoting and teaching catch-and-release—especially of big walleyes—is essential on many waters. Over time, most folks mature as anglers and choose to release bigger walleyes."

Lindner says he would like to see opportunities for fishing expand instead of merely being conserved through fishing restrictions. "Today we must abide by regulations like length limits and reduced daily bags designed to manage individual bodies of water. On every water I've ever fished, whether a shallow, fertile prairie lake or the Great Lakes, each fishery fluctuates with water level, water temperature, and harvest or forage populations, creating highs and lows in fishing opportunities. Managing fisheries on a short-term basis may be the best option—tweaking management practices to reflect the ups and downs of fish populations.

"Our goal should be to make sure enough fish are present for people to catch. In many waters, stocking walleyes works. I think it's especially important to continue stocking efforts in waters where walleyes aren't capable of reproducing, especially in waters that had healthy populations of walleyes in the past. The overall effect that a healthy fishery has on tourism, sportfishing, and the future of angling is phenomenal. Making sure there are fish for people to catch is a no-brainer, but it isn't always easy. Of course, the whole affair has to be cost-effective, too. Everyone involved must adapt to regulation changes in order for walleye fishing and the walleye industry to remain healthy."

Technology—computer software, detailed contour mapping, GPS, underwater cameras—isn't going away and will continue to evolve. "It's incredible," Lindner says, "how fast information about fishing conditions nationwide can be accessed via the Internet. This has really increased the mobility of anglers. Simply type *www.whatever* into a computer to obtain fishing information about a specific body of water miles away. In spring, for example, I can monitor the status of river levels 1,000 miles away on an hourly basis, so I can actually pinpoint the best time to catch walleyes moving upstream to spawn.

"Tournament anglers will continue to set trends in walleye fishing. Many major breakthroughs in recent history have evolved from tournaments. The question is, will tournaments and technology deplete the walleye population?

"I say no. Walleye fishing generally is as good as it's ever been. Technology won't make fish bite; you still have to go out and get intimate with them in order to catch them."

THE RISING PRICE PER POUND OF WALLEYES

"Forty years ago," says *Walleye In-Sider* Editor Dave Csanda, "my great-grandfather proclaimed that mustard should be $5 a jar so people wouldn't waste their money on it. He didn't like mustard and apparently felt little sympathy for those who did. For comparison purposes, I checked the local grocery store: an 8-ounce jar of brand-name mustard was only 93 cents. Some things, apparently, remain bargains over time."

Times change, however, and time changes our perspectives. Back about 1970, you could buy a state-of-the-art walleye rig—a 15-foot fiberglass tri-hull, 25-hp outboard, and trailer—for about $1,000. Toss in another $100 for a depthfinder, plus another C-note for an electric trolling motor and battery—say, $1,200 bucks total. By comparison, today's tournament-ready 20-footers, decked out with huge engines, dual electric motors, and every conceivable form of electronics, regularly top $30,000.

If you don't like walleyes or walleye fishing, that may not bother you much.

If, however, you enjoy fishing for walleyes, at some point you're likely to ponder the rising cost of involvement. Especially when gas prices shoot to $2 per gallon. Traveling to and from the lake is bad enough, but with big outboards that get 2 to 4 miles per gallon, range may soon be determined more by credit card limits than fuel tank capacity.

So why has the price of fully rigged walleye boats gone up by a factor of 30, while mustard is still affordable—other than those frilly French Dijon designer types? Because after all these years, mustard is still pretty much mustard. The only similarities between the boats of yesteryear and today is that they both float and go where you point them. Otherwise, it's like comparing Model T's with sport utility vehicles or lunar landing modules—there's no comparison.

The same goes for virtually every fishing rod, reel, line, and accessory we use today. They're not just newer and prettier, but much improved over many generations of change. So we must temper our discomfort about higher prices with the realization that we're paying for increased quality, not just lining somebody's pocket with our hard-earned dollars.

Remember back in the early '70s, when gas was about 45¢ per gallon? Today, $2 per gallon seems outrageous, but in reality, that's only four or five times what it cost 30 years ago. Gas is still pretty much gas, though it is now lead-free and has been refined to burn cleaner. (If there's less stuff in there, shouldn't it be cheaper?) We can take some solace in the fact that it has been improved for everyone's benefit.

Which brings us back to the high cost of walleyes. Hourly wages and salaries have clearly risen over the past few decades—but by a factor of 30? No way. What gives?

Once again, think carefully about walleye equipment and who uses it. Those $30,000 rigs are primarily used by leading-edge tournament competitors and serious anglers to run long distances in big waves, fishing every conceivable sea condition from calm to gale-force. The average guy or gal isn't going to do that. They'll trailer to the boat launch nearest their intended fishing area and range only as far as current weather conditions permit. They'll roll with the punches rather than attempt to conquer conditions at any cost.

While we all "ooh" and "ahh" at those fancy boats, rods, reels, and electronics at sports shows, the fact is that their manufacturers don't offer only top-of-the-line versions. They're smart enough to realize that they can sell only a limited number of premium items. Thus, within any product line, from crankbaits and reels to boats and motors, you'll find various levels and models (called price points) ranging from bargain-priced gear for occasional users to better gear suited for average anglers who fish more than a few times per year to premium gear for serious anglers who fish regularly. Something for everyone at every level, from first timer to connoisseur.

We all wish we could drive a Cadillac or Lexus, though the reality is that there are a whole lot more Fords, Chevys, and Hondas on the road. And how many of us can say that our first car was a Caddy? Chances are, most of us started with a used—excuse us, the current terminology is "pre-owned"—rust bucket that nickeled and dimed us nearly to death. Same with walleye fishing. You don't necessarily need a $30,000 rig to catch walleyes, particularly when a more modest setup suits your budget and level of involvement better. At least to begin with. Look around: anglers in leaky old boats still catch fish. They just don't look as good while doing it.

Sure, you can dream and aspire, and if and when the time is right, you can upgrade to the deluxe version. But don't ever let the lack of premium equipment convince you that you can't have fun out there. Heck, on small lakes and rivers, little boats and motors are better suited to shallow bottoms, limited accesses, and fine boat control. The best bet is to invest in equipment that matches the size and types of waters you fish, the frequency of your trips, and your family budget.

Human nature being what it is, we all tend to want a little extra glitz and glitter, so new technology tempts us to upgrade at every opportunity. Fine. That helps keep things exciting, the fishing tackle companies in business, and over the course of lifetimes spurs anglers to invest in better tackle and gear to enhance their effectiveness and enjoyment.

So what's the true cost per pound of walleyes? It depends on how you fish. Among tournament anglers, it sometimes seems like $1,000 per pound. At the grocery store, it's more like $10 a pound—and that's filleted! And if you pursue walleyes with old-style technology, the bargain prices of the '60s and '70s still apply.

Remember, you don't necessarily have to own the most expensive equipment to have the best time, especially right out of the starting blocks. You can still walk down to the riverbank, cast out, and catch a fish on simple tackle. That's part of the mystique and majesty of fishing; we all have to start somewhere, and that's how and where most of us started. A fat wallet doesn't guarantee success. Participation at any level, however, gets results. Catching fish on any tackle is fun, whether you toss 'em all back or keep a few for the table, with perhaps a dollop of still-affordable mustard on the side.

A PRAIRIE LAKE COMPANION

"It's been a quiet week here in Lake Wobegon, out on the edge of the prairie. School's out. Bikes, baseball, and swimming are in. The crops are progressing nicely. Tomatoes have ripened to scarlet splendor, gracing the baskets of Sunday afternoon picnics and glorifying the hot lazy days of summer. Preparations are in place for the upcoming Lake Wobegon Days Festival, though volunteers have been conspicuously harder to come by ever since the walleyes started biting so well . . ."

From 5 to 7 p.m. (Central) every Saturday afternoon, anglers throughout walleye country tune to National Public Radio to catch the weekly live broadcast of Garrison Keillor's *A Prairie Home Companion*, which extols the virtues and simple joys of life in a rural Minnesota farm community. It's a good time to be out on the water, enjoying the typical lull in boat traffic that occurs over the dinner hour. A great opportunity to cruise at gentle speed—perhaps trailing a few lures behind the boat, perhaps not—or to stop and make a few casts in likely places. To kick back and relax on the water. No great expectations. No pressure. A brief version of Lake Wobegon Days, tomatoes strictly optional.

Among walleye anglers, the prevailing notion now runs to bigger waters and bigger fish, with an ever-expanding array of electronic gear and gadgets. We think of deep, clear, classic waters surrounded by pine-studded forests and granite outcroppings. Of huge reservoirs spanning countless miles of terrain. Of mighty rivers teeming with seasonal runs of golden walleyes.

Understandably so. Such waters are the leading edge of the walleye fishing frontier. But just as they epitomize the eternal quest for newer and more glorified angling locales, a great many other, less-glamorous waters, often lying closer to home, provide excellent fishing opportunities. Shallower, dingier, more fertile waters bordered by agricultural communities. Waters teeming with fish, yet seemingly less attractive because of their unpretentious surroundings and less complex fishing patterns.

On these, the Lake Wobegons of the walleye world, your tactics needn't be fancy. You can cast a diving crankbait, a jig, or even a humble slipbobber-and-nightcrawler combo to a rocky shoreline point, plumbing the depths in only 4 feet of water. Or troll a bottom bouncer-spinner-crawler rig through a productive depth range along slowly tapering shorelines. Or longline troll diving crankbaits across the expansive, flat, featureless basin in search of roving schools of suspended fish. You can do these even from a pontoon. Nothing fancy. Just effective.

You may not encounter a hot, fast bite. Often, though, the fishing's better than you expected, and the fish bigger than you'd dream. Fat walleyes grown big on the abundant forage, fed by nutrient run-off from the surrounding agricultural watershed. Today, many shallow, eutrophic lakes even have aeration systems to keep them from freezing out during winter.

As anglers, we dream of adventurous vacation trips to exotic fishing destinations, perhaps placing our baits in front of huge fish that have never seen a lure. But the reality is, most of us have limited time and opportunity to explore such distant waters. If that's true for you, don't ignore angling opportunities closer to home. They may be less exotic, but they're certainly more accessible. And even though they may lack the romance of far-off waters, they can offer the satisfying rewards of a quiet day on the water, a few fish on the line, and a job well done—perhaps while listening to Public Radio International on a Lake Wobegon somewhere near your home.

"And that's the news from Lake Wobegon, where all the walleyes are strong, all the anglers are good looking, and all the children display above-average interest in fishing."

One Final Perspective:

RIVERS OF GOLD

"There's a place up North," my friend said, "where bottoms of rivers and streams glitter with gold." His face glowed as he spoke of this place, his eyes slowly glazing over like those of a man who had been given the worst of news but had not believed it. His faraway gaze was unblinking, and I imagined his mind carrying him to the Yukon and beyond, knowing he'd been there before, swatting mosquitoes and playing dead beneath charging grizzlies.

"Look for gravel," he said. "The white gravel. Quartzite!" His voice was getting excited now. "And bends in the river. Always bends in the river. Places where current washes close to shore and erodes the bank."

"And black sand. Yes! The black sand is always flecked with gold. Look for logjams, too. Check the washout above and behind them. And the feeder creeks. And look where others have found it, because assuredly they didn't find it all."

His excitement was contagious. His voice began to carry a mystical tone like that of a chanting monk. My heart began to race as his words carried me great distances to pristine places I'd never seen and only infrequently had read about.

"I know of such a place, even places," I said, matter-of-factly; my words halted him in midgroan.

"What? Where? Let's go," he begged.

"First, let me tell you all about it, then you can decide if you still want to go," I teased. "It's like this," I began. "There's a place on the Missouri River where cottonwoods grow tall and willows line the banks. It's a place where beaver and eagles and gold can be found all year. But it's not always where you think it should be, or even where it was yesterday. But I know of a spot where the current cuts close to the bank, and the gold is always there. There isn't always much weight to it in this part of the river, but there's usually enough to satisfy.

"I know of another place," I continued. "It's on the dark waters of the Rainy River. It's behind a logjam, just as you said, and it can be loaded with gold in spring and fall. It's not a big washout, but it can produce the Mother Lode, especially right before ice-up. I can take you there sometime, if you'd like, but you have to promise never to show anyone."

I could see that his curiosity was peaking, but I wasn't through yet. "Let me tell you about another place where the gold runs heavy. It's downstream from a dam on the Wisconsin River, where a stretch of gravel is washed by the current. The gold is always there in spring. When the snowmelt gets low, you can see flashes of gold on the gravel in the shallow water. But when the water is high, you just have to trust that the gold will be there for the taking.

"I could take you there sometime, but you just might want to try it yourself. Here, I'll draw a quick map. It's easy to find once you near it. Look for the only big granite boulder on the bank, then move upstream to where the river birch begin to grow. The gravel is right in front of the birch. Don't worry about saving any for me—more will always be there if I go back."

He gave me a puzzled look as I continued. "There's still another spot. It's on the Fox River right in front of a feeder creek—some of the purest gold you'll ever find, especially in April. There's a spot farther downstream, too, where the bottom is black, not with black sand, as you'd suppose, but black silt. The water's warmer, though, and the gold is always there in spring and fall.

"I know of lots more rivers and places," I told him, "but it's late, and we should be going." He thanked me for the stories and the map and disappeared into the darkness.

I never saw him again. I suspect his days are spent wading a creek somewhere in Alaska, catching salmon, panning gold, and trying not to look like a midday snack to *Ursus arctos horribilis*. I doubt he ever used my map or even considered looking for gold on the rivers I mentioned.

And I often wonder, too, if deep down inside, he knew that although our gold is found in the same sorts of riverbeds, it's vastly different.

For while his gold is of rock and metal and flour and flakes and nuggets, mine is of fins and scales and the white-gold eyes that reflect moonlight in the gravelly shallows of North American rivers.

Daryl Christensen